D0965511

A M Y

The World of Amy Lowell
and the Imagist Movement

Other books by Jean Gould

WALTER REUTHER: LABOR'S RUGGED INDIVIDUALIST (*with Lorena Hickok*)

THE POET AND HER BOOK: A BIOGRAPHY OF EDNA ST. VINCENT MILLAY

MODERN AMERICAN PLAYWRIGHTS

ROBERT FROST: THE AIM WAS SONG

WINSLOW HOMER

A GOOD FIGHT

THAT DUNBAR BOY

YOUNG MARINER MELVILLE

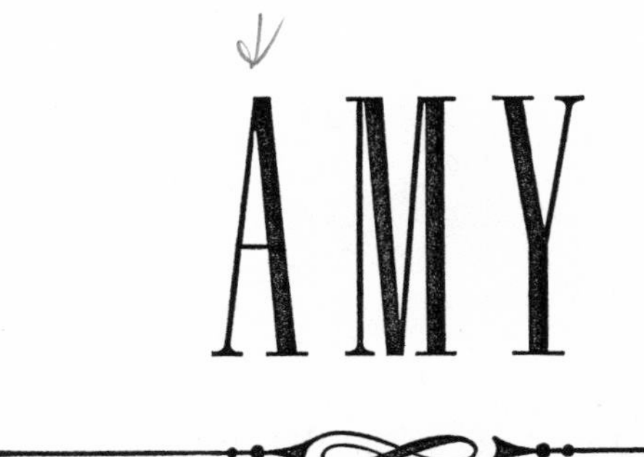

THE WORLD OF AMY LOWELL AND THE IMAGIST MOVEMENT

By Jean Gould

DODD, MEAD & COMPANY
NEW YORK

To

ELEANOR ROBSON BELMONT,

who understood the impassioned heart of Amy Lowell's poetry.

A section of this book appeared in a slightly different form in *Yankee* magazine under the title "Afternoon Tea with Amy Lowell" and is reproduced here by courtesy of *Yankee* magazine, Dublin, New Hampshire.

Printed in the United States of America
by The Cornwall Press, Inc., Cornwall, N.Y.

Library of Congress Cataloging in Publication Data

Gould, Jean, date
Amy: the world of Amy Lowell and the Imagist movement.

Bibliography: p.
Includes index.
1. Lowell, Amy, 1874-1925—Biography.
2. Imagist poetry—History and criticism. I. Title.
PS3523.O88Z66 811'.5'2 [B] 75-11563
ISBN 0-396-07022-1

Acknowledgments

With the passage of years, direct sources of personal or anecdotal material on Amy Lowell have dwindled appreciably. Only a handful of people remain who knew her in her heyday. Foremost among these is Mrs. August Belmont, to whom I am greatly indebted for a close-up view of the intensely devoted relationship between the leader of the Imagist movement and her friend and companion, Ada Dwyer Russell. I wish to express my gratitude to Mrs. Belmont, not only for the information she furnished, but for her interest, encouragement, and sympathy during the trials and tribulations that beset the author in the course of writing this biography. I am grateful also for the cooperation I received from the late Mr. John Farrar, publisher, who, as the young editor of the *Bookman* magazine, met Amy at the height of her fame, came to know her well, and was able to give me a first-hand account of several delightful anecdotes in addition to notes on her career. Lesley Frost Ballantine, daughter of Robert Frost, has been most generous in contributing her recollections of the poet-leader at Sevenels, including some entirely new material, and has given permission to use Frost family letters and photographs. Mary Sands (Mrs. Alexander) Thompson, who was one of Amy's secretaries around the time of World War I, furnished much of the material on the daily routine at Sevenels during the stringent years of food rationing and Amy's method of handling the situation, as well as her regular work habits and demands. And Doris Russell (Mrs. George Luther) Foote, whose family were neighbors of Amy's at her summer home in Dublin, New Hampshire, and who from early childhood until the poet's death was an ardent admirer of "Miss Lowell," gave me the first full account of Rupert Brooke's visit to Sevenels in 1913. To composer Virgil Thomson, who, as friend and colleague of George Foote, suggested my contact with Mrs. Foote, and with Mr. John Marshall, I am greatly indebted. Mr. Marshall, who was the roommate of the late S. Foster Damon, Amy's first biographer, at the time the latter was writing his *Chronicle* of the poet's life, was both prompt and enthusiastic in his response to my questions, presenting a glowing picture of Amy's companion, Ada Russell.* Reverend Donald Amussen, grandson of Mrs. Russell, and his wife, Helen, were both cordial and helpful to me. Mrs. Stanhope Ficke, daughter-in-law of the poet and literary critic Arthur Davison Ficke, furnished a firsthand account of Ficke's reaction to Amy Lowell and her Imagist regime. Mrs. Harvey H. Bundy, Amy's niece, gave prompt assistance in answering my questions about her aunt's debutante years and in supplying the name of the present executor of Miss Lowell's estate. Mrs. Lizette Lewis, daughter of Carl Engel, furnished an unpublished photograph of her father.

Allen Hughes, music critic of *The New York Times,* made invaluable suggestions in regard to source material on Amy Lowell's interest in modern music, and also in his critique of the book after reading it in manuscript, for which I am most grateful. Dr. Robert D. Seely, internist, who furnished pertinent data on the glandular cause and treatment of obesity, deserves a special vote of thanks. I am also indebted to Dr. Arnold T. Schwab, of the California State University English Department, who kindly passed along to me correspondence material involving Amy Lowell from the files of his own research for a biography of Mrs. Edward MacDowell. Writer George Martin gave valued assistance in suggesting personal contacts and research material. A vote of thanks goes to Roberta Peters and Janet Flanner for answering my queries regarding Lina Abarbanell ** and Margaret Anderson respectively.

* No relation to Doris Russell Foote.

** Popular soubrette (and object of Amy Lowell's attentions from 1908 to 1912), later a concert manager, one of whose clients was Miss Peters at the start of her operatic career.

I am greatly indebted to Mr. Rodney G. Dennis, Curator of Manuscripts, and to the staff at the Houghton Library of Harvard University, which houses the Lowell collections of letters, photographs, and memorabilia, and where a large portion of research for this book was done. Staff members were always prompt and helpful in furnishing materials from the Lowell files. In selecting photographs, much assistance was given by Miss Deborah Kelley, Miss Hinda Sklar, and Miss Carolyn Jakeman. In the gathering of photographs, I am also grateful to Mr. Jack Jackson of the Boston Athenaeum; Miss Janice Gallinger, Librarian of Plymouth State College, New Hampshire; Mr. Robert W. Allison, Assistant Curator of Manuscripts and Archives at the Regenstein Library of the University of Chicago; Miss Charlotte LaRue, Curator of Photographs at the Museum of the City of New York; and Mr. Louis Rachow, Librarian of the Walter Hampden Memorial Library at the Players.

Finally, I am most grateful to Director Conrad Spohnholz and his able staff at the MacDowell Colony, for residence periods during which the manuscript for this book was begun in the summer of 1973, and revised in the summer of 1974.

Contents

Illustrations

Following page 180

CHAPTER I

Foreground (Stage Center)

On a bright spring day in 1919, the Hotel Belmont in New York City was galvanized into action by news that traveled like an electric shock through the building: "Miss Amy Lowell of Brookline, Massachusetts," poet and lecturer, was coming to town again. As usual, she had engaged the corner suite she and her companion occupied several times a year. Her impending arrival was a melodrama in itself, a frenzy of preparation for this important "regular guest." The eighth floor, especially, was all in commotion. In half an hour, every large mirror in the corner suite was swathed with folds of black cloth, and every clock was stopped. The housekeeper supervised the preparation of Miss Lowell's wide double bed, seeing to it that exactly sixteen plump pillows were laid over the mattress, covered by carefully stretched sheets; and woe to the one who had not taken out the fine old soft linens kept for Miss Lowell's express use.

In the dining room, waiters were alerted, and woe to the one who did not deliver two pitchers of ice water in a trice whenever she ordered it during her stay. The maître d' warned them about prompt, efficient service in relation to tips as he began sharpening steel dinner knives for the private parties Miss Lowell customarily gave in her suite. Woe also to the switchboard operator who failed to answer when the signal light flashed from there, whether it was broad daylight or the middle of the night. Even the engineers and electricians in the cellar stood ready for nightly summonses, and for the sizable tip they had come to expect from the poet-leader who was both regal and fraternal.

Some time after all was in readiness, a large taxi, laden with luggage, drew up in front of the hotel, and, with the driver's help, a lumbering figure emerged, slowly extricating her bulky body through the cab door. A low groan escaped her, but she quickly stifled it by a laugh and a hearty "Made it!" to the driver. Scarcely more than five feet tall, she was almost as broad; though she had some difficulty maneuvering her body, once out, she moved with dignity. She wore a mannish suit with a long skirt and a loose-fitting three-quarter-length jacket which hid her bulk somewhat, and the high pompadour of her hair style gave her a little added height. The pince-nez perched on the narrow bridge of her nose lent her a commanding, professorial air. Also, the steady stream of animated, running comment she kept up served as a distraction from her size. This was Amy Lowell, at the crest of her fame. Her remarks were directed at her beloved friend and companion, Ada Russell, a handsome, middle-aged woman who followed her out of the taxi with a springy gait, offering her arm in support as soon as Amy had paid the driver. Meanwhile, a second taxi with more luggage had drawn up in back of the first, and Elizabeth Henry, Amy's private maid, signaling the porters to take the bags, jumped out and offered support on the other side of Miss Lowell. New York was the last stop on a tour that had taken them south as far as Richmond, Virginia, and had been carried out against doctor's orders, right after Amy had suffered a bout with pneumonia, in addition to a "nasty little umbilical hernia," as she called it, which had already required two operations.

In a kind of ritual, the little cortege moved majestically into the hotel. Amy loved ritual and retinue, partially relying on them as a panacea to a life plagued by illness. Just before they went on tour, she had climbed out of a sickbed to lecture, at the invitation of Harvard's music department, on the subject, "Some Musical Analogies in Modern Poetry." She was the first woman ever to deliver a lecture under the auspices of that exalted university. It had been a great success, and now, as she earnestly discussed with Ada the next few days' schedule, a radiance spread over her face and her hazel eyes sparkled with anticipation. She planned to see the editor of *The Musical Quarterly* about publishing her lecture. Also, she intended to beard the lions among editors of leading literary magazines for publication of individual poems in advance of her next volume. "Come hell or high water, I'm going to place every one of those poems before the new book comes out . . . we'll call the *Bookman* first," she might be saying. "That nice young editor, John Farrar . . . and Ellery Sedgwick at the *Atlantic,* of course. . . ."

As soon as they were settled, the calls began. Amy seated herself in an armchair beside the writing desk where the phone stood, lit one of the little Manila cigars for which she was famous, and, with a pitcher of ice water handy at her elbow, went to work. (To her, the telephone was one of the necessities of existence, as editors of magazines well realized. It signified the direct word. She could not endure delay, even on unimportant questions.) Appointments were made with friends and editors; in most cases the terms were synonymous now, but some editors were still her enemies and had to be badgered into seeing the formidable Amy Lowell, "demon saleswoman" of poetry, as T. S. Eliot called her.

After business was taken care of, social engagements were set up. Ada, who had been a distinguished character actress, usually got in touch with her great good friend from her theater years, Mrs. August Belmont, the former stage star Eleanor Robson. "Nell" nearly always arranged to see them, either at the hotel or at the Belmonts for dinner. Amy's most recent book, *Can Grande's Castle,* published the previous fall (September 1918) to wide acclaim, included two poems of different wars,* based on stories she had heard from each of the Belmonts during the long conversations they enjoyed on these visits. (Frequently Nell spent a weekend at Sevenels, the old family home of the seven Lowells in Brookline, of which Amy was the proud owner.) Since Amy was to give a public reading of the air-raid poem inspired by Nell's description, they probably arranged for the Belmonts to attend.

* "Guns as Keys: and the Great Gate Swings," dealing with the opening of the Orient by U.S. Naval forces under Comdr. Joseph Matthew Perry, Mr. Belmont's grandfather, and "The Bronze Horses," containing a section about an air raid Mrs. Belmont had witnessed while with the Red Cross in World War I.

Amy usually called Jessie Rittenhouse, secretary of the Poetry Society of America, to let them know she was in New York. Jessie would pass the word around: "Amy's in town again," and soon members friendly to Amy and her "Imagist" movement would keep the switchboard operator busy. Messages might come from the Untermeyers (Jean and Louis); Sara Teasdale; Alfred Kreymborg; Archibald MacLeish; William Rose Benét (and, in a couple of years, Elinor Wylie); Conrad Aiken and William Carlos Williams (both friendly enemies, who enjoyed a bristling conversation with Amy); and a close friend, Elizabeth Sergeant, writer for the *New Republic,* who seemed to know everyone in all fields of the arts. Often, if Amy was busy preparing last-minute notes for a lecture, Ada took all incoming calls in her room. Some inquired after Amy's health; others wanted to see them. Amy and Ada were accepted as a pair by everyone.

On this short trip, besides the reading of her long poem, "The Bronze Horses," at the MacDowell Club (which had recently appointed her a member of the Committee on Literature), Amy sold no less than seventeen poems to various editors. She met and entertained for Percy MacKaye, the well-known dramatist. She had a conference with her publishers, and, after some hassle, signed the contract for her forthcoming book on her own terms. She received requests for future readings, one from Columbia University, another from the Brooklyn Institute, where she had delivered a series of lectures the previous year. Jessie Rittenhouse wanted to arrange a Poetry Society luncheon for her. If it had not been for news of a tragic death in the family, which caused her to cancel all engagements, she and Ada might have done much more during this stay.

Amy Lowell had not always enjoyed such attention. It had taken five years from the time her second book was published in 1914 for her to reach this recognized place. Her first encounter with the Poetry Society, a mere five minutes she had been granted to explain her Imagist movement, ended in a two-hour barrage of attack which she fought back singlehanded. Her second, a year later, was the scene of an even greater row—"a wild beast show and gladiator's fight," she called it. But, through her efforts, the "new" poetry took hold, and was still spreading in spite of all opposition. Before her championship of Imagism, her first book of poems (in 1912) received no more than a polite acknowledgment. Earlier, she had known years of vague yearnings and various diffuse efforts in the theater, in poetry; and before that, a seven-year period of recovery from a nervous breakdown. Though, like Jane Austen's Emma, Amy was "rich and well-born," of a proud family name, her beginnings were far from auspicious.

CHAPTER II

Backdrop: The United States in 1874

AMY LOWELL WAS a self-liberated woman whose birth, as she implied in her famous poem, "Patterns," was surrounded by "stiff, brocaded" mores regarding her sex. Yet she became a militant literary leader in the development of modern American poetry, a vociferous advocate of revolutionary rhythms and free verse. When she was born, scarcely a decade had passed since the end of the Civil War. Ulysses S. Grant, former commander-in-chief of the Union forces in that bloody conflict, was taking up his second term as president. The United States, though still licking its self-inflicted wounds, was at last recovering its unity. A new feeling of national pride was evident in the North. The Fifteenth Amendment was taking effect in the federal government, and Negro faces began to appear in Congress, a trend soon to be aborted. Walt Whitman, whose "Songs of War and Peace" celebrated the peace by condemning war, had sounded the first notes of modern poetry in his earliest edition of *Leaves of Grass,* some years before the Civil War broke out. They would be taken up in a different key by Emily Dickinson's as yet unheard, hidden lyrics. And his "Beat! beat! drums!—blow! bugles! blow!" would be echoed much later in Amy Lowell's "Bombardment."

The year was 1874, one that was marked by a number of notable births of creative personalities in literary and other fields, as if heralding a future renascence in the world of art in addition to astonishing developments in the worlds of science and industry. The year began with the birth of poets. Amy Lowell and Gertrude

Stein were both born in the second month, Stein on the morning of February 3, and Amy on the morning of February 9; and Robert Frost arrived on March 26 (though for many years, through an error in records, his birth date was thought to be 1875). Two giants in the realm of music, Charles Ives, a fellow New Englander of Amy's and the outstanding precursor of modern American music, and Arnold Schönberg, who in the 1920s, established the twelve-tone system of musical composition, were both born in 1874, as well as Serge Koussevitzky, years after Amy's death conductor of the Boston Symphony Orchestra (supported by Lowells). The towering figure of Sir Winston Churchill, world statesman and Nobel Prize winner in literature, was ushered into the world in 1874, as were the English novelist W. Somerset Maugham and the American novelist Ellen Glasgow, later a friend of Amy's. A rival, and sometimes "friendly enemy" of Amy Lowell, the popular Boston poet Josephine Preston Peabody, famous for her dramatization of Browning's *The Pied Piper of Hamelin,* came along later in the year, as did Zona Gale, journalist, novelist, and Pulitzer Prize playwright, whose winning play, *Miss Lulu Bett,* dealt with the emancipation of the spinster sister-in-law. Mary Heaton Vorse, pioneer woman labor-journalist, who was covering the textile strike in Lawrence, Massachusetts, mills, a Lowell family vested interest, when Amy's first book of poems appeared in 1912, was born in 1874. All four women advanced the freedom of their sex in varying ways and degrees through their literary careers.

The city of Boston had expanded after the Civil War, absorbing the suburbs of Roxbury, Dorchester, West Roxbury, and Brighton, and broadening its horizons culturally as well as physically. Although one of its founding fathers, clergyman John Harvard, had established in 1636 the college that eventually became Harvard University, Boston itself had little to offer besides its schools and libraries for generations. The Boston Museum of Fine Arts was not founded until 1870, four years before Amy's birth. Billboards announced with a flourish the new repertory company of the old established Boston Museum-Theatre,* which, with its

* Originally a historical museum with an auditorium in which the plays were offered, disguised as "operas" or lectures to satisfy Puritan critics.

weekly stage attractions, was to have a profound influence on Amy Lowell's life and work.

Amy's father, Augustus Lowell, had settled his family in the suburb of Brookline on a small estate, eventually named "Sevenels," for the seven *L*'s of his branch of the Lowell family tree, but they spent the deep winter months in a Beacon Hill townhouse in Boston, where gas lamps still lined the city streets and lit most homes. When these dimmed around eight o'clock in the evening as the chandelier of the Boston Museum-Theatre was lighted, the prosperous families in the neighborhood of Beacon Hill knew it was time to start for the play. Those fortunate enough to live in such upper-class neighborhoods ordered their carriages sent round; those not so fortunate took the horse car or set out on foot; and those even less fortunate merely looked up from the evening paper when the lights dimmed, to check their kitchen clocks. And over all of them, from the straitlaced elegance of rose-brick houses on the hill to the chimney pots and flat roofs of tenements across the Common on the west side of town, the golden dome of the State House was reflected by sun or gaslight, proclaiming day and night that Boston was the capital.

One of the dominant strands threading through the history of Massachusetts, and a major force in creating its oddly combined intellectual and industrial fabric, is the unique history of the ubiquitous Lowells. The story of the Lowells in America begins with Percival "Lowle" and his sons, John and Richard,* his daughter Joan, and their spouses and families, who landed on the shores of Massachusetts some twenty years after the *Mayflower* arrived, in 1639, bearing their coat of arms and a grudge against the high taxes in England. Percival had come to America to escape the taxes. He was of Norman stock, a direct descendant of William the Conqueror on his mother's side. He soon changed the spelling of his name (probably to avoid payment of taxes due the mother country) and proceeded to overcome the obstacles facing the early settlers. He and his descendants through his son John emerged

* The family and descendants of Richard Lowell moved inland, where they multiplied and led useful lives, but never attained the prominence of the branch to which Amy belonged.

victorious in various fields, from the professions to the more lucrative ones of merchandising and manufacturing, to the arts and sciences.

The sixth descendant of Percival Lowell married Susan Cabot, and the male descendants of his son John married their Cabot cousins. Between the two families, they filled the city of Boston with so many distinguished persons that the famous epigram, "the Cabots speak only to the Lowells, and the Lowells speak only to God," was not without foundation. (It has been said that in quoting the epigram, Amy reversed the order of Cabots and Lowells, but the gesture hardly seems characteristic of any Lowell, least of all Amy, who was to call herself more than once "the last of the barons.") Her first biographer, S. Foster Damon, has rightfully pointed out that to understand Amy Lowell, one must know her forebears, which included clergymen, judges, poets, scholars, critics, and horticulturists as well as manufacturers, merchants, and bankers, for, "not only did they bulk large in her own consciousness, but actually she was what they made her."

Tracing back the family heritage which shaped the mold of her highly individualistic personality, the first in the family to attend Harvard was John Lowell, fifth-generation descendant of Percival. He graduated at seventeen in 1721, received his master's degree three years later, and became a pastor at Newburyport, a post he retained till his death in 1767. His son John also graduated from Harvard at seventeen. He took part in the Revolutionary War, and in the preliminary Bill of Rights of 1774. He initiated the idealistic statement that "all men are born free and equal, and have certain natural, essential, and inalienable rights, among which may be reckoned the right of enjoying and defending their lives and liberties." The single word "enjoying" could have been used by Amy Lowell to justify her own life-style if she ever thought about it. Frequently she had to defend her literary style, but the mere fact that she was a Lowell was, from her point of view, license enough to live any way she pleased. She bore a remarkable resemblance, facially and otherwise, to "the Old Judge," as he was known in the family.

He became a member of the Continental Congress, a Fellow

of Harvard, and a founder of the American Academy of Arts and Sciences. The year before he died, President John Adams appointed him Chief Justice of the U.S. Circuit Court of four states. This hardy ancestor had three wives (one of whom was Susan Cabot), and by each wife he had a son: John III, Amy Lowell's great-grandfather; Francis Cabot Lowell, for whom the town of East Chelmsford was to have its name changed to Lowell; and Charles, the father of James Russell Lowell. It was these three eminent sons and their descendants whose names were to fill the Lowell files in library catalogs down to the present time. A fact which may well account for the dominance of masculine genes in Amy is that, as her brother Percy was to observe in an article after their father died: "The family has proved a singular instance of prepotence in the male line." He does add: "while the temperament has been as strikingly a maternal gift"; but he goes no further, nor does he record achievements of any substance from the maternal side.

John Lowell III, Amy's great-grandfather, was known as "the Boston Rebel" because of his liberal views in pamphleteering. His country estate in Roxbury, Broomley Vale, was laid out in long walks, and had specially grafted trees, through extensive hybridizing; according to Amy, he invented many new species of flowers and fruit trees. The first orchids in America were grown in his greenhouse. John III was also a founder of the Boston Athenaeum, the great library supported by shareholders, of which he was eventually president. He received an LL.D. from Harvard in 1814, and was an innovator in giving free legal advice to the poor.

His only son, John Amory Lowell, also became an honorary LL.D. after graduating from Harvard, but he abandoned the family profession of law for cotton manufacturing because of the strange genius of his uncle, Francis Cabot. This second son of "the Old Judge" traveled in England after his graduation from Harvard and brought back to America a thorough knowledge of the spinning jenny. Merely from his observations he proceeded to "re-invent the machine," no small feat of memory, as well as science. These machines, built and tested by the Lowells, were the foundation of the factory system of New England, for which he was equally cursed and blessed, as those states where the industry flourished gained the reputation of having ugly towns in contrast to beautiful villages. John Amory Lowell built the Boott Cotton Mills and the Massachusetts Cotton Mills, serving as treasurer and president-director of both. He was also president of Pacific Mills for six years and an official of the Suffolk Bank for fifty-nine years. (Small wonder that these two branches of the family were variously called "economic royalists" or "robber barons.") He distinguished himself in the field of arts and letters as well, principally in his devotion to the Lowell Institute, an intellectual enterprise founded by his half-cousin, John, Jr., who made John Amory its sole trustee. In this capacity, he succeeded so well that the institute prospered financially as well as academically.

His two real passions were algebra and botany. Soon after college, he took up his father's interest in flowers and fruit trees, and in 1845 started a noted herbarium and fine botanic library. But the financial panic of 1857 forced him to return to business, so he gave the books to Harvard and the herbarium to the Boston Society of Natural History. He was a member of the Linnean Society of London, and of the American Academy of Arts and Sciences—altogether a well-rounded, prominent personage in Boston society. Although his last-born grandchild, Amy, was only seven years old when he died in 1881, she was often in her Lowell grandfather's house, where there were many objects to catch an impressionable child's eye. One that she always admired was the bas-relief of panels of fruit painted into the dining-room ceiling, bunches of grapes, pears, and apples looking as if they must fall onto the table. When she redecorated Sevenels as its sole owner, she had those panels placed over the dining-room doors, a symbolic link she maintained with her Lowell ancestry while she was breaking loose from many of its traditions.

The third son of John III, the Reverend Charles Lowell, beloved pastor of West Church in Boston for half a century, gentle and refined, purchased the historic residence of Elmwood, and made it famous as its genial host. He was the father of the eminent journalist, poet, and statesman, James Russell Lowell, who, though only fifty-five at the time of Amy's birth, was already past his prime as a poet, but was looked upon as a much-revered relative during her childhood. Since his birthday was the day after hers, February 10, 1819, it is likely that some of the large family parties the Lowell clan often held at Broomley Vale, Elmwood, or Sevenels, were in celebration of both birthdays. (James, like Amy, had been the last-born in his family, and Ferris Greenslet's description of him as "the problem child of his family and of American literature" could easily be applied to Amy.) * His wit and charm were relished by his cousins as they had been earlier by his classmates and then by his students at Harvard. Family stories of "Cousin James" were passed around from one Lowell household to another, and his poetry, by the time Amy came along, was accepted and well known to all of them. Indeed, when asked what her favorite poem was, Amy at age ten answered at once, *The Vision of Sir Launfal,* and she was sincere. If she spoke partly out of family pride, it is true that poetry in the last third of the nineteenth century was generally static, particularly the sort taught in schools, and *The Vision* was at least a romantic tale.

Amy's father, Augustus Lowell, born January 15, 1830, was John Amory's son by his second wife, Elizabeth Cabot Putnam. Although not much of a scholar by Lowell standards, he graduated from Harvard in 1850. Four years later he married Katherine, the daughter of his father's business partner, Abbott Lawrence, a self-educated man, but eventually a congressman, and U.S. minister to England. The wedding on June 1, 1854, brought together two of

* Greenslet, in *The Lowells and Their Seven Worlds,* cites Havelock Ellis's conclusion that in large families the talented one is usually the oldest or the youngest. In two Lowell families it was both. James was the most famous, in his triple career as poet, professor, and diplomat. As minister to the Court of St. James's, he developed a warm friendship with Sir Leslie Stephen, a rather quixotic man of letters. There were stories of the literary arguments the two men would have, shouting quotations and hurling books at each other across Sir Leslie's library, making the argument an athletic as well as an intellectual contest. Sir Leslie was so fond of Lowell that he asked him to stand godfather to Stephen's youngest child. With the usual gift Lowell sent a poem, "Verses to go with a Posset-dish to my dear little God-daughter." Among the contents of the posset-dish poem was the wish that she might have "Her father's wit veined through/with tenderness." The wish came true, for the little girl was to become the famous novelist Virginia Woolf. Stephen paid Lowell a long visit at Elmwood in the summer of 1890, a year before the poet died, when there were Lowell clan gatherings. Her Cousin James's connection with the Stephens family forms a link between the Bloomsbury circle and Amy's Imagist enclave.

America's oldest families. The Lawrences had come over from England almost as early as the Lowells and had settled at Groton as farmers. Some time in the late eighteenth or early nineteenth century, Amos and Abbott Lawrence started an import business, A. & A. Lawrence & Company, which became famous throughout the world. The firm would ship purchases anywhere and boasted in a slogan that the company "spanned the globe." Katherine, Abbott's second daughter, received the cultural education her father did not have. She spoke seven languages, played five instruments, and sang. (Very little of this knowledge was put to practical use, except when she tried to tutor her obstreperous youngest daughter in French, with minimal success.) Through the Lowells, the Lawrences became cotton manufacturers, and another Massachusetts mill town, Lawrence, notorious for its textile strikes, was established in the name of the family who furnished the capital to build the factory.

Augustus and Katherine Lowell's first child, Percival, was born on March 13, 1855, about nine months after they were married; his name harked back ten generations to the original immigrant ancestor. Another son was born within a year and was named for his maternal grandfather, Abbott Lawrence, whom the family always called by his second name. A boy-and-girl set of twins came next, Roger and Katherine, but the boy died about the time another daughter, Elizabeth (always called Bessie), arrived. Too many childbirths, plus the strain of Roger's illness and death, brought on a serious malady, Bright's disease, in Mrs. Lowell, who had shown a tendency toward it from the time she was a girl. Pictures of her show a pretty, rather frail-looking young woman with a thoughtful, mild, pleasant face, a figure of medium build, and moderately fashionable dress. One would guess that she accepted her place as wife of Augustus Lowell, the hard man of business, with some trepidation, though she was from an equally solid family background. There can be no doubt that she did not question his decisions in regard to the family or the household any more than she would have questioned his business affairs or other interests. For his part, Augustus, concerned about his wife's health, decided that the spas in Europe might cure her of her chronic condition, and they spent two and a half years at these watering places.

When they returned, they learned that the estate at Roxbury where they had lived from the time they were married was soon to be mutilated by a railroad, so Augustus sold the home at once and bought a smaller place, only ten acres, at Brookline, not too far from Boston, but at a safe enough distance not to be absorbed by the city. Situated on the western slope of Heath Street, a country road, it was ideally suited to landscape gardening, and Augustus gave full expression to the Lowell love of horticulture. In Amy's words, "He covered it with beautiful and exotic flowering shrubs, and many rare and lovely flowers. The planning of his garden was done entirely by himself. He never allowed anyone to . . . decide any matter of change or addition . . . he got up at six o'clock every morning and cut his favorites, the roses, with his own hands." (He once cut a thousand roses in three days.) "In the rear were three greenhouses which supplied fruit and vegetables for a household of sixteen people. Two hothouses of grapes helped to shield the sunken garden. . . ." She also wrote a more detailed and vivid description of her father's landscape design, but the above gives some idea of his careful planning and meticulous habits. This was his home, the place for carrying out his ideals of living; the townhouses were only conveniences for the winter months. They lived in several townhouses: on Beacon Street, Park Square, Commonwealth Avenue, and Tremont Street.

The Brookline home had garrets for storage trunks that could stay for generations. There were stables for horses and cows, plenty of countryside for children to play in and explore, and a garden Augustus could cultivate for decades. When his father died, Augustus became sole trustee of the Lowell Institute. He also was a founder and corporate member of the Massachusetts Institute of Technology. Like the Lowells before him, he was an official of the American Academy of Arts and Sciences and participated in civic affairs generally. He was a methodical man, who was always punctual, and insisted on punctuality at meals. According to Bessie, he used to rise at 4:00 A.M. in the summer and at 4:30 in the winter. In the summer he spent the before-breakfast hours swimming or fishing during the weeks the family were at a private resort place near Lynn, both before and for some time after he bought the Brookline estate. When the boys discovered a swimming hole, he was likely to plunge in it nude along with them after his pruning or cultivating was done. He went swimming every summer day until he was eighty; and, whether to show his hardiness or constant warm-bloodedness, he never wore an overcoat during the winter. In the winter he spent prebreakfast hours reading, or writing tracts; when he left for the office, he put on only a topcoat and scarf. Yet emotionally he was not warm-blooded, nor was he cold or unkind; but he was remote, taciturn, and bound to a strict routine, as he expected his children to be. Like his father before him, he refused to accept Darwin's theory, and he would not allow a volume of "that atheist" Shelley in the house.

Some years after the family moved to Brookline, Mrs. Lowell became pregnant again, and a daughter born on May 1 was named for the merry month, but the birth was hard, and she lived only a day. Katherine Lowell was not well, and her chronic disorder was exacerbated by this latest drain on her system. It is possible that she was beginning an early menopause, and, like many women, was going through a second period of fertility. Little was known about contraception in the 1870s and less was practiced. Two and a half years later she was pregnant again, and on February 9, 1874, the daughter that was to be her last child arrived under even greater duress than the previous girl. Augustus wanted to call her Rebecca Amory, after a spinster sister of his father, his doughty Aunt Amory, who had recently died and whom he had regarded with affection for her forthright opinions. Katherine, however, exhausted though she was by the rigors of childbirth, protested that she did not like the name "Rebecca," and "Amory" she thought too masculine. It would not do to call a daughter by a surname. She compromised by suggesting "Amy," which was almost the same, but softer, and truly a girl's name. (Years later her daughter expressed her distaste for her mother's choice in no uncertain terms: "Amy" was a "foolish, fancy" name; she would much have preferred her great-aunt's; "Rebecca Amory Lowell" had a ring of strong character to it, and, since it was a family name, would have been more meaningful. If she had thought, she would have taken it when her first volume of poetry was published, but once the book was out, it was too late.)

In any case, Amy it was, and, with her arrival, her father decided his family was complete. It was then that he devised the word "Sevenels" for his home base in Brookline, a name that Amy considered more appropriate than the one *she* was given. Sevenels was her home from birth to death, no matter how far she traveled in between; she enjoyed living there and returning there after a journey. The place meant much more to her than to her brothers and sisters, who would begin to leave it before long. The age gap between her and her brothers was nearly a generation: Percy, nineteen, was a sophomore at Harvard; Lawrence, seventeen and a half, was a freshman. Her older sister, Katie, at sixteen, was already a young lady, preparing for her debut, and Bessie, the closest to her in age, usually charged to "look after the baby" on family outings, was already in her adolescence by the time Amy was talking and, according to Bessie, "running wild" in the nursery, teasing and tormenting her nurse (whom she hardly ever obeyed although they adored each other) because she had no small playmates.

Her mother, a semi-invalid during most of Amy's life, and particularly in the first few years, would come into the top-floor nursery for a little while each day to hold the baby, to make sure she was properly cared for, and, as soon as she was old enough, to show her picture books; but almost the entire care was left to Medusa May, the governess-nurse better known as "Mu," Amy's name for her. Augustus Lowell, involved with multiple interests as he was, had little time for a baby daughter until she was able to respond with something more than a smile or gurgle or a shouting cry of hunger, pain, or anger. There never was anything wrong with Amy's lung power, and during infancy, she was apt to smile frequently, especially when hugged, as any well-fed baby tends to do. When she began to respond with words and could toddle up to her father, as she did soon after her first birthday, he spent more time with her. He began to show her the garden and to teach her things about it, though she paid little attention. One of her earliest memories was "helping Papa gather the seeds." She would watch, fascinated, while he folded pieces of paper into flutings to hold the seeds; then she would tag along after him as he went from one bed to another selecting the best specimen for seeds, and he would let her hold the paper while he slid them into the pleats. She would soon get tired of waiting and start chasing a butterfly or grasshopper. Then, irritated, he would admonish her: "If you can't pay attention to what I'm doing, run away and play, child!" And off she would go. (Later she wished she had paid closer attention while a child to the knowledge of gardening her father could have taught her instead of taking it all for granted. Yet she learned a great deal by osmosis, as it were, from being around her father or simply by playing in the garden by herself as she did on many summer afternoons till she heard the carriage coming up the drive and ran to meet Papa, back from his office in Boston.)

Born late into a family of illustrious forebears, Amy rebelled yet conformed. She basked in the limelight of a ruling house while resenting some of the rules in her immediate family, one cause of her emotional conflict to come.

CHAPTER III

"The Postscript"—Amy in Childhood

WHEN AMY LOWELL BECAME AWARE of the world around her, it seemed to her that the whole outdoors was a bright-colored garden and that all the people in the big house where she was born were grown-ups. Even her sister Bessie, who, she was told, was the "youngest" of the "older children," seemed grand at times, and the others, especially her two brothers, seemed very grand indeed. To them she was a novelty, and her parents had almost forgotten what it was like to have a baby in the family; everyone laughed at her lispings, her funny, clever sayings, which only inspired her more. Percy, the oldest and most exciting, nicknamed her "the Postscript," and the others took it up. She did not realize fully what it meant until in later years when, for various reasons, she found it impossible to be on time even for family dinners, and they claimed it was not her fault: She was born late. The phrase was almost symbolic of her entire life-experience, including her career.

According to her own testimony, her "earliest recollection was a mocking-bird" in that flower-filled garden; her father, holding her small hand in his, led her through the paths bordering the bewildering maze of varicolored beds while the trilling of a bird grew louder and louder until at last he stopped at the bottom of a low hill with the fruit garden growing up its sides. Here on a pear tree hung a bird cage; as they approached, the trilling stopped. Then all at once it became louder than ever, with a burst of song in a different tone. "Hear that, Amy," her father said, listening to the notes with an approving wink of satisfaction. "He's our mocking-bird." He adored these birds and always kept one in a cage, whether in the little apple-and-pear orchard during the summer or in the greenhouse or a sunny corner of the long dining room in the winter. Amy listened and soon became used to the mockingbird in the Lowell menagerie: There was always a dog or two, barn cats, cows, a few chickens, and, best of all, horses; but she never could understand why the mockingbird was in a cage. She never said anything to her father, however, for this was "Papa's" pleasure, just as the pruning and cutting of the roses was his special province, and she early learned that the Lowells let each other alone as far as individual interests were concerned. Besides, "Papa" was head of the house, whose preferences and set rules were not to be questioned or disputed, except possibly by Percy; certainly not by a girl child, who was the baby of the family. That she learned to circumvent some of his rules could be attributed to the fact that Amy, seemingly as much boy as girl, was so much like Augustus himself at times that it was as if she had literally sprung from her father's loins.

From the time she could walk without being held she began to explore the gardens and grounds of Sevenels by herself, and if the farm was Augustus Lowell's principality, it was a paradise to his youngest child. During the month of June she loved to wade in the wide meadow kept for mowing just inside a broad belt of trees, plunging waist-deep into "a glory of daisies and buttercups nodding in the wind," accompanied by her dog, Buff, a brown spaniel, nosing along beside her, only the tip of his plumed tail waving above the meadow flowers and grasses. Both were stalking prey, the dog perhaps a mole or woodchuck, she an Indian or enemy outlaw (by the time she was seven or eight). Beyond the meadow, the grove began. In her own words, "One could put the whole grove in one's pocket, but as a child it seemed to me limitless, and many are the Indians I have shot when out scouting with my bow and arrows as they peered for a moment behind a distant tree trunk, and, in spite of a little confusion in my mind as to whether I were Robinhood or the Last of the Mohicans, I delight to record that I never missed my man." (A typical reaction on her part.)

A path led to an old-fashioned arbor covered with wisteria and trumpetvine—the perfect hideaway—and from there down two flights of stone steps to the sunken formal garden. Amy never knew whether the garden had been artificially blasted out or made from a natural basin; she never thought to ask, for by the time she came into the world and first saw it lying some twenty feet below the south lawn, she felt sure it had always been there. The paths were so clearly cut that you could walk or run all around every bed, and the garden was kept in bloom from April until October. Here Amy rolled her white hoop; caught bees in canterbury bells, holding them prisoner while they sucked and fought to get out; pinched the snapdragons to see them gape, open-mouthed; and tried to catch white moths or butterflies. Gradually, she learned the names of all the flowers strewn throughout her poetry, often used in weird ways: foxglove and dahlia; asters and anemones; larkspur and blue salvia; heliotrope and night-scented stock; poppies and *Pyrus japonica,* as well as the "daffodils and bright blue squills" she made famous in her "Patterns." Amy Lowell used to complain that she took flowers so for granted as a child that she was "annoyed at her own ignorance," but no one who was ignorant of flowers or "the caprices of nature" could make the choices she did for her poems or ask, as she did, "Why . . . will clematis Jackmani flourish year after year on two of my trellises and die annually on the third?" And she added: "I know every tree, every rock, every flower, as only children know these things. . . ."

On the other side of the house were well-kept lawns and wide shrubberies of magnolias and lilacs, all shades of lilacs, their "great puffs of flowers" * with the rich, sweet fragrance filling all the pores of her plump child's body as she ambled past them some soft May mornings toward the fruit and vegetable gardens on her way to one of her favorite haunts—the stables. She loved and accepted the fragrance of lilacs without realizing it, but the "horsy" smell of the stables, combined with the mystery of the dark stalls and

* From Amy Lowell's famous poem, "Lilacs."

the fascination of the great lithe animals, never failed to fill her with excitement and love of the whole surroundings.

Here Burns, the coachman, was king, and she never doubted his authority or wisdom. Between these two there was a subtle empathy and a mutual admiration from the time Amy was a tiny child taking her first drive. She showed no fear of horses. In fact, the commotion caused by the harnessing—the neighing, snorting, and pawing of the pairs as they responded to Burns's orders (given with a pat on the nose, a slap on the rump)—seemed to delight her. When the carriage was brought out and he perched her on the box beside him, she shouted for joy. Burns was a colorful character around Brookline, since he had been a noted jockey at Newmarket as a boy. After that first drive, her place was on the box beside Burns, and one fine Sunday morning when she was not yet three, she drove the horses to and from church; of course, Burns kept the reins hung lightly over his forefinger, but it was remarkable how naturally she "took to driving," he said.

Amy spent hours planted on an overturned bucket in the stable, watching Burns while he curried and otherwise tended the horses. She listened to his stories and asked him questions about breeds, points, and habits. "All she knew about horses, and she knew a great deal, was learnt from him," Bessie commented in her memoir.* Sometimes he would let her help him, so she would get the feel of horses, and she accepted his instructions quickly, never doubting his orders. A family tale arose from the October day both sisters were going for a drive, and, just as they were about to start, Bessie thought Amy might get chilly sitting up on the box, so, with her seniority of twelve years over "the Postscript," she told her to get a coat. Amy refused flatly: "No, I don't want to."

Burns, about to lift his crop to the horses, repeated Bessie's command, and Amy obediently went back to get a coat. At supper Bessie related the incident, and Augustus, his sharp eyes staring into hers sternly, asked Amy why she obeyed the coachman and not her sister. She answered seriously, "Oh, Burns was *born* to command." The flicker of a smile crossed Mr. Lowell's face briefly,

* Mrs. William Lowell Putnam, "A Glimpse of Amy Lowell's Childhood by Her Sister," unpublished manuscript.

but Percy and Lawrence hooted with laughter, joined by the older girls. Amy, sensing she had somehow scored, moved in quickly with, "On the strength of that, can't I sit up an hour later tonight?" (She always wanted to stay up later than her bedtime.)

Her father didn't answer, but her mother, with a wan smile, said, "We'll see," so she knew she would get around them again. (The habit of bending her wits to get around the grown-ups—or people in authority—was one that stayed with her all her life.) Her parents were half a generation too old to discipline her properly, as her first biographer pointed out: They had brought up too many children to cope with a new and stubborn personality.* Except for his set of rules and regulations, her father was too remote. Her mother was either too sympathetic or too irritable. Amy virtually disregarded her nurse, and Bessie's discipline she resented. In Burns, however, Amy found a camaraderie and an authority, so she responded to his directives with a docility that baffled her elders. In fact, a favorite Boston quip was that "Amy Lowell was brought up by the coachman." There came a day on which she really drove without Burns's guiding hand on the reins, and nothing made her prouder than his admiring comment that she "handled the horses like a man."

In general, she preferred outdoor games and activities to indoor diversions and was a true tomboy before she was eight. Books were the one exception. From the time she learned to read, she loved to curl up with a good book, especially on rainy days; and she spent hours reading in bed at night. Her mother thought she should be more feminine and tried to interest her in dolls and sewing, things Amy "abhorred," according to an early friend. She enjoyed making paper dolls, or watching Bessie make them for her, because of the inventiveness the process involved. But once they were finished, she didn't care to play with them; and the usual French doll that small girls of her era received for Christmas left her indifferent. She scorned the little girl's game of playing house.

Undoubtedly the reason for her tomboy trait was that for the first five years of her life she lacked the companionship of children

* S. Foster Damon, *Amy Lowell: A Chronicle* (Boston: Houghton Mifflin Company, 1935).

her own age; she was lonely, and, left to her own devices, she chose to do the things that would make her seem like the grown-ups she most admired: her brothers and her father, in that order. As she went along the footpath outdoors, she tried to imitate her brothers' walk, pounding her heels down hard. Indoors, she watched her brothers playing billiards with their father; she even liked to watch her brothers study and write, with books and papers all around them. Whatever they were doing, "Can I watch?" was her persistent question. Sometimes, watching them play chess, she would ask, "Can I play, too?" But they waved her away, saying she was "too little to play chess." Once in a while they would relent and play jacks with her, but Percy was such a whiz that he always won. Then he would show her a few tricks to improve her game.

Percy was her idol. Everything he tried, he did easily and skillfully. Percy had a certain dash that was lacking in Lawrence, who more closely resembled their father. Augustus, ever immaculately dressed, was arid in his neatness. Beneath his steel-gray eyes and short, well-shaped nose his tight-lipped mouth was half-covered by a walrus mustache always well groomed, like his neatly combed hair. (His double-breasted waistcoat was always neatly buttoned, his tie neatly tied. Even in his shirtsleeves, pruning his roses, he had the look of a neat, well-ordered individual.) And as the director of his cotton mills he was paternal, distant in attitude, respected but unloved. Lawrence, although he had some of their mother's attributes, was almost as dry, tight-lipped, and insistent on well-ordered stability as Augustus. Lacking in humor in comparison to Percy, he was too busy studying law at Harvard to show much interest in his baby sister or to take the time, as Percy did, to try to understand and entertain or instruct her occasionally.

One of the objects Amy adored in the big house was the panel of carved-wood animal heads in the front hall, and it was usually Percy who lifted her up to pat them on the way to and from dinner. (All her life the nose on the deer head nearest the dining room shone with the multiple patting she had given it.) At the large family dinners of the Lowell clan, it was Percy who could best keep up with Cousin James (although all the Lowells were famous for their brilliant conversations) and who would make things even livelier with some crackling joke, which was Amy's cue to join in with a joke of her own.

She listened to these conversations whatever the topic, but there was one recurrent subject she dreaded—the Civil War. The war had been over for ten years before she was born, but feeling in the family still ran high against Southern atrocities on the battlefields and in prison camps like Libby, Andersonville, or anywhere Northerners had been mistreated. She listened to the grisly tales, the war songs like "Tenting on the Old Camp Ground," and "the whole thing assumed at once the horror of actual happening and the mysticism of a legend," as she wrote later. To an impressionable child like Amy, the grim aspect of the Civil War was both terrifying and fascinating, but it engendered a fear so great that she was never able to touch upon anything approaching it in her work. Perhaps because the Lowell legends of her own ancestry were often repeated at these family gatherings, the ghosts of the past were very real to Amy, and, with the single exception of those originating in the Civil War, became an appreciable part of her poetry.

In general, however, these early years were the happiest of her life. It was true that she often felt lonely, but not for want of attention. She did her share of maintaining the family tradition of brilliant conversation by concocting a series of puns so clever that she would be called downstairs to amuse her mother's guests. After her audience had laughed a few times, she would ask eagerly, "Want to hear some more puns?" If they did, she had a fresh supply ready, but if they said no, she was just as glad to run back up to the nursery or outdoors to play. She seemed to have been born with a sense of audience reaction. Although she loved to perform, she was too intelligent to be an exhibitionist, as her detractors were to claim in the future; and while she enjoyed appreciation, she was too self-confident as the spoiled darling of a Lowell to be downcast if she didn't receive as much as she expected on occasion. Perhaps because she associated frequently with distinguished people of an older generation—besides Cousin James, other important relatives and famous men from abroad who came to lecture at the Lowell Institute were entertained at Sevenels—

Amy Lowell tended to be precocious intellectually but somewhat old-fashioned in other ways.

Augustus and the family moved to a rented townhouse at 97 Beacon Street when Amy was about four years old, so the winters from then on were spent in Boston, but the family returned to Sevenels in time for May Day and stayed until late October or until the weather became very cold in November. As a result, in her recollections of her childhood, Sevenels seemed to be in a state of perpetual summer. Boston was associated with school, the Boston Museum-Theatre (where she loved to see the relics of the American Revolution, the whaling industry, and old clipper ships almost as much as the performance in the auditorium), and other important events. One of these was the marriage of her brother Lawrence (typically, to a third cousin, Anna Parker Lowell) which took place at King's Chapel in Boston when Amy was only five. Another in the same year was a certain dinner party her parents took her to, actually a meeting of the literary Saturday Night Club, to which they belonged. The party was eventful for a lovely, memorable incident: Mr. Longfellow, the venerable white-haired, bearded poet, carried her around the table in a scrap basket. She never quite knew how it came about, but "the recollection of that ride is quite as vivid as though it were yesterday," she wrote in 1919.

It must have been about this time—when she was five or six—that her governess began teaching Amy to read and write. She learned to read easily enough because she wanted to: She had been longing to get her hands on a book and go through it herself. Her mother had been reading aloud to her during her daily visit to the nursery, but that was all too short a time for Amy. In particular, at first she coveted one of a series of books about a typical New England boy, the first of the Little Rollo books. The whole set was in a fine-grained morocco edition illustrated with woodcuts; to Amy, the mere touch of the morocco was a delight, and she soon determined that all those books should be hers. There was an ancient yellow-ash bookcase in the nursery, but it contained only a few fairy-tale volumes—well worn, for she had the stories read to her many times—and she wanted the Rollo books for "that bookcase." * "The passion of her covetous desire" to own *Rollo Learning to Read* was so great that she learned to read in a remarkably short time, perhaps to use her knowledge as another tool in wheedling the treasured copy out of her mother. She started by demanding, "Read it again!" a great many times, so that her mother probably grew weary of it and was glad enough to relinquish it when her youngest child could read by herself. Eventually she managed to acquire the whole set. She also learned to form the letters of the alphabet, but her governess, Mu, could not teach her to spell words any way but phonetically, and even then it was hard to tell how she arrived at certain misspellings. The truth was that spelling bored Amy, and she didn't want to bother to learn it.

She stood alone in her enthusiasm for Rollo; none of her small acquaintances took to him, though obstinate Amy tried to make them like him by reading select passages out loud. But her friends' scorn did not diminish her admiration. She cherished those hard-won copies all her life and kept them in "that bookcase" for her nieces and nephews to read not many years later.

The children who refused to be a captive audience were probably some of Amy's classmates at dancing school. Like the other Lowell daughters, she was enrolled at an early age at Papanti's, *the* Boston dancing school for generations of Back Bay families. Besides the feminine grace that every future debutante was supposed to acquire in learning to dance, Mr. Lowell thought the lessons would provide enough exercise for Amy to control her weight; she was, as Percy called her, a "pleasingly plump little girl," but her father and mother hoped she would not become any plumper. In spite of her outdoor activity, the child had a lazy streak: She hated to get up in the morning and was often late for breakfast. Her father's scoldings and lectures on the benefits of early rising seemed to have no effect on Amy. She would always say, "I'm sorry, Papa," but after a few mornings she would forget about his strict schedule and take her time getting ready to go downstairs. She was a natural dawdler and dreamer in the morning, and no amount of

* "That Bookcase" was the title of the second of two articles published in the *New York Evening Post*, 1920.

nudging from her nurse could make her dress any faster when she could read more easily she began reading in bed, and this brought about a twofold scolding from her father: The third floor was not yet wired for electricity, so she had to read by kerosene lamp (which she relit after Mu had gone to bed), and her father told her she would ruin her eyes if she didn't stop it.

The brief exercise she did at Papanti's with its spring floor, which sent up great clouds of dust on state occasions, didn't help her much. Mr. Papanti was a frail old gentleman "in a wig, who fiddled while he demonstrated the steps," as she said. To Amy, he was a comic figure, especially if his toupee went askew as he made mincing runs and turns to illustrate the schottische or the german. She would start to giggle, which set off the others in her small ring of beginners, so precious little was learned in the first season; usually, a young lady kept on going to Papanti's till she "came out," so there was plenty of time.

She was still struggling hard with writing and spelling when she made one of her bright remarks, which, after circulating through Boston society, found its way into print as a joke in *Life,** the original humor magazine founded by a group of Harvard graduates in 1883 who had earlier founded the Harvard *Lampoon* (one of whose contributors was Lawrence Lowell). Amy's remark, given as explanation for her chronic misspelling, was entitled, "A Short Way Out of It," a two-line dialogue: "Papa—'But why do you sign it: Your loving son, Amy?' Amy—'Why of course mamma will know, and I couldn't spell daughter.' " She might have added that she was always wishing she had been a boy and so was doubly prone to sign herself son in a note she had written to her mother when her parents went out of town for a few days. At any rate, she was evidently delighted with her first taste of publicity, judging by a reprint of the *Life* joke found in one of her childhood books. She was encouraged to do more writing and wrote a series of character sketches, which provide clear examples of her misspelling.

In the summer of 1882, Mr. Lowell took his wife and three

* Henry Luce, founder of the photography and news magazine, *Life,* which folded nearly a century later (1972), bought the title from the owners of the earlier publication in the 1930s.

daughters on a tour of Europe. Katherine had come out and, as a popular debutante, had received several offers of marriage from eligible young men, but she needed some time to make up her mind. In such a case, a trip abroad was customary, and would be educational for Bessie and for Amy, who, at eight years, he felt, was "old enough to behave herself." However, they went dashing through so many countries—Scotland, England, the Netherlands, Italy, Germany, Norway, Denmark, and Sweden—that she was overwhelmed by myriad impressions and found it tedious and difficult to sit through long train rides. Her parents, who had been letting her do about what she pleased, changed their tactics and went to the other extreme. They put up with no nonsense. She had to go to bed and get up and dress promptly so they could keep to the tour's schedule. Bessie, however, had charge of keeping her occupied during the endless railroad trips, and it was then that she created whole families of ingenious paper dolls, with all they needed, from dustpans and brushes to umbrellas—all devised under her "baby's sister's" detailed directions. Amy was not much help in making the dolls, but she seemed fascinated by seeing them take shape under *her* supervision, and the process whiled away many a listless hour. These were the only dolls she ever really liked; she took them on trips everywhere afterward.

She was so stimulated by the kaleidoscopic succession of sights, however, that she became fearfully ill before the end of the journey. She might have withstood the impact of multiple experiences better if her governess had not taken her to see the instruments of torture on display at Nuremberg one afternoon when the others were attending an opera thought to be too heavy for a child. She was almost traumatized by those monuments of torture, and by one in particular. As she wrote later, "for months afterward," her "nights were made horrible by visions of the Iron Virgin." * Her family never realized how terrified and shaken she was, but in her opinion, only the return voyage and the quiet life at Sevenels averted a severe breakdown or brain fever; it was in-

* A controversial piece, then thought to be a relic of the Middle Ages; it was actually created in 1867, of tin instead of iron, depicting the agony of a martyred saint.

deed several years before she regained her nerve sufficiently not to be afraid of the dark.

Autumn had set in by the time the Lowells returned to Sevenels, so Amy could not play outdoors. But indoors there was a pleasant hustle and bustle going on, for Katherine had decided to accept the hand of Alfred Roosevelt in marriage. He was a first cousin of the Teddy Roosevelt whose exploits would be making headlines in a few years, and there were several names of that prominent family on the guest list for the wedding, which was to take place December 5 at St. Paul's Church in Brookline. Seamstresses came to Sevenels to prepare the trousseau, and bridesmaids met with Katie to discuss their gowns. Parties were given for her, some of them by the other branches of the Lowell clan. It may have been at one of these family parties that Amy, who loved to eat, consumed all of a large dish of rice pudding set before her with such zest and gusto that laughing remarks were made about her capacity for food. Amy, laughing with the rest, bragged that she could eat another plateful right then, and it took only Percy's "I dare you!" for her to prove her prowess by eating a second helping, to everyone's amusement. But when they prepared to go home, her coat simply would not button across her middle. "And it never buttoned again," she declared humorously in relating the incident. Although they joked about it at the time, this was the first evidence of the obesity that was to plague her throughout her life.

The following summer Amy was taken on a cross-country tour to the West Coast. Percy had just left for the Far East, and she missed him dreadfully; her parents thought the trip would be both educational and entertaining for her. They persuaded her to start a journal (as all well-educated people were expected to do from the time they could read and write). Her *Notes of my trip to and from California,* dutifully jotted down, are notable mostly for her description of the first night in a berth on a Pullman, which shows her eye for detail, giving an accurate account of an experience that is rapidly becoming a vanishing part of Americana. Her mention of waking in the night to a beautiful moon is unusual in a child of nine. It marks the beginning of her ardent moon worship, a lifelong love.

After this burst of energy, however, she slackened off. The diary dwindled to a mere list of eating places, significantly enough in her case. And in Santa Fe, which they reached on the tenth day of their journey (having stopped over several days at various points, including "Chicago"), she was fascinated by the sight of the Indians riding donkeys down the streets, "arrayed in gaudily striped blankets and feathers," as she wrote to D. H. Lawrence thirty years later. She was even more excited by the sight of horses in a corral and of the lassoing of a spirited colt by a cowboy. Horses in any setting never failed to stimulate her. The journal ended abruptly when they arrived in Los Angeles and from there "took stages to go into the Yosemite," where "the wild dash in a coach along the steep roads" delighted her.

Following the final entry in this journal, Amy wrote her first poem, the subject of which, surprisingly, was "Chacago," out of all the places they had visited, and, even more curious, was set down like the "new" poetry she later championed, in one-, two-, or three-word lines: "Chacago. ditto/ the land of/ the free./ It is on lake/ Mich'gan, and/ not on the sea./ It has some/ fine houses/ in the suberbs/ I'm told/ And its people are rolling in/ silver and/ gold./ . . ." But she concludes, after citing a few more features of the Windy City: "I'de rather/ go home./ To Boston,/ Charles River,/ and the/ State houses/ dome."

Percival Lowell, true to his reputation of cutting a dashing figure and making a name for himself (as a Lowell, a fact he never forgot), wrote home before the year 1882 was out that officials in Tokyo had just appointed him counselor and foreign secretary to the special mission from Korea to the United States. He would be coming home soon, bringing with him as his own secretary, a seventeen-year-old Oriental boy, Tsunejiro Miyaoka. The news filled Amy with joyful anticipation. Percy was her hero; his every act was touched with glamour in her eyes, and she could hardly wait till he and his secretary arrived. She was not disappointed. Percy brought presents for everyone, including Amy, whom he introduced as "the baby" of the family to Miyaoka. His young secretary, with his black hair, almond-shaped eyes, and broad toothy grin, captivated Amy. He teased her as Percy did, and told her fascinating new fairy tales of fox-sprites and spider demons and two-sworded nobles and camellia trees that walked and sobbed. Every day, when his duties for Percy were over and Amy came home from the private school she had started attending, Tsunejiro would gladly play games with her, boxes of which she had inherited from her parents; or they would swap stories of East and West, Amy being only too willing to give her versions of Hans Christian Andersen—a favorite of hers—to such a receptive ear. To him she was an "eager sympathy in a foreign land," and, although her mother rebuked her for being too familiar with an adult, he was grateful for her boyish friendliness in making him feel at home.

All too soon the special mission terminated, and Percy returned to the Far East, taking Tsunejiro with him. It would be forty years until she saw the secretary again, and almost that long until she heard from him. By then he was *Doctor* Miyaoka, distinguished in his own field, and he wanted to see "the baby" who had become so famous. In one of her letters at that time, she recalled her mother's rebuke, adding, "But you were so good to me and played with me so delightfully how could I resist considering you a play-fellow of my own age!"

It would be ten years until she saw her older brother again, for Percy stayed in the Orient, chiefly Japan, until 1893, and wrote four books describing the country as well as relating his experiences.*

During those years Percy frequently wrote to his "little sister" detailed letters on notepaper decorated with Japanese designs. Very often the postman brought a package for "Miss Amy Lowell," which made her feel important. A "constant stream of pictures, prints, and kakemonos flowed in upon her," she wrote later, which undoubtedly stimulated her imagination to the point where, as she said, she could not realize that she had not actually been there, it was all so vivid to her as seen through Percy's eyes.

* His *Soul of the Far East,* published in 1888, inspired Lafcadio Hearn to go to Japan.

The packages that came from him, mailed with exotic Oriental stamps, were especially welcome on days when school seemed too trying to bear. At school she was beginning to experience a discipline even stricter than the sort she now received at home (since she was nine, old enough to behave herself, her father thought). At the first private school she attended—there were several of them between the years of eight and twelve because she could not get along with her teachers and resented their authority—she made friends with the children, but was the terror of the faculty. Precocious, knowledgeable, a tomboy, and a smart-aleck, too impatient to "grub" for grades. Amy did not bother about spelling any more than she did with Mu at home; and the multiplication table was still a mystery to her at middle age. In vain did various teachers try to drum these subjects into her head, and inevitably they sent reports to her parents stating that "Amy was the ringleader in fun and mischief," which was disrupting to the class. Then her parents would send her to another school.

Disrupting or not, Amy made friends among her classmates by amusing them with her tendency to clown. Then she bossed them and often angered them, but won their devotion by her own. Her forthright admiration for any distinctive attribute * or accomplishment was irresistible, but her enthusiasm did not survive once the subject was exhausted; at that point, the friendship was often broken up by a violent quarrel. Her growing stockiness was an embarrassment that hindered her from developing the maturity that other girls entered into with grace and ease. Her heart longed for the beauty and charm she envied in other girls, but as her hopes grew dimmer and dimmer, she began to imitate her adored brothers more and more. In games and outdoor sports, at least, she could be somebody, and saw to it that she was, especially when they played Indians at the Lowells' park, or prisoner's base, the favorite at the Cabots'; she set the rules and led off whether she was supposed to or not. In winter, her own favorite was "punging," partly because her parents frowned on it as being an unnecessary risk. A group of children would take themselves into the streets of Boston to hitch free rides on the runners of the slow delivery

* She seemed to gravitate toward the prettiest girls in school.

sleighs that replaced grocery wagons in the winter; an added thrill was lent by a surly driver who would holler, "Git off there!" or "No pungers allowed!" and could be teased with retaliatory hoots and catcalls.

At eleven, she was already twice an aunt, with a niece and nephew * nearer in age to her than any of her sisters or brothers, so she considered herself in a position to give orders, whether she was or not. Her best friend of this period, Katherine Dana ** has used "obstreperous" as the one word to describe Amy Lowell then. The two met during the summer of 1885, when the Danas came to live on the next estate to Sevenels in Brookline, and "a very roly-poly little girl with a brown spaniel named Buff" came up to a gate in the fence, full of curiosity about her new neighbors. After they had exchanged names, Amy asked her stock questions: "How old are you?" "What time do you have to go to bed?" and "What books do you like to read?" They discovered they were the same age, had about the same bedtime, and, while their reading tastes were not exactly the same—hardly anyone besides Amy read or liked the Rollo books—they were close enough to satisfy Amy. Soon the two girls were fast friends, running back and forth through the gate in the fence with some plan dear to the hearts of eleven-year-olds.

Amy was always ready with schemes to affront authority. It was her idea to climb up on the roof to watch the sunrise once when Katie came to visit her for a week while the Lowells were away. Because Bessie forbade it, Amy convinced her friend to go through with the scheme. Then they crept down to the nursery—or, as Amy now called it, the "sky parlour"—again. The household had not yet stirred.

Amy felt a sense of triumph because they had succeeded without being caught. "If we were boys," she told Katie, "we could do a lot more things like that, and nobody would ask any questions."

* Her sister Katherine's children: Elfrieda, born December 1883, and James A. Roosevelt, born a few days after Amy's birthday, in February 1885. She was "Aunt Amy" to them within a year.

** Katherine Dana White, "Recollections of Amy Lowell in Childhood," unpublished manuscript.

Before long, her friend realized that "Amy was deeply grieved that she was not a boy. She always tried to walk exactly like her brothers, Percy and Lawrence, striding along with her head down and yellow straw hat, round as a cheese, crammed over her ears. She loved horses and dogs. Jack, her favorite, a black cocker spaniel, was her inseparable companion. Though not fond of riding horseback, she loved to drive, and her father gave her a horse of her own as soon as he thought she was skilled enough to handle him." To hasten that day, she put Jack to good use. "I can see Amy driving her dog Jack in harness all over the place, or sliding down the hay in the barn loft, or struggling to play baseball." (Although she was tomboyish, she was not athletic, probably because she wouldn't discipline herself enough to learn skill in outdoor games; and although full of energy, she was careless, and her movements were clumsy and awkward or wildly off balance.) What she lacked in skill she made up for in lung volume and directorship. She was one of the younger members of the crowd of boys and girls who always played together, but also one of its most vociferous. At baseball she argued with the umpire, or she made up rules to suit herself. When she became too exasperating, the others would all rise up with a strident shout of, "Shut up, Amy Lowell!" which she always took with good nature, no doubt because she was pleased at getting the attention of all, and so was content to subside, at least for a while.

The same characteristic held true at the school she and Katie attended in Boston. She was the clown of the class, particularly in the French division, where she was the despair of a succession of madames who tried in vain to teach her. Learning a language by rote bored Amy. Her mind would not receive it even when her mother, who had been fairly proficient in languages, tried to tutor her privately. Too, in school there were many diversions. Among the best were whispering jokes or making wisecracks about the lesson in an audible whisper. The teacher, almost in tears with exasperation, would beat on the table for silence. *"Ne riez pas des bêtises d'Aimée!"* she would command, but her words had little effect. Amy had an impish desire to shock people which remained with her. But, as her friend wrote, "at heart she was sound, and would cut off her right hand rather than do a dishonorable action." She could also show self-sacrifice in her devotion to close friends, as she did when Katie was disabled for a few days after a minor accident. Amy came to see her every day, bringing along her collection of paper dolls even though she didn't care to play with them, because she knew Katie admired them and could not do anything strenuous.

Similarly, she expected Katie to listen quietly when, in a more tranquil mood, she read aloud from "the immortal Rollo books," * which she clung to long after she had progressed to a higher level of reading. She also loved fairy tales. There was no halfway mark or mixture in her choices: The stories she liked best were characterized either by full-fledged realism or by fantasy, and from the age of five or six she had begun writing stories of her own in both categories. At the age of ten she started a mimeographed magazine, "The Monthly Story-Teller." The lead story concerned a wholly realistic boy, and was entitled "A Day of Misfortunes," a narrative about a child whose plans for the Fourth of July go awry. Although fictional, it might have reflected her own general misadventures. She also composed versions of fairy tales that Bessie often told her. (These efforts show a marked influence of her love of food, especially sweets. In her adaptation of one classic, it was not the shoemaker, but the grocery-store keeper whom the elves saved, by filling his shelves with glasses of currant "jeley." Apparently a favorite, currant jelly appears more than once in her stories. Chocolate was a lifelong addiction.)

Her mother, noticing Amy's steady concentration on her story-writing, was struck with the idea of putting them all into a book to be sold at the charity bazaar for the benefit of the Perkins Institute for the Blind, and offered to help her. Amy was more than happy. This was one of the few times her mother participated in a project with her instead of merely giving passive approval, or trying to teach her something, or reprimanding her for some misdeed. They planned the book together, and decided on the method of selling it. Printed by Cupples, the slim little volume, *Dream Drops,* was sold at a bazaar booth by young Amy, all dressed up

* Amy's term.

in a fancy costume. She collected fifty-six dollars, which she then turned over to the Perkins Institute, as a contribution to a fund for blind children. The cause was worthy, if not the book. But another childhood effort, based on her favorite fantasy tale, *Moonfolk,* a story she had read over and over, was more creative. In the book, one moonlight night a lonely little girl meets an elf, who takes her away in his boat; they sail across the sea on a broad silver glade all the way to the moon itself; there they meet the folk of legends, including King Arthur and his knights. Amy could easily identify with a lonely little girl and her moon fantasy; but in her own story the child is a boy, and his adventures on the moon are original, much more so than her inventions in the *Dream Drops* tales.

At some point in these childhood literary endeavors, Amy put together a "Private Scrapbook," which contained the first of her many prefaces, already provocative, in its challenge to prying eyes. She ended with a warning to the "naughty reader" who dares to go further: The book will interest nobody but herself, and he had best "not imagine he will like it because he won't." What better way to lure the reader on! Significantly, following the title, the credits read: "Arranged by Amy Lowell, published by Lowell & Co., Skyparlor, Sevenels." Before the second seven-year cycle of her life ended, Amy Lowell revealed signs of the whimsy, the romantic realism, the moon madness, the thunder and lightning and brilliant color prisms of her poetry, as well as strong signs of her sexual drives and of her imperious sense of leadership.

CHAPTER IV

Sloughing Off the Swaddling Bands

ALTHOUGH HER WIT and repartee could match that of her elders, Amy Lowell was slow to mature in more ordinary ways, in part because of her pampered home life. Since her parents were a generation older than those of her classmates, she was not exposed to the new ideas of child rearing, and she was as old-fashioned in some respects as she was advanced in others. A lover of adventure novels, she had read all of Sir Walter Scott by the age of eleven or twelve. Her father, who had started her on the Waverley series by reading Scott aloud in the evenings, read Cooper aloud next, beginning with the Leatherstocking Tales, which he considered the American author's best novels; but Amy obstinately preferred Cooper's sea stories. She also read R. H. Dana's *Two Years Before the Mast* and was so fascinated by it that for a time sea stories became a passion; her great favorite was Jules Verne, whose *Twenty Thousand Leagues Under the Sea* stirred the depths of her being, "so much so as to be notoriously potent as a bribe" in connection with her schoolwork.

No doubt her brother Percy, whose book *Chosön, the Land of the Morning Calm,* an account of his travels in the Far East (particularly the Hermit Kingdom of Korea), was published by Macmillan in 1885, and whose letters and gifts kept coming steadily, had a good deal to do with Amy's passion for sea adventure stories. They also provided an escape from the staid Victorian atmosphere of the Lowells' Boston-Brookline households, conforming to the exclusive social set of the last decades in the nineteenth century. It was a life that might have been pleasant enough if Amy Lowell had been less imaginative, or if she had been slim and popular, like the girls she admired in dancing school. With the advent of puberty, it was evident that she was not going to "stretch out" the way most of the girls did. Instead, she was growing wider. It was true that her hands and feet were small and her ankles slim, and she retained the distinctive fresh complexion that had been hers as a child. Her friends often remarked on the clear, almost transparent smoothness of her skin—but she was built more like a freighter than a clipper ship, and she still could not dance very well. Her attitude was reflected in a publication called *The Wall-Flower Society Mirror,* which had only a single issue, in May 1888 (its title was indicative of Amy's increasing problem). A choice item was her first book review, "The Editor's Bookshelf," dealing with her own book. "One of the latest, and also one of the most interesting literary productions of the year," she wrote, "is the charming little book, by Miss Lowell, entitled 'Dream Drops by a Dreamer.' We understand that Miss Lowell is to be one of the writers for this paper, and as she is, perhaps, the greatest of the century's geniuses, we hope that this sheet will be patronized by many of the fashionable set." Ostensibly satire, she might well have been joking in earnest, partly to buoy up her spirits, and partly because she probably felt she *was* a genius of sorts. In French class she continued to be the *enfant terrible,* and only the promise of being permitted to read aloud from her current favorite novel in English class would make her more tractable in other studies.

A month later Amy was faced with the fact that she was the only one of Augustus and Katherine Lowell's children left at home. Bessie was married, on June 9, 1888, to William Lowell Putnam, a third cousin of the interrelated Lowells, at St. Paul's Church in Brookline. Amy longed for Percy to return from the Orient. She forgot her troubles somewhat, however, when she was invited to the annual boat race between Harvard and Yale. This would be her first college crew race—the great event she had heard her brothers talk about for years—and she was most impressed with the importance of being able to attend one at last. On June 29 the party met at her "Aunt Mary" Putnam's, sister of her great-cousin James Russell Lowell, and, as luck would have it, Cousin James was there. At fourteen, Amy was much more excited about being on her way to the boat race than speaking to her famous cousin, but she was "hauled into the library to say how-do-you-do" to him. He was standing in front of the fireplace, his white hair and long white beard giving him a venerable appearance. They had less to say to each other now than when she had seen him while she was still a very little girl. She was eager to be off and was "frightened to death" of the old poet, whom she was seeing for the last time, as fate would have it; and he was "obviously bored." They were "the old and the new, meeting in furious conjunction," but they did not know this. She was afraid of his grandeur, and she felt he considered her a poor little girl. After a few minutes they said good-bye, and she hurried away to join the others. ("He went on his slow and steady way to the grave," she wrote long afterward, "and I to my boat-race, where my side lost; and the stars went on in their courses—to what end, I wonder, alas, I wonder.") *

For a term or two she applied herself to her schoolwork, particularly to English composition, perhaps with the idea of going to Radcliffe, then known as the Harvard Annex, which would be almost like attending the same college her brothers had. Just as she called the Harvard crew *her* team, she felt that Harvard was her school, the Lowells having been connected with it for generations. She wrote themes on social problems. One was on the "Inconvenience of the Horse-Car Strikes," just then being waged in Boston (not far removed from transportation strikes of nearly a century later); another, in four flaming pages, dealt with "Man's Inhumanity to Man." Beginning with Cain and Abel, and proceeding to the New Testament persecutions and the tortures of the Middle Ages (a reference to the Iron Virgin of Nuremberg, which still haunted her), the paper was notable mostly for its ending with "the women who still work in cheap clothing houses" —the only time she ever showed concern for female sweatshop

* This account, fragmentarily quoted, was contained in a letter Amy wrote c. 1919.

labor. Her teacher's comment was that the last topic might have been expanded, "as it is a practical one at the present day," an indication that unfair labor standards and women's rights were already coming to the fore, although the violent strikes in the Lowell cotton mills did not begin until the 1900s, and Amy was hardly aware of them then. The teacher's other notations, often repeated in the margins, were: "Penmanship and punctuation faulty," or *"Spelling!"* But Amy ignored them.

Her reading may have aroused her interest in social justice, for after *A Tale of Two Cities,* which was assigned in class, Amy went on to read all of Dickens, and followed with the novels of Thackeray. If interested, she needed no prodding and did not shirk her schoolwork. Her composition book contains various clues to her outlook. The most telling answer to a series of questions she copied in her notebook is her reply to "What is your idea of happyness [sic]?: *To be loved."* It marked the beginning of a long, painful, and awkward period of adolescence that seemed endless to her. A diary begun in 1880, the year she turned fifteen, reveals Amy Lowell's utter frankness about her inner and outer defects, her despair over her physique, the despair of many adolescents—especially young girls—who have a physical defect; in her case, it caused humiliation and self-hatred.

Girls in her crowd like Katie Dana and Florence Wheelock (later Florence Ayscough, the noted writer on China, who was to help Amy with translations of Chinese poetry) were fast developing the hour-glass figure so popular around the turn of the century. With lengthened skirts and tight lacing, they pulled in their waistlines to achieve it; but Amy, whom Florence described as "a rather square little girl with a very fresh color" when they first met,* had practically no waistline to draw in: Her girth was wide; her figure still bulked square, short, and stout. The other girls were purposely accentuating their budding beauty and grace in unadmitted preparation for marriage. But she, who had witnessed her two sisters' weddings and watched them leave the church in their white gowns, radiant on the arm of the bridegroom, had already begun to despair of such happiness. Most of the girls seemed

* Probably at about the same time Amy met Katherine Dana.

to be able to attract boys merely by smiling at them. But when Amy found herself alone with a boy, she was either the obstreperous clown she had always been or, worse, she was struck dumb, a stupid gawk. "I was a fool, *as usual!!*" became a frequent entry in her diary. And, with amazing insight, she once wrote: "If I were not so self-conscious, I would be much better. Everybody thinks I'm a fool (& it's true) & nobody cares a hang about me." She despised herself as "a great, rough, masculine, strong thing."

Dancing school became her worst trial. She was now in the "Friday Evenings"—ballroom classes for sub-subdebs—which meant that she had progressed or at least had not been eliminated from the class, but to her this was, instead of a consolation, an added humiliation. She only felt more awkward and neglected. "I was left over in the german, *as* usual!" her diary read. The german, the most complicated of the dances, a cotillion with constantly changing partners, could be a joy if she was picked as a partner right away, but for Amy was usually the most dreaded moment of the evening. More often than not, when the pairing was done, she was left over or found herself with a dreary little clutch of girls resting on the gilt chairs against the wall. And it did not help to see Mr. Papanti nudge some equally awkward boy who had not been lucky enough to nab some girl for himself and persuade him to ask one of the wallflowers to dance.

Riding school was scarcely better. As much as she loved horses, and as skillful as she was at driving, Amy could not seem to acquire the rhythm of riding. Whether she was supposed to be posting, trotting, or galloping, she just bumped along, her buttocks flapping over the saddle, her insides shaking. She endured the riding lessons because they were held outdoors, but she never enjoyed them. Still, one went to riding school as to dancing school: It was *comme il faut,* in the language of the times. She wished she could do as she pleased. She envied her brothers their freedom, and other girls their slim or softly rounded figures and attractive ways.

There was no one to whom she could confess her most confidential thoughts, so she poured them into her diary. One of its most important entries is dated May 25, 1889: "I feel very much in need of a *very* intimate friend," she scrawled on a fresh page, "a friend whom I should love better than any other girl in the world, & who would feel so toward me. To whom I could tell all that is in my heart, and she would do so to me. We should love to be alone together, both of us."

Certainly her emotions were conflicting, her impulses fired by the longing "to be loved" and admired by companions of both sexes. Her main sources of solace were the theater, to which she had been taken from an early age, and books. "I could go to the theatre every night," she told her diary after a performance on January 2. She was "thrilled" by the play and by the beauty of the leading lady. And when curled up with a book, she was invariably late for dinner, despite her father's strict rules regarding promptness at mealtimes. She lost all sense of time and place until the parlor maid knocked on her door with word that "the dinner-bell rang a quarter of an hour ago," and Amy would put the ribbon marker in place, closing the book before running down the two flights of stairs without stopping to fix her hair or straighten her blouse. As impetuous as she was about most things, Amy never slammed down a book face open to keep her place (as some of her friends did) for fear of "breaking its spine." From the time she was a very small girl she always took good care of books. She had too much reverence for them to misuse them. She had vague longings to be a poet, to be literary; although she had made only one or two attempts at writing poetry, it seemed to offer her the greatest surcease from her youthful unrest and melancholy. "What I would not give to be a poet!" she wrote on January 13, 1889; and, on March 19: "I should like best of anything to be literary. Ah, me! I'm afraid I shall never be. . . ." But there were hints of occasions for laughter and fun in between these sighs. She listed invitations to dances at a fraternity house (DKE) and to Harvard's Hasty Pudding shows. She had sporadic crushes on boys, and she enjoyed a moment of triumph when she and "Paul H." won a tennis tournament. And always in her diary she recorded her hour of rising and the phase of the moon. She knew of no one else who felt impelled to follow the lunar course, but it held a secret fascination for her that she could not resist.

Later in the year she found herself in love—unrequited—with

the tennis partner with whom she had won the tournament, and the diary becomes even more revealing of her androgynous conflict. The entry on October 28 reads: "Do you know I was 'struck all of a heap' the other day by discovering that I love Paul H.***** How long I have loved him I don't know, but I must have loved him for some time." Pathetically, she set down her feelings on discovering that Paul preferred her friend Mabel, whom she also admired.

"It is so silly, but when Paul asks Mabel to walk with him I feel just like going off alone somewhere & crying. <u>This feeling is mixed by a kind of a wish to hit Somebody.</u>* If there was any chance of Paul's ever loving me it would be different, & I should not be ready to pound myself for being such a fool as to love him.

"But I am ugly, fat, conspicuous & dull; to say nothing of a very bad temper. Oh Lord, please let it be all right & let Paul love me, & don't let me be a fool. . . ."

After the Lowells moved to their townhouse late in November, she spoke of missing Paul, and, in a fit of self-pity, somewhat falsely lamented, "I have no faculty for making friends. . . . Paul!" On the twenty-fourth she tried to analyze her situation: "I don't think that being all alone ** in here is good for me. In fact, I have been building my-self castles in the air, & thinking, thinking! I think that to be married to a sweet, tender, strong & good man would be the nearest approach to perfect happiness, of course provided that you love the man. To be his sole, & whole, confident. In short, my ideas of what a husband should be are very exalted." She followed this speculation on the ideal mate, in whom she would find a combination of feminine and masculine characteristics, by a complete reversal to realistic self-abuse: "No! I shall be an old maid, nobody could love me I know. Why, if I were somebody-els, I should hate my-self. I am doomed, for how can it be different?—To see the man I love marry somebody-els." Then, under the heading "Private," she goes on: "Bessy H**** take pity on me for you love Fred.—But you are loveable, He may, *will,* love

* Amy's diary was full of underlining.

** The diary reads "along," but obviously Amy meant "alone"; she usually had to adjust to the move from Sevenels each fall.

& marry you. But Paul! Oh! I feel queer! But, but Goodnight!"

These are surely the reactions of an emotionally agitated if not deeply disturbed adolescent. It is remarkable that she was able to record her heartache so clearly. She also felt she was stupid in school now. And on December 13, evidently referring to an incident in class, she was seized by another fit of self-castigation: "It doesn't make any difference to me. I am rough and strong & can bear anything that would bear down sweeter and more delicate natures. But somehow I can seem to bear it very well. I hate to hear Patty and that kind of sweet girl getting sat on, & I have got into the habbit of thinking myself cast iron. I don't like to find I'm not.

"Lotty told me last Sunday that I affected hoydenness, & was really the opposite, I did not let on, but I knew it was true." Amy often defended some girl she admired with a fierceness she did not actually feel and so gave the impression, even to herself, of being cast iron. But inside she was as full of quivering fears and tender passions as any of the girls, as she had to admit when Lotty confronted her with the truth. To suffer an unrequited love is difficult for anyone, but if one is young and the victim of a physical handicap, real or imagined, such a love can become impossible to cope with, and only Amy Lowell's native intelligence and the confidence inspired by her family background—the fact that she was a Lowell—could overcome it.

For the next year, 1890, although the dark moods recurred, the general tone of the journal is livelier. For one thing, there was much theatergoing, a diversion that could take her out of her personal world into the artistic one of the drama. The Boston Museum-Theatre appears frequently in the diary pages; and, as it was located directly across from Papanti's, it seems to have served as an antidote to Amy's misery in dancing class. The doldrums of a Friday evening were followed by the pleasures of a Saturday matinee; and, even if the play or the actors were not always of great merit, they more than made up for the humiliation of being left over. But her love for the theater was also doomed to disappoint her occasionally. She and Dolly Brooks, her best friend of this period—a bland young girl with a bland but very pretty face—

often went to the matinee together. Both girls thought the leading lady at the Boston Museum-Theatre was "divine." She was especially delicious as Lydia Languish; after the performance, Amy and Dolly decided to write fan letters to Miss Sheridan—but it was Dolly who received an answer and not Amy, alas! However, the theater still held a magic for her. She started writing a play and worked on the script through the spring recess. With a group of friends she planned to produce a series of plays, starting with *She Stoops to Conquer*. Amy was cast as Tony Lumpkin, a role that seemed admirably suited to her ability to clown. But after a few weeks, she wrote regretfully in her diary, "Mamma does not want me to act as a man so we have given the play up."

She was less disappointed than she might have been had she not sprained her ankle and was hopping around on one foot at rehearsal anyway. This was an accident that was to be a frequent occurrence: During the years that followed, she was to sprain one ankle nine times, the other ten, and break the bone of one of her legs three times before she reached her mid-forties. She may have been prone to such accidents because her top-heavy body imposed too much weight on her small-boned frame, but no explanation of them was ever given in so many words.

Another revealing diary entry begins: "I am *in!* for the Saturday evenings next year.* Oh, Joy!!" But her joy was almost immediately superseded by a masochistic tirade: "I don't know why I'm glad; of course I shall be an awful pill, as I was at the Friday Evenings last year. I think that I should like parties quite well if only I could dance well and was sure of having a *very* good time. But of course I am doomed to be a dreadful pill; doomed to blush very visibly, and waste my sweetness in the vicinity of the wall. But then, you know, I don't care a rap!" And the next day she concluded: "Really, you know, I am appaulingly fat."

Amy had the soul of a sylph but the body of a hippopotamus. How she envied those skinny girls who were always chosen first. She must often have pictured herself swaying like a slender reed, as they did, in the arms of some handsome boy during the waltz, which partners danced together. Most of all, she longed to learn

* The dances for subdebs and Harvard sophomores.

to waltz *well* and was determined to do so somehow. At least her ankles were slim, her feet small—and she could move as fast as any-one "els" on a tennis court.

The diary makes no further mention of the young man who caused her so much anguish; evidently she either decided he was not worthy of it or she was trying to sublimate her passion for the opposite sex. She also had crushes on girls; just then it was "Louly W.****," to whom she wrote a poem. And in her diary she confessed frankly: "I cannot help admireing, & generally falling in love with, extreme beauty." Needless to say, it was a great help to be able to express her inmost thoughts and feelings in her secret journal, and probably these private airings did as much as anything to stabilize her emotions. Her acknowledgment at being "appaulingly fat," for example, was followed two days later by a significant entry of literary interest. She went to see the exhibit of old and rare books brought to America by "a Mr. Quarritch" of London, the well-known book dealer. Eventually, he became the main source of her fabulous library of handsome volumes and rare manuscripts.

Her confirmation in Trinity Church, which occurred at about the same time (1890), meant far less to her than the exhibit. Earlier, regarding Reverend Parks's sermon, "You Are God's Child," she had written, "Well, that was very nice, but he said that one's aim in life was to 'save your soul.' Now I don't think it is. I think that is a very selfish view to take of life. I believe that you had better not think at all about your hereafter but do what you think you ought to do in that particular instance and trust to God for the rest. . . ." And that youthful statement of her attitude toward religion remained in large measure her attitude throughout her life. Her confirmation as a member of Trinity Church did not last long. She renounced conventional Christianity after a few years. Indeed, if the occasion demanded, she would declare herself an atheist, although she was more of an agnostic, doubting the existence of a benevolent deity. Although she later dealt with the subject of religion as it related to sex and fanaticism in various religious orders (e.g., in "The Book of Hours of Sister Clotilde" and other poems), she herself could never accept the idea of life after death. Moreover, according to Foster Damon, who once sat up half the night discussing religious mysticism with her, Amy became convinced through her own sufferings and those of others that the god of this world, if there was one, was a devil and "she did not hesitate to reject demonstrations of deity." If she had a religion, it evolved from, and revolved around, poetry. And if she worshiped anything, it was the moon goddess. Such religious aberrations developed from events in the future, but the seeds were sown in the agonies of her adolescence.

At fifteen and sixteen, she was still resentful of teachers and of formal education. She wrote a series of poison-pen portraits, entitled "Sketches of my Teachers—Made During History recitations at School." While pretending to take notes on class recitations, she scribbled these scornful caricatures of those who should have been her mentors right under the nose of one teacher she could easily fool, and then surreptitiously passed the slips of paper to her friends to hear their stifled giggles. The portraits contained little outside the usual invective against teachers mixed with tomfoolery that schoolchildren often write. But the very fact that she was so little inspired by the teaching she received was, in Amy's view, justification enough for her attitude toward the whole educational system, as she was later to point out in an article published in the *North American Review*. Emphasis was on gaining useful knowledge, on the "materialities" instead of the humanities. Imagination, the power behind all great achievements in the world (whether in the arts or science), had to take second place to utility. Even the poetry the class was assigned to read was treated in such a way as to stifle the imagination of a student like Amy. "Memorize the first five stanzas of Grey's 'Elegy' and be prepared to give the salient points," or a similar directive, was typical of teaching methods, hardly apt to inspire creative ability in any pupil, let alone one of her quixotic, erratic temperament.

In the same article she especially inveighed against the Harvard professor whose lectures on Shakespeare she attended at the Annex for two years. "He left an indelible impression," she remarked sarcastically: He nearly wrecked Shakespeare for her. She and the other girls who attended his lectures had to learn everything about the plays they studied except "the things that mattered." The professor pointed out or told them to ferret out all the unimportant facts to such an extent that these plays became "mines of valueless information." Not once did the professor bid the students to notice the poetry in the lines of a *Hamlet* soliloquy or of Ariel's songs; not once did he offer an aesthetic analysis of a play or a scene. And the psychological implications of Shakespearean drama were ignored. Amy grew bored with the course and wondered why on earth every actor's supreme ambition was to play Shakespearean roles.

It suddenly dawned on her that in all the schools she had attended she had learned very little—nothing, really, except how to read and write. She was still trying to learn the multiplication tables (and would be for the rest of her days). What little she had managed to learn came from her habit of reading on her own. If the teacher assigned one chapter of a book and Amy found it interesting, she would read the whole book, so the smattering of knowledge she had gained was "learnt round the cirriculum," not within its narrow channels. She realized that she was one of those people who cannot have knowledge pumped into them. She simply could *not be taught;* she *had to learn.* She had a strong impulse to write poetry, but she had learned nothing of the basic principles or practices in poetry-writing at school. The little reading that was assigned in English literature she did not care for, nor would she ever like it. She had not been able to master a foreign language, not even French, though her mother had tried so hard to tutor her. The Harvard professor had taken away any desire she might have had to go to college. At the age of seventeen, she announced to her parents that she was not going to enroll for the coming term, and she left school for good.

Since she would soon be coming out and, if she followed the usual pattern, her debut would be the doorway to marriage, her parents saw no point in urging her to go to college. Amy could hardly be called a scholar; and if the Lowells had any doubts about her chances as a debutante, they put them aside with the hope that, as a Lowell, she would make a suitable match. She would take her place in Boston society, so what need was there for an academic degree? In a letter to Archibald MacLeish, dated October 16, 1924, she outlined the "extent of her formal education" and added, with her usual frankness: "It really did not amount to a hill of beans."

CHAPTER V

Self-education of a Self-determined Debutante

IN HER SECRET LONGING to be "Somebody" in the literary world—a poet above all else—Amy Lowell educated herself by browsing in two havens: her father's library and the Boston Athenaeum. She felt proprietary toward the old library because a Lowell had been one of its founders, her father was a board member, and her brothers were its patrons. After she dropped out of school, she began going there regularly every day when the family moved into the townhouse, just as she would have gone to class, except that this solitary education was much pleasanter. It was rather a painful climb up the little spiral stairway, which her wide girth spanned so that she had to twist her body when rounding the turns. But she really didn't mind it because the best books were on the top floor, and, once there, she found some secluded alcove where she was sure of privacy.

When she located the books she wanted, she sat on the dusty floor, reading and dreaming the hours away. She usually stuffed a couple of apples into her pockets, or a bar of the French chocolate wrapped in silver foil that was her favorite, and she would munch absentmindedly as she read. Leaving Thackeray of her school days, she discovered Charlotte Brontë; Anthony Trollope, whose subtle and often salacious wit gave her an unexpected jolt of joy; and Jane Austen, whom she found wholly delicious. (That none of these had been on the "corollary reading" lists her English teachers had recommended, surely confirmed Amy's suspicions of the limitations of the curricula of the academic world she had encountered in the private schools she had attended, supposedly the most advanced anywhere at that time. Now she was finding undreamed of riches in these novels alone.)

Her greatest discoveries, however, were in poetry, particularly in the poetry of Keats, and that providentially through a book in her father's library. One day while browsing among the shelves near the ceiling, she came across Leigh Hunt's *Imagination and Fancy; or, Selections from the English Poets,* an aesthetic analysis and answer to the question, What is poetry? The volume was like the Book of Revelation for her, opening "a door that might otherwise have remained shut," as she said, and it turned her definitely to poetry. She devoured it avidly, reading it over and over, and then looked up the poets whose works were discussed and tried to read them in the light of her new perceptions. She felt as if she had stumbled upon and uncovered a hidden storehouse of treasures. And, being Amy, she inveigled her old school friends into going up to her room where she read them long "stretches" of Shelley, Keats, and Coleridge, and of Beaumont and Fletcher. (Of course her father wouldn't have Shelley, the dissolute atheist, in the house, but Amy didn't let that stop her, or let him know that she had borrowed the volume from the Athenaeum, or mention the fact that a book in his own library sanctioned that poet and others of whom he probably disapproved.)

Through Hunt's guidance, moreover, she found a new Shakespeare, one of whom she would never have dreamed if she had not discovered this artistic interpretation, and so the plays were saved for her: Nothing was left of the Harvard professor's lectures but bitterness for the time she had lost in digging up inconsequential data when she might have been enjoying the music and meaning of the lines. Her esteem of Leigh Hunt was unbounded. She was convinced that *Imagination and Fancy* would make an excellent textbook for proper teaching of literature, especially poetry. Later on, when the literary world began listening to her voice, she shouted her ideas in print.

At present, still troubled by her amorphous yearning to be a poet, she realized that her instinct had been starved: She knew nothing of Chaucer, Spenser, Herrick, Herbert, Donne, Blake, or later poets, including great Americans like Walt Whitman, Emily Dickinson, or even Emerson or Poe. Her father read very little "modern poetry" when he read aloud in the evenings and possessed even less in his library. (Emily Dickinson's poems had been published only a year earlier, in 1890, in a collected volume, and were considered alien to the accepted ideas of poetry by traditionalists like Augustus Lowell. It would be a few years before Amy Lowell came to appreciate fully the magnitude of that work, but when she did she was unstinting, placing her "sister" poet above any other as precursor of the "new" poetry.) In school, the poets she had studied—Gray, Goldsmith, Burns, and Cowper—were foreign to her flamboyant nature, and happily none of them appeared in Hunt. That one book, which introduced her to the poetry of "imagination and fancy," defined as "images of the objects of which it treats," including "whatsoever of painting can be made visible to the mind's eye, and whatsoever of music can be conveyed, without singing or instruments, by sound and proportion," became her bible. She studied it, chapter and verse, as she had never studied a book before.

Most important of all, *Imagination and Fancy* led her to Keats. And in so doing it opened another door to freedom from the emotional upheaval brought on by her trying, awkward adolescence, freedom from the guilt associated with sex as related to religion and belief in the hereafter. In Keats she found a skeptic like herself, and his creed became hers: From now on she would be "certain of nothing but the holiness of the heart's affections and the truth of imagination." The effect of *Endymion* especially was like balm to her turbulent spirits. That erotic narrative clarified for her the relative values of the physical and the spiritual in love and, fusing the two elements into one, showed her that both are essentially pure. She discovered that there was nothing evil or disgusting in sex, contrary to the precepts the Victorians believed. The love scene in the second canto affected her for days. "How many boys and girls have found solace and joy in this passage!" she declared when she came to write about it. Also, in *Endymion,* her own adoration of the moon was justified; she need not feel sheepish or secretive about recording the phases of the moon, its effect on her huge, misshapen body. Its symbolism was to run through her own poetry from the first volume to the last.

Finally, her literary discoveries freed her in one sense from the prison of her body. Although she never was free from the physical tortures of her excessive weight, psychologically she was able to bear it with greater objectivity and so overcome much of her self-consciousness. She badgered her friends to practice dancing with her privately, and because she began to apply herself at Papanti's, she found she could perform the steps with ease. By the time her debut date was set, she was as skillful as any other member of her class.

That summer—on July 2, 1891—the sudden heart attack and death of Alfred Roosevelt, her sister Katherine's husband, was a shock to all the Lowells. Katie was so stricken by the blow that she was invalided for some time. Amy kept the children entertained as much as she could to help her sister. She took them up to her room and gave them her own childhood books (from "that bookcase") to read—but not to take home; they must read them there in her room and put them back in the bookcase. (The rule, once formed, was one she kept and applied to the vast library she eventually acquired: Relatives and friends were always welcome to read books at her home, but she never loaned them out.) She had not paid much attention to her nephew and nieces before because she did not like babies and never learned to like them. A squalling infant, or even a fairly tranquil one, made her feel uncomfortable because all babies seemed uncomfortable to her, frustrated in their efforts to be understood, often in discomfort or pain. But, like her father, she began to love the children as soon as they were articulate, and they in turn were always fond of "Aunt Amy."

One day she invited her favorite, James, the oldest at age six, to go for a drive. On the return trip, when she goaded the horses to go faster to give her nephew an extra thrill, one of them suddenly turned runaway just as they rounded the sharp curve that led to the Lowells' long driveway. The horses went wild. The carriage lurched crazily, nearly tipping over, and for once, Amy could not control an animal. Seeing the scared little face of her nephew as he clung bravely to the side of the carriage, she thought in her panic, "Oh, God, Katie has just lost her husband, and now I am killing her boy!" And indeed they might both have been killed had it not been for her brother Lawrence, who happened to be talking to her father on the portico at Sevenels when they saw the careening carriage. He leaped into action and reined in the runaway, bringing the pair to a halt. Amy, ashen and trembling, was full of admiration for her brother's feat of strength. She never forgot the incident, and afterward she regarded her second brother in much the same light as she did Percy.

Not long afterward, word came to Sevenels that her great-cousin James had died (August 12, 1891),* and Lawrence was asked to be one of the pallbearers. James Russell Lowell's prominence in the literary, academic, and diplomatic worlds warranted a state funeral, which Amy attended with her parents. She was later to be annoyed at having her name constantly linked to her eminent cousin's, but now as she watched her brother moving in the slow, stately procession accompanying the bier, she hoped she could some day be one-tenth as famous a poet as James. Listening to the eulogies spoken at the memorial for him, she wondered whether she would be, or if she would even get into print; but the thought of Keats and her recent discoveries gave her courage, and she determined to learn somehow to write enough poems for at least one volume. She would some day be "Somebody," too!

In the fall, despite the deaths in the family, Amy Lowell came out formally. She was presented to Boston society in a white silk ballgown, demure with its short cap sleeves and designed to conceal her oversized bosom and broad hips as much as possible. (During her debutante year, her cousin Sarah Putnam painted a

* It is interesting to note that Herman Melville, who died the next month (September 1891), was born the same year as James Russell Lowell, 1819. Both men became famous as writers in different fields during their lifetime, but Melville, by far the greater artist, had led such a secluded life during his last twenty years (as an obscure customs inspector who wrote only at night, mostly for himself) that his death received very little notice in the press—many had thought him dead long before. His masterpiece, *Moby Dick,* was not even mentioned. (*Billy Budd* was still in manuscript form.) Lowell, on the other hand, was lauded and eulogized as the outstanding figure of the literary world in the nineteenth century.

portrait of Amy in her ballgown, and, while it is probably a slenderized version of her figure, she hardly resembles the "great, rough, masculine strong thing" she described herself in her diary.) In a way, she was more prepared for the great event than some of her classmates at Papanti's: She was entering a circle that prided itself on its sparkling conversation and wit, gifts that came naturally to the Lowells. It was a circle led by such bright, quick-witted beauties as Rufus Choate's two daughters, Mrs. Bell and Mrs. Pratt, both in constant demand at parties and social events as much for their liveliness of wit as for their looks. (It was Mrs. Bell who was credited with the classic remark in regard to privately owned motor cars: "The automobile is speedily dividing mankind into two classes: the quick and the dead.") There was Sarah Wyman Whitman, of French descent, whose home was a veritable salon; she herself painted and was a pupil of William Morris Hunt, a friend of John La Farge, one of whose stained-glass windows added to the artistry of her home. She made a policy of entertaining celebrated guests distinguished in the arts, and invited young people recently "out" to meet them. Soon after her debut, Amy was often a guest at these gatherings, and at those of Mrs. Bell, who took an immediate liking to her. Too, there was the fabulous Mrs. Jack Gardner, whose Fenway Court drawing room Amy came to know well. In Boston society gossip, Mrs. Gardner's name did not have to be mentioned for those in the know to recognize "a certain lady who had a room lined with black velvet in which she posed nude before a select company of gentlemen"; or that it was she who "scrubbed the steps of the Church of the Advent on hands and knees to atone for that and other sins" connected with John Singer Sargent, painter of beautiful society women, as Foster Damon pointed out.*

To her own vast surprise, Amy was a popular debutante. According to the favors carefully preserved—for she kept everything, including invitations, programs, and announcements—no less than sixty dinners were given in her honor. No doubt the Lowell name accounts for much of the festivity planned for her, but she added

* His friend John Marshall definitely identified Mrs. Gardner in a letter to this author.

her own flair: Now that she had finally learned to dance, she could keep going for hours and enjoyed every minute of it as much as Jane Austen ever did. Like many stout people, she was amazingly light on her feet once she acquired the knack of keeping time. The very knowledge that she could do it went to her head like wine, and her boisterous good spirits as she joked at the top of her lungs and shouted at other couples whirling past in part made up for her lack of glamour. She still longed to be an alluring figure, but it didn't seem to matter so much since she was never deserted by her partners or forced to sit out every other number. She learned the latest dances such as the newly invented two-step, to match Sousa's marches, and the popular "coon-songs." The waltz remained her favorite, however, and until her mid-forties, when surgery stopped her, she never missed a chance to whirl in three-quarter time, especially at informal gatherings.

On these occasions she was the life of the party. She knew all of the Gilbert and Sullivan lyrics by heart, and would often organize an impromptu chorus to sing them around the piano. (She even got her nieces and nephews to sing them along with the grown-ups at family gatherings.) In 1891 a woman national golf champion, Louisa Wells, made sports generally fashionable among the debutantes. And intercollegiate games were begun in the nineties. Amy became a roaring spectator. She rooted for her team—Harvard—with all her might. Her enthusiasm was infectious, and those around her were usually shouting and jumping up and down at crucial moments, wildly happy over a victory. But bicycling was the biggest, most influential sport of the 1891 season. As the "safety bicycle" (equipped with a brake) came in, bustles went out of fashion with the increased popularity of bicycling that resulted. Bloomers were brought back for cycling, and skirts were shortened to ankle length, shorn of entangling trains. According to Foster Damon, "Bicycling freed women from more artificial fashions, and gave them the means of getting away from the house on a summer afternoon; it was the beginning of their emancipation." * This may be an exaggeration, but it has a grain of truth and indicates

* S. Foster Damon, *Amy Lowell: A Chronicle* (Boston: Houghton Mifflin Company, 1935).

to what extent bicycling became the rage in the 1890s.* Like many Bostonians, the Lowells rode regularly and well. Mr. Lowell, who would not deign to bend over the handlebars, but sat bolt upright, sped along as fast as any "scorcher."

Besides the debutante dances that winter, there was sleighing as well as tobogganing at Corey Hill and skating on any number of ponds in and around Boston. Amy did not go in for the last for fear of turning her ankle and not being able to dance at the next ball. There were also luncheons, theater parties, and concerts, all of which she enjoyed more than skating.

Amy was free to ask one or more of her friends to come stay with her. Now that her brothers and sisters had households of their own, the whole top floor at Sevenels was at her disposal. She made it her lair and never changed quarters even when she owned and ran the house. One of her favorite friends was Bessie Ward (Elizabeth Ward Perkins), who had gone to school with Amy at one point but was now living in New York. Bessie was fascinated by the Lowell family, their varied interests and opinions. Mealtimes were "as good as a play," she would say, especially if any of Amy's brothers and sisters were there to lead her on. With the overabundant menus of the era, dinner was never less than six courses, and with the Lowells' gift for conversation, it was an evening's entertainment. "Any two members of that family could talk and listen simultaneously," she declared; customary New England reserve was hardly noticeable when the family board was large. Another house guest, who was at Sevenels during the uproar of controversy over the Lizzie Borden trial, testified to a typical Lowell scene at table: Midway through dinner in the midst of a heated discussion about the trial, Amy's brothers suddenly jumped up and "began to act it out: Percy was the prosecuting attorney, while Lawrence in a brilliant speech, proved that the axe committed the double murder all alone, then went and buried itself in the garden!"

However, when the middle generation left and the household

* For a hilarious account of the enormous popularity of bicycling in the 1890s, see Samuel Eliot Morison's description of couples learning to ride on the "quiet" street where his family lived for three generations, in his memoir, *One Boy's Boston: 1887–1901* (Boston: Houghton Mifflin Company, 1962).

was reduced to Amy's parents and two girls, the old reserve descended like a fog, to Amy's distress as well as to her visitor's. Her mother's invalidism, expressed in her wan presence at table or in her marked absence, combined with her father's stern convention as to time and order, stifled the natural zest of the girls, both examples of perennially nonconformist youth. An unexpected terror seized the guest and an angry embarrassment was stamped on the face of his spoiled youngest daughter when a portfolio left on a forbidden heirloom table brought a tirade from Mr. Lowell, or when their late arrival for breakfast was greeted by his cold silence in disapproval, which considerably lowered the temperature of hospitality. Amy might have made a scene of her own, but her father was old * and her mother was ill. The only solution was to get out of the house as often as possible. She would tell Burns to hitch up the horses, and the girls would go buggy-riding all over the neighborhood. Amy might drive furiously, letting out her anger and frustration, but she never lost control of the horses. The near-accident she had experienced with her nephew was enough for her. There is no record of a horse ever running away again when Amy Lowell held the reins.

Her good friend Florence Wheelock also described driving for miles with Amy through the countryside. It was somehow symbolic of her nature that Amy Lowell preferred driving to riding—symbolic of the way she was to drive herself and others, goading them on for whatever reason she felt it necessary. Seated in a carriage and handling the reins "like a man" made her feel in command, and at the same time freer to socialize with her companions. As she and Florence drove along, they talked about everything imaginable—from books of poetry to religion (about which they argued endlessly)—and always about love. Florence observed that Amy's "keen common sense and true sense of values came to the fore" during their young, earnest haranguing. Once, when Florence was trying to decide about a beau of hers, a young fellow who had "taken her fancy" but not much more, Amy was vehement in

* Augustus Lowell was actually only sixty-one in 1891, but, so far as Amy was concerned, he had always been old.

her advice: "Never marry any man *unless you can't help it!*" Her voice boomed out as she cracked the whip for emphasis.

She went visiting, too, when invitations came from school friends and neighbors who had been at Sevenels. The Cabot sisters, who lived down the road on Heath Street and were part of the crowd, asked her to come to the family place in Dublin, New Hampshire, in the summer of 1893, an invitation she was more than happy to accept: The region around Monadnock and Dublin Lake was noted for its fashionable (but nonetheless genuine) artists' circle. Painters like Abbott Thayer and Joseph Lindon Smith (whose home at Loon Lake, decorated with his well-known Egyptian scenes and pyramid paintings from his travels in that land fascinated Amy) and Alexander James (son of William) drew others interested in the arts, and made it a lively spot for a young debutante with artistic ambitions. At the home of Mrs. Charles MacVeagh, who gave theatricals on an improvised stage in the drawing room, Amy acquired her first taste for private or "little theater" productions, which she later developed. (The Smiths, too, had a tiny theater—"Teatro Bambino"—at Loon Lake that enchanted her and became the subject of a poem.)

Another place she loved to visit was Dolly Brooks's. Her friend's parents were the owners of the famous Francis Brooks estate at West Medford; the house dated from 1660, with the original Indian deed to prove it. Here, too, were extensive, exquisite gardens, among the oldest in America, that vied for perfection with the Lowells' at Sevenels. Amy's favorite haunt was a shaded corner sheltering rather curious painted lead statues of Paul and Virginia, the legendary lovers who drowned, which later served as inspiration for her weird tale, "The Statue in the Garden." And beyond the landscaping was a field full of fringed gentians, in bloom like a miraculous blue lake. Mrs. Brooks, who knew the value of that rare wildflower, never allowed children to pick the gentians, although she made very few hard-and-fast rules and was known for her warm hospitality. Indeed, the Brooks estate bore a close resemblance to the great houses of Jane Austen, with a constant coming and going of high-spirited guests.

Beginning a few weeks after she came out, Amy Lowell acquired the book-buying habit, with assistance from Percy. For Christmas in 1891, her mother, who was too indisposed to do much shopping, gave her a "cheque" * sizable enough to buy something she had been wanting for a long time: a good set of books. Percy, who had come home for the holidays, took her to the Cornhill Bookshop, known among collectors for its rare books and fine bindings. She always remembered that snowy December morning when they walked into the bookshop and she saw a gold and leather complete set of Sir Walter Scott lying on the floor among a shipment of books that had just arrived. She fell in love with the beautifully bound volumes and made up her mind at once, though Percy suggested that she make sure there was nothing else she would prefer. But she knew what she wanted right away. She bought the complete set of Scott, and she often returned to the bookshop, where she found some of her best buys—copies of Shelley and Keats—her Waterloo, because she could not resist their handsome bindings. She loved the contents of both, particularly Keats, and to possess their works in richly bound volumes became an urgent desire. She also bought a second bookcase to hold the set of Scott. Standing beside the "hideous ash bookcase" in her room, it marked the beginning of her passion for collecting books and manuscripts. Amy Lowell's reactions were rarely mild: Her loves were passionate; her dislikes, violent. Though she had periods of depression, she seldom suffered from apathy, and her enthusiasms, especially at this time of self-discovery, were wild and explosive.

One of these, which eventually led to her life's career of writing poetry, began in April 1893, with the first appearance in Boston of Eleonora Duse at the Globe Theatre, newly built and boasting that it was "illuminated by the Edison incandescent light." The event was heralded weeks in advance, and Amy made her reservation early. At this performance, she felt the greatness of Duse's art, but she did not fully appreciate its tremendous force then, or at Duse's second appearance in 1896. Nevertheless, the pull was strong enough so that she would not have missed any

* Her spelling here and elsewhere was "cheque." She also used the *-our* ending for words such as *honor* and *color.*

appearance of the extraordinary actress; and at the third (the actress's tour of 1902), Duse brought forth an "overwhelming vision" in Amy's mind and soul which sent her leaping into the realm of poetry for her own creative expression. As she wrote of the inspirational force of Duse's acting, "It loosed a bolt in my brain and I knew where my true function lay," * she was unconsciously giving a significant example of her emotional attitude toward life in all areas of experience.

And if, in the spring of 1893, she could not fully understand what was happening to her, she sensed it, and was both troubled and elated by it. News that sent her spirits soaring and brought a certain reassurance was that Percy might be coming back to America to live. His letter of May 11, 1893, was his last to Amy from Japan, for he soon decided definitely to return home to stay. His first activity was to give a series of lectures on the Far East at the Lowell Institute that winter. (Lawrence had lectured there the winter before on the legal aspects of government, his special field. There may have been the usual sibling rivalry between the brothers, but their interests were so widely separated that it apparently was not a problem.) However, as soon as the lectures were over, Percy announced that he was going to Flagstaff, Arizona, perhaps to settle. He hoped to resume his early academic love for astronomy: As an undergraduate, he had chosen astronomy for his minor, developing a boyhood ardor, and now recalled "seeing the white snowcaps of Mars crowning a globe that was spread with many colors." He founded the Lowell Observatory soon after he arrived in Flagstaff, and devoted himself thereafter principally to planetary research. He spent his spare time completing a book, *Occult Japan,* a fascinating study of Shinto trances and other Eastern religious practices based partly on his own experiences with them. Published in 1894, it caused almost as much comment as his earlier *Soul of the Far East,* the book that strongly influenced Lafcadio Hearn. No wonder Amy had little less than hero worship for Percy.

She was disappointed, not to say disconsolate, at Percy's de-

* In a letter to Eunice Tietjens, of *Poetry,* for a special issue on early years of poets.

parture for the Southwest so soon after he had come home to stay. She had hoped desperately that he would remain a few years at least, especially since their mother's condition had been growing steadily worse. He knew it. Mrs. Lowell was in bed much of the time now, the painful nephritis becoming more and more severe; to ease her, the doctor gave her morphine, and the drug sometimes made her vague or slightly delirious. After Percy left, the burden of keeping her company fell most of all on Amy, who, with her new emotional problems regarding her own self-expression, was scarcely equipped to provide solace for a sick mother who had never been much of a mother to her. Her father, worried as he was about Mrs. Lowell, was morose as well as taciturn now, but did not alter his business schedule because of his wife's illness and was of little help in the sickroom beyond seeing to it that the nurse or somebody was there. He expected Amy to look in on her mother frequently or sit with her to relieve the nurse. So like a dutiful daughter Amy went into her mother's room every morning before she left for the Athenaeum or elsewhere and in the afternoon when she came home. But she never stayed long, for there was little she could do beyond seeing that her mother was properly cared for by the nurse (ironically, a complete reversal of the situation when Amy was an infant).

Mrs. Lowell would often complain that nobody loved her. Or she would scream with pain and tell Amy to go away, that she did not want her daughter to see her suffer so, which was even more disturbing. Amy felt sorry for her mother. She tried to comfort her, but she could not reach her. She tried to imagine herself in her mother's place, but she could not; she could have identified with her father more easily. There were times when her mother would utter cries no one could understand, and it was clear that she was temporarily deranged. At such moments Amy feared she would lose her own mind; this was her greatest fear, but she overcame it by the force of her will. If ever there was a triumph of mind over matter, it was hers at this crucial period, and it served as a preparation for later trials.

She could not have achieved such objectivity except for her self-imposed habit of self-education. And, quite by accident, another door to poetry was opened to her one night, again indirectly through the theater. She attended a performance of *Ruy Blas,* perhaps with some young man she had met at an Assembly ball, for Amy Lowell had had the usual number of eligible suitors since her debut. She was so taken with the actor's superb interpretation of the title role that it sent her on the run for the works of Victor Hugo on the shelves at the Athenaeum the next day. She read the English translation of *Notre Dame de Paris* with the joy of fresh discovery and was moved to read it in the original. She regretted not having paid attention to her language course in school, but that did not stop her. Inspired by Hugo's book to study French, as her teachers' tirades and her mother's tutoring had never done, she learned the language so well that she read Hugo's novels straight through without stopping to look up words; oddly enough, she preferred Hugo's novels to his poetry or plays. She read the rich stories avidly.

"Many a night did I sit up in bed, reading by the flickering light of two candles!" she wrote enthusiastically. She was engrossed not only by the plot but by the style of the novels: His prose style opened new doors of poetry for her far more than his poems did. (That style no doubt was part of the groundwork for her own "polyphonic prose." An odd assortment—Walter Scott, Duse, Victor Hugo, and Keats—combined to form her most peculiar muse.) At the moment, she was fired with fresh zeal to learn more of French literature.

She wished her mother could know that she had finally mastered vocabulary and syntax to read in French with ease, but her mother's condition suddenly became crucial, and she died on April 1, 1895, just after Amy's twenty-first birthday. Whatever grief Amy felt must have been tempered with relief that her mother was at last released from the long siege of Bright's disease, which had been a trial for everyone. Now Amy could pursue her course of learning to her heart's content, but she had to decide what she was going to do with the knowledge she was gathering. Many of the debutantes who did not marry within a few years turned to teaching, and while Amy Lowell had her own ideas about education and probably felt she could surpass the teachers she had had, her longings to be "Somebody" in the literary world, somebody as important as Percy had become, superseded all others. Percy's four books on the Far East had made him famous in America. His latest, *Mars,* published shortly after their mother died, was so controversial in its theories about life and the certainty of canals on that planet that it was rapidly making him world famous as "The Martian." His rise to fame was indeed meteoric—or seemed so to Amy—and it was her dream to emulate and surpass him if possible. Lawrence, too, was gaining a reputation, with one published book on government and another nearing completion. Even Bessie wrote poems and other pieces, but since she was married and had a family, she did not consider it necessary to seek publication of her work. So it was only natural for Amy to decide that she would be a writer of some sort. She did not yet dare to think of herself as the author of volumes of poetry, much as she adored her new-found idols, Shelley and, most of all, Keats.

In the next few years Amy experimented with plays, novels, and short stories to find out if she had writing talent in any of those fields, but none of them took. And all the while she was leading the life of the debutante in the nineties along with others in her crowd. In the summer of 1896 she went abroad again, with Katie Dana and one of the Miss Dabneys as chaperon. (The Dabneys were old friends of the Lowells, from an equally reputable and early Boston family.) It was a typical late-Victorian grand tour of Europe: They sailed to Naples, and from there traveled through the rest of Italy, where Amy fell in love with Venice, and went on to Austria, France, the Netherlands, and England. From her letters to "Dear Papa" and other members of the family, Amy seems to have thoroughly enjoyed the journey—certainly far more than the one she had taken with her parents and Bessie when she was only eight.

In London, Amy straightaway sought out the firm of Bernard Quarritch, Ltd., where she bought books and made a friend of Quarritch's associate, E. H. Dring, who was responsible for many of the future treasures of her library. And also in London, she was taken by her friends, the W. Heinemans, with whom Whistler was then living, to visit the venerable painter in his studio. She bought a picture from him—not the one he recommended, but one that had caught her eye right away and which she preferred in spite of his promotion of the other—and she was always convinced, from a slight gleam in his eye, that he was "secretly pleased by the perspicacity of her choice." (When she renovated Sevenels, she hung it "on the chimney-breast" in her library, where it remained the rest of her life.)

Katie Dana became Mrs. White not long after their return; one by one, the girls who had shared Amy Lowell's coming-out year were being tapped for marriage. (Some wag had dubbed a debutante ball the "market-place for brides," and it seemed an apt metaphor.) Amy herself had received two proposals, but neither one had interested her. Then, some time in 1897, according to the prevailing story, she received another proposal of marriage from a young (and evidently "proper") Bostonian who had been coming to call regularly. Amy, pleased, and grateful for his consistent attention, had fallen in love with him. She gladly accepted his offer of marriage; her father approved the match; and the engagement was "all but announced" when the young man had to leave town. Evidently, no word came from him for some time until a brief letter arrived, confessing that he had unfortunately "become entangled elsewhere," and he was breaking off the alliance with her.* It was a terrible blow. Amy had probably wanted to be married, like her sisters and her close friends. Moreover, when she loved, she loved hard, and she longed for affection to be lavished upon her in return. Too proud to grieve outwardly for a lost love, she shut herself up in her room for days, coming downstairs only for meals. The family could do nothing to protect her except guard tenaciously the name of the errant suitor. Her father felt very sorry for her, but what was there to say? Other members of the family have suggested that the name was never revealed because the suitor never existed.

One can only speculate on what Amy Lowell went through during those days of self-confinement, but she must have been

* "A Communication," a poem published in a posthumous volume, *Ballads for Sale* (1927), was apparently addressed to the young near-fiancé; it expresses both an almost wistful dejection and a fine show of bravado.

bitter, realizing perhaps that she had received marriage proposals for reasons of prestige, not of real love. Men probably thought she would be a good match, but changed their minds quickly, perhaps scared by her tendency to dominate and her sense of family arrogance. Some of her self-hate and self-consciousness about her overweight body must have returned with this rejection. She was still struggling to escape from it, still "sloughing off the swaddling bands," as she said later. At any rate, she must have blamed this failure in love on her oversized body, for she determined to decrease it.

CHAPTER VI

"Banting" Aboard a Dahabeah, "God of the Rising Moon"—and Disaster

THE REDUCING-DIET FAD of the day followed a formula of Dr. William Banting, who prescribed an extreme diet of nothing but tomatoes and asparagus, preferably on a trip up the Nile, where the heat would help one sweat off excess weight. Medical science knew little of glandular diseases or ways of combating them. It was true that Amy Lowell had always had a large appetite and loved to eat; one look at the menu of a typical dinner party of the day makes one wonder why the entire upper-class population did not suffer from obesity as Amy did. However, most of Amy's debutante friends suffered from no serious weight problems. It was obvious that her trouble was glandular, but most doctors believed the cure lay in diet alone. And the popular one was that restricted to tomatoes and asparagus; people who found themselves putting on weight talked about "banting" for a few weeks or months. And, if they could afford to travel, they tried the diet on a trip up the Nile. Even if the diet didn't work, they could enjoy the beautiful scenery, to say nothing of the wondrous sights—the ancient temples, the shrines, and the historical sculptures.

Amy, humiliated by her recent rejection and eager to get away from Boston and Sevenels for a while, must have gone through some such reasoning when she announced with her usual flair that she was taking a trip up the Nile to try "banting." Whatever deeper motives she might have had were not mentioned. Ostensibly, she was making this voyage to try to reduce, for there was no denying that she was abnormally, "appaulingly fat," as she had frankly phrased it in her diary. And now she had to face the fact again. No matter how much she might surmount her defect psychologically, she still had to be realistic about it.

She resolutely put aside the sadness in her heart and set about organizing a party of five women who would be interested in hiring a small boat—a dahabeah—to make the voyage. There would be no Cook's tour for her!

As usual, Amy arranged everything, persuading a cousin who was ailing to join the party, and urging that they start at once. It was late November of 1897, and her father was reluctant to let her go on a long journey just before Christmas; she had never been away over the holidays, and it would mean that he would be alone. But her sense of urgency was too strong: She felt she *had* to get away; she needed a drastic change of scenery to help her forget the fiasco of her love affair. Thank heaven they had not announced the engagement, she told her father as she said good-bye a few days after Thanksgiving. She promised to write to him every Sunday.

She kept her promise. The early letters to "Dearest Papa" read like a travelogue, with descriptions of their dahabeah, *Chonsu* (which means "God of the Rising Moon," an appropriate title for a moon worshiper), an elegant little craft, sumptuously outfitted with velvet curtains and divans in the cabins, and overmanned with a crew that seemed to be swarming all over it. "Seventeen men to take five women up the Nile!" she exclaimed in her account of the start of their journey. The scenery was almost inexpressibly beautiful, in no small part because of the river itself, especially at sunset. "It seems to me that the color that best expresses the Nile is my pink diamond," she wrote, referring to a present her father had given her. "It is really just like that," she added, gazing at the silvery-pink sheen of the river. She wrote on deck, as she wanted to be outside as much as possible. But a little farther along, she expressed annoyance at the unsavory attitude of the special "cataract Arabs" of the crew, seasoned sailors of the Nile, who, supposedly, were the only ones who could get the dahabeah safely over the cataracts.

They kept staring at her while she was writing, evidently

fascinated by her fountain pen, a recent invention. They looked with awe at her scribbling away without ever dipping her pen into an inkpot, and sometimes crowded around her, jabbering and pointing. Earlier they had put on an act she had been forewarned about, predicting the dire fate facing them when they reached the cataracts, clasping their hands in prayer, chanting, moaning, and beating their breasts, and always ending with a plea for baksheesh in return for such risks of life and limb. (The captain explained that this was their usual procedure.) The next time the cataract Arabs came crowding around as she sat writing, Amy had a sudden inspiration: She rose up wrathfully and advanced on them menacingly, the point of her pen held on a level with their scared, rolling eyes. Her brandishing pen cowed them. They backed away as if hypnotized, but she kept advancing, ordering them to continue the journey at once, without further "nonsense or delay." And off they scurried to do as she commanded.

The incident had a comic-opera aspect, but it somehow restored Amy's self-confidence and gave her a sense of power. She could—and would—make her force felt in the world of men. As it turned out, all aboard survived the ordeal of the cataracts; despite some crucial moments during the descent of the most turbulent waters, there were no serious mishaps. Later, on the return course downriver, Amy was seized with a consuming desire to visit Philae, one of a cluster of islands off the far shore. But the natives refused. It was a hazardous crossing, it was too far off course, the winds were not right, and so on—they could only manage it for a large baksheesh. This time the captain sided with them. He said that the currents were tricky and dangerous in that part of the river; few tourists ever wanted to try it. Incensed, the redoubtable Amy Lowell took over the dahabeah herself and sailed directly to the island of Philae. From then on, the crew was far more docile and respectful toward the rich, fat American lady whom they had thought they could fool.

As for Amy, she spoke of herself as "running a party consisting of an invalid friend and 17 recalcitrant natives. . . ." She was running the show, though she was supposed to be the failing one for whom the trip had been planned. And indeed the tomato-and-asparagus diet was not agreeing with her, but she gave no hint of its ill-effect in her letters or actions. She did not want her father to worry or tell her to give up the journey, because in spite of all the aggravations, she was able to forget her emotional troubles among the strange and beautiful sights. For her, the high point of the trip was their arrival at Abu Simbel in Nubia, their main goal. "Never shall I forget Aboo Simbel as our dahabeah swung around the curve in the river and those four colossal figures sat gazing calmly down upon the blue river with that bright orange tumble of sand beside them," she wrote. To her, the most perfect piece of Egyptian sculpture was at the portal of one of the temples, "The Kiss of Athon Ra and Thutmoset." She was so entranced by the figures that she took photographs and commissioned Joseph Lindon Smith to do a painting of them when she came home. (She brought back five albums of snapshots.) Her description of the Libyan Desert, into which they made a day-long trek to view temples, is full of the mention of the changing hues of colors as the sun took its course. (One aspect of this side trip that was almost frightening was the way the poverty-stricken natives—men, women, and small children—approached the party en masse with outstretched palms, begging, crying, "Baksheesh, baksheesh!"—by now an all-too-familiar wail. The guides told the travelers to ignore them, and it was the only thing to do, no matter how annoyed or compassionate one might feel.) Her observations were to appear later, in one form or another, in poems. Typically, she noticed that "the moonlight on the Nile is more beautiful than any I have seen." On some nights when she could not sleep, she sat up on deck, watching its silver magic like one bewitched.

Her overall conclusion, however, after relating graphically the fuss and howl the Arabs had made over "descending the cataract" and the destitute state of so much of the population, was emphatic: "I am glad I am an American, & was brought up like a boy, . . . There!" She had voiced the sentiments clearly indicating the character she was to become, partly because of innate masculine tendencies, partly because of her background and upbringing, and in no small measure because of her "banting" aboard the dahabeah.

The trip proved to be a terrible mistake physically. Amy had lost very few pounds, and she returned to Boston in mid-winter of 1898 with a gastritis condition brought on by the heavily acid diet; it weakened her constitution, producing a nervous prostration that lasted for the next seven years—"the real thing, the kind where you live with a perpetual headache, & the slightest sound jars you all over"—so she later described it to John Farrar in 1921.

She felt limp; her insides were a quivering mass; at times she was painfully bloated by hyperacidity; at other times it seemed as if the inner lining of her stomach would burst open. Her formerly iron nerves were ragged, as frail as tissue paper. Her head throbbed constantly. Her father, puzzled and concerned, refrained from saying, "I told you so," but Amy had to admit that the experiment in Egypt had proved a complete disaster. For the first time, she entered a period of lassitude. She didn't care what she did. Perhaps the return to Boston and to her father's townhouse, the scene of her failure and heartbreak, brought on the dejection. While she was seeing new, strange sights and having adventures in Egypt, she was too occupied to realize what was happening to her body, beyond realizing occasionally that the diet was not working and often caused her distress. But she kept thinking that the benefits would appear after the diet was completed. Now, in addition to the recent physical damage to her health, all her psychological stumbling blocks came flooding back and proved to be too much. Certainly she could not face the remainder of the Boston winter social season of entertaining.

The Dabneys owned property in southern California, twenty miles north of the Mexican border—Fayal Ranch (named after Fayal in the Azores, where for eighty-five years three generations of Dabneys served as the American consul—and an adjoining fruit ranch that had a house Amy could occupy. It was small, but adequate for "Miss Lowell, and her chaperone, maid and cook," the Misses Dabney said. They were going out to spend a few months, and would be close by—a mile and a half away—but not close enough to interfere with the peace and quiet she needed.

Hoping to regain at least a modicum of health, Amy decided to go. She found the house pleasant and the life extremely quiet. She spent most of her time sitting on the "piazza," immobile, "which seems to agree with me better than anything," she wrote her father, commenting on the beauty of the "ipomeas" twining through the trellis on the porch. (The use of the botanical name for blue morning-glory came naturally to her as part of the horticultural lore she had acquired from her father; this was one area in which they spoke the same language.) She spoke, too, of riding over the hills and trails all day long when she felt strong enough, "amid the flowering roses and orange blossoms." (She loved heavily scented flowers, the fragrance of orange blossoms, jasmine, and tropical night-blooms, like the exotic cereus.) She fully enjoyed the open-air life and was able to regain some of her lost strength and spirit.

But the summer of 1899 found her still in search of health, this time in Devonshire, England, where the mild climate was supposed to be good for the nerves—and the rich Devonshire cream was supposed to counteract hyperacidity. It also helped her to put on weight, but she no longer cared how large she was as long as she could feel like herself. She swore she would never diet drastically again, and she kept the vow with pleasure. There might have been a middle course of moderate, well-balanced meals, which, if started early enough, could have prevented the obesity and certainly would have avoided the recurrent illnesses she suffered. But Amy Lowell was never one to do anything by halves. She was a person of extremes, and now, although she occasionally refrained from sweets, she gave way indulgently to all the foods she loved. While she was in Devonshire, settled for the summer in a charming little cottage where the fuchsias hanging over the doorway provided a profusion of color,* if she indulged herself to the full with rice pudding covered with Devonshire cream, both were good for her stomach—and her psyche.

* As she recalled in a future letter to D. H. Lawrence.

CHAPTER VII

Amorphous Ambitions of a Literary Amateur, from the American Upper Class

BESIDES HER OBESITY, Amy Lowell had other bars to attaining a successful life: her wealth and social position. She described it as "one of the greatest handicaps that anyone could possibly have. I belonged to the class which is not supposed to be able to produce good creative work." In the future some would claim derisively that it was a handicap she did not overcome; many others were to cite her achievement as a triumph of creative talent over material gifts. When she returned from Devonshire in the fall of 1899, however, she was soon to be confronted with even more personal, immediate concerns. She was just beginning to emerge from the grizzly aftermath of her health experiment in Egypt and was wondering vaguely what she should do next when she found that her father was ailing.

Augustus Lowell had been bothered by a troublesome gall bladder for some time. It had never been serious, but was annoying to a man who held that good health was simply a matter of regular habits, hard work, and a little common sense in eating. But during the first months of 1899 the condition began to grow worse, and after they moved to Sevenels on May 1, it was Amy, not Augustus, who supervised the gardening; and in other ways she also did as much as she could herself. Neither, however, was able to be very active. In June, Augustus was stricken by a severe attack and had to undergo an operation. It was pronounced successful, and he had returned to Sevenels to convalesce when he had a sudden relapse and died there within twenty-four hours. All of his children and grandchildren were around him—Percy had come from Arizona—and it was decided to hold the funeral in the parlor there, the room which was soon to become the front half of Amy's famous library. Even during the memorial service for their father, Amy, realizing she was alone, made up her mind to buy Sevenels from the estate (which presumably was left to the five children). She alone had been born there, and she loved it as much as her father had. Now she wanted it, and her brothers and sisters were agreeable. The purchase was quickly made, and as soon as the family dispersed, Amy set about remodeling the old square stone mansion to suit herself.*

The tasks of planning, selecting, and pleasing her decorative tastes provided beneficial therapy for the time being. Amy Lowell, like her father and grandfather, had a strong sense of property, and redoing Sevenels once it was hers was a labor of love and, as such, was completely absorbing. The first thing she did was to create a baronial library. She directed the architects to tear down the wall between the already spacious front and back parlors. Each room had a large fireplace, which she embellished with intricate wood carvings imported from England, and she installed heavy oak paneling along the wall space that was not lined with floor-to-ceiling built-in bookshelves—the latest thing in home libraries. In a touch worthy of Sir Walter Scott, she had a huge safety vault built at one end of the middle shelves, camouflaged by dummy books that formed a sliding panel. The safe held her greatest treasures: her rare books and original manuscripts. The furnishings of this exceptionally large library were also capacious and comfortable. There were big, deep chairs; "Amy's chair" was leather, like a man's, with an ample footstool or hassock at its base—not only for ease and comfort, but for health reasons, as she had to keep her feet elevated. Soft, plump sofas flanked the fireplaces, and highly polished mahogany tables reflected the exquisite bouquets of flowers in select vases; Amy loved fine porcelain and china, as well as crystal and silver. These tables were soon to be stacked

* The actual renovation was not completed until 1906 or 1907, but Amy began thinking about it as soon as she was in sole possession of Sevenels.

with recently published books, which were regularly sent to Miss Lowell by the Old Corner Bookshop for her perusal. She kept those she wanted and returned the rest. It was seldom that one did not see new books on the library tables. Numerous lamps and two large chandeliers kept the room at whatever level of light was desired, for the extrafunctional feature of Amy's extraordinary library was that it could easily be turned into a little theater. She probably had such a purpose in mind when she remodeled the ground floor, remembering the Lindon Smiths' Teatro Bambino in Dublin. Home theatricals became her avocation for several years.*

If the baronial library evidenced Amy Lowell's masculinity, the music room—a miraculous conversion of the old billiard room—accented the feminine side of her dual personality. Here the decor was eighteenth-century Adam in blue and white trimmed with gold. The dainty Adam chairs and delicate crystal chandeliers, which burned candles; the polished parquet floor; the Chinese wallpaper—all reflected in antique gilt mirrors—was a perfect setting for the home musicals and piano and song recitals Amy was to give. With her flair for shocking the world around her, the programs featured "modern" music, strange to most Boston ears: Debussy, Béla Bartók, Stravinsky, even Eric Satie, and George Antheil (who set to music one of her poems) were the composers whose works were most often heard in Amy Lowell's jewellike music room.

Because she could not bring herself to part with the time-honored antlered heads that had given her so much pleasure as a child, Amy did not redecorate the entrance hall. And she did little to the dining room except to have it papered in a landscape-patterned fine wallpaper. She also acquired the painted bas-relief panels of luscious fruit from the ceiling of her grandfather's house in Roxbury; she had them placed over her dining-room doors, thus providing herself with links to the past even while breaking away from it.

* Perhaps because of its use as a theater, Amy did not adorn the library panels with paintings. Her Whistler hung "on the chimney-breast" of one fireplace and a small Constable on the other. Later, she added Japanese wood blocks, and the Egyptian scenes she had commissioned from Joseph Lindon Smith.

Another tie she could not relinquish was her third-floor bedroom quarters. She decided to keep her old nursery inviolable so that she could always retire to her childhood if she chose. It was not a sanctum sanctorum, however; rather, it became her headquarters when necessary—a frequent occurrence—for she rarely rose before 1:00 P.M., and usually later. Here the domestics came for their daily orders, beginning with the cook (who had been with the family from the time Amy was a little girl, and had had a share in pampering her with cookies and other treats between meals), to discuss the daily menus, especially when there would be guests for dinner. When she began her writing career in earnest, her secretaries would appear next, with typed manuscripts for approval or corrections. Since she was still suffering from headaches and nerves, she also received representatives of various committees while still in bed. (Now that she was the head and sole family occupant of Sevenels, she could stay up and get up as late as she pleased, and in this respect she indulged her childhood desire to the fullest.) According to Elizabeth Sergeant, when close friends arrived to spend the weekend they found themselves being "hallooed upstairs" by a hearty greeting from Amy to "share the mysteries of the bedchamber." But from all accounts, there was less mystery than conviviality in Amy's third-floor domain.

When redecorating, she had it wired for electricity (some said she "electrified it in more ways than one"); she had the walls painted a sky-blue and hung them with the deeper blue Hiroshiges Percy had sent her from Japan. And she also installed a huge, outsized tile bath—which may have marked her "a sybaritic empress," as her friend Elsie Sergeant said—but it also gave her much simple pleasure and beneficial hydrotherapy.

Being a woman of means, she bought a townhouse and an automobile (wanting to be also "the first by whome the new is tried"). She soon found that getting to and from Boston by motor was so easy that she sold the townhouse and bought a sixty-acre place in the country, near Dublin, New Hampshire, from her distant cousins, the Frank Crowninshields. There she would be close to the artistic circle of friends she most admired. And the location was a choice one: on a wooded slope overlooking Dublin

Lake, with a view of Mount Monadnock in the distance. With such a view, there was no need for extensive landscaping, though she did keep a few rows of flowers along the front veranda and a back garden for cuttings, which she herself tended for the most part. The house was spacious but simple, a brown-shingled one typical of the period. She called it Broomley Lacey, a term derived from the name of her great-grandfather's estate, Broomley Vale. (Since her house was not in a valley, she varied the title by using the Old English word for "woods," but she was still maintaining ties with the past and her identity as a Lowell.)

In Brookline, Amy stepped into her father's shoes by becoming the new sovereign of Sevenels, and she continued the Lowell tradition of civic leadership by looking after the town's interests. She became chairman of the library committee of the Brookline Educational Society and a member of its executive board, an activist in the Women's Municipal League, and president of the Committee for the Suppression of Unnecessary Noise. She attended town meetings faithfully, as her father had, and the first two of her public offices came about as a result of making her voice heard and her power felt in town hall early in 1902. Amy spoke out at a meeting called by the school board to retire the elderly superintendent of schools, whose ideas were outmoded and inefficient. However, everyone was so afraid of hurting the old man's feelings that they all kept praising his past record, and could not bring themselves to criticize him. He was about to be reappointed when Amy's amazonian figure rose from the audience and ascended the platform. As she began to speak she was hissed—she was the first woman in the Lowell family to make a speech in public, and she was antipathetic to the general feeling—but she took it that she was being applauded, and plunged ahead with her usual forthrightness, stating all her reasons for being against the reappointment. In the end, she was really applauded and won her point; the older official was retired and replaced by a younger man. After she became a member of the executive committee, she gave another address on, "Is the Present System of High School Education Prejudicial to Individual Development?" in which she stated her case in detail and was fully quoted in the *Boston Transcript.** Percy sent her a letter of congratulations, telling "Miss Postscript" to keep up the good work. But other members of the Lowell family were shocked at her public speech. After the meeting that night, Lawrence's wife, Katie, Bessie, and a couple of Cabots had gathered around her in mixed admiration and dismay: How *could* she stand up there and talk like that? A woman—and a Lowell! What would people say? But her triumph convinced her (as had her success in dealing with the crew of the dahabeah in Egypt) that she had power over people; it was a feeling that gave her confidence and poise for further jousts. In civic affairs, her male Lowell heritage came to the fore.

Later in the year—October 21, 1902—an event took place which was to develop her self-confidence on a different plane. In fact, it marked the beginning of her life as a poet. The date was the opening night of Eleonora Duse's third, and triumphant, tour. She was appearing at the Tremont Theatre in Boston in a series of plays written especially for her by Gabriel D'Annunzio, a renowned novelist of the day, known to be her lover. Amy, regal in sequined black satin in the Lowell box, sat through the entire performance like one entranced. She had been deeply impressed with Duse in her earlier appearances, but now she was spellbound. When she came home, she found herself trembling with churning emotion, compelled "with infinite agitation" to write a poem. There, at midnight, at twenty-eight years of age, she sat down and dashed off line after line, inspired by the miraculous vision the great actress had given her. The poem was not a paeon of praise to La Duse, but rather an outpouring of emotion—"Seventy-one lines of bad blank verse," Amy admitted frankly years later. Only the last three lines concerned the actress herself: "And through the studied anguish learnt by rote/ We feel the throbbing of a woman's soul,/ A woman's heart that cries to God and fears."

During the Boston run, Amy attended all nine performances

* Recalling her own inadequate schooling, she said, "Nature cannot be hurried, there is no such thing as cramming. . . . And what can we think of a primary school taught by one teacher, in which the children were taught seventeen subjects, with fifteen minutes given to each subject, as was the case in one school in Brookline!"

of the cycle and, with masculine aggression, followed her idol to Philadelphia. There she contacted a Dublin friend, Katie Dunham, who had theater connections, and arrangements were made for Amy to visit Duse at her hotel. It was a sacred moment for Amy when she entered the room and found the luminous-eyed actress resting in bed, clad in a filmy dressing gown that made her fair skin look paler and more translucent than usual, as if her delicate bones shone through it. She held out her hand with the long tapering fingers—so expressive in her acting—and in greeting Amy her voice was as low and intimate as it was onstage, one of the elements of her rare charm. Though she spoke in Italian, of which Amy knew very little, it did not matter: "She talked as if soul to soul," or as though it was "a spirit, scarcely a woman, that spoke through her lips." Amy felt exalted by the touch of that hand, the sound of that velvet, throaty voice; she came away from the visit "almost on air," she told her friends. Filled with the same fever of poetic vision that prompted the "seventy-one lines of bad blank verse," she decided that her calling must be writing poetry. In commenting on the length of time it took her to find her true self, Amy Lowell remarked on the value of remaining a child longer than usual; it enabled her, she said, to develop into a "more mature man." In more general terms she observed, "The longer a child can remain comparatively fallow, the better it will be for him; we must never forget to allow the greatest possible development to the subconscious."

Yet the impropriety of a woman seeking a public career, even as a poet—frowned upon by her father during his lifetime—was still a factor she had to grapple with, in her own mind, as well as externally. Most of her friends were married now, occupied principally with raising their young children and entertaining in their social set. She did have one ally in Bessie Ward (Mrs. Charles) Perkins, who enjoyed writing poetry for her own gratification. Together they studied Leigh Hunt's book, analyzed Keats, and criticized each other's poems. Percy, to whom Amy had confided her ambitions, sent her some good advice: "Amy, do not forget that no matter what you write about, a book is a failure if it is not interesting." Dependable, dear Percy was always with her; she wished he were not so far away, or would come from Arizona more often.

She had occasion to appreciate his moral support soon again, when a stormy controversy arose on the issue of moving the crowded Boston Athenaeum from its Beacon Hill building to a new site across the Public Gardens. As its most prominent founding members, the Lowells had of course been connected with the old library for generations, and to Amy the building itself, with its spiral stairway and dusty stacks, was a symbol of escape from authority to freedom of thought. Moreover, since most of the directors were for the move, she realized that they must be hoping to make a profit on it; and to her, a Lowell of the first order, profit made at the expense of a venerable historical landmark was undesirable. So in this instance she, who considered herself avant-garde and ready to try anything—the latest and most daring for women was smoking—proved herself conservative, but for strong, valid reasons. She presented them in no uncertain terms, and those who agreed with her rallied to form an opposition committee. In her fervent need of loyalty, she wrote a poem, "The Boston Athenaeum," later published in full in her first volume, and in part at the time in the *Transcript,* along with an account of her position. Percy wrote: "Bravo! Bravo! I know you did it well. . . . So with you heart and soul that I have just written a piece to the *Transcript* and sent it to them. Macte virtute, virgine! And continue to be a dear girl to—Your affectionate brother, Percival."

She was glad to receive his unsolicited support, but meanwhile had called a meeting of the opposition committee with a scheme of her own in mind. The "virgine" received the astonished members in her bedroom, sitting up in her queen-sized bed, wearing an old-fashioned woolen nightgown and smoking a pipe. A large black umbrella set up in back of her shoulders shielded her from the drafts of open windows on either side of the headboard. Her breakfast tray, the contents of which she had just demolished, although it was three o'clock in the afternoon, rested on the pillows at her side. Before the committee could fully digest this bizarre scene, she outlined her strategy to them with such briskness and aplomb that their astonishment subsided and they entered into discussion. Part of her plan was to buy an extra share of Athenaeum stock to increase the strength of her vote, and at the next meeting of the board of directors the opposition, spurred by her spirit of spunky courage, carried the day: The Athenaeum building was to be preserved, and alterations made to accommodate the spate of new books. (Another beloved building, the old Boston Museum-Theatre, where Amy had spent so many happy hours as a child, was doomed, however, that same year. She and others of the Lowell clan were opposed to its being razed, but they could not save it. Amy, however, bought two of the double doors, which she put up between the entrance hall and the music room at Sevenels.)

Thus she filled her days and nights with activities to forget the headaches, the attacks of nerves, the depressions that subconsciously seethed beneath the surface. After the interview with Duse, she felt more inward calm than she had before. She acquired a deeper goal than the civic interests, the chitchat of lunch clubs, the teas, or even the theater provided. And along with poetry and live drama, the beauty of flowers and art objects, her books, the building of her library and store of rare books and manuscripts, plus eating good food—the enjoyment of all these made up for the lack of the passionate love she had dreamed of in adolescence. When she wrote the repeated refrain, "I am a woman, sick for passion," in "Appuldurcombe Park"—one of her most revealing narrative poems of later years—she must have been speaking from experience; but she sublimated so well that few suspected how poignant her pangs were.

Amy Lowell turned thirty on February 9, 1904, so there was no denying that, in Victorian terms, she was a spinster, and had been one for five years. In the nineteenth century, a young woman became an old maid if she was not married by the age of twenty-five, and a young man became a bachelor if he was unmarried at thirty. For at least the first decade of the twentieth century, these tags were commonly strung on single people over twenty-one, often with strangling effect on their sex life. In the case of a young man, however, who was given five more years of grace to begin with, the term "bachelor" added a certain dash even to a dullard, probably because he was still eligible. (Percy—handsome, accomplished, and wealthy—had been one of Boston's most eligible bachelors for years.) There was a definite stigma attached to the terms "spinster" or "old maid," implying that one was undesirable or a discard: a girl that had been left "on the shelf" while the flower of her youth withered away. It is unthinkable that a nature as aware and impassioned as Amy Lowell's should not feel this implied stigma and also that, with her love of the exotic, she should be equally defiant of it in her life-style. Her first published volume speaks of ". . . the curse/ That never shall I be fulfilled by love!" And in her last, she daringly depicts a fantasy or a deviate love, "For which unreasonable reason/ I am determined to remain a virgin."

She celebrated her thirtieth birthday by attending Whistler's Memorial Exhibit at Copley Hall, and in the next few years sustained herself by emphasizing the things of the spirit and by exercising her strong and active mind. With Duse as her artistic ideal, she turned for companionship ever more toward women, although she never became hostile toward men; in fact, every so often a hope for marital love with a man flared up, exacerbating her old conflict. Obviously, she had bisexual tendencies without knowing it; but her capacity for enjoyment and her sense of power and property kept her from being destroyed by the duality within her. In 1905 she bought the complete Keats collection of Frederick Locker Lampson, famous for its original manuscripts, which were to form the basis for her own remarkable Keats collection. She began taking an interest in women's colleges, particularly in Radcliffe. She donated books to help build up its library and aided in strengthening its independence as a separate entity instead of being the Harvard Annex. She studied Wellesley College as a place of higher learning for women and assessed its needs. She was always to hold to her contention that the purpose of teaching should be to inspire students to learn on their own, a theory on which she and Robert Frost found common ground.

During the summer, Amy divided her time between Sevenels and her country place, with an occasional trip to Europe or to the Carolinas to visit the great gardens there. Her deep love of flowers, like her love of horses and dogs, was a passion she could openly display without fear of frustration or being considered queer. Not that she minded her reputation for eccentricity and iconoclasm—she rather enjoyed it and, indeed, invited it—but she wanted to be respected and respectable at the same time. This part of her nineteenth-century Lowell heritage she never wholly lost. She was delighted to find that her neighbors at Broomley Lacey, the Russells, were horse fanciers, and particularly that Mr. Russell raised show horses. She immediately became friends with the whole family, including the Russells' small daughter, Doris, who always enjoyed going to see Miss Lowell in her big brown cottage above the lake. (When she was old enough, Doris drove her own pony and cart, and one of the first places she went was to Broomley Lacey to show Miss Lowell, who would appreciate the accomplishment more than anybody.) As for Amy, she never took her car to Dublin because she preferred driving with horses through the country lanes and woods. She spent a good deal of time at the Russells' stables and, after two or three years, was one of the judges at Dublin's annual horse show. If she found some activities interesting, Amy was bound to lead wherever she was!

In the late spring of 1908, she took a short trip to Greece (after visiting Naples again) to view the source of inspiration for so many works of art; uppermost in her mind was Keats's "Ode on a Grecian Urn," in its reverence for ancient Greek art. She had nothing especially notable to say about Greece itself except, typically, that Athens was "just like Boston"; there was a "Clean, cozy, provincial friendliness all over it." But on an excursion through the islands of the Aegean she breathed in the ancient beauty of Delphi, and she had a strange yet serene experience at Olympia: She fell asleep in the warm, golden sunlight, "woke to perfect quiet and the gentle blowing of the poppies, and walked into the house where Praxiteles' Hermes is, and his striking my tired eyes almost as the real god might have done had I met him in a grove of olives. . . . I have never gotten over the almost breathless effect its beauty had on me."

She arrived home just in time for Percy's wedding on June 10 to Constance Savage Keith. With the marriage of her perennial bachelor brother—Percy was fifty-three—all her siblings were now married. Her sister Katie had emerged from widowhood six years before to wed Thomas James Bowlker, British dean of the College of Hertford and priest of the Anglican church. That event took place just as Amy was being swept off her feet in adoration of Eleonora Duse (November 24, 1902, probably the date she had been with Duse in the latter's bedroom), so it did not really affect her at the time, but with Percy's becoming a family man, her single status became more pronounced in her mind.

It was inevitable that rumors would circulate from time to time among the Boston clubwomen regarding some attentive or frequent caller at Sevenels as a "lost lover" of Amy Lowell. There was Berkeley Updike, for example, expert in graphic arts and typography as well as rare-book dealer, who designed and printed the programs for the Sevenels concerts and theatricals. Updike was a dapper little man from Providence, Rhode Island, who had set up shop in Boston with an eye toward Beacon Hill society women. Always impeccably dressed, brisk and bright in manner, he knew his trade and his customers well. He remembered to compliment women on their appearance, but he was neither obsequious nor obvious, and he was well versed enough in the arts to be an interesting dinner guest as well as an efficient adviser on matters of typography, paper stock, and design. In fact, Amy was so confident of his ability that she came to consult him in the production of all her books. His frequent visits to Sevenels, supposedly a sign of romance between the two, undoubtedly filled many a lonely hour for her with pleasant, busy activity; but their relationship, if anything more than a business connection, was certainly platonic.

A far deeper, more significant, and more lasting friendship—just short of romance—was the one Amy formed with the musicologist, composer, and music publisher Carl Engel. She had undeniable feelings for him as a member of the opposite sex. Based on some recently published letters,* it is apparent that Amy Lowell's love for someone she admired transcended sex and also that, until 1912, she suffered from extreme loneliness and had a longing to be loved. Equally interesting is the fact that she met Carl Engel

* William C. Bedford, "A Musical Apprentice: Amy Lowell to Carl Engel," *The Musical Quarterly* (October 1972).

through an actress on whom she had one of her habitual crushes. In late August 1908, *The Merry Widow* came to the Tremont Theatre. Amy, who rarely missed an opening, was so delighted with the gaiety of the operetta that she went again on the night when Lina Abarbanell performed the part of Sonia, and, proving herself a charming soubrette—the hit of the show—became its star. Amy was completely enchanted by Abarbanell and straightaway gave a party at Sevenels for the new leading lady. The party set the tongues of Boston society ladies wagging for weeks, for Mme Abarbanell chose to present a scene from a melodrama depicting the miseries of courtesans. This in itself shocked the parents whose daughters had been invited to the party; and then, to cap it, the star proceeded to sing—to accompaniment by Mrs. Langdon Frothingham—some risqué Bavarian songs (though no one could understand a word). Some gentlemen were amused, but their wives told the hostess frankly that they wouldn't have come if they had known what the entertainment would be. "And on a *Sunday,* too!" ran the refrain from a chorus of voices in Boston drawing rooms.

Amy was unabashed and was so taken with Lina Abarbanell that she invited the actress to come to Sevenels as often as her schedule would permit. On one of these occasions, Abarbanell brought with her a young French-trained composer and musician who had recently come from Europe and was now with the Boston Music Company.* It was Carl Engel, and the meeting was one of the most fortuitous in Amy Lowell's life and literary development up to that point. Engel—not handsome, but pleasant-faced, urbane, charming, and sympathetic, as well as talented and knowledgeable in his field—soon became one of Amy Lowell's most valued and valuable friends. Both he and Amy knew that Lina Abarbanell's was a light talent and that hers was a somewhat frivolous and irresponsible character, especially where money was concerned; but both were fond of her, and more than once helped her out—Carl, professionally, and Amy, financially. Amy made a pet of her, followed her to New York when she became the star of musicals

* A branch of G. Schirmer, Inc., New York music publishers, of which Engel eventually became president (part time from 1929 to 1932; and full time from 1934 till his death in 1944).

at the Irving Place Theatre, gave her a pearl necklace from Tiffany's, and entertained her in Dublin as well as Brookline. She was blonde, pretty, and merry as the widow whose part she played and sang so disarmingly, and Amy found her a delightful diversion, as the lord of a manor house might sponsor a court entertainer.

But with Carl Engel, Amy's attitude was almost that of a pupil: He was her mentor in musical matters; her kind, sympathetic, and gallant friend in emotional channels. He was always happy to advise her regarding music scores for her concerts. When she needed parts for the compositions to be played, he told her which publishers might have them and how many she would need ("three first violins, two violas," etc.). He helped her plan the concerts. It was he who led her to modern French music (which he himself played brilliantly) and to other moderns: Bartók, Stravinsky, Schönberg, Albéniz, Eric Satie, composers scarcely heard of in America in 1908. He introduced her to Heinrich Gebhardt, concert pianist in the music department at Harvard (from whom Virgil Thomson would be taking "keyboard lessons," as he called them, in another ten years or so), and around whom the series of piano recitals were given at Sevenels.

Socially, Carl Engel came promptly whenever Amy Lowell called him to fill in at dinner, or to escort her to the Boston Symphony concerts or to the theater, or simply to talk her out of the doldrums when she despaired of her ability to write. She wrote earnestly and relentlessly, usually in the deep watches of the night when she couldn't sleep. The result was mostly tentative, timid poetry, because she was unsure of her ground, bound by conventional form, but some of it was valid, and Engel could sense her potential. Best of all, he introduced her to the French *Symbolistes,* which again opened up a new world of poetry for her (and eventually led to her critical study, *Six French Poets*). Indirectly, this new interest led to the Imagist movement that made her famous, since the Symbolists were the forerunners of *Les Imagistes* in France. Foster Damon merely states that Engel, "until he became Chief of the Music Division of the Library of Congress was a regular members of her circle," * but evidence that he was much more lies in the fact that Amy requested that all his letters to her, which she kept locked in her desk drawer, be burned after her death, along with those of the person who was to become closest of all to her. This is an incalculable loss, and Engel evidently culled her letters to him as well; but fortunately he saved some thirty holographs from her, with a few cards, invitations, and the like—enough to pull away the curtain to show the development, climax, and denouement in the drama of their relationship.

Obviously her acquaintance with Engel in the fall of 1908 quickly blossomed into friendship. Amy, with such encouragement from Carl Engel in regard to her poems, gave up her committee posts in order to devote more time to her writing and other artistic pursuits, the concerts and theatricals. Between Berkeley Updike, who persuaded her to put on a production of Oscar Wilde's *The Ideal Husband* and play the lead herself, and Carl Engel, she had two staunch supporters for her salon, which she now launched in full sail. Throughout the late fall and winter she and Carl consulted on the music to be played at the monthly gatherings. A typical program might include Debussy, Fauré, Max Reger, Ethelbert Nevin, perhaps a song of Engel's or E. B. (Edward Burlingame) Hill's, head of music at Harvard, also French trained, and a family friend of the Lowells'. (Actually, Amy had probably learned about French modern music from E. B. Hill before she met Engel. Hill and his wife were often guests at Sevenels, and he was later to set to music Amy's famous poem, "Lilacs," a choral work often played by the Boston Symphony.) According to Virgil Thomson, whose faculty adviser, professor, associate, and friend Hill was later to be, he was "aloof, but not unfriendly, tall, athletic, well-to-do—the Bostonian's ideal of the gentleman artist. But he also had a straightforwardness of statement . . . and a thoroughness of knowledge" that influenced Thomson and no doubt had its effect on Amy to the point of making her receptive to Carl Engel's suggestions. She and Engel did not always agree, but for the most part theirs was a rich and glowing friendship. As it grew, however,

* S. Foster Damon, *Amy Lowell: A Chronicle* (Boston: Houghton Mifflin Company, 1935).

her characteristic fervor overpowered her, and her manner toward him was deferential yet demanding.

In 1909 her life was going reasonably well, her health virtually restored, when she had a horrible experience that shook her to the vitals: On March 25, shortly after midnight, she was working on an idea for a poem when she suddenly heard cries and yells outside. One of the servants burst in to tell her a fire had been discovered in the stables. It was already blazing, too uncontrollably to rescue the horses; even as she rushed toward the stables, she knew from the frightful neighing that they were doomed. All, including her beloved mare, Aura, burned to death before the Brookline volunteer fire department could get there. The flames, the smoke, the terrible smell of burning horseflesh mingled with the horror and shock she felt. Perhaps even more shaking psychologically was the arrival the next day of some ugly, anonymous letters addressed to Amy Lowell, rejoicing in her misfortune and assailing her arrogance. These were followed by others, which, while not actually threatening, except by indirection, expressed a wild, insane glee that disaster should befall the house of Lowell, and as such they were extremely disturbing.

So far as anyone knew, the fire had not been set by an arsonist —but who could be sure? Feeling was probably still high against Augustus Lowell, the hard man of business. Only a year and a half had passed since the panic of 1907, which had wiped out the hard-earned savings of so many, while the Lowells with their wide holdings had not suffered. Strikes in the Lowell mills were quickly quelled, but unrest was rife, and labor organizations were rousing the people to the need for unions, to form a strong, united voice of protest against the inequities between the very rich and the very poor. Undoubtedly there was resentment against the heirs of Augustus Lowell living in luxury, especially against his huge, loud-mouthed daughter and her lavish entertainments at Sevenels. Ever since Henry George's single tax program, outlined in his *Progress and Poverty* (1879), people had been uniting to form the Populist movement to rid the country of its "economic royalists." The epithet "robber barons" was coined somewhat later, but "barons of industry" was an often heard term, and Amy Lowell considered herself one of them. She said more than once that the Lowells were among the few families who had the right to carry their coat of arms.

She had too many personal problems to worry about conditions in the Lowell cotton mills. She was interested, like her forebears, her father, her brothers and sisters, in the cultural and educational life of the city of Boston (and Brookline, of course)—indeed, of the nation—but the plight of the poverty-stricken touched her very little. The tone of the anonymous letters was fanatic, citing biblical passages, implying that the wrath of the Lord had visited itself upon her in the burning of her stables, a flaming sign of the fate that would befall her if she did not mend her ways and share her wealth with the poor. Amy Lowell, like Augustus, was too imbued with the precepts of capitalism—the hard world of business, which expected a "just return" on its investment—to pay much heed to such warnings. But she was shaken nevertheless. The episode left her so upset and despondent that she could not bear to rebuild the stables. (She had her Pierce-Arrow in Brookline, and in Dublin she could get horses from the Russells' stables.) She realized that the temper of the times indicated an upheaval that would topple the empires of the wealthy at some future date, but she was not ready to relinquish hers. Sevenels was her citadel. It gave her the self-assurance she needed to face the world outside (though few would have suspected she required such assurance from her manner). After every emotional bout, Sevenels was her refuge, her stronghold of comparative peace and comfort. She defended her position as a baron, even though the exalted ranks of the rich were being reduced in every decade by new inventions and other fruits of the continuing industrial revolution. But many a night she shivered at the thought of what might happen to her fortress.

During this period of despondency, Carl Engel must have been a main source of sympathy and strength as well as a diversion for her. She made no move to lessen the number of her "entertainments"; instead, she increased them. Carl started calling her "Baronne," perhaps in fun, to help her laugh at her fears, and she in turn dubbed him "Marquis." Perhaps this practice came about during Amy's production of Alfred de Musset's *A Caprice,* which she translated (not "Englished," as she said in the program notes), directed, and acted "so brilliantly that one quite forgot her figure," a spectator commented. At any rate, in her letters preserved by Engel, three distinct stages of their relationship are indicated in the manner of greeting. The earliest was simply, "Dear Mr. Engel," usually requesting certain scores or information. But in one, in a tender note of admiration, she tells him how "beautiful his songs were, . . . like the fragrance of some beautiful flowers in a moonlight garden . . ." (a sentence all-inclusive of her overt passions—flowers, gardening, and moon worship). She speaks of hearing and loving music, especially "modern," which appeals to her strongly, and asks if he will play his songs "on Thursday night."

By the following spring, beginning in March 1910, the letters salute "Cher Marquis" and are signed "Baronne." Two of these sent from Broomley Lacy reveal a feeling of unrequited love. In the letter from Dublin, undated, she begins by confessing that she "feels badly about today, sending him the milage" (evidently a misspelling of "mileage") and continues: "It is more than a pleasure to have you come up, it is almost a necessity, for I am having a discouraging fit about everything, and I turn to you, on account of your constant and ready sympathy. But now I feel as if I had *forced* you into an extravagance, a thing I never meant to do. Am I making the same mistake I made last winter and expect you to like doing things with me when you really are a shade weary of it? Indeed, in this world there seems to be nothing I can trust. Why can't I learn my lesson, *and realize that I must always be in every sense, absolutely alone?* You will say I am imagining things. But I am not.

"I know how good a friend you are, but it seems that I have been importunate when I only meant to be cordial. . . ." She begs him to let her know that he understands, to keep in touch with his "Baronne."

Then, also from Dublin, "Wed. afternoon," possibly a week later and also addressing "Cher Marquis," she wrote:

"Your letter has just come, dear Boy, let us forgive, and try not to tread on each other's toes in future. I do not need your telling me to know my faults. I know them very well, alas. But it is hard to cure one's faults, even when one tries. Do you not care enough for me, enough for the Baronne, to put up with Amy Lowell? I care enough for Marquis to bear with Carl Engel. Is not friendship made up of mutual forbearance? I know you are too fine a man to let such things rancour in your heart. I am deeply grieved at having hurt you, and will try to be more considerate in future. But I ask you as my dear & considerate & understanding friend to remember now the things I have done, and not only the inconsiderate ones. I have tried to give you some pleasure since you have been in Boston, and I have often succeeded.

"In remembrance of those times, be generous, as I am trying to be, for you have wounded me terribly, too. Have we a right to deprive the Baronne & Marquis of a happiness because Miss Amy Lowell and Mr. Carl Engel don't get on? The mails take so long, why have you not the kindness to phone?

"If I could see you, you would realize that this is wrong and foolish for both of us. We must not clash, ever again. We must both try for that. I think we shall succeed, Dear, if we both try. Will you help me, Dear Boy, so that we both may get the comfort we can out of each other?"

Signing herself "Baronne," she added a postscript: "P.S. Oh, my Dear, my Dear! If either of us were to read of the other's death in the paper, how should we feel? Let us not make the mistake of hugging anger to our hearts in place of so many loving thoughts and deeds on both sides. Let us try again & feel that it is *forever,* our friendship, through all changes and vissisitudes [sic], & no matter where our outward life shall lead us, *Remember only the Baronne and answer her."*

If the references to "Baronne" and "Marquis" as romantic sobriquets seem rather coy, they are also appealing, and the pleading note of the whole letter gives the lie to Amy Lowell's outward bravado. In the realm of romance with the opposite sex, she was the same overeager, bumbling, confused adolescent she had been at sixteen. One more letter to Engel notable in this respect was written scarcely a month before she met, by pure chance, the one person who was to transform her emotional insecurity into self-assured fulfillment. Sent from Sevenels on February 26, 1912, to Engel in Paris, where he had evidently gone on a combined business and pleasure trip, while she had just returned from New York, her words contain the same plaintive cry of loneliness and self-reproach: "I have not written before because I had not the heart to—I have been awfully blue since you left. . . . And now that I have got home and you are not here, it is almost unbearable, the loneliness. In vain I tell myself you will come back entirely changed & that is a fact I firmly believe, nevertheless I want you back dreadfully, and as soon as possible. I knew that I had been fool enough to count on you too much, and now I am reaping the harvest I have sown. I wonder why I, with all my natural appetite for love and happiness in a superlative degree, should have managed so badly as to carve out for myself a life made of ashes & fog.

"I envy you in Paris.—Envy you anyway; if only I had your powers, your talent." (Engel had set to music two of her poems, "Sea Shell," and "The Trout," published by G. Schirmer in 1911.) "How mad you will be at my saying that! I have been collecting my poems for the book, and they do seem to me so bad. Barely a half a dozen which I like at all. Tonight it seems to me I should put them all in the fire and take up crocheting. Only of course I should crochet badly!" Luckily her sense of humor came to the fore occasionally to restore her objectivity. "You can just ask all the affection and tenderness you want, it will always be there for you," she wrote a little further on. "You told me once that I made a sacrement [sic] of friendship. It was prettily put, but it is also true. You know how few people I care for, but it is also true you are one of the few."

(The "Cher Marquis" letters continued for a time even though Amy had found closer ties; and after Carl Engel married, in the third stage of their relationship, when they were simply good friends, the greeting changed to the fond nickname Bibi, as all his intimates called him.)

In the years before she had recovered from the loss of her beloved horses, two factors were added to the stories that eventually became the legend of Amy Lowell. One was the inauguration of her brother Lawrence as the twenty-fourth president of Harvard University on October 6, 1909. It was a warm day, and the ceremonies were held outdoors in front of University Hall. Amy was only a *little* late, but she could see the look of disapproval on her sister-in-law's face; Anna merely "tolerated" Amy's habits, never approved them, and openly disapproved of some. Smoking was one of these, and out of deference to Lawrence, Amy did not yet smoke in front of her. As she watched Lawrence being sworn in as president, she was again struck by his close resemblance to their father. Except for his longer legs, it might be Augustus standing up there —he had the same neat features, the same taciturn expression. Abbott Lawrence Lowell was already distinguished for his published articles on government, for his good, solid views on education; Amy agreed with the latter, which stressed less teaching and more independent study, with the student working for honors by himself, out of love of a self-chosen subject. Lawrence had been a favored pupil of Henry Adams, but he tempered Adams's ideas with practicality; and he was to carry out his ideas after he was in office, borrowing from the tutorial system of Oxford.

Amy had the uneasy feeling as she listened to his speech that she might have another stumbling block to face in her own career; and in fact, she was to be known in Cambridge, Boston, and Brookline—if not the whole country—principally as "the sister of Harvard's president" for a number of years, even after her first volumes were published. It was a designation that, in spite of her annoyance, also served as a spur: She determined to work harder than ever to be "Somebody" in the literary world until Lawrence would be known as "Amy Lowell's brother"! And before five years had passed, she was to find the route to fame in her own right.

The other event was the acquisition of a troupe of sheep dogs, which she started shortly after Lawrence's inauguration. She still felt the loss of her beloved horses keenly, and when her friend and cousin Barbara Higginson suggested that they start a kennel of English sheep dogs, she was delighted, and went into the project with her usual ardor. She and Barbara began with a pedigreed pair of the huge, rough-haired, high-strung dogs housed in their kennel, Hylowe (for the first syllables of their surnames), which was set up at Sevenels. The breed required extreme and loving care, which Amy was more than ready to give. Her first "children," as she called them, were whelped in late fall (November 28, 1909), and christened Hylowe Sir John and Hylowe Prue. Both were fine specimens, perfect enough to show. (Prue was her favorite, and was the last to die, in 1918.) Amy spent a great deal of time with the dogs, training them and tending them if they fell ill. More than once she sat up all night with a sick puppy, and she lost very few out of each litter. She bred them until she had seven of show caliber, for Sevenels. (Like her father, she stopped with seven; but, unlike him, she lavished affection on her "children" almost to the point of lasciviousness.)

When the pack was complete it became as much of, if not more than, an integral part of Amy Lowell's household as any children could have been. Every day they consumed nine pounds of top-round beef, along with side dishes of fresh, mashed vegetables, more than enough to nourish and keep a large family of children in radiant health. The meadow where Amy played as a child was given over to them; they could romp all over it, but were trained never to jump the low wall surrounding Sevenels. At dinner, they accompanied Amy in her late appearances—a female Henry VIII, surrounded by hunting dogs—but they charged no farther than the doorway, where they remained in a semicircle, waiting until the guests had finished, and then preceded everybody into the library. Each visitor, who on arrival had been met at the gate by a guard to escort them to the front door and to fend off the fiercely barking dogs, was furnished with a large clean turkish towel to protect dress clothes from the hearty, lubricated caresses of the well-fed sheep dogs, now ready for a romp. (It must have been more of a trial than a treat for her guests, replete from a seven-course dinner, to sit watching the seven dogs slurp up their food. Often an "incident" occurred during the after-dinner hour, but the hostess seemed oblivious to all this, and beamed upon her "children" while she puffed contentedly on her little Manila cigar.)

In summer, the dogs went with Amy to Dublin in a haycart, barking all the way. Here she took the same care for their health and comfort that she did in Brookline. Doris Russell drove over in her pony cart one blistering hot August afternoon to see Miss Lowell and found her standing in the side yard on the hilltop, wearing a starched white dress with leg-o'-mutton sleeves, holding the nozzle of her garden hose, from which a fine white spray poured over her pets—she was "trying to cool 'em off a little, poor things!" she called heartily. "They can't stand the heat any better than I can." But she looked cool and collected in spite of her stiff, long dress. Doris, who had asked her aunt to drive over with her, never forgot the picture Amy Lowell made, standing there as they drove up on that hot August afternoon, spraying her sheep dogs. Whether her partner lost interest or established her own kennels is not clear, but obviously Hylowe was Amy's by right of devotion.

She continued to give theatricals in the library. The group called themselves "Amateur Professionals," and Amy was instrumental in turning it into the "Toy Theatre," one of the first "little theaters" in America. (She was partly inspired by George Pierce Baker's English 47 Workshop, then at Harvard, where it originated.) She continued to produce, act, and direct the plays with a firm hand, and no one except a close friend like Carl Engel would have suspected her inner quaking, her fits of despondency and loneliness. During rehearsals for *The Ideal Husband,* one young ingenue, practically in tears after having been dropped from a role, went around Boston spreading the tale, "She's rehearsing Henry Higginson with a horsewhip." Actually, it was her riding crop, but the principle was the same: Amy found it handy to crack when she wanted the prompt attention of her cast.

However, the group broke up after the successful production of Musset's *Caprice.* For Amy, satisfied that she could never have a real career as an actress, and encouraged by Carl Engel's enthusiasm for her poems, realized that she had been writing verses for eight years and more: It was time to get some of her lines in print. She recalled that a school friend, Mabel Cabot, whom she had so envied because of "Paul H.," had finally married Ellery Sedgwick, the perceptive young editor of the *Atlantic Monthly.* With a palpitating heart, she sent him four poems, which, to her astonishment, he accepted at once. The first to appear, "A Fixed Idea," was printed in the August 1910 issue of the magazine, and became for her a beacon shining through the clouds of self-doubt and emotional insecurity, lighting the course she must follow.

CHAPTER VIII

The Advent of Ada Dwyer Russell

AND SO IT WAS (as mentioned in the letter quoted earlier) that Amy Lowell sat writing to Carl Engel two weeks after her thirty-eighth birthday, telling him that she was at last collecting her poems for *the book,* and wondering if she should throw them all into the fire. She knew well enough that she would not allow them to be licked up by the leaping tongues of flame shooting from the crackling logs in her library fireplace—she always worked at a narrow table in her baronial library—and she probably figured that Carl Engel would know it, too, and would realize that she was dramatizing her despondency. Yet she showed no sign of her discouragement in arranging for publication of her work.

Casting around in her mind for the most likely publisher, Amy considered Houghton Mifflin Company one of the most desirable. It was a good, solid house, and readily accessible with offices near the Boston Common. But she did not know how much poetry the company published, or whether they looked upon poetry with any degree of cordiality. Light verse was marketable, but she knew that most reputable publishers regarded serious poetry as a high risk. While she was pondering the question, she ran into a friendly rival, the popular Boston poet-playwright Josephine Preston Peabody, one snowy January afternoon in a florist's shop. (During those winter months when her greenhouses did not yield enough to fill her cut-glass and porcelain vases, Amy frequented the florist's shop, where she kept an account.) While the two were selecting bouquets (Amy with an eye toward a floral centerpiece for her dinner table), they exchanged the latest literary gossip. After commenting on Josephine Peabody's success with her play, *Piper,* and her volumes of verse, Amy, as casually as she could, asked her what chance of acceptance her own poems might have if she submitted enough for a volume to "Houghton and Mifflin." The catty, evasive answer was that it would not hurt to try—Houghton Mifflin "did not care much for poetry that had no human interest, but why should they?"

Amy was miffed. Josephine Preston Peabody (in private, Mrs. Lionel Marks, wife of a professor of mechanical engineering at Harvard) was the antithesis of Amy Lowell in background, bearing, and accomplishment. Only a few months younger than Amy, she looked at least ten years her junior. She came from a respectable but struggling New England family. She had been brought up in genteel poverty, her parents straining to make ends meet in order to give her a proper education at Boston Latin School. She was the kind of a little girl whose beauty was often described by the phrase "pretty as a picture," and, as she was also bright, her parents tried to give her such advantages as they could from a "mean, dark, lower-middle-class suburb" like Dorchester, as she described it in her memoirs. She was quick, ambitious, and romantic and showed an ability for acting in school productions of Shakespeare and an amazing facility for dashing off verses in a romantic yet lighthearted vein. When her father died, and there was no money to send her to college, she won two scholarships to Radcliffe; on graduating, she taught poetry (its reading and writing) at Wellesley for several years, until her marriage in 1903. She and her husband spent a honeymoon year in Europe, with Dresden as their headquarters. On their return, she had no difficulty getting her verses published, and she read manuscripts of other poets for various editors, who looked upon her as an authority. When her dramatization of *The Pied Piper* won the Stratford Prize and production in England, she had "arrived" at home and abroad. She did have a knack of promoting her own work and that of other poets—in 1901 she succeeded in finding a publisher for the first of

Edwin Arlington Robinson's long narrative poems, *Captain Craig* —but her work possessed little substance.

Actually, Amy did not think much of either *Piper* or the poetry its author turned out; but the success of the play had prompted her to continue the theatricals at Sevenels, and the wide publication of the poems won her respect inasmuch as it was the sort of work editors wanted. Still, the offhand advice Mrs. Marks had given her, with its implied criticism, worried her. But more than that, it rankled in her soul, making her more determined than ever, as a Lowell and as a poet of larger potential than Josephine Peabody, to have a volume of verses published as soon as possible. After all, her poems had been printed in the *Atlantic Monthly* with little hesitation; there was no reason why some respected publisher should not bring them out in book form. By the time she kept her appointment with Ferris Greenslet, the new editor in chief at Houghton Mifflin, all her faculties were girded for the encounter.

Greenslet, who was to become one of the deans among American editors, has recorded that meeting with Amy Lowell early in 1912. He was not a Bostonian, having come from New York State, and having held an editorship on the liberal weekly, the *Nation*. However, he already knew that the Lowell name was to be reckoned with in the business and academic worlds and that Augustus Lowell's youngest daughter owned and ran the family estate with a firm if eccentric hand. He also knew that she had literary and artistic leanings. He, too, had such tendencies as well as a fondness for Jane Austen and poetry, in spite of his businesslike attitude toward publishing. He had found Amy Lowell's batch of poems interesting enough to warrant an interview, if not particularly startling; but he was not prepared for the ponderous figure that entered his office at the appointed hour (for once). Almost as wide as she was tall, wearing an old-fashioned black serge suit with a loose-fitting three-quarter-length jacket to conceal her bulk; a stiff net collar whose stays held her neck up and her head high; and a professorial pince-nez perched on her nose, her hair in a sleek shining pompadour, she looked as if she, herself, might be the president of Harvard rather than his sister. Certainly, the last thing she resembled was a poet.

As soon as she sat down, however, her enormous size seemed to diminish if not vanish: One forgot it completely when she started to talk—as she did almost immediately. Her comments were lively and lighthearted and edged with a sharpness Greenslet sensed rather than heard. Behind the pince-nez her eyes glinted with intelligence and piercing humor, and her hearty laugh proclaimed a zest for living. He noticed that her face, though round as a full moon, was delicate in feature, with an upturned, slightly snubbed-nose and well-formed mouth. Her small hands (adorned by several rings, including one on her index finger) were graceful in gesture, and she used them to good advantage. In short, she was charming, excellent company, and Greenslet had the impression that *she* was conducting the interview; certainly she was in command of the occasion. In the course of the meeting, she brought up and settled all the questions regarding publication of her poems that had been on her mind, and Greenslet found himself acceding to her suggestions before he realized what he was promising.

One facet she went into explicitly was the design of the book itself. She wanted the format of her book modeled after the first edition of Keats's *Lamia,* and she wanted Berkeley Updike, and no one else, to handle the whole job. Greenslet agreed; they got along famously. He understood her worship of Keats and divined that she, like her poetic idol, was a moon worshiper. As the title for her book, she had chosen the phrase "a dome of many-coloured glass," from *Adonais,* Shelley's elegiac tribute to Keats—which Greenslet considered appropriate.

As soon as she reached home, Amy got in touch with Berkeley Updike, and the little typographer came hustling out to Sevenels where the two spent hours busily planning the design of her first volume.

By a singular coincidence, in this same year of 1912, Robert Frost was culling the little pile of poems he had collected for his first volume. He did this sitting on the floor of his temporary home in rural England, also in front of the fireplace, and actually throwing into the flames "all those he could spare" and still have enough for a book. At the same time, in Chicago, an enterprising literary and art critic, Harriet Monroe, was trying to secure backing for a new publication to be called *Poetry: A Magazine of Verse.* One of the newest features of it was that Miss Monroe intended to pay the poets for works published. Elsewhere, an anthology called *The Lyric Year,* already in the press, contained a poem entitled *Renascence* by a very young poet, Edna St. Vincent Millay. By *not* winning the first prize for the best poem in the anthology, her entry caused such controversy that its author was catapulted into fame, and her poem symbolized the start of a new era in American poetry. So much has been written about the renaissance that took place in America and, to a lesser extent, in England, in 1912, that it seems hardly necessary to discuss the circumstances. Amy herself, although she did not seem to be aware of it—and indeed there was less sign of it in Boston than in other parts of the country—had probably read Henry Adams's words of the year before: "The twenty-five years between 1873 and 1898 were marked by a steady decline of literary and artistic intensity, and especially of the *feeling* for poetry." And she was able to put her finger on the trouble in 1919, when she wrote: "After the days of Whitman and Poe, there was a decided slump in the poetry of this country. The main tendency seemed to be toward a diluted Tennysonism, and it was not until 1912 that a new vigor became visible."

The phenomenon of 1912 has been explained in numerous ways, not the least of which was the discovery of Emily Dickinson's iconoclastic and at the same time mystically religious poetry. But in Amy Lowell's private life, it was the advent of a new personality, a new friendship that was to change her whole life, which brought about a rebirth of spirit just three weeks after she had written so despairingly to Carl Engel that "barely a half a dozen" of her poems had any merit and she had "managed so badly as to carve out for herself a life made of ashes and fog."

On March 12, 1912, a group of accomplished women to which she belonged, who called themselves simply the Lunch Club, was meeting at the home of Bessie Ward (Mrs. Charles) Perkins, Amy's poetry partner. (One of the poems in *A Dome of Many-Coloured Glass* was entitled "To Elizabeth Ward Perkins.") This was no ordinary lunch club, and since Amy looked forward to its meetings, she usually got up before noon to attend them. That day she wanted to get some advice about spring plantings at Sevenels from Rose Nichols, a club member who had published books on landscape gardening. She was excited, however, at the prospect of meeting the guest of honor. Bessie had invited to the meeting Ada Dwyer, the actress who was playing the character lead in the current hit, *The Deep Purple,* a drama by Paul Armstrong, which had begun its Boston run on February 25. Amy had attended the opening night performance. She had seen the actress in *The Dawn of a Tomorrow,** Eleanor Robson's final hit before leaving the stage to marry August Belmont. Amy admired the character actress's ability to take on the personality of whatever role she was assigned and hoped to get a few pointers on technique from her in the event she resumed presenting theatricals at Sevenels. She dressed with extreme care. (It always took Amy Lowell a long time to dress, even with the help of her private maid, Elizabeth Henry, whom she adored and abused.) There were extra things that had to be done—like placing the braid of hair that had to be pinned on "just so" in order to raise her pompadour, giving her an added inch of height. It was with a feeling of great expectation that she left for Bessie Perkins's that morning in 1912.

And she was not disappointed; rather, she was enchanted beyond belief. The moment Ada Dwyer, a handsome brunette, walked in, the room seemed to light up with a suffused glow from the warmth of her presence. Not that she made an entrance, or was in any way stagy, but she had infinite grace and charm, coupled with a subtle sense of humor and with a poise that was evident even in her acknowledgment of the introductions. She was not beautiful in the conventional sense, but she had remarkable eyes—large, soft brown eyes that "could look right through you at times," her friend Eleanor Robson said—or that could embrace you with a calm, bright gaze of fond understanding. The serene expression of her whole countenance, with its generous mouth and long upper lip, was one that had the effect of beauty. Amy noticed, too, her graceful, rounded arms, and her hands, long and slender, and the deep half-moons of her fingernails. Those hands were to be-

* A dramatization of a famous novel of the same title, by Frances Hodgson Burnett.

come the pivotal subject of more than one poem and the inspiration of some of Amy Lowell's loveliest images:

Your hands moving, a chime of bells across a windless air.

The movement of your hands is the long, golden running of light
from a rising sun:
It is the hopping of birds upon a garden-path.*

Her figure was moderately tall and well proportioned, and she held herself erect but not to the point of stiffness; she walked with the ease that spoke her long experience on the stage. Ada Dwyer—in private life, Mrs. Harold Russell, divorced soon after her only child, a daughter, Lorna, was born—had an interesting history. Born in 1863 in Salt Lake City, Utah, just after Brigham Young had begun his experiment with communal marriage, Ada was the oldest of the five children her father had with his only wife. He was a "jack-Mormon," ** an imaginative Irishman who had brought his bride cross-country in a covered wagon from Philadelphia to open up the first (and for years the only) bookstore in the Far West. Dwyer's Book Store was a landmark among the pioneers, who relied on it for their book-learning (outside Brigham Young's version of the Bible), and its proprietor kept the shelves well stocked with secular literature. When Ada was eight years old, he began taking her with him on buying trips to Boston, where her education commenced while her father made his selections. She would sit for hours perched on a high stool, dangling her legs, reading the classics, from *Alice in Wonderland* to *A Midsummer-Night's Dream*. She developed a love for reading, especially poetry, to equal the warm, glowing love for people that had been imparted to her by her parents.

Her father was wise enough to realize that such a daughter should have a good education, so he sent her east to attend Boston Latin High School. There she performed so outstandingly in school Shakespeare productions and dramatic clubs that she re-

* From "In Excelsis," one of the finest love poems in the Lowell canon. See also "A Sprig of Rosemary," in the section "Two Speak Together," from *Pictures of the Floating World*.

** A colloquial term for those who did not practice Mormonism, but were tolerant of it, and so were accepted as part of the community.

ceived offers to go on the stage. She joined the company in which Madge Carr Cook, Eleanor Robson's mother, herself a well-known actress, was the leading woman. The two became friends, and one week when they were between runs Mrs. Cook took Ada with her when she went to visit her small daughter, Eleanor, then only eight years old * and living in the convent where she stayed until her early teens, when she, too, joined the company. The little girl took to Ada Dwyer at once, for the character actress had a way with both young and old. She had just become engaged to a British actor, Harold Russell, and was radiantly happy. Unfortunately, her marriage went to pieces shortly after their daughter, Lorna, was born, when Ada returned to the United States and the American theater. Leaving Lorna with her family in Utah, Ada began trouping, and it was inevitable that through the paths of friendship and the theater she was soon reunited with Eleanor Robson and her mother in one production or another. Although Ada was seventeen years older than Eleanor, they were the same age in spirit and outlook. Ada was always *there:* for guidance when the younger actress needed it, onstage and off; for care when she was ill; for advice in troubled moments and laughter in merry ones. It was Ada who first gave her an interest in reading poetry for its own sake, a gift for which she was always grateful. When Eleanor Robson became world famous in *Merely Mary Ann,* by Israel Zangwill, and formed her own company, Ada Dwyer became a member; if there was no part for her in a new play, one was written into the script.

When Nell, as Ada usually called Eleanor Robson if she didn't use the endearing term, "child," left the stage in 1910 to marry August Belmont, Ada Dwyer Russell was too sterling an actress to give up the theater, in addition to the fact that she had been maintaining the family home in Salt Lake City for a number of years and needed the income. When an offer came to join the British company of Gertrude Forbes-Robertson, she accepted, and she

* Horace Gregory, in an erroneous account of Ada Russell's history in *Amy Lowell: Portrait of the Poet in Her Time* (New York: Thomas Nelson & Sons, 1958), makes the misstatement that she and Eleanor Robson Belmont were "girlhood friends" (p. 72).

took Lorna, now in her teens, to England with her, where the girl went to boarding school while her mother was on tour (which took her halfway around the world to Australia). After a highly successful season with *The Deep Purple* in New York and Chicago in 1911, she had gone back to England to spend the summer with Lorna. On the ship coming home, she met Mr. and Mrs. Thomas Ward, Bessie Ward Perkins's parents, and promised them she would send a card to their daughter when she was playing in Boston, for *The Deep Purple* was scheduled to go on tour right after the first of the year.

During lunch at Bessie's that day in March, Ada recounted some of the highlights of her career, no doubt including one hilarious incident during a performance of *The Gentleman from France,* when she was playing the duenna to Eleanor Robson's "Mademoiselle," and a "grand old actor" who, as Henry of Navarre, was trying to speak a dignified, imperious line through the click-clacking of an ill-fitting new denture, all but lost his false teeth! The audience could see them plainly as he clutched wildly at his mouth, and the curtain came down amid howls of laughter from both audience and actors. Ada told a story well; she had a way of being gently scintillating as she spoke, and she mimicked an actor with just the right touch of caricature that was utterly delicious. The Lunch Club members were so delighted with her that they changed their club name to the Purple Lunch Club (after *The Deep Purple*). In later years, it became a dinner club which met only once a year—because Amy was unable to get anywhere by noon as time went on—and then it was to celebrate the birthdays of both Amy and Ada, for, as chance would have it, the latter's was February 8, the day before Amy's.

The affinity Amy and Ada felt for each other was apparent immediately. Ada was as good a listener as she was a storyteller; she would put her head a little to one side when listening to someone, as if she didn't want to lose a word, while her eyes rested on the person speaking, registering her perception and understanding. In her completely natural awareness lay her art of putting others—especially one of Amy Lowell's high-strung temperament—into a mood of easy calm. And when, as it inevitably did, the talk turned to books and poetry, she listened intently to Amy's story of her recent interview with Greenslet and the plans for the forthcoming volume; poetry was her second love after the theater, and she made no secret of her interest. Amy was ecstatic and immediately asked Ada if she would like to hear the poems on her free evening. There was no Sunday night performance; perhaps Ada could come to Sevenels for dinner.

A date was arranged, and after she had heard all the poems, Ada gave her thoughtful approval to the majority, but there was one which she felt definitely should be excluded—"Petals," a weak, sentimental piece of bathos. Amy, who was surprisingly ready to accept criticism if she believed it valid, knew full well that Ada was right. "Petals" was one of the poems she had been most dubious about, and now wished she had consigned it to the ash heap. She tried to get Houghton Mifflin to delete it, but the book was already in press, and Amy was too eager for publication to want to cause any delay. However, the utter congeniality with her new friend brought her unbounded joy. Mrs. Russell's Boston run (during which Amy saw *The Deep Purple* several more times) was over by March 23, when she had to move on to the next tour engagement. But she did not leave without promising to pay a long visit to Amy in Dublin during the summer. This visit was the beginning of a lifelong alliance. Amy felt that at last she had found the friend she had been seeking—one who understood her needs, and whom she could thoroughly trust. Their friendship was still in the formative stage, but she sensed that Ada was to be, as she had written in her diary, "a very intimate friend, a friend whom I should love better than any other girl in the world, and who would feel so toward me. To whom I could tell all that is in my heart, and who would do so to me. We should love to be alone together, both of us."

In the meantime, another influence was about to change the direction of her poetry. Carl Engel, probably in answer to her letter of February 26, had sent her from Paris a copy of Albert Samain's *Chariot d'Or,* which led her to the French Symbolists, and post-Symbolist poets. Their vers libre fascinated her; in fact, she was so stimulated by the vistas opened by their free phrasing that she wrote a new poem, "Before the Altar." As the title implies, the stanzas were written to her idol, John Keats, expressing through him her own worship of the moon. Completing the lines at the crest of her enthusiasm, she recognized the poem as her best to date and sent it posthaste to Houghton Mifflin. She wanted it to be the opening poem in the book, instead of "Apples of Hesperides," as in her original manuscript. The publisher must have agreed with her, for when the final version of the contract came—Amy had exacted a number of changes before it was settled—an accompanying letter told her the arrangement had been made. She also insisted, after seeing the proofs, that the printers drop the first stanza down an inch or two from the top of the page; the printers were more difficult to handle, but she won her point, and the format proved so successful that all her subsequent volumes were modeled after it.

During the summer of 1912 she happily entertained Ada Dwyer at Dublin, and the affinity between the two new friends became more pronounced. They took long rides together through the New Hampshire countryside, rowed on the lake, gardened—Ada displayed the same love for flowers that Amy had, and she embraced the family of sheep dogs without hesitation, which alone would have endeared her to Amy's heart forever—and they read and talked poetry day and night. During her visit, Amy received the prospectus of Harriet Monroe's new magazine, which was rapidly taking shape. Miss Monroe had seen Amy Lowell's sonnets in the *Atlantic,* and her prospectus included an invitation to contribute to the proposed publication—financially as well as artistically. No doubt Amy and Ada discussed the prospectus, Amy seeking her new friend's opinion. As a result, she sent a check for twenty-five dollars—a token contribution. But Amy Lowell was not so much a patron as an activist in the arts, and she included a note promising to send some poems later.

A Dome of Many-Coloured Glass was published on October 12, 1912. Although her primary aim had been to prove that she actually could get a volume of poetry published, and she doubtlessly experienced the thrill every writer feels holding a first author's copy in trembling hands, she looked forward with great anticipation to the reaction of readers, critics, and the general public. She did not know what to expect. *Dome* contained largely conventional poetry, and some were good, promising poems. They were more personal than most readers could realize—their outward tameness concealed an inner torment—and many of the lines held glints of the splendid splash of color that was to come. The book began, after the Keats poems, with memories of her relatively happy childhood: her grandfather's house in Roxbury, the fruit garden in Brookline, a Japanese wood carving and a Shokei * print Percy had sent, and other possessions she had loved. But with "The Fool Errant," which is surely the poet searching for love and acceptance in vain, the poems take on a tone of disillusion, brought by the stark face of reality. "Roads," descriptive of the dear, familiar paths around Sevenels, was one of the few poems which include her attachment to horses and dogs: "the rhythmic beat of a horse's feet/ And the pattering paws of a sheep-dog bitch . . ."; again the up-and down march of the roads is "beaten into a song/ By the softly ringing hoofs of a horse/ And the panting breath of the dogs I love . . ."; finally, the song and countryside become one, the land of desire, which "beats in my listening ears/ With the gentle thud of a horse's stride,/ With the swift-falling steps of many dogs,/ Following, following at my side." Yet these roads lead only to the "opaline gates" of "the Castles of Dream," not to the real happiness they seem to promise. And "A Fairy Tale," belying its bland title, is a bitter tale indeed. This was the poem in which Amy Lowell likened herself to the princess at whose christening some uninvited guest has brought a curse instead of a gift; but in the poet's life there is no one to rescue her or to lift the curse. The poem, which started with a touch of Longfellow's *The Children's Hour,* turns into an acrid lament for a lost paradise: "all is changed,/ I am no more a child, and what I see/ Is not a fairy tale, but life, my life." And she lists its assets: health, wealth, "long-settled friendships, *with a name/ Which honors all who bear it,*** and the power/ Of making words obedient. . . ."

* Classical Japanese painter.
** Italics mine.

But overshadowing all is still the curse,
That never shall I be fulfilled by love!
Along the parching highroad of the world
No other soul shall bear mine company.
Always shall I be teased with semblances,
With cruel impostures, which I trust awhile
Then dash to pieces, as a careless boy
Flings a kaleidoscope, which shattering
Strews all the ground about with coloured sherds.

Between these two, in "New York at Night," there are signs of Amy Lowell's unconscious imagisms, though she herself did not yet recognize them. The art of description in a single precise word or phrase had been her aim in the opening lines: "A near horizon whose sharp jags/ Cut brutally into a sky/ Of leaden heaviness . . ." and "I hear the sigh/ The goaded city gives . . ." certainly represent New York or any metropolis with originality and unerring precision, perhaps even more applicable today than they were in 1912. And in the poem to Bessie Ward Perkins (which again shows disillusion and self-flagellation regarding "the bitter wind of doubt" that has chilled her religious belief) there is a calling off of colors that fortells her future palette, but the tones are a pale radiance of those to come.

Here was "The Boston Athenaeum," a personal record in valid poetry, but only a faint outline of the broad, sweeping tridimensional picture she achieved in "The Congressional Library" of a much later volume. *Dome* ended with a delightful section of "Verses for Children," two of which Carl Engel set to music, and George Antheil asked permission to do the same with a third. The last poem in the section (and the book) was "The Pleiades," in which Amy again refers to herself as a "boy."

In short, her first volume was perfectly acceptable poetry, but, according to the few reviews it received, that was the trouble. There was nothing to excite or arouse the reader, even to anger. Such was the gist of the comment in the *Chicago Evening Post*'s monthly column, "And Other Poems," by Louis Untermeyer, then one of the bright young men entering the scene of literary criticism, with a flair for poetry himself. Mr. Untermeyer has admitted that his review was "not only generally patronizing but cruel in its particulars." * Unaware of Amy's utter and continuing devotion to Keats, he implied that she "had not freed herself from a fatuous, fancied kinship to Keats" and, worse, that the tone of her bland talent was "belatedly Tennysonian."

None of the notices was enthusiastic, but Untermeyer's was not only disappointing but damaging to all Amy Lowell's dreams—particularly the accusation that she could not "rouse one at all." She must have recalled Percy's warning—"Always remember, Amy, if a book is not interesting, it is a failure"—and her morale was shattered. She took to her third-floor bedroom, where she shed scalding tears of anger and shame. As always, her despair was accompanied by an attack of gastric neuralgia, and the doctor prescribed complete rest for "nervous exhaustion." She stayed in bed, which was cushioned with exactly sixteen pillows to ease her quaking nerves. (She usually made it up herself, with faithful Elizabeth Henry standing by to plump up the pillows; even if the hour was 1:00 A.M., her devoted Irish maid was on hand to insure Miss Lowell's complete comfort.)

Amy stayed in bed in her nursery quarters through the Christmas holidays trying to overcome her grief and her physical illness—a psychiatrist would probably say it was her way of returning to the womb in a time of stress. She could not bear to face even the traditional family Christmas dinner. Like Coleridge, and her more contemporary colleague in the literary world, her great-cousin's goddaughter, Virginia Woolf, Amy Lowell found the onslaught of reviews, good or bad, traumatic. (However, with the exception of one period during her mother's last illness, she never had nightmares of insanity; nor, so far as is known, did she have suicidal impulses. She was, in fact, eminently sane, in spite of all her madcap eccentricities.) She felt lonely—Ada Dwyer was on tour or she might have come to Sevenels over the holiday—and she missed her "grandchildren," missed seeing a new litter of her sheep dogs come into the world; but she obeyed the doctor's orders. "My children are well," she wrote in a note to Josephine

* In "A Memoir," his introduction to *The Complete Poetical Works of Amy Lowell* (Boston: Houghton Mifflin Company, 1955).

Peabody, "and I hear their eyes are open, but alas! it is a week since I have seen any but the older members of my family." Then, on December 27, the doctor allowed her to go to a symphony concert, and word came that Ada was going to be playing in Atlantic City, in a run extending over the New Year holiday!

On December 31, Amy wrote to "Cher Marquis," telling him that she had come to Atlantic City, where "Miss Dwyer" was playing, to complete her recovery from the shock of publication, and that she was already feeling much better.* No doubt these two, already closely allied in feeling, talked over the chances Amy might have for future success in the face of the cool reception her first attempt had been given. *Dome* was a financial failure of course. Only eighty copies sold the first year, but it did go into a second printing in 1915 after her second book came out. Ada Dwyer Russell was one of those rare people who are both compassionate and wise. She had a philosophic outlook on life, and her counsel, her calm presence, enlivened by her gentle humor, had a beneficial effect on Amy. Moreover, during the time she had spent resting, Amy was also reflecting and planning her next approach to the hall of fame. None of the reviews had been downright bad. Nobody had said she couldn't write poetry, and the judgment of friends like Ada and Carl—both intelligent artists who knew poetry and were not given to idle flattery—convinced her that she had enough talent to tear her way through the thorny path of criticism. She would blast her way if need be! She was sharp enough to notice that it was the controversy over a single poem, *Renascence,* that had brought fame to Edna St. Vincent Millay and the anthology *The Lyric Year;* she also realized that new forces were at work in Harriet Monroe's experiment in publishing a magazine of verse devoted to fresh ideas of creativity from poets as yet unrecognized. If notoriety and sensationalism were needed, she could provoke them in plenty! She made up her mind that she would not be carelessly dismissed or overlooked again.

* This letter is one that has recently come to light; the Atlantic City trip is not mentioned in Damon's or in other biographies.

CHAPTER IX

Professional Poet at Last

EXHILARATED BY HER VISIT with Ada, whose personality was like wine and honey to her wounded feelings, Amy returned to Sevenels and began writing vigorously, with a kind of fierce joy. Three of the poems she had written in 1912 prior to the publication of *Dome,* she had sent right off to Harriet Monroe, who had accepted them, but had not printed them in the next issue of *Poetry,* nor the following one. There was no word of explanation from the editor or her assistant, Alice Corbin. Amy did not know that lagging publication (and laconic communication) was a characteristic, not only of the new *Magazine of Verse,* but of most "little magazines." Each issue was put together on a perilously thin financial thread, even though Harriet Monroe (who came from a family almost as prominent in the Middle West as Amy Lowell's in the East, and had entrée to the offices of established businessmen, bankers, and philanthropists) spent half her time bearding the lions of finance in their dens for assistance in her venture.

A close friend of Mary Cassatt's, the noted American painter living in Paris, Miss Monroe (who had been an art critic for a time) used the same approach to these men that Mary Cassatt had employed. By appealing to their sense of civic pride—they could, she said, bring the remarkable "new" art to American culture—she had convinced them to help build the outstanding collection of modern French paintings now in the Chicago Art Institute. Harriet Monroe argued that they could now be instrumental in bringing a fresh new element to American poetry. She was fairly successful, but in order to pay her literary contributors she constantly had to tackle the financial ones. As wraithlike as Amy Lowell was monumental, Harriet Monroe (who was fourteen years older than Amy)—with her pale sandy hair and rather stern, aristocratic face, her concise, no-nonsense attitude toward fund-raising for the arts—had the ability to impress prospective patrons as an authority on the arts. Yet they always required nudging, and consequently *Poetry* lagged behind, particularly in the matter of correspondence with anxious poets eager to see their creative efforts in print. (A few years hence, Edna St. Vincent Millay would be going through the same experience as Amy Lowell, and the situation continued for decades. However, *Poetry* survived, while many other "little magazines" passed into oblivion.)

One of Harriet Monroe's principal aims was to make her magazine an outlet for new American poets, whether they were living at home or abroad; both groups were important to her, since she wanted the publication to be international in scope. She had traveled extensively, and on a world tour in 1910 she had picked up in London two slim volumes of poetry, *Personae* and *Exultations,* by Ezra Pound, an expatriate American originally from Idaho. The little books were certainly different from any she had encountered, and when she set up the prospectus for *Poetry,* Pound was one of the first poets she contacted. He had already become a legend in London for his fiery tongue and almost as fiery appearance. With his shock of reddish hair, his mustachios and vandyke beard, his outlandish clothes and ivory-headed cane, he was the embodiment of a Romantic concept of the creative artist stemming from the days of the young Oscar Wilde and Whistler in London, characterized as bohemians in Thackeray's "Artists' Life in Paris," and perpetuated the later Impressionists of Montmartre and Montparnasse. Pound had definite ideas, and some of them were sound enough to make sense to Harriet Monroe, who was so delighted with the young rebel's sharp scorn of established magazine verse in his native country that she appointed him "foreign correspondent" for *Poetry*. He also led a group of young poets in England who, trying to find their way, loosely banded together under Pound's leadership and called themselves *Les Imagistes,* at his suggestion. Pound, in his capacity as foreign correspondent, sent some of their poems to Harriet Monroe, and in the January 1913 issue, Amy (after momentary disappointment at not finding any of her own poems) looked to see if there was anything more of this intriguing group she had been reading about in the magazine. A short description of them had appeared in the issue announcing Pound's appointment. She found some poems that took hold of her with tremendous force: The lines were unrhymed, clear-cut, classical in the Grecian references, spare in form (with their three-to-five and single-word lines), and exact in the use of visual images. The poems were signed, mysteriously, "H.D., Imagiste." Suddenly the revelation of Amy's own identity came over her in a great surge: *She* was an *Imagiste,* too! This was the sort of poetry she had been unknowingly striving to write. It was startlingly clear to her that she was a born *Imagiste.* She immediately set out to discover all she could about the London group and its origin, which obviously was French. She knew something about Verlaine, Baudelaire, and the circle of younger French poets, who advocated vers libre, the freedom of form being its basic principle.

It so happened that she had been invited to attend a small banquet in Chicago, where her brother Lawrence was being honored at a dinner by the Harvard alumni; and according to custom, a separate and lesser affair was planned for his wife. (It was this custom of sex segregation that enraged Edna Millay so much fifteen years later that she refused to go to a dinner in her honor; but in 1913, it was still accepted without question.) Amy was not sure whether she had been asked because she was the sister of Harvard's president or because she was now the author of a book of poems, but she decided to go. She would seek out the editor of *Poetry* to learn more about the *Imagistes* and to ask about the publication of her own poems. Luck was with her, for Miss Monroe was also a guest at the dinner for the wife of Harvard's president.

As usual, Amy was late, and Harriet Monroe in her memoirs recorded the scene of their meeting graphically: "As we were beginning dessert, an imposing figure appeared in the remote distance, at the top of a half-flight of stairs, and, 'Oh, there's Amy!' said Mrs. Lawrence Lowell, in a voice accepting resignedly anything Amy might do." At first, Harriet Monroe did not connect her with the poet whose verses she had accepted; she was absorbed in listening to the melodramatic words of greeting and in watching the "ponderous and regal figure slowly descend the steps. . . . She took possession of the occasion and the company—no one else was of any account. Our hostess presented her to each of the dozen or so women at table. . . . On hearing my name, the newcomer turned a powerfully reproachful eye on me with the query, 'Well, since you've taken 'em, why don't you print 'em?' " Her tone was demanding, but as she "literally sank" into her chair, she beamed good-naturedly at Harriet and everyone around the table, disarming them as she usually did. Miss Monroe, like the others, was charmed with her forthright personality, which was "half-magnificent, half-humorous." From then on, the conversation was directed toward *Poetry,* the new poetry, and Amy Lowell's poetry and her ideas and ambitions for the future not only of her own work but of all American poetry. It was a typical Lowell approach, but it worked. Not too long afterward, her poems appeared in the *Magazine of Verse.*

Once her interest in vers libre was aroused, Amy determined to learn more about French influence on modern culture. Her "Cher Marquis" had returned from Paris imbued more than ever with the music developing along parallel lines with the art of the Impressionist school: Foremost was Debussy—*Clair de lune* was just then being included on recital programs by concert artists—and the compositions of Gabriel Fauré, Eric Satie, and others were also closely allied to recent developments in poetry. The March 25 musicale at Sevenels featured piano works by these composers, and four songs by Carl, one of which was his setting of Amy's "Sea Shell" (the verse for children beginning, "Sea Shell, Sea Shell, / Sing me a song, O Please!"). They were sung by the noted French tenor Edmond Clement, who was appearing at the Metropolitan Opera that season. Amy, who had to approve every number, wanted Berkeley Updike to design a special cover for the printed program, and he outdid himself. She talked to her friend

E. B. Hill about the interdependence of French composers' music and the group of poets who gathered around Mallarmé every Tuesday afternoon, who called themselves *Les Symbolistes.* (Debussy had taken the story of Mallarmé's poem for his ballet music, *L'Après-midi d'un faune.*) When the famous International Art Exhibit came from the Armory in New York to Copley Hall in Boston, she went to the opening full of anticipation; but she came away puzzled and slightly nettled. "I had a faint idea of what the idiom of cubism might be," she told Carl, "but I could get no clue to the other schools."

However, the element that really piqued her interest was the set of principles published in the March issue of *Poetry* by Ezra Pound, outlining the method used by *Les Imagistes* to achieve the effect they were striving for in poetry: the emotional impact of things seen. Amy had been following their work since reading the poems by H. D., but nothing had so excited her as this set of do's and don'ts by *Poetry*'s foreign correspondent. She considered his article the soundest commentary on technique since Leigh Hunt's *Imagination and Fancy.* But to her annoyance, Pound declined to publish the doctrine he called the "most important," claiming it was not for the "general public." His words gave the impression that the *Imagiste* circle was a sacred cabala that must preserve a mystic secrecy concerning its essential concept.

His arrogance was enough to send Amy to London to find out just what this mysterious school consisted of, and to learn all she could from its members. Ada Dwyer was still on tour, so Amy took her niece (by marriage to her favorite nephew), Mrs. James Roosevelt, with her. Armed with a letter of introduction to Ezra Pound from Harriet Monroe, Amy set sail with a purpose in the early summer of 1913. If she had any real power over men, and past experience had shown her she did, she would manage to wangle the secret ingredient of *Imagisme* out of Ezra Pound somehow—even if she had to shake it out by sheer force! She took a suite of rooms in the Berkeley Hotel, Piccadilly West, and proceeded to operate from these impressive headquarters.

Pound, meanwhile, whose history as a dashing, cocksure, quarrelsome, if brilliant figure in the London literary world was only twelve months old,* though he made it seem much longer, was bragging to Robert Frost (who wanted no alliance with *Les Imagistes*): "When I get through with that girl [Amy Lowell], she'll think she was born in free verse!" He may not have known that Amy herself had already made that discovery, but he must have been aware from Harriet Monroe's letters that Amy Lowell wished to meet him and the other *Imagistes*—especially H.D.—primarily for information and instruction; she needed no convincing. Pound had been trying his damndest to win Robert Frost over to free verse. Pound had just previewed Frost's forthcoming first volume, *A Boy's Will,* in *Poetry* and probably wanted to impress that laconic individualist with the importance of the *Imagiste* movement as a force in modern poetry in addition to his own power as its leader. Actually, the size of Pound's ego was much greater than the influence of his leadership, and the members of *Les Imagistes* were loosely held together. *Imagisme* was hardly a true movement. It had originated with Thomas E. Hulme, a philosopher and poet-aesthete, whose formulation drew on French vers libre, ancient Greek and Roman poetry, and translations from ancient Chinese and Japanese works, as well as on other ancient poetic forms such as the Hebrew poem from the Hagadah** which tells the story of the Exodus in a "This-is-the-house-that-Jack-built" narrative. Hulme had set forth his principles before Pound made his "escape from the iamb," as he called his conversion, and the flamboyant American was quick to grab hold of them and make them his creation. The *Imagiste* movement was simply a series of weekly meetings in Soho cafes or teahouses, where the struggling new poets gathered to talk over tea and cakes and to sit around by the hour writing Japanese tanka or haiku for their own amusement (as poets have continued doing more than half a century later). The secret tenet was nonexistent, evidently a trick of Pound's fertile gift of gab.

At first, all went well between Amy and the self-styled leader of *Les Imagistes.* Amy gave a dinner party in her suite at the Berkeley to meet him and others of the group: "H. D., who

* In leaving America, he had fled to Italy first.

** Sacred book read on the first Seder night of the Passover celebration.

turned out to be Hilda Doolittle," a tall, willowy blonde American girl from Pennsylvania, serious, sensitive, and incisive in her thinking; Richard Aldington, a young British poet whom Hilda was soon to marry; and John Gould Fletcher (another American)—all of whom Amy was to be closely associated with. As Pound had hardly a ha'penny to spare, he could not have taken her anywhere except to the cheap cafes in Soho and was glad enough to let her lead off; he was also pleased to find her such a willing and apt pupil, although each sensed in the other a domineering streak that could lead to friction between them.

Afterward Amy wrote to her "Cher Marquis," giving him an account of the meeting and her impressions. Her description of Pound is quite different from others on record, showing more perception than he would have given her credit for. "I have just met the erratic young poet, Ezra Pound," she wrote Carl. "He is the oddest youth, clever, fearfully conceited, &, at the same time, excessively thin-skinned; & I imagine that never, since the days of Wilde, have such garments been seen in the streets of London. He arrays himself like the traditional 'poet' of the theatre." She spoke of the "stimulating" talk of London poetry circles and of Pound's suggestion that she send a poem she had written since learning of the *Imagiste* technique, following a concert she had attended with Carl. It was called "After Hearing a Waltz by Bartók" and tells the story of a jealous lover who murders his rival while the three-quarter beat of the music drowns out his cries. (Amy Lowell, it might be said, reversed the usual process and set music to poetry. She was criticized for borrowing from Browning's *Porphyria's Lover* in this poem, but the story is one of the basic plots in literature and certainly Browning had no copyright on it.) She told Carl that Pound had suggested she send the poem, which he liked, to the *English Review;* if not, he would include it in a small anthology the *Imagiste* group occasionally published. To do Pound justice, he did try to place the work or review the work of anyone who interested him; and, Amy closed her letter, "the water thing"—"In a Garden"—which Carl had liked, was to be published by the *New Freewoman,* a Suffragist paper started in

1913; Amy was not an active Suffragist, but she was not averse to publishing her poem in a Suffragist organ.

She booked passage home about midsummer, a voyage which proved to be the cause for widespread notoriety. Her stateroom was hot; it was impossible to sleep; aside from the heat, the ship's dance band made such a racket she could not think when she tried to write. She finally appeared in the doorway of the saloon one night and shouted at those inside: "Stop that outrageous noise!" Another night she invited a young man to hear her read her new poem, "After Hearing a Waltz by Bartók," and when she reached the last lines, "Beats me into a jelly!/ The chime,/ One! Two! Three! And his dead legs keep time./ Air! Give me air! Air! My God!" the mounting heat of her rendition in the hot, stuffy stateroom was so realistic her young listener paled with fright, and the steward came running to see what was wrong: he was afraid Miss Lowell was choking to death!

Usually, in the small hours, when the dancing and the blaring band had stopped, Amy would go up on deck to smoke her cigars in the cool air when no one was around to stare at her. She had stopped trying to deceive her sister-in-law; Anne knew Amy smoked, and it seemed hypocritical not to light up a cigar in front of her. But, out of respect for the Lowell family's reputation, Amy still did not smoke in public places. However, on one of her night promenades on deck someone saw her bulky figure pacing the deck, the glowing cigar like a rosy beacon revealing her face every time she took a puff. This bit of shipboard gossip was noised around the floating community, and when the ship docked, she was met by newspaper reporters clamoring for the facts. Amy, thoroughly exasperated by this time, admitted angrily that she smoked cigars—and what of it?

In these times it seems incredible, but the news made headlines the next morning in the *New York Tribune* and other dailies. Amy would not have minded the publicity if it had only been about herself, but the news value of the story seemed to be largely based on the fact that she was Harvard President Abbott L. Lowell's sister. She decided to make the most of it, however, partly because of the pleasure she took in defying the shibboleth that made a sin of women's smoking, partly because of her desire to shock people, and finally because her sense of showmanship told her it could be a means of getting notice for her next volume, which, from the poems that were piling up, was going to be a complete departure from *Dome*. From now on, the "big, black cigar" became part of Amy Lowell's image.

In the interest of accuracy, the newspapers' adjectives, "big, black" were misleading. But, probably because the phrase was suitably dramatic, she never bothered to correct the description. As late as 1973, the veteran book reviewer, Fanny Butcher, blithely states in her memoirs that "Amy Lowell's favorite was a big, black Corona-Corona," and it is possible that Amy smoked that brand in Chicago when she either could not get her own or ran out of them, but her favorites were a small, very light Manila brand, imported from the Philippines. They were elaborately wrapped in tinfoil and tissue paper; one evening, in a mischievous mood as she was preparing to smoke, she told a shy young poet that unwrapping her little Manila was like undressing a lady: First, one removed the belt (the outer cigar band), then the ballgown (the silver paper), then the shift (the thin tissue), and finally the girdle (the inner band). And with that she lit up, sucking in the smoke seductively while the blushing young man looked on.

Amy was so fond of the little Manilas that she ordered ten thousand of them when World War I threatened to mean a cutoff in her supply. She didn't want to take the chance of running out: She had tried both cigarettes and pipes, but the former were too quick and messy, and they distracted her when she worked. Moreover, the doctor had told her that the burning paper of a cigarette or prolonged contact with a pipestem could produce lip cancer.* (She did keep a rack of pipes and occasionally smoked one in her bedroom; but it was a bore to keep sending them into Boston once a week to be scraped and cleaned, as she did for a time. Besides, in Boston only the "shanty Irish" among women smoked pipes.) Psychologically, smoking, which she began on a dare, became a pleasure, then a necessity—"to calm her nerves," she said. Actually, the stage business of unwrapping it and cutting off the tip

* This was rather advanced medical advice in the early 1900s.

("like a man," her friend Elsie Sergeant wrote), helped give her self-confidence. Even the serene, rocklike presence of Ada Russell did not always quell Amy Lowell's inner quaking, her nameless anxiety, nor quiet the driving nervous energy that was like a scourge of Furies within her.*

Soon after her return from London, Amy invited Ada, whose tour was over, to spend the rest of the summer with her in Dublin. The joy the actress's company gave her was great, and Ada offered her inspiration and encouragement as well as critical judgment, particularly of the new "experimental" poems Amy was writing. Thus, their closeness developed during these weeks to a greater degree than ever. She hated to think of her friend's leaving, and one day, toward the close of summer, she asked Ada to come back to Sevenels with her. She wanted her to stay with her always, to share her home and her life. At first Ada refused; she had a tour commitment in the late fall, and as an old trouper, she considered a tour contract inviolable, even though life on the road was rough. Amy tried to persuade her to stay, but she said it would not be right. Ada Dwyer Russell was strong-minded in her own way, firm in her decisions, so Amy had to be satisfied with a promise that after this tour they would see.

She missed her friend sorely when she returned to Sevenels, and as a compensation she entertained more than usual. One night she called the young Dublin composer, George Luther Foote (a cousin of the well-known American composer, Arthur Foote, whom he admired and liked). George had recently become engaged to Amy's Dublin neighbor, Doris Russell, now a lovely young girl; they were planning to marry as soon as George got his music degree from Harvard. Amy felt a proprietary interest in him as a composer, as a Dubliner, and as the fiancé of her favorite Dublin neighbor. It was late at night, but the customary hour for Amy's phone calls: One reason she worked at night was to avoid the ringing of the phone at Sevenels, but she didn't hesitate to make calls during *her* working hours, rarely giving a thought to

* After Amy's death, Ada found a closet stocked from floor to ceiling with boxes of the little Manilas. She gave some to Amy's friends: to John Farrar; Foster Damon and John Marshall, his roommate; and many others. John Farrar found them too strong.

the fact that she might be rousing someone from a sound sleep. "Did I waken you?" she would ask. "Oh, I'm so sorry!" And then she would blithely proceed, either extending an invitation to the theater, or launching into some literary discussion before her listener was fully awake. This time she called rather early, about 11:30 P.M., before starting to write.

"George, I want you to come for lunch tomorrow," she began peremptorily, "and bring a young man from Boston. He will be ready about 12:30, and will be waiting for you at the Hotel Bellevue."

George thanked her, but before he could get the young man's name she had hung up. She had other calls to make before settling down to write.

The young man was waiting practically at the door of the hotel when George drove up in his touring car. His passenger was exceedingly tall and handsome—with blond, auburn-glinted hair waving softly back from his high forehead, clear blue eyes, and classic features—and exceedingly shy. From his dress, the Norfolk jacket, open-shirt collar, and loosely knotted wide tie, he must be a poet, as indeed he was: The young man turned out to be Rupert Brooke, perhaps the most notable British poet of his time as well as matinee idol among poets. When he settled himself in the car, the lap robe over his knees and legs to protect him from the brisk chilly breezes, George, happening to glance down, saw the longest pair of feet he had ever beheld, extending from the robe, covering the entire floorboard on that side. They were so incredibly long that George, staring at them, nearly lost control of the car. But the poet seemed unaware of his driver-companion's curious looks. He was extremely quiet and murmured only a few words about the scenery as they drove to Brookline.

At Sevenels, he was equally silent at first, perhaps overwhelmed by his hostess's hearty welcome, and when he did speak during luncheon his voice was so low one could hardly hear him. At readings of his poems, especially his well-known "The Great Lover," when he began, "These I have loved . . . ," in a soft, intimate tone, his audiences were thrilled. Now, once his shyness was dispelled by Amy's Johnsonian humor and the delectable Sevenels food, he relaxed in one of the big chairs of the library, stretched out his long legs, and proved to be a diverting conversationalist. In fact, he was such a delightful guest that Amy invited him to come back for dinner one night before his return to England. He accepted, and he charmed everyone with his gaiety and wit.*

(Amy was to find his public delivery too indistinct when she heard him read at Harold Munro's Poetry Bookshop the following summer in London. She called out, "Louder, louder!" He ignored her, but after the reading she went up and talked with him and discovered that he did not know that in America it was considered a compliment to shout "Louder!"—it was meant as a form of encouragement. The Georgians, as the Bookshop poets were known, did not stimulate Amy as much as the *Imagiste* group did. They were more conservative and more independent of each other, so she did not pursue the acquaintanceship with Brooke further, and within a month or two, this handsome young gifted poet would be lying dead in the trenches in France.)

If Amy did not make any written comment on Brooke's visits (although she may have, in letters that were destroyed by Ada Russell), it was because she received startling news just then from the actress, who was winding up her tour in Chicago. Ada had developed a serious medical problem—she who had always been so well that Eleanor Robson Belmont could not remember her having a sick day in all the years they had been on the road together! It was always Dada—a nickname for Ada—who nursed Nell when she was ill so she could be back onstage in short order. Now Ada was keeping up her own performances, but she felt terrible. As soon as Amy heard the news, she made a brief business trip to Chicago, where Ada was staying with Mrs. Chatfield-Taylor, a patron of *Poetry*. Here she learned in confidence that Ada had to undergo a major operation. The actress had hoped to avoid it, but the verdict was that surgery was mandatory.

Amy was deeply concerned. She arranged for Ada to come

* This account, furnished by Doris Russell (Mrs. George Luther) Foote, is the first and only record in detail of Rupert Brooke's visits to Sevenels. Horace Gregory, in his rather hostile study of Amy Lowell, assumes that because neither Brooke nor Amy commented on the visits, they were not congenial, but such was not the case.

to Sevenels for her convalescence and again urged her to live there permanently. When Ada still seemed reluctant, Amy suggested that her friend leave the theater and assist her *on a business basis* with the books she was planning to write. She would pay Ada whatever she would have earned on the stage; at least they could try it for six months.

So at last Ada yielded, and the result was a lifelong attachment that ripened into a remarkable one of mutual love and devotion. As in any alliance between two human beings, it was inevitable that occasional clashes of will would occur, especially in the first year or so. Amy's impassioned nature led her to be overly possessive toward those she loved. As for Ada, Nell Belmont wrote, "It was a characteristic of Ada Dwyer that when she agreed to become a permanent part of Amy Lowell's home, she tried to share with her those she loved best; and Amy endeavored with as good grace as possible to make these friends her own. One result of this was that I went frequently to Sevenels and whenever possible, Ada came to my home; or I saw them both on their many trips to New York."

The trouble was that it was not very often possible for Ada to see her friends or even her relatives, including her daughter, Lorna, by herself, because Amy was reluctant to let her leave, no matter how short the time. She needed Ada's presence, she said. And she depended on the inspiration she derived from the warmth and inner strength of that presence to help her bring forth poems from the new freshets of her fertile imagination which were springing up inside her at such a rate she could hardly get them down fast enough. Her new-found companion was her rock; perhaps that was the reason she soon nicknamed her friend "Peter." (Nobody seems to have known exactly how it came about, but Amy had never liked the name Ada—it was worse than Amy, she claimed. And while few thought the pet name she picked suited Mrs. Russell—who dropped "Dwyer" when she left the stage—"Peter" or "Mrs. Peter" and occasionally "Pete" she was, as far as Amy was concerned.) Ada didn't seem to mind; she was tolerant, and, with her unfailing humor, quite amused by Amy Lowell's latest whimsy.

A clash of wills came about, however, when Ada wanted to visit her family after she had fully recovered from her operation. They were anxious to see her, and she wanted to be with them for a little while. Amy objected: "I can't spare you; they don't need you as much as I do!" And Ada, who had given of herself unstintingly, cried out: "I can't stand it—you're so possessive!"

At that Amy flew into one of her temper tantrums. She was *not* possessive: She wanted to see her friend's family, too. "Why can't they come here?" she demanded hotly. "I've told you I would be glad to pay their fares, and we have plenty of room here!" Actually, she was jealous of all the Dwyers, as well as of Ada's daughter, but she didn't like to admit it even to herself, and this was her way of getting around it. But Ada was not swayed. "You've got to let me go!" she cried out. And she threatened to leave for good if Amy would not.

It seemed like an impasse. Ada might well have been reminded of the time many years before when she had been invited to the Connecticut River country home of William Gillette, the famous actor who created the role of Sherlock Holmes on the stage, and with whom both she and Eleanor Robson had a "lovely friendship"; they had often been in his country place and always enjoyed it. This time, however, he had asked Ada to come and bring a flapperish young girl they both knew. Nell thought she was "a bit gay" (in those days, the word meant "racy" or "fast"), and entirely unworthy of Ada's attention, and since she herself wasn't going along, she objected to Ada's going. When Eleanor Robson disapproved of something, she would freeze, become silent and "cold as ice," * as she did in this instance. Ada asked what was bothering her, and after some prodding, finally learned Nell's feelings. At that the older actress took hold of her shoulders and looked into her eyes with her own all-seeing eyes. "Child," she

* It was this facet of "E. R. B." that probably gave rise to Amy Lowell's "Portrait, (E. R. B.)," which reads, "This lady is like a grass-blade sheathed in ice,/ . . . / She is like violets under the misted glass of a cold frame/ On an autumn morning with the sun scarcely above the trees. . . ./ But what can equal the glitter of the frosty grass-blades,/ Held to a rigid radiance,/ . . . / Answering nothing to the wind?/ No, do not lift the frames./ The violets are a lovely touch of colour,/ And I would rather forego the scent of them/ Than run the risk of their freezing."

said earnestly, "I have no money, no possessions; all I have to give is love. You will always have a secure place in my heart; you don't need to be afraid of losing it. But I must give to people what I have to offer." (In her autobiography Mrs. Belmont, commenting generally on Ada's personality, says, "unquestionably her greatest asset was a warm, radiant love of people which she distributed generously, as a philanthropist pours out his accepted form of wealth.")

Ada may have said something similar to Amy as they confronted each other. Moreover, Amy knew her faults "only too well," as she had told Carl Engel. She had come perilously close to losing his friendship, but had caught herself in time; she wanted even less to lose the person whose presence gave new meaning to her whole life. And so she relented. Ada went to Salt Lake City and came back in time to go to London with Amy in the summer of 1914. Also aboard ship was Amy's maroon Pierce-Arrow, with liveried chauffeur to match. On this second trip she planned to tour the countryside in pursuit of further Keatsiana, not only for her collection, but for an exhaustive study she was planning. She also wanted to consult with Ezra Pound and to consolidate her position with *Les Imagistes,* to be considered a full-fledged member or even an executive.

A third purpose of the summer sojourn was to secure publication in England of her forthcoming volume of poetry. She had already virtually assured this by switching from Houghton Mifflin to the Macmillan Company. Percy and Lawrence were published by Macmillan, and Amy thought she might be wise to use the New York firm that was a branch of the British publishing house, an advantage in itself. Early in 1914, just before Ada came to live with her, Amy had gone to New York and signed a contract with Frederick Marsh and George Brett of Macmillan for *Sword Blades and Poppy Seed,* the intriguing title she had chosen for her new book. They could not help admiring her forthright business tactics. This accomplished, she called on various editors to insure publication of individual poems in magazines before the book came out. (Here again she flaunted convention. Usually, poets had to wait until enough individual poems had appeared in general periodicals or the literary magazines before collecting them in a volume; but Amy used her Macmillan contract as proof that her new poems were worthy of prestigious publication singly. It was to impress Harriet Monroe and convince her to include a few of these in *Poetry* that she had gone to Chicago.)

As soon as Amy and Ada were settled in the Berkeley Hotel in the same top-floor headquarters Amy had occupied the summer before, the poet went to see George Macmillan, head of Macmillan's London office, and came away with a signed contract containing unusual terms: The publisher agreed to distribute one hundred copies of *Sword Blades and Poppy Seed* in England, keeping 10 percent of the retail price and sending 90 percent to Miss Lowell. It was a reversal of the customary publisher-author division of profits. Macmillan, like his American colleagues, was so impressed with her combined business acumen and hail-fellow-well-met approach to talking terms that he asked her to dine at the exclusive Ranelagh Club near Richmond, an invitation rarely extended to authors.

She fared far less well in consolidating her position with Pound. For one thing, in the year that had elapsed between these two visits, Ezra, whose tiny second-floor flat at 10 Church Walk in Kensington had been the setting for so many literary discoveries of poets and poetry-writing,* was now the cradle of another movement: Vorticism. "The Vortex," as envisioned by Wyndham Lewis, a young painter-writer with a year in Paris as his training, was a whirling centralization of all the arts, a rushing revolt not only against convention but bohemianism of the arty variety. Its publication was called *Blast,* and it was explosive, to say the least. If it embraced all the arts, the magazine also blasted all those its editors considered pseudo-artists, and Pound entered into this endeavor with gusto. He, Lewis, and an audacious, atrocious, raffish, if gifted young French sculptor, Henri Gaudier-Brzeska, formed a triumvirate of leaders guiding the newest trend, to the partial neglect of the *Imagistes,* although Pound had not entirely abandoned them. His anthology, *Des Imagistes,* scarcely more than a

* Including Robert Frost, who, Pound decided, had "the seeds of grace" in him, and the early verses of James Joyce.

pamphlet—including poems by H. D., Richard Aldington, John Gould Fletcher, James Joyce, Amy Lowell's "In a Garden," and a few by Pound himself—had just appeared in New York, sponsored by Albert and Charles Boni, brothers who were first booksellers, then publishers.

Altogether, Pound had succeeded in introducing nine little-known new poets to literary circles in his native land, and although he still insisted that they hold to the rules ("A Few Don'ts by an Imagist"), he himself was off on another track, keeping his own set of poetic standards to himself. Amy Lowell was puzzled, not to say bewildered, and more than a little annoyed at Pound's quixotic leaps, his championing of one cultural clique after another while at the same time wanting to maintain a firm, dogmatic hand on all of them. Yet she could not help admiring his boundless activity and enthusiasm, and she did her best to keep up with him. She asked him for introductions to the Vorticists, which he gladly gave her; he also invited her and Mrs. Russell to join them at one of their dinners in the Dieudonne, a French restaurant in London's bohemian quarter.

Amy could not abide Gaudier-Brzeska, the latter part of whose name he adopted from his Polish common-law wife, an older, half-mad hanger-on, who adored, harassed, worked, and cared for the twenty-two-year-old sculptor. He probably nurtured an equal dislike for the regal, immaculate appearance and "vivacious intelligence" * of Amy Lowell. With his lank hair almost to his shoulders, his sparsely bearded cheeks, pointed chin, oddly slanted eyes topping off his slovenly clothes (almost identical to fellow artists of sixty years later), he was revolting to her, no matter how brilliant his sculptures were considered to be by art critics and colleagues. At the dinner she also tangled briefly with Ford Madox Ford, who claimed to be neither an *Imagiste* nor a Vorticist, but simply a friend of Ezra's—or, if anything, an Impressionist. He looked on all these sizzling movements with the objectivity of an older and more sophisticated background, the pre-Raphaelite circle and their descendants. Christina Rossetti was his aunt, and

* Aldington's phrase describing Amy Lowell's curiosity and challenging attitude.

Joseph Conrad his friend. He regarded Amy Lowell as a newcomer and an interloper who wanted to take over the movement his friend had started, and in the round-table discussion that took place at these dinners, he gave her no opening.

Feeling humiliated and left out, Amy resorted to the role of hostess at a dinner, given at the Dieudonne, in celebration of the publication of *Des Imagistes.* All the contributors and the erratic, domineering editor-poet, Ezra Pound, accepted her invitation with pleasure. There was a complimentary copy of the publication at everyone's place, as a souvenir of the occasion. Amy was hopeful that now at last she would learn the secret, basic tenet of *Imagisme* she had failed to discover the summer before. Was there no more to it than she had already grasped? She wanted to make sure. But when they were all around the table, nobody would listen to questions or undertake serious discussions, partly because they were all too busy autographing each other's copies of the book, examining its contents.*

Principally, however, it was because Pound saw to it that she could not assume any leadership while he was around: He rebuffed her attempts at seriousness with ill-bred, impertinent levity. In answer to her question about a precise formula for *Imagisme,* he left the table and came back in a few minutes wearing an old-fashioned tin tub on his head in caricature of a helmet of some knight-errant. He produced hilarious laughter, in which Amy joined, but hers was a hard and a hurt laugh. Was Pound implying that she was tilting at windmills? That *Imagisme* was old hat by now? Or simply that he, Pound, had to be the cynosure of all eyes?

It was well that Amy Lowell was a good sport. She paid the bill with good grace, though she had not fully joined in the high-jinks. She parted from Pound with unmistakable coolness, and with an inner vow to divest him of his impudence and high-handed

* John Gould Fletcher, whose mania for keeping mementos was almost equal to Amy's, preserved his copy, and many years later the late poet Louise Bogan, who was visiting his widow, wrote to Morton Zabel (May 3, 1952): "She has some amazing stuff, since J. G. F. never threw anything away. . . . The copy of *Des Imagistes,* signed by everyone on the occasion of a dinner given on the day of its publication, was also extraordinary to see." (From *What the Woman Lived, Selected Letters of Louise Bogan.* (New York: Harcourt Brace Jovanovich, 1973).

use of power. She was happy, too, that she had someone to turn to, the one she most needed at such moments. When they got back to the Berkeley, she and "Peter" could hash over the dinner to their heart's content, and neither would betray the other's confidence. She also counted on Mrs. Russell's insight and sense of humor to give her support and objectivity, and her companion did not disillusion her. She saw clearly what Pound was trying to do, and she discerned that his own genius needed constant nurturing.

She helped Amy plan another dinner, a kind of consolation prize for the fiasco of the first one, this to be given in their top-floor suite at the Berkeley. Of Pound's *Imagiste* group Amy chose four: H. D. and Richard Aldington, who had just been married and were in a euphoric state; the neurotic, paranoiac American poet, John Gould Fletcher (whose distrust of Pound equaled Amy's); and D. H. Lawrence, whom Amy had not yet met, but whom she knew enough about through Pound and the few Lawrence poems in print to make her eager to use her letter of introduction from Ezra with her invitation to him. Lawrence had just eloped with Frieda, who had left her husband and children for the passionate but penniless English poet. It was a romantic story, all the more since Frieda was the daughter of one Baron von Richtofen, an accident of birth that appealed especially to Amy Lowell's feeling of kinship with the baronial class.

The dinner, planned with care, was as notable in its success as the earlier one for its failure. Amy's apartment looked out from a bay window across Piccadilly toward Green Park and St. James's. She had recently begun to drape the mirrors in hotel rooms in black or red to save herself the painful sight of her massive portliness once she left her dressing room, where she made sure she was presentable before draping that mirror also. As a result, the view outward was emphasized; and as the evening lights came on in London, the shadowy outlines of trees shone with subdued color. The day, July 30, like most of that memorable month in 1914, had been amazingly clear and warm, closely resembling the strange calm before a storm: The "guns of August" were only five days away. Everyone knew that at Sarajevo the archduke of Austria had been shot over a month before, on June 28, but no one expected the incident to precipitate a world war. It was true that newspaper headlines warned that "Germany and Russia Are at War," and news of the British army's mobilization appeared that very day. But to Richard Aldington, who had arrived early with H. D., after having watched posters announcing the news being set up below in Piccadilly, all-out war still seemed remote and unlikely.

Inside, all was serene and charming. As he turned to see an attendant lighting the long tapers above the gleaming silverware and white damask cloth of the dinner table, the quiet atmosphere suddenly became emotionally charged, sparked by the rapid entrance of D. H. Lawrence, who was followed by Frieda close on his heels. Here was the young Lawrence, not the bearded "sly Christ" or "creeping Jesus" of Taos, but a clean-shaven, slim, vibrant young man, with shiny red hair and sharp electric-blue eyes, moving with a lithe, agile, almost agitated step to the center of the room. Without waiting for introductions, according to Aldington's account, he burst out with his news that "Edward Marsh just informed me that the British are going into the war!" * His words crackled with fire, and his lightning glance shot around the company in mingled anger and triumph. It was a typical Lawrence entrance—full of drama and excitement—and Amy loved it.

During dinner, at which Lawrence, as guest of honor, sat at Amy's right hand, she became just as infatuated with his ideas. He was neither Georgian nor *Imagiste,* he declared; he was an independent poet and writer. He was not a joiner of groups or movements, and the emphatic way he said it brought Amy's respect for his position, if it cost her a moment of doubt about her own eagerness to become a full-fledged *Imagiste.* She approved of his scrubbed appearance in contrast to the flaunted unwashed flavor of the Vorticists; of his spirited, sensual discussion of the erotic in poetry, which, though it seemed "some sort of mania" in him, she thought, held her fascinated.

He also knew the art of listening, and he let her have her turn, as Pound rarely did. He kept his bright blue eyes riveted to her face, as if he, too, were fascinated by her opinions, so that she felt

* Marsh was editor of the *Georgian Poetry* anthologies and private secretary to Prime Minister Herbert Asquith.

honored instead of humiliated or slighted. D. H. Lawrence, a coal miner's son, surely had the gift of capturing a woman's soul, regardless of her station in life. Mabel Dodge (Luhan), who was to become his patron in Taos, New Mexico, once remarked that "Lorenzo" could undress a woman with a glance; and while it is doubtful if he had any desire or undertook to undress his huge hostess with his long look, he nevertheless touched the core of her being. And he made a friend that was to help him—not as a patron, but as a colleague and kindred spirit—in many trying moments in the future. She was hardly less taken with Frieda. The former wife of a professor was no beauty, but she was almost as vivid and volatile as Lawrence in expressing herself and maintained a positive Prussian viewpoint on a wide variety of subjects. (Both Amy and Mrs. Russell tactfully avoided the current conflict soon to affect them all, and, although Lawrence vented his anger at British involvement—he was an avowed pacifist—they managed to keep the conversation on a literary level.) Amy quickly recognized the genius in D. H. Lawrence. She believed he would be an asset to the Imagist movement that she was already, half-unconsciously, planning to launch in America.

She did not give much heed to the fact that he had just declared his independence of all groups. She knew that to all these struggling young poets—the Aldingtons, Fletcher, and F. S. Flint, who had all been kind and attentive to her—publication was important. Without it, they could not continue to exist as professional poets. Whether or not he adhered to the strict rules of Pound's *Imagisme* did not matter. She felt in her bones that D. H. Lawrence was among those destined for greatness, and she never forsook her convictions about Lawrence, even in his darkest moments, when he was being castigated by the critics, or worse, ignored by them and by the reading public. It was due to her efforts that Lawrence was known for his love poems at all. He, in turn, was one of the few who saw that Amy's personal poems—those dealing with the things she loved as well as those expressing the deep emotions of her private life—were her finest, and he told her so, advising her "always to be herself." He wrote her: "If it doesn't come out of your heart, real Amy Lowell, it is no good, however many colours it may have."

Some of Lawrence's most perceptive, diverting, and delightful prose is to be found in his letters to Amy Lowell. In the correspondence files of the Lowell collection at the Houghton Library of Harvard University are fifty-five letters testifying to his art, his understanding of Amy's psyche, and the felicitous, enduring literary friendship which began with the dinner at the Berkeley Hotel. (The Lawrences subsequently came there a number of times, and she and Ada visited them at their cottage in Chesham.)

Scarcely any less vivid and memorable (with added reasons of weather conditions) was Amy's visit to Thomas Hardy at his famous country house, Max Gate, in Dorchester. Among her letters of introduction Amy had brought a surprisingly cordial one from Josephine Peabody * to the elder statesman of British literati, but Amy had found too many other important contacts pressing upon her to arrange for a meeting until the tag end of their stay. Only a day or two after the Berkeley dinner, she and Ada set out one morning with her chauffeur at the wheel of her Pierce-Arrow touring car; he had suggested putting the top up, but Amy preferred the more sporty effect of an open car, especially since she was wearing a new hat, trimmed with the bright-colored feathers of a stuffed bird. Unfortunately, the long calm spell was over, and on the way out they drove through a number of summer showers. It was too unwieldy and time-consuming a job to adjust the top to suit the sun and rain, so by the time they reached Max Gate, as Hardy described it, he saw from the bow window in his living room, "two very bedraggled ladies emerging from the motor-car." The bird on Amy's hat, nearly washed away, was hanging by the tail over one side of the brim; Ada's jacket was crinkled with rain spots; and both were generally disheveled.

Amy, with her flair for clowning, made the most of the situation, and her gaiety was infectious. Thomas Hardy, bald and elderly, trim and elegant as the brick walls, bow windows, and well-kept lawns of Max Gate, his eyes twinkling with amusement, welcomed

* Josephine had come to know him five years earlier when her play, *Piper*, was produced at Stratford.

them warmly. He appreciated Amy's exaggerated version of their plight and the straightforward manner in which she asked what his feelings were about *Imagisme,* Pound, and the new poetry in general. He sidestepped the issue by saying that he was old-fashioned. He was pleased to learn that she was acquainted with his poetry as well as his novels; he was impatient with people who were unaware that he had written anything besides *Tess of the d'Urbervilles* and *The Return of the Native.* He, himself, ranked his poems above his novels, and he was delighted to discover that Amy Lowell's estimate of his work was much the same.

Their encounter was on a much more equal footing than the meeting she had had with Henry James the summer before, also just prior to leaving London. James, aging and ill in 1913, and depressed by the drop in popularity he had suffered both socially and professionally, had given Amy some bitter words of advice: "I have cut myself off from America, where I belonged, and in England I am not really accepted," he confided. "Don't make my mistake." He had been a close friend of Amy's Cousin James, and missed the poet-diplomat keenly.* He should have known that Amy Lowell of Brookline had no intention of becoming an expatriate, and his air of patronizing her professionally had irritated her. Yet she had felt sorry for him; and before leaving the garden of his home at Rye, where they had strolled to talk after tea, she had plucked a sprig of lavender, which she kept in her desk at Sevenels. At Max Gate in 1914, however, with Ada at her side, and with the promise of a fruitful friendship with D. H. Lawrence and Frieda ahead, Amy felt on an equal basis with a literary personage in her own field, poetry. And the genial Hardys responded both to her distinct personality and to the warm relationship they perceived between Amy and Ada Russell. Hardy's letters to her, which followed this visit and continued through the years, always concluded with mention of Mrs. Russell, and his words of warm affection were not casually but definitely sent to her as well as to Amy. The same was true of Lawrence's letters and those from H. D. and

* In an intimate letter to Charles Eliot Norton after James Russell Lowell's death, Henry James wrote of his grief: "It is a dim satisfaction to me . . . to say to you how fond I was of him and how I shall miss him and miss him and miss him."

Richard Aldington; in fact, all the personal correspondence in the Lowell files includes mention of Ada from the time she became Amy's companion.

Shortly after the delightful visit at Max Gate, Britain formally declared war on Germany, signaling the first world war in history, a conflict on a scale previously conceivable only in the novels of H. G. Wells and in the prophetic warnings of G. B. Shaw regarding class struggle. Overnight, London became a city of wartime turmoil, a confusion of mobilization mixed with the frenzied efforts of tourists rushing to leave the country. Percy, who had turned up in London a week or two earlier to attend a meeting with British astronomists, had already booked return passage and advised Amy to do the same. But she hesitated. Her new book was due to appear in England momentarily, and she could not believe "the war scare" was serious. She was shrewd enough, however, to ship her maroon Pierce-Arrow back to Boston at once, as the British government announced that all automobiles would be commandeered. Personal danger didn't bother her, and if "Peter" was willing to wait till the book came out, they would secure passage on a later boat. Ada agreed, realizing how much this publication meant to Amy.

They delayed their departure, as did other literary figures for varied reasons of publication. By a curious coincidence, two were among those born around the same time as Amy Lowell: Gertrude Stein, who was with her friend, Alice B. Toklas; and Robert Frost, who, with his family, had been in England since 1912. During the past year the Frosts had been living among a group of the Georgian poets in the Lake Country, but when war was declared, the circle dwindled, their publication ceased owing to a paper shortage, and a source of income was cut off when the dailies ceased printing book review columns and other pieces by free-lance writers. Luckily, *North of Boston,* Frost's second volume and the one that brought him substantial recognition, had appeared in April 1914; however, his eccentric British publisher had sent him hints of an American publisher, but no definite word or statement of royalties on the British edition. And the Frosts did not know how they could afford passage home even if they could book it. He and his family moved in with the Lascelles Abercrombies at Ryton to save expenses. The spectacular reviews of the book, pronounced "revolutionary" in its language and probing content if not in form, had aroused Amy Lowell's interest, and she had gone to the Poetry Bookshop and purchased "the little green volume, and spent an evening reading it with ever increasing delight." She and Ada took turns reading the dramatic scenes aloud. She would follow up her admiration when she got home; at the same time, she voiced loud hopes that her own second volume would be considered just as "revolutionary" by British critics as Robert Frost's, and maybe go his one better. (Ironically, Frost was waiting to see if his book would be an American success before he went home, while Amy was waiting for hers to duplicate his in England before she returned.)

In a suburb of London not too many miles from the Berkeley Hotel, that already famous pair, Gertrude Stein and Alice B. Toklas, were caught by the outbreak of war at Lockridge, the home of Dr. and Mrs. Alfred Whitehead, near Salisbury Plain, where they had been invited for a weekend. They stayed for six weeks because of the war. They also had come to England to discuss a second publication of Gertrude's work, *Three Lives,* which John Lane, Ltd., had expressed an interest in publishing. She had the signed contract in hand when war was declared. (While waiting to return, Gertrude added to the store of anecdotes about her by entering into a heated discussion with Bertrand Russell, Whitehead's close friend and collaborator on their monumental social history of man. In the confrontation with Miss Stein, he was bested more than once, and "fussed and fussed," word of which traveled around the London literary circles.)

The legends about Amy Lowell—after spending two summers among the most notable English avant-garde poets—were legion at this early date also, principally because of her sparring with Ezra Pound. In this connection, Robert McAlmon, literary jack-of-all-trades and avant-garde gambler-publisher, who was to take a chance on an experimental edition of Gertrude Stein's 1,000-page novel, *The Making of Americans,* and also to marry (briefly) one of Amy Lowell's Imagists, Bryher,* a close friend of H. D., tells a story about Amy in his memoirs which may or may not have been true. According to McAlmon, the day war was declared or shortly thereafter, Amy, having sent her car home, got caught in the panicked crowds trying to book passage or withdraw money from banks. Probably feeling trapped herself for a moment, she stormed and raged because a London bobby would not help her find a cab. She was concerned only about being late for an appointment with her publisher at her hotel. Back in her suite at the Berkeley at last, she paced up and down, smoking her cigar and crying, "My book is supposed to come out! A lot of attention it will get now with a war on! What's the matter with England? Why don't they just stop the war?"

If she did say such a thing—and it was like Amy Lowell to be annoyed rather than anxious over such an upheaval—she must have assumed that whoever heard her would know she was merely letting off steam. On another level, which McAlmon did not mention and probably never knew about, Amy acted in true Lowell tradition: She offered her services to Herbert Hoover, who was in London to organize Belgian War Relief and to help stranded Americans who wanted to go home. She aided the latter cause by working in Hoover's office at the American consulate and at Victoria Station, where, with a large placard pinned to her ample bosom, she directed late, bewildered arrivals to the proper bureaus for finding hotel rooms or return passage. She also made a personal donation of $10,000 to Hoover's committee.

Her main activity during these days of turmoil and marking time, however, was to make concrete plans for a new *Imagiste* anthology. She had already consulted the Aldingtons, who were enthusiastic about her idea of a cooperative volume. She sent a prospectus to F. S. Flint and Ford Madox Ford as well as to Ezra Pound, who after all was responsible for the first volume. But he would have none of it. In a letter Amy found waiting for her when she and Ada returned from the visit to the Hardys, he said although

* Pseudonym of Winifred Ellerman, daughter of the British shipping magnate, who later lived with H. D., bringing up the latter's child after the Aldingtons were divorced. She married McAlmon, he discovered, merely as a convenience, so he sued for divorce and received a handsome settlement.

he might sanction such a volume, he would insist that it be clearly stated that he—Pound—had no part in selecting the contents. (Each poet in her outline of the project was to make selections individually; a committee would pass on them, and all contributors would share equally in the profits.) And he would take no responsibility for the views of the contributing poets. His real grievance was that the whole project would deprive him of selecting and promoting the work of stray poets (as he had done in the case of Frost's first book, *A Boy's Will*); and he couldn't see "being saddled with a dam'd contentious, probably incompetent committee," and so on. In other words, he was disassociating himself from the group. If they wanted to form a separate group, he thought it might be done amicably, although he himself was not exactly amicable in attitude.

Amy did not want to hurt him or to alienate him completely, and she did not; but the schism between them widened. She invited the Lawrences to dinner again and persuaded the hesitating Lawrence to join her group. He had contended that Imagism was just "an advertising scheme" (besides which, he hated French poetry). But she convinced him that her purpose in publishing a second anthology was to show that the movement was flexible and that it need not adhere to Pound's dogma. Moreover, inclusion of Lawrence's poems would be a worthwhile outlet for his work. So he consented to contribute. F. S. Flint and Ford Madox Ford were (surprisingly, in the case of Ford) ready to go along with her. She was satisfied that she was accomplishing a good deal. On the long August evenings, she and F. S. Flint discussed the French poets, and Amy read Paul Fort or Henri de Regnier aloud—"she reads French beautifully," he wrote—while awaiting the latest news from the front. On August 14, Amy wrote a war poem, "The Allies," in polyphonic prose, her latest style; and on August 22, Lawrence sent her his contribution of seven poems, along with an invitation to her and Ada to spend a day with him and Frieda at the cottage in Chesham (where he was "having a rare old time whitewashing the upper rooms and grinding over in his soul the war news"). They would have a "perfectly rural and idyllic time." Among the sheaf of poems he included was his lovely, tragic, "Ballad of Another Ophelia," beginning, "O the green glimmer of apples in the orchard," of which he pleaded, "even if you don't like the poem, please put it in an you love me." (Harriet Monroe wanted to publish the "far end of it" and leave out the first half, but he would see her in blazes first.) The rural and idyllic event took place on August 27—and was enjoyed by all. In the months ahead, as the lengthening war took its toll in death and hardship, they often looked back with nostalgia at the happy times of eager discussion and laughter they had together during the tense month of August 1914.

When word finally came that British publication of Amy's book would have to be postponed, she managed to secure passage for two on the *Laconia,* the same ship, even the same cabin, that had brought them over in June, and they reached American shores the first week in September. The American publication date for the book was September 22, and even as she looked forward to the reviews, Amy was buzzing with plans to promote Imagism first of all, but in addition, poetry of every sort, as long as it was fresh and free—like Robert Frost's—from the cloying clichés of the immediate past. If, in the process, she would also be promoting Amy Lowell and her own garden variety of Imagism, so much the better.

As she and Ada approached Sevenels, she had the feeling that she was about to become "Somebody" at last; and she felt strongly that it was largely because she had "a very intimate friend" who knew how to help her, who would share the work and the glory of her life. In a gesture of love and gratitude, often to be repeated in days to come, she reached for her friend's long, tapering fingers with "a quick, necessary touch of her hand." The only cloud on the horizon was that Ada was leaving at once for Chicago to visit Lorna, who in an early, unexpected marriage, had become Mrs. Theodore Amussen. Amy had hoped "Peter" would wait to go till after *Sword Blades* was off the press, but Ada pointed out that Lorna was her only child. Marriage was an important step, and she wanted to get acquainted with her son-in-law. Amy sighed; she was about to say, "Can't they come here?" but she held her peace. Instead, she persuaded Ada to be back at Sevenels by publication day. Then she got out of the car and strode toward the kennels, calling out, "There are my children, my family!" as, with wild, joyful barking, the great sheep dogs came rushing to greet her.

CHAPTER X

Challenger of the Old and Champion of the New Poetry: "Amygism"

AMY'S HUNCH that she was about to become "Somebody" was correct. Her second volume, *Sword Blades and Poppy Seed,* which appeared on schedule—September 22, 1914—brought her an instantaneous, phenomenal rise to fame. The title alone, coming at the outbreak of war in Flanders where the poppy fields flourished, was externally apropos, internally symbolizing "fighting truths" vis-à-vis "lulling dreams," as the ardent new Imagist intended when she chose it. (The title, and opening, poem is a rather obvious tale of an aged, wise peddler of words that are used as sharp-edged weapons and as drugs; he is depicted showing his wares to a rank, awestruck beginner.) However intuitive or inadvertently appropriate the title may have been, *Sword Blades and Poppy Seed* marked the beginning of Amy Lowell's career as an experimentalist and leader of the Imagist movement in American poetry. (Although still greatly interested in the French poets and vers libre, she Americanized and adapted the terms at once; vers libre, for example, became "unrhymed cadence" in Lowellese.)

The book created something of a furor with its varied freedom of rhythms and versification of all kinds, written on the theory that "the sound should be an echo to the sense." Coming as it did only two years after the acceptable but quite conventional *Dome,* the new volume seemed to proclaim, as Louis Untermeyer wrote, "that a wholly new poet, and, what was more, a new epoch had appeared. *Sword Blades and Poppy Seed* sounded some of the first notes in the controversy which raged about the New Poetry. The book heralded the era's growing dissatisfaction with traditional measures and the determination to try new verse forms, strange cadences, and unfamiliar responses to standard sentiments."

Reviews came pouring in—not polite or desultory notices like those that *Dome* had received—but bona fide reviews, some puzzled, some adverse or angry or openly derisive; but mostly they were favorable. Reviewers from William Stanley Braithwaite in the *Boston Transcript* to H. L. Mencken in *Smart Set* had something to say about Amy Lowell's bizarre images and weird inventions in polyphonic prose, a form she had learned through John Gould Fletcher, but which she made her own. One of the weirdest of these compositions, "The Basket," uses an uneven rhyme scheme and sexual symbolism to full effect. The story of unrequited love that a poet with stubborn passion foists on a needlework artist has this strange passage, quoted in a recent anthology, *The Women Poets in English* (1972), and cited as "modern enough to have been written today":

> They are eyes, hundreds of eyes, round like marbles! Unwinking, for there are no lids. Blue, black, gray, and hazel, and the irises are cased in the whites, and they glitter and spark under the moon. The basket is heaped with human eyes. She cracks off the whites and throws them away. They ricochet upon the roof, and get into the gutters, and bounce over the edge and disappear. But she is here, quietly sitting on the window-sill, eating human eyes.*

The symbolic implication would be heady enough in any era, but in 1914 it was sensational, and Amy knew it. Her detractors were many. As late as 1958, Horace Gregory claimed that the verses in *Sword Blades* "were not 'modern' in any sense of the word." He must have had a worse myopia than the poet in Amy's barb-filled "Astigmatism," written about and dedicated "To Ezra Pound with Much Friendship and Admiration and Some Differences of Opinion," also in *Sword Blades*. Certainly those who

* S. Foster Damon, *Amy Lowell, A Chronicle* (Boston: Houghton Mifflin Company, 1935), wrote: " 'The Basket' is a symbolic puzzle which Miss Lowell always refused to explain." A present-day poet (1973), on reading the passage, and the Lowell concept of "the life of the eye," excaimed, "Why, that's the same concept I use in my new book!"

tried to diminish her contribution to modern American poetry could have had no concept of Amy Lowell's psyche. Moreover, to her, the barrage of antipathetic criticism was an exhilarating challenge, and she prepared her battle campaign with joyous fury, which she no doubt confided to the small inner circle of five at Sevenels who dubbed themselves "the Devils." The cabala consisted of Amy, Ada, Carl Engel, Heinrich Gebhard, and Dr. Herman Adler. Carl, especially, was overjoyed with the attention Amy was receiving, to say nothing of the fact that five hundred copies of the book were sold before Christmas. He claimed credit for having recognized her ability and continued to aid and abet her in writing and promoting her own poetry as well as that of others who were taking a new approach to poetry-writing.

For, both in the preface and in "Astigmatism," Amy made clear that, although Imagism had opened the way to freedom of expression for her, she was by no means solely an Imagist. "Schools are for those who can confine themselves within them," she wrote with something of her old antagonism toward the schoolroom. In the poem separating herself from Pound's school she used the figure of the Poet who has fashioned an exquisite cane which he brandishes as a weapon to destroy, while out for a walk, all the flowers—both wild and cultivated—that are not roses. It was natural for Amy to choose flowers as the basis for her figure of speech. Each section ends with the line, "Peace be with you, Brother," and an added line as the Poet lops off the heads of different flowers: after the third section, "But behind you is destruction, and waste places," and, after the last, the tag line: "You have chosen your part." She had shown a copy to Pound before she left London, and he had said it was "all right." However, when Macmillan in its zeal to make the most of the stir the book caused, advertised the author as "the foremost member of the Imagists, a group of poets that includes William Butler Yeats, Ezra Pound, Ford Madox Hueffer [Ford]," he was furious and threatened to sue both Amy and the publisher. She answered him with a letter that, in spite of an attempt to sound apologetic, did not conceal her glee at the row he was raising. She pointed out that "The ludicrous thing is that in my preface I have carefully said that I do not belong to any school. . . ." As to his lawsuit, she had never heard of a school of poetry being copyrighted and doubted if it could be done. "But if you should feel inclined to sue, I should be exceedingly delighted as then they would put new jackets on the book, which I should greatly prefer. Also it would be a good advertisement. And, in the third place, you would be obliged to prove my inclusion in your group * as a libel, and it would be interesting to see whether that could be done." She had him there, and she knew it!

There were other poems in *Sword Blades* that caused controversy. A seemingly simple, naïve narrative is "The Book of Hours of Sister Clotilde," in which a youthful nun, illustrating a sacred manuscript, can find no color divine enough for the robe of the Madonna until she catches sight of an adder in the garden. She allows the adder to bite her, but an old gardener sucks the poison from her wound, and she completes the illumination with the colors of the snakeskin. Amy cherished the meaning too much to explain the poem to those who questioned it, and usually turned off their attempts at guessing what it meant with a laugh; but she did admit that the choice of the ancient symbol of sex, the snake, and of the poisonous adder for the Virgin's robe, was intentional, and that it was the key to the whole meaning of the poem.

The other symbolic tales in the book, although too wordy, have a dual meaning for those acquainted with Amy's background. Outwardly they deal with man's frustrating search for the ideal, which may drive him to suicide; more subtly, however, the salient feelings that Amy in her youthful yearnings to be loved, must have experienced in many such fantasy loves. This is not to imply that they are in any sense factually autobiographical—indeed, the contrivances used, and what D. H. Lawrence called her "banal resolutions," make for artificiality—but emotionally they cannot help being an expression of her early inner loneliness and longing (this is particularly true of "The Great Adventure of Max Breuck"). The best one of these "Poppy Seed" dramas is the shortest, "Clear, with Light Variable Winds" (cited by Thomas Hardy in his letter of appreciation to Amy for the author's copy she sent him). Here she describes a woman's body in the tender terms of a lover:

* A reference to Pound's little anthology, *Des Imagistes*.

Her breasts point outwards,
And the nipples are like buds of peonies.
Her flanks ripple as she plays,
And the water is not more undulating
Than the lines of her body.

Hardy also found "arresting" the poem "After Hearing a Waltz by Bartók," mentioning that "the metre & rhythm keep up the beat of the waltz admirably," as well as "Music" and "A Lady" (in part a portrait of Ada), plus "The Captured Goddess," often quoted as an example of Amy's use of color:

Over the housetops,
Above the rotating chimney-pots,
I have seen a shiver of amethyst,
And blue and cinnamon have flickered
A moment,
At the far end of a dusty street.

Through sheeted rain
Has come a lustre of crimson,
And I have watched moonbeams
Hushed by a film of palest green. . . .

"The Forsaken," a dramatic monologue in polyphonic prose, was attacked because it contained the word "whore" not once but twice, and, although a prayer to the Virgin, was a kind of protest against the church's forbiddance of sexual intercourse outside marriage. Probably because of its controversial theme and the inherent melodrama of an unwed pregnant girl praying to the virgin, not for forgiveness, but for understanding, the piece proved most popular as a dramatic monologue at the public readings that were soon to begin. During these, Amy gave it full theatrical treatment.

Sword Blades contained both metered and free verse, rhymed and unrhymed, as well as her polyphonic prose, which, she explained, "permits the use of all the methods: cadence, rhyme, alliteration, and assonance, also perhaps true metre for a few minutes." She had learned a valuable lesson from the poems of Robert Frost, namely, that the "vaunted *mot juste*" of the Imagists could be employed to equal effect in blank verse. But the best poems in her second volume were the personal ones. Most of them were short lyrics in free verse that revealed her impressions of life and her emotional torments and ties. As D. H. Lawrence had discerned, here was the real Amy Lowell, the straightforward poet, full of gusto and "vivacious intelligence," yet reflective, capable of tender, delicate emotion and warm or sometimes "bitter Puritan passion," as Lawrence called it. "Why don't you always be yourself," he told her (in the form of a statement, not a question). "If it doesn't come out of your own heart, real Amy Lowell, it is no good, however many colours it may have. I wish one saw more of your genuine, sound self in this book, full of common sense & kindness. . . . Why do you deny the bitterness in your nature, when you write poetry? Why do you take a pose? . . . When you are full of your own strong gusto of things, real old English strong gusto it is, like those tulips,* then I like you very much. . . . I hate to see you posturing, when there is thereby a real person betrayed in you. . . . At any rate, thank you very much for your poems, which I like because after all they have a lot of you in them. . . ." Among those he chose were "The Taxi," one of the most successful and frequently quoted of these free-verse lyrics, and, like most of them, having to do in some way with her relationship to her beloved friend. "The Taxi," which has some of the bitterness Lawrence mentioned and maintains its strong metaphor throughout, must have been written one of those times when she saw Ada off on the train, after much protest:

When I go away from you
The world beats dead
Like a slackened drum.
I call out for you against the jutted stars
And shout into the ridges of the wind.
Streets coming fast,
One after the other,
Wedge you away from me,

* A reference to a poem called "A Tulip Garden," inspired by the magnificent garden of Mrs. Bayard Thayer. After giving her the above piece of his mind, Lawrence added, "I suppose you think me damned impertinent. But I hate to see you posturing when there is thereby a real person betrayed in you." He ended, "Saluti di cuore."

And the lamps of the city prick my eyes
So that I can no longer see your face.
Why should I leave you,
To wound myself upon the sharp edges of the night?

"Absence" is in a similar vein:

My cup is empty to-night,
Cold and dry are its sides,
Chilled by the wind from the open window. . . .
The room is filled with the strange scent
Of wistaria blossoms. . . .

But the cup of my heart is still,
And cold, and empty.

When you come, it brims
Red and trembling with blood,
Heart's blood for your drinking;
To fill your mouth with love
And the bitter-sweet taste of a soul.

In "Fool's Money Bags," another of Lawrence's selections, one he liked "very much," she shows an infrequent edge of doubt as she writes to the absent one:

Outside the long window,
With his head on the stone sill,
The dog is lying,
Gazing at his Beloved.
His eyes are wet and urgent,
And his body is taut and shaking.

It is cold on the terrace;
A pale wind licks along the stone slabs,
But the dog gazes through the glass
And is content.

The Beloved is writing a letter.
Occasionally she speaks to the dog,
But she is thinking of her writing.
Does she, too, give her devotion to one
Not worthy?

The "almost bitter Puritan passion" comes out in "Miscast," especially section II:

My heart is like a cleft pomegranate
Bleeding crimson seeds
And dripping them on the ground.
My heart gapes because it is ripe and over-full,
And its seeds are bursting from it.

But how is this other than a torment to me!
I, who am shut up, with broken crockery,
In a dark closet!

A moment of her old self-hate came out in "The Bungler":

You glow in my heart
Like the flames of uncounted candles.
But when I go to warm my hands,
My clumsiness overturns the light
And then I stumble
Against the tables and chairs.

But the moments of doubt and despairing self-flagellation are far outdistanced by the enduring devotion and gratitude expressed in these poems. "A Gift" is not only devout but uncannily prophetic in its vow to the beloved friend:

See! I give myself to you, Beloved!
My words are little jars
For you to take and put upon a shelf.
Their shapes are quaint and beautiful,
And they have many pleasant colours and lustres
To recommend them.
Also the scent from them fills the room
With sweetness of flowers and crushed grasses.

When I shall have given you the last one,
You will have the whole of me,
But I shall be dead.

"Obligation" repeats the desire to shower the beloved with gifts, representing Amy's constant petition, always refused, to dedicate her books to Ada:

Hold your apron wide
That I may pour my gifts into it, . . .

I would pour them upon you
And cover you,
For greatly do I feel this need
Of giving you something,
Even these poor things.

Dearest of my Heart!

And surely "The Giver of Stars" presents a clearly drawn picture of her companion's serene and loving nature:

Hold your soul open for my welcoming.
Let the quiet of your spirit bathe me
With its clear and rippled coolness,
That, loose-limbed and weary, I find rest,
Outstretched upon your peace, as on a bed of ivory.

Let the flickering flame of your soul play all about me,
That into my limbs may come the keenness of fire,
The life and joy of tongues of flame,
And, going out from you, tightly strung and in tune,
I may rouse the blear-eyed world,
And pour into it the beauty which you have begotten.

Amy felt deeply that Ada Russell's presence in her life-scheme was necessarily responsible for any "beauty" she might be able to "pour into the blear-eyed world," and she experienced a new surge of joy when her friend returned in time for publication date and the flood of reviews that they could gloat over with their close friends. She had already produced enough poems to begin planning publication of her next volume. There was the matter of the Imagist anthology to be arranged; and there were letters and challenges to answer. (Amy did not believe in letting attacks like the one by Ella Wheeler Wilcox in the *Boston American* criticizing "Miss Lowell's language" go unanswered.) Poetry readings were requested, and she received an early offer to give a series of lectures on the French Symbolists the following spring (on the six consecutive Thursdays of Lent), which meant that Ada would be doing considerable research, collecting the books she would need.

Amy could now devote all her free time to writing. She hired two full-time secretaries to handle the preparation of her manuscripts and the enormous literary correspondence that began around this time. She kept in close touch with all the Imagists connected with the new venture, as well as with editors, publishers, and critics. Her daytime schedule, as before, began in the afternoon, but if it had not been for Ada Russell's superb organization and calm supervision, Amy could not have carried out all her diverse activities as thoroughly as she did, and Sevenels would not have run so smoothly. It was Ada who saw to it that the household was kept quiet through the morning hours until Amy's bell rang, the signal that she was ready for her breakfast tray—and for action. Foster Damon wrote with pretty conceit that Sevenels, like an enchanted castle, was "silent and motionless" until that moment, but the truth is that the place hummed with semihushed activity while Amy slept.

Ada usually rose about seven o'clock and was downstairs, dressed, and ready to greet the secretaries at nine. There was usually a sheaf of manuscript poems waiting for them on the hall table, verses Amy was in process of perfecting. Some bore corrections on the draft that had been typed the day before; others were entirely in her handwriting, which had to be deciphered and typed so that she could work on clean versions of them in the evening. There were rarely poems, or even letters, that did not receive three or four revisions and retypings, for "Miss Lowell" was an exacting employer. (Until Ada came, she had been known to raise the roof at two o'clock in the morning if she found an unwashed or cracked plate in the pantry while padding around for a snack to ease her hunger during her nightly work hours; woe betide the domestic who had left it there! Ada convinced her that creating such scenes was beneath her as a basically fair-minded and kindhearted person. There was occasional backsliding on Amy's part, and Ada solved this problem by suggesting that a cold-supper tray be brought to the library and placed on a side table at eleven o'clock, when Amy started to work if there were no guests.* Then she could take it

* Company always stayed until midnight; in fact, nobody was allowed to leave until 12:05 A.M., just in time to make the last trolley to Boston at 12:15.

whenever she felt like eating during the night. The plan worked beautifully.)

Discarded drafts of poems were always found on the library floor in the mornings, as Amy considered that to be the most convenient wastebasket. Every piece of paper lying scattered in front of the hearth—a second, third, or perhaps even a fourth draft—had to be burned by the secretaries before they started typing. Only once was a group of second drafts rescued from the fate of the fireplace by a daring secretary, who gathered them up and hid them in her handbag; they are now in the Lowell files of the Harvard Library. The girls, who also kept accounts, checked bills, and called creditors, worked steadily until twelve-thirty, when they had lunch with Mrs. Russell, a welcome interruption. Ada was always considerate of their likes and dislikes: She would see that the cook prepared their favorite desserts when she could. Served in the dining room by the parlor maid, who doubled as waitress, lunch was the most delightful part of the day for the girls. Mrs. Russell was excellent company, and her stories of the old days in the theater were always entertaining. (Most of Amy's secretaries—and there was a succession of them; only one or two stayed for any length of time—were Radcliffe alumni or graduate students, and at least one had studied for the stage in Professor Baker's English 47 Workshop.* Ada took an interest in the girls' lives and ambitions, and they often confided in her. Then they would return to their typewriters until they were summoned to the upper chamber by the head of the household.

Amy almost always received them while still resting in bed, her breakfast tray on one side, puffing pensively on her first cigar of the day. Often the cook was leaving as they came in, her note pad in hand with jottings of Amy's orders for the day's, or week's, menus. As a parting command, the imperious voice might be calling after her, "And don't forget the after-dinner ginger-and-peppermints tonight!" Only rarely was she up and dressed in the severe

* This was Mary Sands (Mrs. Alexander) Thompson, sister of actress Dorothy Sands; the above and other relevant data of Amy's dealings with her secretaries, given to me in an interview, form the only firsthand record of this facet in the daily life of Amy Lowell at Sevenels.

suit, with a man's collar and stock that she wore for a business appointment, or in the shiny satin with a net collar and lace dickey, her dress if she and Ada were going to a matinee. Usually she was wearing an "innocent blue" dressing gown, like a sixteen-year-old girl's, her hair brushed and pinned in a flat little twist, with no sign of the imposing pompadour. Elizabeth Henry usually helped Amy dress for the day, but it was always Ada who put the crowning touch to the process. When Amy combed her hair, Ada stood behind her, ready to pin on the braided "switch" Amy wore under her pompadour to give her added height, and more body to her naturally fine, thin hair. "God didn't give me much on the outside of my head," she joked to Mary Sands (the secretary who was waiting to take dictation) one day as she puffed up her pompadour over the braid, "but he gave me plenty on the inside!"

She never wasted time in getting down to business, and immediately began dictating letters, personal and professional, and reviewing typed copies of the letters she had dictated the day before. She was as particular about personal notes as she was about everything else—business correspondence, essays, lectures (each of the lectures on the French Symbolists ran to forty typewritten pages), and the prefaces that preceded every book. She never went over the poems with the girls; these were checked during the work hours of the night. She indicated corrections in the margins, or she crossed out and rewrote portions; sometimes she rewrote them completely in longhand. When she felt she had perfected a poem, she would mark it "Final copy," although sometimes even that copy was changed.

How she would have decried the charges made by so many after her death that "Amy was careless"! She accused her beloved Keats of being careless in *Endymion* (which she called "a magnificent failure"); but it is clear that she thought of herself as being meticulous, painstaking, and scholarly. She probably never realized that she *over*wrote, driving herself and others needlessly, in a kind of compulsion to prove the worth of her own and all modern poetry. In doing so, she diminished the portion of her work that was truly art. She questioned the smallest details, the spelling of various words *she* had misspelled to begin with, but she wanted to be sure the correction was correct!

She also quizzed the girls about their other chores. Once she wanted to know if a girl had called S. S. Pierce to protest the charges on her grocery bill; she received the reply that the company had said the bill was correct. "Well, call them again; I know they're overcharging. And don't be afraid to scream at them! After all, they're only tradespeople, even if their name is S. S. Pierce!" she said and laughed. Amy had often screamed at them and other tradespeople. The row over the butcher's bill was a regular event: The nine pounds of beef every day for her "children" cost her sixty dollars a week, more if one of the bitches whelped and puppies from the litters weren't placed as soon as they were weaned. (At one point, there were fifteen barking dogs at Sevenels, seven big ones, and eight smaller ones; during this period a secretary called the place "Seven Hells.") Since Amy paid her bills only once every three years, that amount alone, aside from the dinner-table roasts, ducklings, and other delicacies that she offered her guests, was enormous, and the total always shocked her. She would protest loudly but in vain, and in the end she always sent a check.

After dictation, usually mostly of letters, which Amy, in Mary Sands's words, "dictated like a streak," quickly becoming impatient if she had to repeat a word or phrase, the girls would go back to their typewriters downstairs and work till five. Then the freshly typed manuscripts were neatly piled on the center mahogany table in the library, ready for the nightly creative session. Ada served as a buffer between Amy and the servants and secretaries. It was she who quelled the kitchen quarrels and soothed the ruffled feelings of secretaries, as well as those of guests who objected to Amy's tardy entrances or to the doubtful affection of the sheep dogs. In the afternoons, unless she and Amy had an appointment or went shopping together, she would go to the library to gather books and check research items for Amy. Few knew how much of Amy Lowell's output was due to Ada's quiet assistance. Once, when Nell Belmont was spending the weekend at Sevenels, Ada went into town to the library right after lunch, promising to be back in "a couple of hours." She was not back by the time Amy appeared downstairs and visited with Nell, talking of poems and poetry for more than a "couple of hours" longer, but still Ada did not return. It was growing dark, and Mrs. Belmont began to worry about her friend, but Amy assured her that "Peter" had just lost track of the time. "You know how she is about books—an addict, like me! I'm not worried; she'll soon be along, loaded down." And sure enough, when Ada finally got back, she came in staggering under a huge load of library books, followed by the chauffeur, carrying another load! They all had to laugh.

Ada read proofs for all Amy's books, correcting the galleys carefully. In the evenings, if they were alone together, she listened, head a little to one side, to every composition, poem or essay, before it was declared completed by the author: She was Amy's best and most critical audience, and the burgeoning poet-leader trusted in and abided by her judgment, even if Ada suggested no more than some change in punctuation. Often it was simply her moral support—her being there, sewing or reading—that Amy needed to start the wheels turning in her fertile brain. In those quiet moments, they worked in harmonious unity. Small wonder that Amy thought they should put up a sign just below the Genoese statue of Flora that stood in a niche above the doorway at Sevenels: "Lowell & Russell, Makers of Fine Poems" the sign would say to all the world. Ada would shake her head, laughing, her beautiful, melodious laughter like bells in Amy's ears. She would protest that she was only the associate and chief appreciator of Amy Lowell, poet and specialist in polyphonic prose. "Nonsense!" Amy would probably declare. They were partners in life and art alike; she didn't see why poets, painters, composers—or performing artists like Ada Dwyer and Eleonora Duse—shouldn't make a business of producing art. What better way was there to spend their lives?

In the fall of 1914, the business at hand was to place manuscripts. Amy had promised D. H. Lawrence that she would get after Mitchell Kennerly, the procrastinating, shoddy (if not shady) publisher who had done nothing about bringing out Lawrence's novel, *The Rainbow*, as he had promised. Lawrence had written: ". . . please abuse Mr. Kennerly for me and *please* make him send me some money, even if it is no more than the bad cheque for £10 that he sent me and I sent back." He had not even sent word that he had received the manuscript. The Lawrences' little cottage in Chesham was not so idyllic now that the chill, damp weather had set in, Lawrence had written, and they could not go to their equally small place in Italy because of lack of funds as well as because of the war. (Lawrence was already beginning to suffer from consumption and tried to spend the winter months in a warm or dry climate.) Harriet Monroe had also failed to send him a check for poems she had already accepted. "Nobody will pay me any money," he complained bitterly. He had not been able to write; his nearest approach to poetry had been some first-rate blackberry jelly that he and Frieda had made. He had let Amy know earlier that he needed a typewriter; it would make the submission of manuscripts a lot easier if he had one. So Amy sent him a typewriter she was going to discard—"as I can make this appear that it is of no use to me and he might as well have it," she wrote to Harriet Monroe in a letter urging her to print the Lawrence poems and pay him for them as soon as possible. She did not want to send him money; that would be too close to charity, which, she felt, neither he nor Frieda would accept. And she didn't want to be a Lady Bountiful to, but a colleague of, other poets. The typewriter was a happy solution.

On October 16, 1914, two months after Amy's return from England, Lawrence expressed his joy over the news that she was sending them a typewriter: "I have got quite tipsy with joy. Already my wife and I are pushing each other off the chair and fight as to who shall work it." He wondered when it would come, if it was already on the Atlantic, and "if it will be small enough for me to smuggle into Italy. I always say that my only bit of property in the world is a silver watch, which is true. Now my realm is a typewriter: I am a man of property. I feel quite scared lest I shall have incurred new trouble and new responsibility. But I hope it won't be long in coming.—the typewriter,—not the trouble. unberufen, unberufen.

"By the same post has come a cheque for 50 [pounds], a grant to me from the Royal Literary Fund. But that bores me. There is no joy in their tame, thin-gutted charity. I would fillip it back in their old noses, the stodgy, stomachy authors, if I could afford it. But I can't.

"We are also curiously awaiting your book of poems. You'll see me prowling through your verses like a beast of prey; and oh, the hyaena howl I shall send up when I seize on a lameness. You wait. But for the Lord's sake, don't be modest, and say you'll listen to me. Disclaim me to start with or I won't say anything at all.

"And don't talk about putting me in the safe with Keats and Shelley. It scares me out of my life, like the disciple at the Transfiguration. But I'd like to know Coleridge when Charon has rowed me over." He said it was good of her to see Kennerly, but: "I don't want him ever to publish me anything, ever any more as long as either of us lives. So you can say what you like to him. Pinker, my agent, is anxious to get me free of him, as there is an American publisher wants to make terms with Pinker for me.

"We have had a beautiful, dim autumn, of pale blue atmosphere and white stubble hedges hesitating to change. But I've been seedy and I've grown a red beard behind which I shall take as much cover as I can, like a creature under a bush. My dear God, I've been miserable this autumn, enough to turn into wood, and be a graven image of myself." In a tribute to Ada, he ended: "Greet Mrs. Russell from us. I can feel her good will towards us very real over there."

In a letter of November 18, 1914, Lawrence told Amy that "The typewriter has come, and is splendid. Why did you give it away? I am sure you must have wanted to keep it. But it goes like a bubbling pot, frightfully jolly. My wife sits at it, fascinated, patiently spelling out, at this moment, my war poem.

"Oh—the War Number of 'Poetry' came—I thought it pretty bad. The war-atmosphere has blackened here—it is soaking in, and getting more like part of our daily life, and therefore much grimmer. So I was quite cross with you for writing about bohemian glass and stalks of flame, when the thing is so ugly and bitter to the soul." (The day before, he had written to Harriet Monroe in a rage over the War Number: "how dare Amy talk about Bohemian glass and stalks of flame?"—and, in "a real fury," he had written a war poem, "because it breaks my heart, this war.")

"I like *you* in your poetry. I don't believe in affecting France. I like you when you are straight out. I really liked very much the Precinct, Rochester. There you had a sunny, vivid, intensely still atmosphere that is very true." Then he continued to discuss *Sword Blades,* the poems he did not like, and those he did, including the queries and the advice about "always being herself" in her poetry (already quoted), and adding, "I suppose you think me damned impertinent. But I hate to see you posturing, when there is thereby a real person betrayed in you.

"Please don't be angry with what I say. Perhaps it is really impertinence.

"At any rate, thank you very much for your book of poems, which I like because after all they have a lot of you in them—but how much nicer, finer, bigger you are, intrinsically, than your poetry is. Thank you also very much for the beautiful typewriter, with which both myself and my wife are for the moment bewitched.

"We are still staying on here—scarcely find it possible to move. It is cold, as you predict, but I think quite healthy. I am well, and Frieda is well. I am just finishing a book, supposed to be on Thomas Hardy, but in reality a sort of Confessions of my Heart. I wonder if ever it will come out—& what you'd say to it.

"I wonder if you saw Mitchell Kennerly. Pinker, the agent, is always worrying me about what he is to do with the American publishing of the novel Kennerly holds at present, in MS. Tell me if you saw him, will you.

"We are not so sad any more: it was perhaps a mood, brought on by the war, and the English autumn. Now the days are brief but very beautiful: a big red sun rising and setting upon a pale, bluish, hoar-frost world. It is very beautiful. The robin comes onto the door-step now, to watch me as I write. Soon he will come indoors. Then it will be mid-winter.

"I wish the war were over and gone. I will not give in to it. We who shall live after it are more important than those who fall.

"Give our very warm regards to Mrs. Russell. Saluti di cuore, Tante belle cose from my wife to you and to Mrs. Russell."

A month later, December 18, 1914, one of his most brilliant and graphic letters came from Lawrence. Commenting on the depressed tone of a letter he had just received from her, he comforted her about critics being "stupid": "But there, they are always like that, the little critics. If the critics are not less than the authors they criticise, they will at once burst into equal authorship. And being less than the authors they criticise, they must diminish these authors. For no critic can admit anything bigger than himself. And we are all, therefore, no bigger than our little critics. So don't be sad. The work one has done with all one's might is as hard as a rock, no matter how much one suffers the silly slings and arrows in one's silly soft flesh.

"Thank you very much for going to Mitchell Kennerly for me. I hope you were not serious when you say that in so doing you have spoiled the 'Forum' for yourself as a publishing field. Is Kennerly indeed such a swine? As for what he owes me—he does not send it, even if it is only ten pounds. I haven't kept proper accounts with him, because Duckworth made the agreement and all that. I will write to them. I will also write to Pinker, to see what he can do. I *must* get the novel out of Kennerly's hands that he has in MS.

"I am re-writing it. It will be called *The Rainbow*. When it is done, I think really it will be a fine piece of work.

"My book of short stories is out. I am sending you a copy. I don't think it is doing very well. The critics really hate me. So they ought.

"My wife and I type away at my book on Thomas Hardy, which has turned out as a sort of Story of my Heart, or a Confessio Fidei: which I must write again, still another time: and for which the critics will plainly beat me, as a Russian friend says.

"It is Christmas in a week today. I'm afraid you may not get this letter in time: which is a pity. We shall be in this cottage. We shall have a little party at Christmas Eve. I at once begin to prick my ears when I think of it. We shall have a great time, boiling ham and roasting chicken and drinking Chianti in memory of Italy. There will be eight of us, all nice people. We shall enjoy ourselves afterwards up in the attico—you wait. I shall spend 25/— on the spree, and do it quite rarely.

"England is getting real thrills out of the war, at last. Yesterday and today there is the news of the shelling of Scarboro. I tell you the whole country is thrilled to the marrow, and enjoys it like hot punch.—I shall make punch at our Christmas Eve party, up in the attico with a Primus stove.

"We have been in the Midlands seeing my people, and Frieda seeing her husband. He did it in the thorough music-hall fashion. It was a surprise visit. When we were children, and used to play at being grand, we put an old discarded hearthrug in the wheelbarrow, and my sister, perched there in state, 'at home,' used to be 'Mrs. Lawson,' and I, visiting with a walking stick, was 'Mr. Marchbanks.' We'd been laughing about it, my sister and I. So Frieda, in a burst of inspiration, announced herself to the landlady as 'Mrs. Lawson.'

" 'You—' said the quondam husband, backing away—'I hoped never to see you again.'

"Frieda: 'Yes—I know.'

"Quondam Husband: 'And what are you doing in *this* town?'

"Frieda: 'I came to see about the children.'

"Quondam Husband: 'Aren't you ashamed to show your face where you are known! Isn't the commonest prostitute better than you?'

"Frieda: 'Oh no.'

"Quon. Husb.: 'Do you want to drive me off the face of the earth, Woman? Is there no place where I can have peace?'

"Frieda: 'You see I must speak to you about the children.'

"Quon. Husb.: 'You shall *not* have them. They don't want to see you.'

"Then the conversation developed into a deeper tinge of slanging—part of which was:

"Q.H.: '*If* you had to go away, why didn't you go away with a *gentleman*?'

"Frieda: 'He is a *great* man.'

"Further slanging.

"Q. Husb.: 'Don't you know you are the vilest creature on earth?'

"Frieda: 'Oh no.'

"A little more of such, and a departure of Frieda. She is no further to seeing her children.

"Q. Husb.: 'Don't you know my solicitors have instructions to arrest you, if you attempt to interfere with the children?'

"Frieda: 'I don't care.'

"If this weren't too painful, dragging out for three years as it does, it would be very funny I think. The Quondam Husband is a Professor of French Literature, great admirer of Maupassant, has lived in Germany and Paris, and thinks he is the tip of cosmopolitan culture. But poor Frieda can't see her children.—I really give you the conversation verbatim.

"It is very rainy and very dark. I shall try to get back to Italy at the end of January.

"Give my sincere sympathy to Mrs. Russell. I hope things aren't going very badly with her." Ada was then in mourning for her father, who had just died, and she was planning to go to Salt Lake City to be with her ailing mother, a situation that was the principal cause of Amy's depression. Lawrence signed his letter, which must have been a real diversion for Amy during her anxious moments, by sending, "All Christmas greetings to you." And as an afterthought: "I do wish we might have a Christmas party together. I feel like kicking everything to the devil and enjoying myself willy-nilly—a wild drunk and a great and rowdy spree."

Frieda added a rather long note, with Wagnerian overtones, leading off with Amy's seeing Kennerly for them. "Don't bother any more, only he is not going to have the new novel—Lawrence hates the whole business. He shouts at me every time he thinks of it. I feel a grudge against Kennerly—not only has he done me out of 25 pounds, but every time Lawrence thinks of *Kennerly,* he gets in a rage at *me,* the logic of men and husbands. You know about my nice children, and what I have had to go through. I wish I could tell you all about it, you are so big-hearted, we think of you with great affection, one of the few oasis in this desert world! We will go to Italy soon—as soon as we have a little money."

On a business trip to New York, after writing a review of Edwin Arlington Robinson's new book, *Van Zorn, A Comedy,* for the *Boston Herald* and presenting the first Gebhard concert of the season at Sevenels, Amy approached two prominent publishing houses. One of them was then her own publisher, Macmillan, where she went, with little success, on behalf of *Some Imagist Poets,* Robert Frost's *North of Boston,* John Gould Fletcher's *Irradia-*

tions, and to make arrangements for a new volume of her own. In Boston, she sought out her first publisher, Houghton Mifflin, and convinced Ferris Greenslet that the poetry renaissance in the United States was on the rise. He accepted the Imagist anthology at once, as well as Fletcher's *Irradiations;* in addition, she persuaded him that he should issue a New Poetry series, small volumes of various poets' work, bound in paper covers like the little French books sold in the stalls along the Seine; it would cut costs way down. They compromised on cardboard, and eight volumes of the series were published in 1915. Nor did she forget to track down the elusive Mr. Kennerly, from whom she extracted a promise that Lawrence's novel would be published as soon as he could arrange a date for it with the printer.*

She also tried to do something for Remy de Gourmont, perhaps the most famous poet of the Symbolist school, and one of those on whom she was going to lecture. Ruined by the war, he was ill as well as penniless, Aldington had written. Amy, who had met and liked the man as much as his poetry, was extremely sympathetic. She broke her rule and, through Aldington, sent him $200, which she insisted must be anonymous; and she persuaded the editors of a magazine just then coming into being, the *New Republic,* to commission six articles from de Gourmont on the current state of literature in France. At the same time, she asked—"nay, demanded," as she wrote later—that she review Robert Frost's *North of Boston* for the new magazine. She had made the same request of the *Atlantic Monthly,* but Ellery Sedgwick had turned her down as well as some poems Frost had sent him. He later regretted both rejections, particularly the latter, since the same poems, which the *Atlantic* later printed, cost much more after Amy Lowell's review of *North of Boston,* which had much to do with making Frost's second volume a best seller in poetry. Ferris Greenslet had been considering publication of the volume in the New Poetry series, but while he was deliberating, they all learned that Henry Holt was going to publish the book in hard cover.

* Kennerly had already acquired a reputation for dishonorable practices, but was undaunted, and kept on bluffing his way until the early 1920s. Edna St. Vincent Millay was another of his victims.

Amy Lowell did all she could for those in whose poetry she believed, and although her judgment was far from infallible, it served her well in the case of Robinson, Frost, and D. H. Lawrence, whose worth she realized before it was recognized by any but a few readers. John Gould Fletcher a poet whose genius not only she but Pound and Harriet Monroe overestimated, returned to the United States about this time, and Amy, meeting him in New York, invited him to spend a week at Sevenels; they could work on the preparation of *Some Imagist Poets*. In December she gave her first public reading before a large audience. Josephine Preston Peabody, who had written an early enthusiastic review of *Sword Blades,* was organizing a program at Steinert Hall as part of the Belgian War Relief. She and Amy would recite their poetry, and Hans Ebel, a young Russian pianist, would play.

Amy was only too glad to participate. She felt she was qualified to read her poetry better than anyone else; and with Ada to coach her concerning voice projection and modulation, she decided to make the most of the occasion. Josephine generously placed her first on the program, and Amy selected a generous sampling of her work: fourteen poems, some of them quite long, listed as "Narratives and Adventures"; these were followed by "Lyrics," "Images," and "War Poems." The finale, completing the last group, was a dramatic narrative in polyphonic prose she had recently completed, a graphic description of a city under the relentless hail of bombs during a heavy rainfall. Starting with bombing of a cathedral, there is a kaleidoscopic shifting of scenes, each punctuated by a roaring "Boom!" as the bombs hit * and the flames flare up. As Amy was reading the poem aloud a few days before the recital, she said she was afraid that the "Booms!" wouldn't have the proper effect she intended. Either Carl Engel, who may have been present then, or Amy herself came up with the idea of having "Bibi" stand concealed behind a backdrop onstage and beat on a bass drum to simulate the sound of a cannon, accompanying her "Booms!" (At one point, there were three in a row.) Ada rehearsed them together to make sure he came in on cue; and the night of the performance,

* An old lady's living room, a frightened child's bedroom, a dedicated scientist's laboratory, and so forth.

the poem was a stunning success—a true "holocaust of noise and terror," Amy termed it. The performance marked the beginning of Amy Lowell's superb showmanship on the lecture and recital platform; neither her friendly rival, Josephine, nor the pale young Russian pianist could hope to compete with her success!

Other appearances followed shortly. She and Robert Haven Schauffler, a well-known poet and critic, were invited to the December meeting of the Twentieth Century Club to discuss "The Failure of American Poetry and Its Remedy." Schauffler declared that this failure was due to the economic struggle most poets had to endure and held that subsidy of poets was the remedy. Amy disagreed on two counts. She did not think that American poetry had failed. It had been stagnant for a generation, but it was rapidly renewing its vigor. And though the economic struggle was real enough, she felt that doing some work was beneficial for any artist. "There is more danger of pampering weaklings than of breaking great men!" she said in ringing tones that brought both hisses and applause, and provided fodder for an alert reporter. Hers was a strictly capitalist view, inherited from her father, and Schauffler had Socialist leanings. Amy did agree with Schauffler that the overall attitude of the public was "simply abominable" toward anything new in art. Her emphatic, forthright delivery of such sweeping statements gave them an authority and invested them with drama as well as news value, accelerating her rise to fame. Ada's advice concerning the proper way to move and maintain an upright but unstrained posture onstage added to her poise before audiences, and her own experience in home theatricals stood her in good stead.

She was still active in theater projects, the latest being an opéra bouffe production of Rostand's *Pierrot Qui Pleure* and *Pierrot Qui Rit,* which she had translated along with the text of another short French light opera. The production was to benefit the Women's Municipal League, of which her sister Katie was president. They planned to hire a public hall in Boston and to ask the renowned Maggie Teyte to sing the lead. And Amy, besides acting as translator and chairman of the artistic committee, had offered to underwrite the production. The inner circle of "the

Devils," to which Magdeleine Carret, a French teacher at Wellesley College, had been added, was involved all during the fall and early winter of 1914–15 with the details of putting together this unusual operatic offering that was planned to be both an artistic and a financial success.

Meanwhile, further trouble cropped up over the title of the Imagist anthology, which was almost ready for the press. Pound, who apparently did not know that Houghton Mifflin was publishing it instead of Macmillan, had written a scathing attack on the latter house, which he planned to publish in *The Egoist* (the English "little magazine" of new literature, run by some of the same group connected with Amy's). Aldington, one of its editors, stopped the article by threatening to resign. Pound evidently resented Amy's takeover of the Imagist movement in America, though she had made it plain she was *not* the editor of the anthology but merely the coordinator of a cooperative venture, and she had given Pound credit in the preface for initiating the *Imagiste* movement in England. Ezra was not mollified, and Ford (who had withdrawn) thought they should drop the name "Imagist" from the American anthology. Aldington came up with the title "Some Twentieth Century Poets," and H. D. with "The Six." Amy was in a quandary about the matter, so, for the moment, she deferred action.

Another commotion was caused by the fact that Remy de Gourmont's first two articles were so pale and devoid of interest that the editors at the *New Republic* did not want to publish them, and Amy could hardly blame them. She felt sorry for the French writer who had once been so dynamic;* she knew he was terribly ill, but she was still disappointed, and, with her usual forthrightness, was honest about it: "There wasn't a damned thing in it that any tyro could not have written," she wrote to Aldington, who was furious (de Gourmont was his idol), and she sent a hot letter to Herbert Croly, of the *New Republic.* The Crolys were personal friends of Amy's, and the whole tempest in the literary teapot embarrassed her. It also put her in a pivotal position of the poetry-

* He was considered risqué, partly for the Gallicisms in his poetry, partly for his book, *Les Amazones,* dealing with lesbians.

storm center on both sides of the Atlantic. In England, and to some extent in America, such battles were being waged as a diversion from the very real and tragic battles threatening to rage in Europe for a much longer time than anyone had expected. And the conflict kept her name constantly before the literary enclaves of the Western world.

In addition to everything else, Amy was toying with the idea of trying to secure a post for herself comparable with Pound's on *Poetry* magazine. When the *New Republic* consented to her writing a review of Robert Frost's book, she immediately suggested that she become poetry editor for the new periodical, but she was as quickly turned down. Undaunted, she decided to contact Margaret Anderson, the very young editor of still another new "little magazine," recently founded in Chicago, which was called in fact the *Little Review*. It differed from *Poetry* by specializing in the experimental, and it advertised that it "made no compromise with the public taste," so it seemed to Amy just the place for her. She knew that Margaret Anderson, like Harriet Monroe, was in need of funds to continue publishing: Like *Poetry,* the *Little Review* had, with its prospectus, solicited both poems and money from Amy Lowell.

Amy sent some poems with a note to Miss Anderson telling her that she was coming to Chicago and wanted to discuss the possibility of becoming the magazine's poetry editor. On January 4, 1915, she and Ada left on the *Twentieth Century* for the Windy City, where Amy took a suite in a hotel. She wasted no time in going to see the attractive young editor, who described her visitor's manner as "somewhat more masterful" than a Roman emperor's, whose first words were: "I've had a fight with Ezra Pound." Naturally she received Margaret Anderson's rapt attention. The editor's quotation of her caller's monologue hardly sounds like Amy Lowell, but her conclusion was quite accurate: "I gathered that she wanted to subsidize modern poetry and push it ahead faster than it could go by its own impetus. A little review would be a helpful organ for such a purpose," Miss Anderson wrote in her autobiography, *My Thirty Years' War.*

Amy's directness charmed and disarmed her, but not to the

point of accepting the offer of $150 a month for the poetry editorship of the *Little Review.* "No clairvoyance was needed to know that Amy Lowell would dictate, uniquely and majestically, any adventure in which she had a part," she said in her account of the meeting. Without hesitation, she said she "could not think of it." When Amy demanded to know her reasons, she answered: "I have only one. I can't function in 'association.'" Of Amy's reaction, she wrote: "Amy was furious. She argued and implored. . . . But she had a redeeming trait—when she was finally convinced that I meant what I said she dropped the subject and never reverted to it."

Furthermore, it was like Amy to admire the tenacity with which Margaret Anderson steadfastly refused her offer, and she promptly invited the young editor to lunch the next day. Just as she had been pleased long ago when her playmates shouted, "Shut up, Amy Lowell!" so she felt a certain kinship with those who stood up to her now; and, as Miss Anderson also remarked in her autobiography, in describing Amy's appearance: "Culture and good taste were stamped upon her." If feelings of urgency often caused her to attack a project precipitously, she was keen enough to know when to subside and shrewd enough to realize that she must not make an enemy out of anyone who was willing to publish the new poetry,* especially her own.

During their stay in Chicago, Harriet Monroe gave a poets' party for Amy, at which Carl Sandburg, Edgar Lee Masters, Vachel Lindsay, and other midwestern poets were present. She and Ada had met the Sandburgs previously and had spent "two good evenings" with them before leaving for London in July.** An immediate rapport had sprung up between Sandburg and Amy Lowell, which was to develop into a lasting friendship, but she never felt quite at home with either Masters or Lindsay, although both poets were among the principals she discussed in her volume, *Tenden-*

* In the course of its years of publication, the *Little Review* published poems by all the poets originally scoffed at, including, besides Amy and her Imagists, James Joyce, Gertrude Stein, Wallace Stevens, e. e. cummings, Marianne Moore, as well as Frost, Robinson, and Yeats, and others less experimental. It also printed Joyce's *Ulysses* serially.

** From a letter to Engel, written from the Berkeley Hotel, July 1914.

cies in Modern American Poetry, and she had great respect for *The Spoon River Anthology.*

Amy still had hopes of making a connection with some literary publication, but her many other pressing interests did not allow her time to pursue these hopes persistently. If Ada sometimes cautioned her friend to slow down, Amy would answer, "Peter, dear, I can't! There's too much to be done, and too little time!" Nearing forty-one, she considered herself middle-aged, and although Ada was eleven years older, Amy acted as if she were the senior partner in their alliance. Whether she had any premonition that her days were numbered is hard to say, but a feeling of urgency seemed to be driving her even more now than before, and Ada was wise enough not to argue with her about her multiple activities. From Chicago they went to New York for a few days of singers' rehearsals of her opera librettos; and when they returned to Brookline about January 15, a welter of correspondence showed that the Imagists were still stewing over the title of their anthology, which was already in press. Fletcher agreed with some of the others that the name should be dropped from the title, suggesting "Allies" in its place, along with a fighting foreword. At Houghton Mifflin, Ferris Greenslet brought up "Quintessentialists," which Amy thought delightful but too esoteric.

Cables and letters flew back and forth in the flurry, but the problem was finally solved by F. S. Flint, whose letters pointed out that Pound "had no more invented Imagism" than he had the moon; the most he had done was to give a name to an order that had existed for a long time. In fact, Pound was a latecomer to the old Thursday meetings started by T. E. Hulme, when they talked of nothing but the *image,* and Pound had added *nothing* to those meetings. And it came out now that Pound had been loath to let Flint in on the "secret" of the *Imagiste* "doctrine," although Flint himself had been one of its inventors! (Amy was glad to learn that she was not the only one who had been excluded from learning the "secret," the existence of which she had doubted for some time.) Flint called for a history of the movement in a preface that would put Pound in his place. With such ammunition from Flint's sector, Aldington urged Amy to "go ahead in the name of God and

St. George!" The publisher advised her to leave the title intact; her decision regarding the preface was to strike out all references to Pound and to keep the rest without change.

Next, she and Ada plunged into the final rehearsal period for the light opera. Besides Maggie Teyte, there were two noted tenors from the Metropolitan Opera and a thirty-five-piece orchestra drawn from the Boston Opera Company; Professor Arthur Shepherd, from the New England Conservatory of Music, conducted. Costumes and scenery were designed by Livingston Platt, a foremost American costume and stage designer; Berkeley Updike was in charge of the tickets, invitations, and programs at his Merrymount Press. With such lavish preparations, paid for in advance by Amy, everyone looked forward to large crowds and a respectable profit for the Municipal League. However, nature conspired against the venture, sending the worst blizzard Boston had seen in generations: It snowed for the entire run, February 2, 3, and 4. Trolley cars stopped running; few people budged from their fireplaces, even to hear Maggie Teyte; and the performances, on a high plane artistically, were a dismal financial failure. Katie was heartbroken, since she had initiated the project for the benefit of her beloved league. Amy comforted her sister, disappointed as she also was, and took the fiasco philosophically by throwing herself into the preparation of her lectures on the French poets.

Her greatest regret over the thousands of dollars she lost was that she could not take advantage of an offer that came to her in the midst of this situation through Aldington and George Plank (designer for *Vogue*) to collaborate on launching a new magazine. It was just the sort of publishing set-up she had been seeking—and now she was quite sure she could not afford it. (True to Bostonian upper-class tradition and to her father's hard-businessman outlook, Amy Lowell would not dip into capital for an uncertain venture; she couldn't prevent the snowstorm, but she did have control over her bank account.)

On the matter of Remy de Gourmont's articles for the *New Republic,* Amy remained firm: They were too elementary for the new, liberal, idealistic magazine. "If you warn a Frenchman about his 'Gallicisms' [as she had warned de Gourmont] he can't write about anything!" she wrote to Aldington. The articles would have to be rewritten; she was preparing a lecture on de Gourmont, and she had great respect for his writing as a French Symbolist, but Americans were not on a kindergarten level as readers, at least not those of the *New Republic.* She had persuaded Herbert Croly to send a check for all six articles in advance in order to assist de Gourmont, and she felt some responsibility for the quality of the material. In the end, through Ferris Greenslet, the *Boston Transcript* (whose readers were not so intellectual) took over the whole series, paying the same rate for them, and the *New Republic* check was returned. Her conscience eased, Amy settled down and slaved away for the next eight weeks, preparing each lecture as its turn came up. Even with Ada to gather needed material from the library, it was a terrible strain.

She worked "nine, ten, eleven, sometimes fifteen hours a day," she wrote Magdeleine, preparing for the first one on February 18, and almost as long, on each subsequent one. An hour-long speech required forty pages of typewritten script, and more than once her secretary would hand her the last typed pages just as she was stepping into the car to leave. And she also had to be up, dressed, and out by midday. She admitted that "real systematic study" was a terrible strain on a temperament like hers. "Since I began to do these lectures I understand why I was so rotten in school," she wrote candidly in the letter to Magdeleine Carret. She had never felt obliged to "bother with silly dates in chronological order and similar details before." However, as the series proved highly successful, even to the point where her reading of Paul Fort's "Chant des Anglais" moved her listeners to tears at the final lecture, she felt that the whole undertaking was worthwhile. Moreover, in the process of preparing the lectures she had accumulated the first draft of a book that needed very little rewriting.

CHAPTER XI

The Road Taken

TWO DAYS AFTER the first lecture, on February 20, 1915, Amy Lowell's review of Robert Frost's *North of Boston* appeared in the *New Republic,* and indirectly marked a turning point in both of their careers.

Nearly every biographer of Robert Frost * has told the story of his return from England with his family, all of them trudging up from the West Street docks after landing in New York that bleak February day in 1915. On an impulse he stopped at a newsstand, where he chanced to see the issue of the *New Republic.* He bought a copy out of curiosity and discovered Amy Lowell's long review of his second volume of poems. It was a good review, though he had a few quarrels with it, the main one being that he "lacked humor"; but it was intelligent, solid criticism, which had the ring of authority. (This was largely because Amy felt on solid ground in reviewing "the uncompromising New Englander" revealed in the book, one she considered, in her closing words, "a book of unusual power and sincerity.") The piece "seemed like a welcome to his native land," Frost told her later; and his daughter, Lesley Frost Ballantine, said in 1973: "Why, if it hadn't been for Amy's review we wouldn't have known the book was out, or who had published it!"

However, neither Frost nor most people who saw the article

* Including the present author, in the first biography following Frost's death, *Robert Frost: The Aim Was Song* (New York: Dodd, Mead & Company, 1964).

realized that Amy still felt like "a mere struggler" herself, battling her way to recognition. Nor did they know that this review was to be instrumental in establishing Amy Lowell's reputation as a critic and leading literary figure when *North of Boston* became a best seller in poetry. As she said much later (March 5, 1925), "I believe I was the first to proclaim the book's amazing quality on this side of the water." (Pound had reviewed it in the December issue of *Poetry* but was much briefer in his discussion than he had been in his earlier article on Frost and *A Boy's Will.*)

About a week after the notice appeared, Amy received a phone call, and a laconic voice said: "I am Robert Frost; I want to see you; I have read your review." Amy lost no time in inviting him to Sevenels for dinner; John Gould Fletcher was spending the week there again, helping to proofread the galleys and tend to last-minute details of the Imagist anthology, which was to be released in April, so there would be a poetry evening. Frost and Fletcher did not have much to say to each other, but for Amy Lowell and Robert Frost the meeting was the beginning of a kind of sparring friendship, a mixture of admiration, rivalry, and wit—"which, on my part," Amy was to say in her future tribute—"has been an ever increasing admiration of his work, and a profound attachment to the man." (For all that, she was not above saying openly, "Oh, I wish I could beat Frost in having a best seller just once!") The San Francisco-born but heritage-bound New Englander, although only six weeks younger than his hostess, looked at least ten years her junior. He was a handsome man, whose sculptured head and classic features, with his deep-set blue eyes, penetrating yet dream filled, caused Elizabeth Sergeant to call him "a good Greek out of New Hampshire." * His manner was most appealing to both Amy and Ada: Admittedly aware that he was more or less on trial, he was quiet, but by no means shy. If he found the food too abundant as the meal progressed from oysters through soup, fish, meat, salad, dessert, and fruit, and the wine (except for the traditional sherry with the soup) too free-flowing,

* Elizabeth Shepley Sergeant, *Fire Under the Andes* (1926; reprinted, 1966, by Kenikut Press). The book also contains a portrait of Amy Lowell, written long before Sergeant's full-length biography of Frost. She met both poets while on the staff of the *New Republic,* c. 1917, and became fast friends of both.

he enjoyed the dinner-table talk his hostess offered in equal abundance. She was as sparkling as her cut-glass crystal and polished silver (on which an electric buffer was used, Amy once told Jean Untermeyer). When he knew her better, Frost would twit her about these "cut-glass" affairs. Now he fiddled with his food and partook with genuine, if amused, gusto of the talk generously dispensed by this genial autocrat of the dinner table. Afterward, in the library, the conversation positively crackled in competition with the fire on the great hearth. (The fire was lighted by Amy in a kind of ritual, with pitch-pine splinters, after she had adjusted, with a feminine hand, the specially made light shields suspended over every lamp shade. With masculine joviality, she lit up one of her little Manilas and saw that cigars and cigarettes were passed around. This was followed by the ritual of the feeding and fondling of the dogs.)

Whether or not she knew that Robert Frost was one of the all-time great talkers of the literary world, Amy took him on without hesitation in her zeal to convince him that he was at heart an Imagist, at least in his use of language, his choice of the "exact word," one of Imagism's basic tenets. Frost agreed with her on that point, but said he wanted no part of the Imagists' vaunted free verse; and they argued about the relative merits of what Amy called "cadence" and the confines of meter. She had pointed out in her review that "he writes in classic metre in a way to set the teeth of all the poets of older schools on edge." Now, with the pungency that Elsie Sergeant was to call "that forthright, buccaneering maleness of hers, that 18th century gusto for meeting and defeating others in talk," * she attempted to prove that cadence was much more effective than meter and that *his* variety of blank verse was merely a step away from cadence and free verse.

Frost probably laughed at her and remarked that he was only "riding easy in harness." And when she demanded an explanation, he discovered that she was also a good listener, for as he expanded on his theory of creativity in poetry—seeing how much liberty he could take and yet keep within the confines of the iamb—she kept still, her alert eyes intently on his face. And she answered intelli-

* In the aforementioned "Portrait" of Amy in *Fire Under the Andes.*

gently, if stubbornly, insisting that he could join with them anyhow in educating the public to the new poetry. He countered by saying that was *her* job—she had been quick enough to take it away from Pound! Now and then Fletcher put in a word, but for the most part he and Ada were content to let the discussion remain a duo, enjoying the duel of wits. The sparks that flew did not always come from the fireplace.

In fact, the only time Frost had a chance to talk to the other two came when Ada remarked that despite the slender four-foot logs Amy had occasionally added to the fire (lifting them easily, since they were cut to a thinness of four inches in diameter so she could replenish the fire while she worked during the night), the February winds were coming through the casement windows. Even the blast of the heated discussion didn't take the chill off the library.

"You're right, Peter! Something must be wrong with 'Matilda!' " Amy agreed. And she rose from her armchair in a cloud of cigar smoke to pad down cellar like a man to look after the furnace ("Matilda"), perhaps adjusting the drafts or shaking down the coals. "Matilda" had a perfectly capable attendant, but Amy felt she knew her household better than anybody, Ada explained, laughing.

When she returned, Amy might have some behind-the-scenes story to tell, and she could make a hilarious tale out of an ordinary mishap; or she might take up the argument where they left off; or, with her insatiable curiosity about books, plunge into some entirely different aspect of writing and literature. At any rate, she and Robert Frost formed a lively friendship which soon included his whole family, and, in spite of sundry disagreements, was based on their common interest in writing new and vital poetry. As he wrote to her in August from Littleton, New Hampshire, "the great thing is that you and I and some of the rest of us have landed with both feet on all the little chipping poetry of a while ago. We have busted 'em up, as with cavalry. We have, we have, we have! Yes, I like your book, and all I lay up against you is that you will not allow me a sense of humor. . . ."

The book Frost referred to was the first anthology of *Some*

Imagist Poets, which was finally published in April, and just before its appearance, was the cause of Amy's first public row over Imagism at a Poetry Society meeting in New York. Following the whirlwind schedule Amy had set for herself, she gave the last of the French-poet lectures on March 25; assembled to give to Macmillan as a manuscript for a possible book; and arranged with Jessie Rittenhouse, secretary of the Poetry Society of America, to give a five-minute reading from the forthcoming Imagist anthology. She was determined to plug her poets in every way, and on March 30 she and Ada left for New York, primed for presentation, but hardly for the battle which followed the five minutes allotted to her at the end of the program. She was preceded by a discussion and reading of Edgar Lee Masters's *Spoon River Anthology,* a work almost as free in both form and content as the Imagists' compositions; but Hamlin Garland and Richard Burton, who presented Masters's work, were so skillful in conducting their discussion of their selections that even the society's most conventional members warmly applauded their rendering of the "novel," as Amy called it.

She, however, opened her "five minutes" with a highly provocative discussion of Imagist principles that was so bristling from the outset it stirred the society's conservatives to action, gearing them for rebuttal. Then, in giving example, she opened by reading "Bath," the first of five poems in polyphonic prose constituting a narrative, "Spring Day," from her new volume. The work depicts the poet's activities from morning till night; it is one of her most successful short works in this medium, a delicious, playful, and sensuous poem, beginning:

> The day is fresh-washed and fair, and there is a smell of tulips and narcissus in the air. . . .

The third paragraph reads:

> Little spots of sunshine lie on the surface of the water and dance, dance, and their reflections wobble deliciously over the ceiling; a stir of my finger sets them whirring, reeling. I move a foot, and the planes of light in the water jar. I lie back and laugh, and let the green-white water, the sun-flawed beryl water, flow over me. The day is almost too

bright to bear, the green water covers me from the too bright day. I will lie here awhile and play with the water and the sun spots.

The bath scene closes with the next short paragraph:

> The sky is blue and high. A crow flaps by the window, and there is a whiff of tulips and narcissus in the air.

The poem then moves on to describe the "Breakfast Table" in the next polyphonic-prose scene; "Walk," in the third (during the course of which she remarks significantly, "I smell tulips and narcissus in the air, but there are no flowers anywhere"); then on to "Midday and Afternoon," and finally, "Night and Sleep."

But taken out of context as it was, "Bath," projecting an image of Amy's obese nude body cavorting in her huge bathtub, produced gasps and continuing waves of literary chortles. Though she kept on reading, it is doubtful if any of the right wingers present listened to or cared about what the rest of "Spring Day" was like. Nor did they grasp the finely etched love lyric, "Venus Transiens," recently written lines of restrained, yet eloquent emotion, with the quiet opening that is both a question and statement; which she gave as an example of free verse:

> Tell me,
> Was Venus more beautiful
> Than you are,
> When she topped
> The crinkled waves,
> Drifting shoreward
> On her plaited shell?
> Was Botticelli's vision
> Fairer than mine; . . .

It was of this passage that John Livingston Lowes, professor of literature at Harvard and source biographer of Coleridge, was to write (in *Essays in Appreciation*): "If these eight lines of 'Venus Transiens' were the only fragment left of an unknown poet, we should recognize that the draftsmanship which wrought their cool, controlled and shining beauty was unique." But at the March meeting of the Poetry Society that beauty fell on deaf ears. Nor did the audience pay much attention to samples from other Imagists' work included in the anthology, like the classic "Oread" by H. D., or one of John Gould Fletcher's "Irradiations."

As soon as she stopped reading, Amy Lowell was attacked from right, left, and center by a barrage of hostile questions from the audience, its members evidently forgetting the society's rule that poems by guests were not supposed to be discussed. Amy was at this point still an outsider—and a Boston Brahmin to boot. It was true that most of the questions came from conservatives, demanding to know if this was supposed to be poetry, but many came from moderates as well; and almost all had to do with the first section of "Spring Day." Ripples of "Bath" kept spreading through the turbulent discussion. They spilled over into the press the next day, providing hilarious copy as news then, and, for a couple of years afterward, provided a dependably risible and risqué item for columnists from coast to coast—eventually to Amy's annoyance. She must have realized beforehand the effect that this poem would have; in fact, she admitted as much to her intimates, as she felt a triumphant pleasure at first. She had defended her poetry, and poets of her persuasion, singlehanded, and she had stood her ground firmly: perhaps too firmly. Part of the reason for the uncalled-for ruckus may have been that though the New Yorkers—with the exception of Jessie Rittenhouse—had heard of Amy Lowell, they had not seen her, and probably expected her to be a sylphlike, frail, nerve-wracked, intense creature instead of the amazonian chieftain who rose majestically to read what seemed at the time a shocking poem. Perhaps because of her very bulk the effect of it was almost as shocking as if she had actually appeared in her bathtub in public; the uproar was an unconscious tribute to her ability for making things "real" in her poetry.* They could not know—and many never did know—that hers was a highly intense, nerve-wracked, and passionate nature, inwardly, if not outwardly, extremely fragile and sensitive.

The truth is that "Bath" is neither as sensational nor innocuous, nor is it as harmless and childish as its friends and de-

* S. Foster Damon, in discussing *Dome,* her first volume, remarked that its value lay in having "real things in it, real flowers and real weather." *Amy Lowell, A Chronicle* (Boston: Houghton Mifflin Company, 1935).

tractors implied. (An interesting sidelight is that Amy's friends and enemies both made light of the poem for the opposing ends of defending and attacking her, respectively.) On the surface, that "green-white . . . sun-flawed beryl" bathwater describes the sheer pleasure of bathing on a bright spring morning with the sun pouring in the window; but surely it was not by accident that the flowers the poet picked to mention there, and through the other parts of "Spring Day," were tulips and the narcissus, especially since, it must be remembered, no flowers were in bloom yet. Amy Lowell knew her legends too well not to realize the significance of narcissus and the water. The self-hate she expressed in her diary and in devious ways in her poems is the other side of the coin of self-love, often born of it. Anyone who has a physical deformity or handicap loves as much as loathes the body that inflicts so much distress. Amy's background had given her a generous portion of self-love which overpowered the self-hate much of the time, and this poem is an example of it. Luckily, her ego was almost as large as her body, and this, coupled with Ada Russell's devoted love and understanding, kept her from self-destruction, a fate which overtook several of her colleagues whose physical attributes were far more blessed than hers. Her close friend and cosponsor of Imagism, John Gould Fletcher, was one; Sara Teasdale, soon to become a member of her inner circle of kindred spirits, and Vachel Lindsay, an associate in the new poetry movement, were two more; and there were a number of others who could not manage their inner stress as well as she.

Before they returned to Brookline, Amy reviewed the manuscript of *Six French Poets* with Magdeleine Carret to make sure of her French spelling of proper names and colloquial phrases. Then she gave it to the editorial board at Macmillan for consideration as a book. And, already regarded as an authority, she was invited to speak at the Round Table Club on "The New Manner in Modern Poetry," a lecture treating of both past and present.* Part of the speech was published in the *New Republic* and served as

* Her reference to Emily Dickinson as "the precursor of the modern day . . . so modern that if she were living today I know just the group of poets with which she would inevitably belong," is typical of Amy's constant promotion of the Imagists.

forerunner of a later book, *Tendencies in Modern American Poetry* (1917). She ended neatly by promoting *Some Imagist Poets,* which was released on April 17.

Of the 750 copies in the first edition, 481 were sold in advance, an excellent showing for a book of verses by relatively unknown poets. Each of the six poets—three British and three American—made his own selections, which were subject to veto by the others. The feature that made the anthology different from most was its provocative preface, written by Aldington but tinkered with and revised by everyone. In its final form, containing the soon to be famous 1915 Imagist credo, the preface seemed no more than logical to its creators, who stated that their aims were:

> 1. To use the language of common speech, but to employ always the *exact* word. . . .
>
> 2. To create new rhythms. . . . We do not insist upon free verse as the only method of writing poetry. We fight for it as a principle of liberty. . . .
>
> 3. To allow absolute freedom in the choice of subject. . . .
>
> 4. To present an image [hence the name Imagist]. . . .
>
> 5. To produce poetry that is hard and clear, never blurred nor indefinite.
>
> 6. Finally, most of us believe that concentration is the very essence of poetry.

Although the credo is cited in sharply abbreviated form, it is easy to see why Amy and her colleagues were stunned by what followed: Storms of controversy soon blew up and kept thundering for several years. She did expect a mild success among the initiated, but she thought even their approval would require two or three years, till several anthologies had come out. At first, all was calm. Amy lectured in the book's behalf before the Writers' Equal Suffrage League at the home of Mrs. Robert Gould Shaw. She was not particularly interested in equal suffrage, but would lecture on Imagism (and new poetry in general) whenever she was asked. Ada's good friend, Eleanor Belmont, who was now Amy's as well, wrote in her autobiography: * "She loved poetry and was its advo-

* Eleanor Robson Belmont, *The Fabric of Memory* (New York: Farrar, Straus & Cudahy, 1957).

cate at a time when poetry was not generally popular. It has always seemed to me that for poets of her day she performed the service of a barker at a circus, as from the lecture platform, in the press, and almost the street corner, she cried aloud, 'Poetry, Poetry, this way to Poetry!' "

Barker she certainly was, and generous enough to plug the work of her contemporaries as well as her own. A few days after the lecture, she wrote to Harriet Monroe that she had just finished reading *Spoon River* "from cover to cover" and agreed "that it is one of the most remarkable books ever published in this country." And a month later, in spite of the widening breach with Pound, who now referred scornfully to the American branch of Imagism as *"Amygisme"* (with an *"e,"* as in the French spelling of Imagism, thereby implying it was *his* movement she took over), she wrote to the same editor: "By the way, Ezra's new book 'Cathay' is full of the most beautiful things. I have seldom read anything finer. What a pity the boy does not confine himself to working and leave strictures on other people's work alone. I would rather like to review it, but I am a little afraid that, if I do, he will think I am trying to curry favor with him. What do you think?"

The note reveals a good deal about the professional as well as the emotional conflict that plagued Amy. She was glad to be a flamboyant barker for poetry she considered worthy, but she did not want to become known or billed as a lecturer, and said so in no uncertain terms later when she was invited to speak before women's clubs in Chicago and several other midwestern cities. After all, she was primarily a poet, she felt; and in regard to her own poetry, she was both humble and proud. She wrote to the London office of Macmillan about the sorry sale of seven copies that *Sword Blades* had had in England as compared with 700 copies in America; she said she thought sales would follow as a matter of course if she could reach readers who appreciated poetry, although she would never expect to be as popular as John Masefield or Rabindranath Tagore. Yet she was so deeply convinced of the merits of her work that she could not understand why others didn't appreciate it fully—and at once. "What's the matter with those people?" she would demand of Ada rhetorically if an unfavorable or derisive review appeared. She took adverse criticism almost as a personal attack and often bullied editors into giving her work a second chance.

Two weeks after the anthology appeared, the New England poets, mostly from the Boston area, decided to form a New England Poetry Club, and Amy was elected to the executive committee, which, at a second meeting, promptly appointed her its first president, a mark of her growing prominence. From Robert Frost came a bit of doggerel by way of congratulation:

Hail first President of the
Poetry Society of New England (bis).
If I liked your poetry before,
You can imagine how much
More I shall like it after this.

Note rhyme. believe me, Seriously yours, Robert Frost.

It was this kind of professional kidding that characterized the friendship of Amy Lowell and Robert Frost; she took it in good part: It made her feel right in the swim of things, accepted as an equal and even as a force in turning the cultural wheels of the country toward the new poetry. In line with her goal, she repeated her talk on "The New Manner in Modern Poetry" before the senior class at Wellesley. News of Rupert Brooke's death in France had just arrived, and, in tribute to him, she read his last sonnet. She was happy over the cordial reception she was given by the girls, as well as over assurance from the faculty that she would have made a first-rate teacher. She was invited to appear there again.

Then on May 22, the attacks on Imagism flared into prominence in print, and from an unexpected corner—in an article in the *New Republic,* the magazine that had been so prompt in giving her an opportunity to review *North of Boston,* and whose editors had seemed so friendly toward the new poetry! The article, "The Place of Imagism," was written by Conrad Aiken, who had already suggested an ignominious "place" in his satirical "Ballade of the Worshippers of the Image," published in the *Boston Transcript.* Amy was hurt and angry and protested loudly. Philip Littell, editor in chief at the *New Republic,* said she should reply to Aiken, but she persuaded William Stanley Braithwaite, who, as poetry editor of the *Transcript,* was also involved, that he should answer Aiken. She did, however, send a steaming, aggrieved letter to Herbert Croly of the *New Republic.* She let him know what a "surprise and blow" the "hostile and ignorant attack" had been, added other grievances she had against the magazine she had counted on from the beginning, and demanded to know if she had "enemies" on the board.

There were other counterattacks and favorable signs. Alfred Kreymborg, well-known member of the Poetry Society and smiling experimenter, a troubadour who accompanied himself on a "mandolute," was about to start his third or fourth "little magazine," *Others,* in memory of all those "that died to make verse free." He had already lined up such contributors as William Carlos Williams, Edna St. Vincent Millay, Orrick Johns, and the Untermeyers, to name a few. Amy was delighted: Such varied support in the face of attack showed that free verse must be taking hold suddenly and spreading like rich clover gone wild. Not since Whitman had there been such a rash of free versifiers in America. People discovered that they had been speaking in poetic terms unconsciously for years: In the new poetry, you could write lines of "cadence" about anything you pleased, from autos and airplanes to skyscrapers and shoes. (Amy's "Red Slippers" caused almost as much commotion as her bathwater.) The difficulty was that few people had an ear for true cadence, so that anything unrhymed and not in blank verse passed for "free"; moreover, the tendency was to connect free verse with free love, a license freely taken by would-be poets happy to call themselves Imagists. Amy Lowell, for all her frenzy to get things done, knew the difference between trash and true verse, free or otherwise. Now, like Pound, ironically, she found herself trying to protect the movement. "Apparently all the questionable and pornographic poets are trying to sail under the name just now," she wrote to Aldington early in June. Still, it was better than being ignored; and, knowing she could trust Kreymborg's judgment, she sent a check and some poems to *Others.* She was busy trying to prepare an appendix for *Six French Poets* containing translations of selections from each, which Macmillan had suggested she add as a condition of publication.

Bostonians still regarded her as President Lowell's queer sister, who had taken up another freak. (How familiar it all sounds: pornographer, poetry-freak, queer—in the sexual connotation or otherwise.) At the Harvard Commencement, late in June, e. e. cummings spoke on the "New Art." After dealing with modern music and painting, he turned to literature and quoted Amy Lowell's "Grotesque" * to point up "a clear development from the ordinary to the abnormal." To the 1915 audience in Sander's Theater the distortion of a traditional pure beauty to an ugly menace with the opening query, "Why do the lilies goggle their tongues at me/ . . ./ Why do they shriek your name/ And spit at me . . ." seemed nothing short of a sacrilege, causing a shudder of horror close to a hiss throughout the reading. One aged lady asked audibly: "Is that our president's sister's poetry he is quoting? . . . Well, *I* think it's an *insult* to our president!" Naturally, all eyes were fixed on the president's face, which remained stonily straight. Amy, watching for signs of disapproval or agitation, could not discern any emotion in her brother's expression. But one of the Boston papers carried a story headlined, "Harvard Orator Calls President Lowell's Sister Abnormal."

Abnormal or not, she had tremendous capacity for work once she got started. Now, between the time she mailed the text portion of *Six French Poets* and did the translations, she wrote a poem destined to become a classic—her classic at least. The idea grabbed her so forcibly that she scarcely noticed the absence of Ada, who had gone away for the weekend. Perhaps because she knew her friend would be back soon, Amy had not raised the fuss she usually did when "Peter" left; and, as the poem unfolded with such precision it might have been automatic writing, she grew more and more elated. Cloaking her own situation in seventeenth-century "stiff brocade," she endowed the poem with a twofold purpose, and she called it "Patterns." She was so buoyant over achieving exactly the effect she desired that she could hardly wait for Ada's opinion, and she met her at the door with it when her friend came

* A poem printed in *Poetry and Drama* in 1914, but not in a book until 1919.

Amy in a white party dress with a pink sash, the way she probably looked as a plump eight-year-old at the fateful family party when she stowed away two big helpings of rice pudding, with ominous results.

HARVARD COLLEGE LIBRARY

HARVARD COLLEGE LIBRARY

In formal school clothes with her dog, "Jack," the pet she often harnessed to a wagon and drove around her father's estate, Sevenels.

Augustus Lowell—Amy's father, the hard man of business, during whose reign as head of the senior branch of Lowells, the family prosperity was at its peak. In private life, he was an expert horticulturist, an interest his last-born child, Amy, perpetuated with a vengeance.

LOWELL OBSERVATORY PHOTOGRAPH

HARVARD COLLEGE LIBRARY

"Miss Amy Lowell," the reluctant debutante. c. 1892.

Right: Great Italian actress Eleonora Duse in 1903, as Francesca da Rimini, the title role in a play by her lover, the notorious Gabriel D'Annunzio. Her performance inspired Amy Lowell's first poem and her impassioned ardor for Duse from that date forward.

THE WALTER HAMPDEN MEMORIAL LIBRARY

Opposite: Percival Lowell, the first-born child and adored brother of Amy, is shown at his telescope in the now-famous Lowell Observatory he established in Flagstaff, Arizona. Through his observations with this telescope, he discovered and located the planet Pluto, but did not live to see it.

DORIS ULMANN

Carl Engel, musicologist, composer, and Amy's adored mentor in modern music; a member of her inner circle, "the Devils," he was her devoted friend from 1908 till the end.

THE WALTER HAMPDEN MEMORIAL LIBRARY

Ada Dwyer (Russell), character actress, in a publicity "cabinet-photo" c. 1909, when she was a member of Eleanor Robson (Belmont's) company.

Ada Dwyer in the character role of the cockney lodginghouse keeper she played in *Merely Mary Ann.*

BOTH PHOTOS: MUSEUM OF THE CITY OF NEW YORK THEATRE AND MUSIC COLLECTION

Eleanor Robson played the title role in *Merely Mary Ann* that made her a full-fledged star, after which she formed her own company. Ada was a member of the company from its inception till 1910, when it was dissolved directly after Miss Robson's marriage to August Belmont.

Ada Dwyer as the character lead in *Mrs. Wiggs of the Cabbage Patch,* a role that took her half-way around the world.

MUSEUM OF THE CITY OF NEW YORK THEATRE AND MUSIC COLLECTION

Ada Dwyer Russell, c. 1916, two and a half years after she became Amy's housemate and companion, "Madonna of the Evening Flowers."

HARVARD COLLEGE LIBRARY

HARVARD COLLEGE LIBRARY

Photo portrait of Amy Lowell at about the year 1916. This is one of the few photographs in which the imagist leader is wearing a low-cut gown instead of her high, boned collars and severe suits.

HARVARD COLLEGE LIBRARY

Sevenels—front porte-cochere, French windows, and driveway.

The sunken garden at Sevenels, terraced and designed by Amy's father, and preserved according to her own preferences when she owned the estate.

HARVARD COLLEGE LIBRARY

HARVARD COLLEGE LIBRARY

The baronial library created by Amy at Sevenels by combining the front and back parlors, adding built-in bookshelves and imported carved panelling, as shown on the mantels of the fireplaces.

East end of the library.

HARVARD COLLEGE LIBRARY

HARVARD COLLEGE LIBRARY

HARVARD COLLEGE LIBRARY

Left: West end of the library, showing Amy's man-like leather chair and hassock. Right: Amy (in later years) in the garden, beside the bed of oriental poppies she loved, which undoubtedly figured in the title of her second book, *Sword Blades and Poppy Seed.*

East end of the Music Room, also designed by Amy (replacing the old billiard room), delicate and feminine in its Adams décor, in contrast to the library.

HARVARD COLLEGE LIBRARY

The Hotel Belmont, Park Avenue at 42nd Street, showing 8th floor corner suite, where Amy and Ada usually stayed when in New York.

MUSEUM OF THE CITY OF NEW YORK

Amy Lowell at the height of her career, as usual, when she was not writing or lecturing, reading a book.

HARVARD COLLEGE LIBRARY

Amy in her small, cut-flower garden at Broomley Lacey, her summer home in Dublin, New Hampshire, which she owned from 1903 to 1919.

HARVARD COLLEGE LIBRARY

Left: Standing by the lattice work near the porch in Dublin. Right: Sprinkling the Dublin garden on a hot summer day; note the man's shirt and straw "boater," her usual garb in Dublin. The man in this snapshot is Sumner Appleton, a descendent of Massachusetts Senator Sumner.

HARVARD COLLEGE LIBRARY

HARVARD COLLEGE LIBRARY

D. H. Lawrence, c. 1912, as he looked when he and Frieda met Amy Lowell and Ada Russell in London, 1914, just before World War I.

MONTAGUE WEEKLEY

Frieda Weekley (Lawrence), c. 1912, as she looked when she met D. H. Lawrence, while she was still married to Ernest Weekley.

A later picture of D. H. Lawrence, right, with Witter Bynner, center, and Willard ("Spud") Johnson, Bynner's secretary, in Santa Fe, 1923.

Amy at the farewell dinner given by the Poetry Society of America for John Masefield in New York in 1916. Standing, left to right: Lawrence Housman, Witter Bynner, Percy MacKaye, Edwin Markham, Cale Young Rice, Louis Untermeyer, Vachel Lindsay. Sitting: Amy Lowell, Josephine Dodge Daskam Bacon, John Masefield, Alfred Noyes.

HARVARD COLLEGE LIBRARY

THE JONES LIBRARY, AMHERST, MASS.

Left: Ezra Pound, one of the initiators of the group he called *Les Imagistes,* as he appeared in 1913–1914, when he and Amy Lowell met. Right: Robert Frost at work in his Morris chair with writing board, c. 1916, in Franconia, New Hampshire, the farm he bought shortly after becoming acquainted with Amy.

The Robert Frost family at the Webster farm near Bridgewater, c. 1917, the time they began to know Amy and Ada well—a rare picture of all members of the Frost family together.

GEORGE H. BROWNE-ROBERT FROST COLLECTION. PLYMOUTH STATE COLLEGE.

THE WALTER HAMPDEN MEMORIAL LIBRARY

Left: Edna St. Vincent Millay, c. 1918–1919, during her years at the Provincetown Players, when she wrote *Aria da Capo,* which Amy Lowell considered Millay's finest work. Right: Elizabeth ("Elsie") Sergeant, author of the first biographical portrait of her close friend Amy, after her death (1926). Photo taken by the present biographer at the MacDowell Colony, September, 1955.

One of the last photographs of Amy Lowell, taken by her girlhood friend, Florence (Wheelock) Ayscough. Worn with pain from a recent hernia operation, overwork, and eyestrain, she still shows ability to concentrate on any project she undertook. (Note the high-powered reading lamp she always used).

THE JOSEPH REGENSTEIN LIBRARY OF THE UNIVERSITY OF CHICAGO LIBRARY.

home. "Never mind your bag—I want you to hear the latest!" she commanded, after giving "Peter" a quick bear hug. And she began reading from the freshly typed sheets (which needed hardly any revision), as Ada, laughing, sat down on the bench beneath the antlered heads to listen.

Written with an irregular but unmistakable rhyme scheme, the "pattern" of the poem itself was designed to reveal Amy Lowell's inner conflict as well as her outer rebellion against world values and armed conflicts between nations. The analogy is clear in such lines as:

> Not a softness anywhere about me,
> Only whalebone and brocade.
> And I sink on a seat in the shade
> Of a lime tree. For my passion
> Wars against the stiff brocade. . . .

And metaphor is equally graphic in the fantasy love scene of the narrator, who pictures the pink-and-silver brocaded gown lying crumpled in a heap upon the ground, and the pink-and-silver of her naked body as she runs laughing and teasing through the maze of patterned garden paths while her lover gives chase and finally bruises her yielding body in a passionate embrace. (Probably no other woman poet of her time described the female nude body as often or as sensuously as Amy Lowell.) Then, as the "plot" discloses that the narrator had just received an official died-in-action note concerning the fiancé-lover who should have loosed her from the stiffness of her stays, she gives way to bitter profanity in the final line: "Christ! What are patterns for?" And the reader cannot help realizing the tragic plight of the writer, whatever the cause. (In 1915, the last line was a shocker, and it carries considerable impact even today.)

Ada Russell recognized, as Amy herself had, that "Patterns" possessed that rare combination of finely wrought form and romantic content that was bound to strike a universal chord among poetry lovers, peace lovers, all sorts of lovers. But they agreed (incredible as it seems) that the piece was a trifle risqué for the general public, so Amy sent it to the *Little Review*. Margaret Anderson accepted it at once for the August issue. The poem was an instant success and became, after its publication in her next volume, more widely quoted and anthologized than any other Amy Lowell poem. One might be tempted to play on the title and claim that "Patterns" merely delineated the fashionable trend of the era; but it has withstood the test of time. Among its recent appearances, it was included in a 1972 anthology of antiwar poems.

Another pleasant surprise was William Rose Benét's acceptance of "The Paper Windmill," a polyphonic prose poem, for *Century Magazine*. The story was based on an incident August Belmont had related one evening when she and Ada were having dinner with the Belmonts. They were discussing the indelible impressions made by childhood disappointments. The story seemed to Amy to be a promising subject for her polyphonic prose technique and the fact that *Century,* a traditional literary magazine, had accepted it, showed that the medium was taking root. Fresh attacks were to come in the near future, mostly in the British press, but Amy was beginning to feel prepared. She had girded on her armor and was ready for further jousts.

Just then, however, Ada became ill. Amy had planned that they would spend July and August in Dublin; having spent the past two summers in England, she had not made use of her country home since 1912. But during the first week in July Ada contracted a fever that was very similar to typhoid. Amy was worried, and she watched over Ada, caring for her all day long, and spending five hours every night finishing up the translations of French poetry. (For one who was so pampered, both by herself and by those around her, Amy was a surprisingly good nurse, especially of someone as close and dear to her as Ada; but even with a comparative stranger who was ill, she had shown quiet understanding and concern, doing what had to be done without fuss or impatience.)

"Peter" was very ill; but when the doctor advised a typhoid inoculation, they were both wary of it. Finally, after discussing the matter with Eleanor Belmont, who called to find out how her friend was feeling, they decided to let the doctor try it, and Ada began to improve. By the end of the month she was so much better that she insisted on going to Salt Lake City, as she had promised

Lorna, who was visiting there, that she would come to help her daughter with a large tea she was giving. Amy objected strenuously: "Peter" was just out of a sickbed; she was not strong enough to make the long trip. She herself was worn out from nursing her. And so on.

There might have been a scene if Eleanor Belmont had not been at Sevenels; she had come up for an overnight visit to see how her friend was coming along and preserved her icy coldness when a temper tantrum threatened. (Mrs. Belmont was genuinely fond of Amy, and thought her "a great lady, in spite of her cigar-smoking and frequent exhibitions of ungovernable temper.") She served as a buffer between the two, and, in the end, Amy relented. Before Eleanor Belmont went home, she paid the parlor maid for her outgoing phone calls, a custom of hers, and said she was sending a book. Amy dashed off a piece of doggerel, along with her check for one dollar (never cashed), which read in part:

Received from Nell
This money. 'Tis well
She pays her debts with promptitude
With an exactitude almost rude. . . .

But any money's welcome as honey—I admit these verses do not go well
But my name is valid! Amy Lowell—

She also included a brief thanks for the book and then she made a stormy departure for Dublin, accompanied by her barking dogs. Her arrival there was literally stormy: Torrential rains ruined the house, flooding the cellar and wrecking the roof. On August 7, after a miserable week, in a letter that tells a great deal about Amy's emotional makeup, she wrote Mrs. Belmont: "What must you think of me for the casual way in which I received the book? Do you know, it never occurred to me when you said you were sending out a book, that it was not intended for Ada. Indeed, I should have deluged you with thanks had I known, instead of letting you go out of the house with a joke poem. . . . I have already enjoyed the pictures, which is all I had time for before the world upheaved with Ada's departure & my removal up here.

"Life has been anything but beer and skittles since I saw you. First, Ada went, an occurrence which one would suppose happened sufficiently often for me to get used to it; but, *having gotten used to her presence, I find it quite impossible to accustom myself to her absence. . . .*" *

After listing all her woes in the Dublin household, she continued: "Surely Ada's vacation is not proving exactly a joy-ride for me. Not that she could have stopped the leaks, or staunched the brook in the cellar, had she been here, but all these things are worse when our only human propinquity is a group of startled and unhappy servants. I knew the Summer would be a trial. . . ." As if to rationalize her feelings and make Nell rest easy regarding her old friend, she continued: "Ada will be better, I am sure, now she is on the spot, & Lorna's tea-party cannot possibly go on without her. She writes in good spirits, says the journey tired her a little, but that she is getting rested, that most of her particular friends are away so there are *no* invitations. . . . I verily believe Ada would have been in bed now, if we had not had that inoculation. I do hope she will pick up, it worries me to have her off there, but I do believe it was the best thing for her to go. She would have worried so about Lorna if she had stayed that that would have made her sick. . . ." Then she twitted the lady herself about having a high pulse count and told her to "Go slow, . . . Be a good, self-sacrificing girl, and 'go gently,' even if you don't want to." In closing, she promised to send a copy of "The Paper Windmill" as soon as her secretary had typed it, and she again thanked Nell for the book.

The villagers who recalled her arrival in Dublin that August probably would not have believed that Miss Lowell was capable of such a concerned, considerate letter. She roared and she roused the whole town, phoning down for every available hand to come and bail out the cellar. When they got there, she had a fire going in the furnace to dry out the house, and she would not let anyone extinguish it. Baffled, one of the men asked how they were supposed to bail out the cellar. She snapped: "Break up this concrete floor and let the water drain out into the ground!"

* Italics mine.

That and many similar tales went the rounds in Dublin for years. No doubt about it, Miss Lowell was a "character"! Nobody, not even delivery boys, dared appear on her driveway before eleven, and her lights burned nightly until three. Dubliners did not realize that these were early hours for Amy, who relaxed her summer schedule even more when the weather was fine in order to spend time outdoors. She had been seen smoking a large calabash pipe on her front porch, and the size of her phone bill, according to Dublin's only operator, scandalized the whole village. Her dogs terrorized those who were not used to them; and this year, in addition to all the other troubles, there seemed to be more sheep-dog incidents than usual. In fact, one such incident could have had serious consequences.

Randolph Bourne, writer for the *New Republic* whose writings showed definite Socialist leanings (with which Amy was not sympathetic to begin with), was spending the summer in Dublin working on a new book that Houghton Mifflin was publishing. Amy, out of regard for Ferris Greenslet and Herbert Croly, invited him to dinner one night. Bourne, who was physically weak and bent over by a deformity that made him look enough like a hunchback to be labeled one, had not been warned about the sheep dogs. He was terrified when they set on him by way of greeting and pursued him when he tried to run. He was finally rescued by one of the maids. He stayed for dinner, but, still trembling, he was resentful toward Amy. She was repelled by him in return and considered his ideas "radical," and somehow the result of his twisted body. The psychological implications on both sides of the contretemps are evident, since people with a handicap often feel themselves reflected in the afflictions of others. Her own self-hate came to the fore in her loathing of Bourne, though she did not realize it until a few years later, when she remarked to James Oppenheim, editor of the magazine, *The Seven Lively Arts,* who had asked her opinion of Bourne's work: "His writing shows he is a cripple. Everything he advocates sounds like a cripple." Oppenheim, he was ashamed to admit, answered loftily, "Aren't we all cripples?" His query brought an unexpected reaction from Amy: Instead of "flaying him alive," she took in her enormous girth with a thoughtful glance and said simply, "Yes. I'm as much of a cripple as he. Look at this. I'm a disease!" She must have felt remorseful at the time, however, for she invited Bourne to the house a couple of weeks after the incident, when Edwin Arlington Robinson, with whom she felt much more comfortable, was coming over from the MacDowell Colony for dinner.* There was no further trouble from the dogs, but conversation between Amy and Randolph Bourne was constrained then and always would be.

In spite of her problems, Amy did manage to promote "her" Imagist-and-new-poetry movement by speaking before several hundred Dublin clubwomen. She also wrote some poems in New Hampshire dialect for a group she called "The Overgrown Pasture." As the name indicates, they were after the manner of Robert Frost, except that Amy claimed hers was the true New England dialect. (She and Frost were to have a running battle of the use of colloquial speech; after he came to know her better, Robert told her frankly, "Trouble with you, Amy, is that you don't go out your back door often enough!") She also did some "enraged gardening," she wrote to "Peter" in Salt Lake City, while otherwise marking time until her beloved friend returned.

Not till then, in late summer, did things settle down—as much as they were ever settled in Amy's seething households. They returned to Sevenels in time to do the last-minute work on *Six French Poets,* making additions to and corrections of galley proofs, and helping to prepare advance publicity for it and the 1916 volume of *Some Imagist Poets.* The Imagist anthology had done far better than anyone had expected, and the publishers were more than willing to bring out a second collection of Imagist poets. Amy herself dispensed the royalties, dividing them into six equal parts, and sending separate checks, along with a cheery note, to each of "her" Imagists, at the same time urging them to submit selections for the new volume. Not that they needed any nudging; all were delighted with the results, since most of the poets were badly in

* Robinson, whose work Amy had reviewed and admired, was another of the instant and sympathetic friendships she made after *Sword Blades* appeared. In the summer of 1915, he was writing in the newly built "Veltin" studio at the MacDowell Colony, which he occupied every summer from then on until shortly before his death in 1934, and in which the present biography of Amy Lowell was begun.

need of money. (Besides Lawrence, the fifty-seven letters from H. D. and the hundred or so from Aldington often expressed concern with financial problems.) H. D. wrote that they were "immensely set up over the Imagist money," that Fletcher had written the Aldingtons "very beautifully of your generosity to him, your influence and continuing work on behalf of us and the Imagist ideas in general. . . . The deepest, heart-felt thanks for your generosity." Of their respective work, she said, "I wish I had one-tenth of your output; mine seems to be a most tenuous shoot of this Imagist Tree of Life!" And in a later letter she speaks again of Amy's "wonderful management" of the Imagist books.

Her own portion of the royalties, Amy, like a true investor, put back into the business by helping to support Margaret Anderson's *Little Review;* Harriet Monroe's *Poetry;* and, to a lesser extent, *Others,* which did not last very long.* It is significant that the poetry renaissance, which started under the leadership of men in England,** never amounted to much until it crossed the Atlantic, when it spread with joyful fecundity under the leadership of women, principally these three. This was due in part to World War I, which early took the lives of the most prominent English poets and disrupted the rise of modern poetry, but it was also due to the lack of organization and to what H. D. called "the bungling, stupid things Ezra has done."

Of these three American women—Harriet Monroe, Margaret Anderson, and herself—Amy Lowell was of course the most doughty, not to say aggressive. In the late fall of 1915, she gave her second address before the Poetry Society in New York, on the subject, "Modern Metres and the Poets Who Write Them," which caused a greater row than the first one had, although the material seemed mild enough to her. Since her book of lecture-essays, *Six French Poets,* was about to appear, she began with a history of modern-poetry sources, bringing in the works of modern com-

* Amy, however, had been very enthusiastic about the second issue of *Others,* especially the poems of Wallace Stevens and William Carlos Williams. The former was new to her, and she wanted to hear all about him.

** Indeed, Ford Madox Ford, in a rather hostile review of *Some Imagist Poets,* had complained peevishly regarding the preface that he felt *he* had started the movement and resented the lack of credit given to him.

posers, including Debussy, Stravinsky, Bartók, and Fauré, among others, as examples of the same tendency in another art form. She went from there to discussion of the paintings of Van Gogh (including his letters as well), of Impressionism and Cubism, and on to the modern poets, including the Symbolists and post-Symbolists in France. And finally, she discussed the freer meters of Robert Frost and D. H. Lawrence and the outright free versifiers like Flint, Fletcher, H. D., Aldington, Masters, Lindsay, Sandburg, and herself, giving examples of her shift from one cadence to another, and ending with one of her polyphonic-prose pieces. The moment she sat down the barrage began—at its height, "a gladiator fight and wild beast show," she reported to Fletcher.

However, she stood her ground and, keeping tabs on her hecklers, answered each one with such brilliance that she gained the admiration, if not the support, of a good many members, including Jean Starr and Louis Untermeyer, who soon became her associates and close friends. Jean almost "blistered her palms applauding"; and Louis, who had already written Amy a couple of admiring letters concerning *Sword Blades,* was ready to become an ally right away.* There were still plenty of hisses beneath the applause when the discussion ended, but Amy's views had at least roused the group out of complacency, and she had won a nucleus of support for the future. Exhilarated by the commotion she caused, before she and Ada returned to Brookline she met with Marsh at Macmillan to discuss final publication arrangements for *Six French Poets* and saw and entertained in her hotel suite editors of newspapers and various columnists, to insure reviews and advance publicity.

The new book was an immediate and surprising success in America, perhaps because of the growing American sympathy for France in the war. Also, Americans were eager to learn more of the group that followed the school of "decadent" poets like Verlaine, Baudelaire, and Rimbaud. *Six French Poets* made it easy

* Later he did collaborate with Amy in editing and publishing the anthology, *An American Miscellany;* but at this time, John Gould Fletcher, who took an instant dislike to both of the Untermeyers, would not accept them as members of the Imagist group.

for the average reader, largely because of Amy's conversational style (which was purely accidental; when she began rewriting her lectures, she found that she could not switch over to the essay form and so left them practically intact). Like *Sword Blades,* the appearance of this book was fortuitously timed: Americans were eager to read more about French poets, particularly about Remy de Gourmont, whose Rabelaisian gusto and Gallicisms in his book, *Les Amazones,* a study of homosexual and bisexual women, had caused quite a stir. In her inevitable preface, Amy had paid special tribute to de Gourmont, who had died on September 28, while the book was on press (and who had sent her three fragments of inscribed manuscript when he learned of her anonymous gift to him). In a footnote at the end of the preface, she expressed great admiration for his work and gratitude for the encouragement he had given her, "even under the heavy weight of a serious illness." She concluded the preface: "By his death, France loses one of the greatest and most sincere artists of his generation."

The book came out in November, and within three weeks had sold half of the first edition. Reviews were generally good (until those from England appeared), bringing in their wake a rash of invitations to read or to speak on the subject of the French poets. A source of satisfaction came around mid-December, when she received a letter from Robert Frost, to whom she had sent a copy. He paid her a fine compliment in typical Frostian style. After thanking her for "this large—this spacious—book, especially the Paul Fort of it," he went on: "Between his French and your English I'm not sure that I don't come nearer some idea of him than ever I did of a foreign poet . . . he's the only one of your six who shows with any vividness the sounds I am after in poetry. I'll tell you what we did with Henry III. My daughter * and I read it together, I with my head tipped one way following your English aloud, & she with her head tipped the other way following his French in silence, the book being open at two places at once you understand. And even under those unfavorable circumstances I

* Lesley, the oldest of the Frost children and the closest to her father and most guided by him in her education, who, in a year or so, was to visit Sevenels.

brought tears of excitement to my daughter's eyes. And she is a young thing."

Of the fifteen letters signed "R. F." in the Lowell files, this was the one Amy treasured most, for, as she came to realize, he was very chary with praise of his colleagues' work. She accepted most of the offers to appear before women's clubs and college student groups that winter. Among the modern poems she chose to read, she always included one of Frost's, along with one of Robinson's. Soon another idea for a book on poetry was forming in her mind—a work that would deal with general tendencies in modern American poetry—and she began to do some research for it early in 1916. One day she went to the Athenaeum instead of sending Ada, as she usually did. Typically, she did not arrive till half an hour before closing time; she barely had a chance to locate her material when the bell rang and the librarian said she must leave.

Amy exploded. This was *her* library, the building she had saved from demolition, and supported with Lowell money: She'd be damned if she would leave before her books came, and they could damn well remain open a little longer for once! They did; when Amy got back to Sevenels, she related the incident to "Peter" indignantly but half-humorously, and she forgot about it; but the ruckus she created was noisy enough to be noted in the Athenaeum daily record and indelibly preserved in its archives.

Amy was also preparing a new volume of her own poems, but she continued to lecture through the winter of 1915–16, and in February she spoke to the Harvard Poetry Club on the subject of vers libre and the French poets. The meeting was thrown open to candidates for membership so there would be a larger attendance, and she was pleased to find the room packed when she arrived. She sat at the head of a long table surrounded by student members, graduate and undergraduate. She began provocatively by remarking, "I suppose you boys think Walt Whitman wrote vers libre; well, he didn't." From there she went on to explain the difference between Whitman's free-flowing verse, which the French poets had adapted, rather than adopted, to suit the cadence of their own language. After her talk the boys fired questions at her, which she answered through a cloud of cigar smoke. Several times she cast a longing eye toward the centerpiece of beer and pretzels, but nobody offered to disturb it, so she finally left with one last look of regret.

"Estlin" * Cummings, who, after graduating the previous June had gone to graduate school for a master of arts degree in literature, and had chaired the meeting, saw her to her car. On the way, in connection with the various influences of the new poetry they had been discussing, he asked her if she liked the work of Gertrude Stein. Amy, wary, and Yankee-wise, countered with the question, "Do you?" And Cummings, almost as wary, answered hesitantly, "Ye-es, I do. . . ." In her response, "Well, I don't!" Amy's tone left no doubt of her disapproval. She had read Stein's repetitive lines in Margaret Anderson's *Little Review* and knew that if *she* had been poetry editor, they would not have been accepted. Donald Evans, a young hopeful who in 1914 had published a slim volume of Stein poems, entitled *Tender Buttons,* under the assumed imprint of Claire-Marie, had circulated the volume around Harvard. Foster Damon enjoyed it so much he recommended it to certain students, and he undoubtedly mentioned the title to Amy. In any case, she knew the writing of Gertrude Stein well enough to pass judgment on her in no uncertain terms.

It was inevitable that the author of "Patterns," who spoke of walking up and down the garden paths where "the daffodils/are blowing, and the bright blue squills," should object to a rival poet who chanted, "Rose is a rose is a rose is a rose." More objectionable still was this bit of drollery tossed to the reader from the author of *Tender Buttons:* "A table means does it not my dear it means a whole steadiness./ Is it likely that a change. . . ./ A table means more than a glass even a looking glass is tall./ . . ." Such quirky lines placed beside the quiet eloquence of "Venus Transiens" or the roar of "Bombardment," the definite design of "Patterns," or the strange sexual symbolism of "The Basket," could not be reconciled, no matter how unorthodox Amy Lowell, with her Imagism and polyphonic prose, was at the time, or how tolerant of all new

* Amy always called e. e. cummings Estlin, his middle name, even after he had taken his lower-case, double-initialed professional name, which she found "affected." (His first name, Edward, was rarely used.)

poetry she considered herself. And the feeling was mutual: These two opposing regal personages of the hour were too much alike ever to accept each other, as a closer look will show.

Whether one believes in astrology or not, the amazing parallels in the lives of Amy Lowell and Gertrude Stein are too startling to be ignored. As stated at the beginning of this book, both of these extraordinary personalities of the literary world were born in the second month of the same year, during the same week—Gertrude Stein on February 3, and Amy Lowell on February 9, 1874. It is often hard to believe that two people born the same year under the same sign have anything else in common, but in this instance one might easily be convinced that the stars shape human destiny. For those interested in ascendancy of the stars, both writers were born in early morning. Their family constellations were almost identical.

The births, in each case coming late in their mothers' lives, were precarious and difficult, causing both matrons to become semi-invalids who were unable to take care of their daughters much of the time. Both Gertrude Stein and Amy Lowell were the last children to be born in large families. Although Gertrude's brother Leo was close to her in age, both of these last-borns had siblings nearly a generation older than they, and in both cases two children had died in between. Such discipline as they received came from the sister closest to them in age. Both of the fathers were remote, preoccupied with their own affairs. Both families were well-to-do—although the Lowell wealth was much greater than the Stein—but the source of their financial success differed widely, and there could be no sharper contrast in ethnic backgrounds than those of these two literary tycoons. The Lowell ancestry of English Protestant early Yankee settlers in 1639, whose history can hardly be separated from that of New England cotton mills, courts of law, and education, is the furthest imaginable from the Stein heritage of German-Jewish stock. Both sides of the Stein family had been fairly successful in Europe, but became part of the melting pot of America as immigrants in 1848, to escape the religious persecution of that era.

Amy Lowell and Gertrude Stein were both exceptionally

bright babies who learned to talk at an early age, and were quite voluble by the time they were three or four. Physically, both children were plump. They were petted and pampered because of being "the baby" of their respective families—even as Amy was called "the Postscript," Gertrude was called "the Afterthought" by her family—yet both were neglected by their parents for that reason as well as because of their mothers' chronic illnesses. And both resented discipline, particularly from the sisters closest to them in age, Bertha Stein and Bessie Lowell, respectively. Both were stubborn, self-willed, quick to anger, and as quickly restored to good nature, though Gertrude Stein less so than Amy Lowell: There were times when Gertrude's anger rose as rapidly, yet she was not always prone to forgive and forget, as her final break with Hemingway shows. Amy Lowell, on the other hand, got furious any number of times with the writer-publisher John Farrar; yet she always forgave him: She never cut people out of her life purposely, as Gertrude did.

These two sturdy children had a tendency to be tomboys from the start. Both preferred boys' games to girls', romping outdoors to playing house inside. Neither had any use for dolls. Neither had any fear of animals. When school days arrived, they took similar attitudes toward education. Gertrude was the better scholar, but both were easily bored, particularly in primary school, where they were ahead of their classmates in reading. Where Amy was inclined to be a clown in class, Gertrude was more prone to scoff at the subjects taught in primary school. Neither bothered to work for a college degree. In 1893, Gertrude began attending the Harvard Annex, and it is possible that the lives of these two literary lionesses brushed against each other as they stalked the libraries, since Amy was by then a dropout studying on her own.

As they came of age, it was not likely that either would marry. Both, following puberty, had grown from plump children into huge women, with enormous bosoms and shoulders, forming imposing, intimidating figures, looming over territory they had made their own—in Stein's case, Cubism and the new art; in Lowell's, Imagism and the new music. Both were frequently compared to a Roman emperor. Since neither was much over five feet tall, the total effect of their enormous weight—each tipped the scales at about 250 pounds—was one of tremendous square bulk, so the comparison was well founded, but in neither case quite accurate. Virgil Thomson has said that Gertrude Stein's features reminded him more of a "medieval abbot's" than a Roman emperor's; while Amy Lowell's rather small head but high forehead and delicate features, her fine intelligent eyes behind the pince-nez she wore from the time she was grown, made her look more like a college president than a military potentate.

Both of these oversized figures were dressed to conceal their size. Gertrude Stein sometimes wore a loose-fitting robe when receiving people who came to her *atelier,* but usually she, like Amy, wore mannish suits with long skirts; Amy had plain suits for daytime, and dress ones for evening wear, while Gertrude wore mostly brown or tan corduroys, and her main item of decoration was a vest; as she grew older, her collection of them was vast in color and variety. Amy often draped several chains around her neck and liked to cover her fingers with sparkling rings, pure gems of emerald, ruby, or diamond; without them she felt undressed and indecorous. Both women had small, graceful hands in contrast to the rest of their bodies.

It is not surprising that both of these literary personalities took female companions as mates; but it is curious that the given names of their respective friends both began with the letter *A;* and in both instances, both pairs, at their first meeting, "recognized each other at once," as Ferris Greenslet wrote of Amy and Ada. And it is an even more curious coincidence that when Gertrude Stein wrote her first "portrait," a sketch of Alice, she called it "Ada." There could hardly be a greater contrast than that between wispy, wiry Alice B. Toklas, with the thin line of mustache above her upper lip and her succinct, dry wit, and the almost Junoesque, warm, and gentle Ada, with her quiet humor and great love of people. But both companions completely filled the multiple needs of these two masculine women. Both smoothed the paths of their respective careers. Just as Amy always tried out her manuscripts on Ada, so Gertrude had Alice read her pieces; and each writer abided by her companion's approval or disapproval. In both cases, the working harmony of the relationship was remarkable, both socially and professionally.

There were other parallels. Like Amy, Gertrude preferred nocturnal hours for writing. In each case, when the last guest had left, usually between eleven-thirty and midnight, these two more-than-ample literary leaders, in their respective salons on either side of the Atlantic, would settle down with copybook or manuscript paper and pencil for a night's work; while Alice Toklas and Ada Russell, who were early risers, usually went to their respective rooms for a night's rest. The two writers set down their thoughts with amazing speed and were capable of tremendous output, though both claimed to struggle with words. Despite their own unconventionalities, both objected to obscenities or pornography in the literature of their day, particularly to James Joyce's *Ulysses.*

Gertrude Stein did not approve of movements in general, whether Suffragist or Imagist, and her principal objection to Amy Lowell was that she tried to make the new poetry a *cause célèbre,* and was having a good deal of success, which may have been the real reason for Gertrude's antipathy toward her. Jealous or not, whether she sanctioned movements or not, Gertrude gathered a sizable circle around her, and she probably did not care for competition from another American, even an ocean away. Winfield Townley Scott, who includes a comparison of these two figures in his study, "Amy Lowell of Brookline, Mass.," * observed in conclusion: "Both had a dynamism which was basically rare egocentricity; and it exercised compellant dominance, not only in the women themselves but over most people who ventured near them, and even over a good many who merely read their books." He ends with the fillip: "However they differed in intellectualisms, the two were so much alike we should be grateful they set up shop on separate continents."

In another comparison, Robert McAlmon contended that Amy preferred to surround herself with "second-raters" who would flatter her, while Stein attracted giants like Picasso and Hemingway. One wonders if McAlmon considered D. H. Lawrence or

* Winfield Townley Scott, *Exiles and Fabrications* (New York: Doubleday & Company, Inc., 1961).

Robert Frost "second-raters," or if he was even aware that they were part of Amy's circle, since he knew her mainly through reports from his short-term wife, Bryher, and her friend, H. D. Before his quarrel with Gertrude over publication of *The Making of Americans,* he thought Stein was "a much better specimen than Amy Lowell, though they were both a species of the same family: doubting and spoiled rich children, hurt only when they discover they can't have the moon if they want it." His parting shot was that "one thing was certain: Amy did weigh a good deal more than Gertrude." But this was not true in their early years, nor in Amy's last.

Amy Lowell died almost a decade before Gertrude Stein returned to the United States on her triumphal lecture tour, and there is no record of their having met in Paris or Boston, though their literary paths crossed indirectly. If these two had met, it is likely that they would have clashed in person as they did in their work. Each was too individualistic, too monumental in personality and physical size to give way to the other or to stand together on common ground. But both, in their separate ways, contributed to the freedom of modern American literature, and, by the lives they led, to the liberation of women, lesbian or otherwise, the world over.

CHAPTER XII

Summer Incidents and Accidents: Portentous Shadows

ALL THROUGH THE WINTER and spring of 1916, Amy continued to battle for victory in the poetic war. Ordinarily, one would call a literary assault, dealing as it does with elements of a spiritual nature, a crusade, but Amy Lowell's militant approach made it a full-scale war, whose battle cries, aptly phrased by John Livingston Lowes in *Convention and Revolt in Poetry,** were "War on the 'eloquent' " and "Death to the cliché." ("Eloquent" here refers to the era of "cosmic" poetry of the post-Tennyson period, whose characteristics still clung, like a vine or limp, hanging moss, to some of the more conservative poets.)

She strengthened her support by accepting a dinner invitation at the Untermeyers' in February, when Jean learned that as hostess she must allow at least an hour for Amy and Ada's tardy appearance, that she must have two pitchers of ice water and an individual, well-filled salt cellar at Amy's place, and that the conversation would be well taken care of by the guest of honor herself, who, though she consumed quantities of food with hearty appetite, managed to keep up a running fire of comment on any number of topics. The liberal wing of the Poetry Society was present: Alfred and Dorothy Kreymborg, Vachel Lindsay and his adored but lan-

* John Livingston Lowes, *Convention and Revolt in Poetry* (Boston: Houghton Mifflin Company, 1930).

guishing Sara Teasdale, who the previous August had written Amy an ardent letter of appreciation from a hospital bed in St. Louis, where she was convalescing from one of her frequent illnesses. She wrote that she had a well-worn copy of *Sword Blades* on her bed and had just read "Patterns" in the *Little Review.* (She compared the poem to the intricate beauty of design of an old snuff box whose mosaic colors stayed fresh and gleaming, a rare compliment from one poet to another.) The two soon discovered a mutual admiration for Eleonora Duse, and the friendship was sealed.

Next, Amy broadened her offensives by going to Chicago, where she and Ada had lunch with Edgar Lee Masters and Arthur Davison Ficke. Masters, in the liberal vanguard, was one of those whose work Amy was soon to discuss, but Ficke was in the conservative wing of the Poetry Society; he and Witter Bynner, for years its president, were about to launch a counterattack on the Lowell forces, but Ficke, a handsome and suave Harvard Law School graduate and a charmer of the first water, gave no sign of their plot. Instead, after arguing pleasantly with Amy about the relative merits of metered and free verse, he asked her to read and criticize an article he had written, promised to send her a Japanese print from his prize collection, and arranged a lecture for her at the Maurice Browne Little Theatre. There was an unexpectedly large turnout for the reading, and she read her polyphonic prose to a packed house.

Back in New York in March, Amy herself launched a counterattack on Joyce Kilmer, who had flayed her and the new poetry viciously in his column in the *New York Times.* Perhaps the best example of the difference between the old, conventional poetry and the new poetry lies in the treatment that Joyce Kilmer and Amy Lowell gave to the same subject: trees. The lines of Kilmer's banal, cliché-ridden "Trees" were much quoted and often sung, and were even hung on plaques in every third living room in the land for years.

I think that I shall never see
A poem lovely as a tree. . . .
A tree that may in summer wear
A nest of robins in her hair;

Upon whose bosom snow has lain
Who intimately lives with rain;
Poems are made by fools like me,
But only God can make a tree.

In sharp contrast, in her "Trees," Amy's lines speak the uncommon in expression:

The branches of the trees lie in layers
Above and behind each other,
And the sun strikes on the outstanding leaves
And turns them white,
And they dance like a spatter of pebbles
Against a green wall.

The trees make a solid path leading up in the air.
It looks as though I could walk upon it
If I only had courage to step out of the window.

Today we are used to this sort of expression. For those who have observed the white dazzle of sunshine on leaves, "a spatter of pebbles against a green wall" is an accurate image, and the symbolism of the last lines is apparent. But in 1916, Joyce Kilmer, who was a literary critic of note and wrote better poems than "Trees," could not see what the Imagists and others were trying to do, so he sought to discredit if not destroy the whole movement. Amy was outraged by his attitude. She got hold of Kilmer and *made* him interview her about the new poetry; moreover, she insisted on seeing and approving the result in manuscript before it appeared in the *New York Times* (March 26). Whether anyone but Amy Lowell of Brookline, Mass., could have pulled this off is doubtful. Van Wyck Brooks, in his hyperbolic but captivating study of her,* says in part: "As Robinson was their precursor . . . so Amy Lowell was their militant leader. In poetry, Miss Lowell was all that, in other fields, Elizabeth Peabody and Susan B. Anthony had been. She crowned the line of puissant women of Boston. . . . A born promoter, as masterful as her forebears were, and the shrewdest of salesmen also, like the old China traders; and

* Van Wyck Brooks, *New England: Indian Summer* (New York: E. P. Dutton, 1940).

seeing that America was giving birth to a first-rate product, she put her shoulder to the wheel and pushed it on the market. The product was American poetry, which was plainly on the rise again, and which she handled like any other 'big business.' . . . This Daniela Webster was also an actress, whose earliest idol was Duse, and all her dramatic flair, with her verve and her gusto, went into the great pitched battle that she waged for the poets. She fought in the front rank, when occasion called for her, or, as less often happened, behind the lines, where she mustered her majors and colonels, her generals and lieutenants. For literary soldiership, or literary statesmanship, America had never seen Miss Lowell's equal. Literary politicians had always abounded, but she was the prime minister of the republic of poets. . . . The poets had reason to thank their stars that they had a Lowell behind them, for whom editors and publishers were factory hands and office boys."

On the other hand, neither Brooks nor most others, who saw only the externality of Amy Lowell's armored front, could know that she was deeply hurt by Harriet Monroe's omission of her and her work in *Poetry*'s latest listings of the names of those "most prominent" in the world of poets. Amy had reason to feel grieved, since she had entertained Harriet Monroe for a week at Sevenels and had arranged an appearance for the editor at the Harvard Poetry Club, besides contributing funds as well as manuscripts to *Poetry*. And she shed heartbroken tears on reading the sarcastically cruel critical piece by Lytton Strachey on *Six French Poets,* entitled "A Bostonian Looks at the Symbolists," which appeared in the *London Times.* Strachey pictured "Miss Lowell patiently explaining the French Symbolists to the reader" as if to small children. Obviously he—and the Bloomsbury circle—regarded her as a naïve pretender if not a buffoon who might not even grasp his withering, politely phrased scorn. She had far more sensitivity and intelligence than many members of the intellectual *haut monde* credited her with. If she had not been equipped with the Lowell sense of security and resilience, reinforced by the understanding love of "Peter," she could not, after losing a skirmish now and again, have resumed the battle so quickly without ever letting on, or losing face in the eyes of the general public.

She continued to strengthen her position by entertaining all manner of poets at Sevenels, from Robert Frost—who, with his wife Elinor, spent a weekend there, after which Amy wrote to Fletcher, "They wear very well"—to Maxwell Bodenheim, whose visit took on the air of a comic opera. Bodenheim, as brilliant in his youth, and as unkempt, as Gaudier-Brzeska in London, epitomized the bohemian in the Greenwich Village of the twenties. He might be called the original hippie, with his long, unwashed blond hair, his crumpled suits, and his clay pipe, in which he claimed to smoke opium. Amy had met him in Chicago, his native "heath," and since she was always on the lookout for new recruits (no matter how raw), especially one already in the vanguard of the new-poetry forces, she invited him to be her guest at Sevenels when he came east. Gifted, but erratic and careless about appointments, he arrived at the mansion two hours early on a late spring day. There was no one to meet him at the entrance to the driveway, and the seven sheep dogs, gamboling about the lawn, rushed at him with their typically fierce greeting.

Scared out of his wits, he turned and ran, while they, yelping loudly, pursued him in great sport. He tried to hide in the shrubbery, but one of the bitches, Hylowe Mary, caught his coattail in her teeth, and there was a terrible ripping sound as she gave a hard yank. Bodenheim let out a yell for help loud enough to drown out the dogs, and someone ran to his rescue. He was found unhurt but huddling in the bushes with the dogs prancing around him and barking joyously. Eventually he ceased trembling, and, mollified by Mrs. Russell's concern and sympathy, plus a few swallows of alcohol, his good humor returned by the time dinner was served. But when he found a check for ten dollars under his plate at table, he let out another yell. When Amy appeared he told her the check should have been made out for at least a hundred dollars. She retorted that ten was all she ever paid for one rip and that his jacket wasn't worth even that much. But his nerves, he protested, were shattered; she told him he would recover as soon as he got to know the dogs better. They were as harmless as babies: If they were vicious, they would have bitten *him,* not his coat. In the end, the dinner passed off amiably enough. Indeed, the incident must have been rather quickly forgiven, since the Lowell log shows that Bodenheim was among the dinner guests at Sevenels soon again, and later in the summer joined Robinson and others from the MacDowell Colony in going to Amy's house in Dublin. The story, however, made the rounds in Boston, flourishing as it traveled, until Amy, who heard that the famous Mrs. Gardner had enjoyed it, wrote to John G. Fletcher: "Mrs. Jack Gardner has just caught on to us—it's the best thing that could happen!"

She was soon to lose Fletcher as a close ally, however, for he was married that spring, and did not come east as often as he had, nor was he available for conferences, though he remained in the Imagist movement and helped to arrange lectures for Amy in Omaha, St. Louis, and several cities in Texas. A worse blow came about two months later, when, in late July, Amy's old friend Carl Engel, the most devoted of the inner circle of "Devils," married Abigail Josephine Carey (for some reason, familiarly known as Helen). Amy had met Miss Carey but had not expected Carl would ever marry her or anyone else. She keenly felt the loss of these two ardent devotees to her cause, especially Carl, since his marriage put an end to the long, informal evenings of conversation that sometimes lasted till dawn (for if they "got into something," as she said, Amy would forsake her night's work, and "Peter" would often stay up beyond her usual hour). Amy missed these sessions, and even though the friendship was extended to include his wife and continued all around, she never wholly reconciled herself to Carl's marriage. It was then that the "Dear Bibi" letters in the Lowell–Engel correspondence began. Though the letters that remain after Engel's culling are affectionate, there is never any hint of Amy's earlier feeling of unrequited love for him. In fact, the tone of Amy's letters to Engel changed from the time she met Ada.

In a later letter, sent to him in time to greet him on his arrival in Washington to take up his post as chief of the Music Division of the Library of Congress, she sums up their whole relationship. Half-apologetic for writing, she says: "I want you to feel and know that underneath I am as much with you there as here." She speaks of dining with the Edward Hills, then goes on: "'Ned' said lovely things about you, and that the Congressional Library was lucky to have secured you. He played me his eight new orchestral waltzes."

Here she mentions Engel's training of her "ear" musically and confesses: "You have really done a lot for me, Bibi dear. Years ago, you lifted me out of a slough of despond so deep I thought it would drown me. You cultivated my ear and my mind, and taught me the salutary lesson that Boston was not the only spot on the globe. And more than that, you brought me a true friend at a time when I seemed to be all alone.* *I am not alone now and neither are you,* and pretty soon you will be three instead of two." (His wife Helen was pregnant, and it was in this letter that Amy also confessed that she never was fond of babies; that they made her unhappy and uncomfortable because she felt *they* were; she admired them as much as possible within these limits.) After a few jocular remarks about herself and "Mrs. Peter" as someday growing old and doting on his grandchildren, she closed with some suggestions about his manuscript (with which she had helped him) of his "Report" to the library, and signed the letter, "Lovingly, Amy."

There is no indication that she and Ada attended Carl's wedding. News of the marriage, however, may have precipitated her work with Edwin Arlington Robinson, in a series of interviews for a study of his work, along with Robert Frost's, which she was doing as part of a lecture series later to be published in book form. With Robinson, who frequently came to dinner, especially during the summer when she and Ada were in Dublin, Amy felt both comfortable and interested. Shy almost to the point of diffidence with most women, Robinson understood Amy's inner stress and made allowances for her eccentric behavior that many would not. His tall, slightly stooped, shabby-genteel figure and rather austere face seemed to become both more animated and more relaxed with Amy and Ada than any of the reigning beauties at the MacDowell Colony would have thought possible. There was a dry, wry humor in him that came to the fore after a few drinks, and Amy could appreciate his crusty remarks about his "town down the river." She knew Gardiner, Maine, or its equivalent, well; they were New Englanders together, and she appreciated his candor and his courtesy.

One night she was invited to the MacDowell Colony for din-

* This would indicate that Engel introduced her to Lina Abarbanell, but in Damon it was the other way around.

ner. Robert Haven Schauffler, with whom Amy had sparred earlier when they were on a panel together by disagreeing with his Socialist views, tried to put her on the spot by offering her a cigar after dinner. At first she glared at him, but then said calmly as she helped herself, "Well, you've all paid a nickel to read about me doing this; now you can see it for free!" She sucked on the cigar as he held a match to the tip, after which the resident artists relaxed and were soon pegging her with questions about Imagism. Padraic Colum, the Irish poet, who had criticized her, found her delightful and equal to his nimble and gnomelike repartee. Two weeks later she had the whole Colony to dinner in Dublin. While everyone sat on the veranda watching the changing colors of Mount Monadnock, she and Robinson were asked to recite their poems about the famous mountain. He declined, but Amy was always willing, and she read both his and her own in her resonant voice.

One incident that became legendary occurred around this time (1915–16) when her car broke down in the country and had to be repaired in a local garage. When the proprietor presented his bill, she told him to charge it, and started to leave. "Just a minute, ma'am; how do I know your credit is any good?" he asked suspiciously. Her answer was simply to repeat her name, but he looked so doubtful that she told him, "My brother is president of Harvard University," adding, as a challenge, "Call Harvard and ask him if you don't believe me!" And she walked out of the garage. Calling Kirkland 7600, the man got Abbott Lawrence Lowell on the phone and explained skeptically, "Some big fat dame whose engine broke down wants to charge her bill—claims she's your sister."

"What is she doing now?" asked the president of Harvard.

"She's across the road . . . sittin' on a stone wall, smoking a cigar!"

Lawrence, who was resigned to Amy's habits, assured him, "That's my sister, all right!"

Amy liked to tell this story as she lit her after-dinner cigar, joining good-naturedly in the laughter at her expense.

It was a busy summer, socially and professionally. Besides the interviews and preparations for the new lectures, "Lowell & Russell" read proofs of her new volume of poetry, which was to appear in the fall. They gardened and went boating and, as always, drove through the woods and country lanes in Amy's rig. She now had a skittery mare, Possibly, so named because one never knew whether or not the horse would go on if there was the slightest distraction. Toward the end of the summer, they were returning from an afternoon ride when a storm blew up. Between the thunderclaps and the wind-blown rain, Possibly got confused at the last turn and started going up the hill instead of down. When Amy gave a sharp yank at the reins to turn him around, the buggy went off the shoulder of the road at the rear, and the wheels stuck in the mud of a shallow ditch.

Amy handed the reins to "Pete," got out before she could ask what she was going to do, and, with a tremendous heave, lifted the back end of the buggy onto the road again. She always overestimated her strength, and now she felt such a terrible pull on her stomach muscles that she groaned aloud; but in answer to Ada's "What happened?" she just said, "I don't know, but we're out of the ditch. Let's go!" And she climbed back in, wet to the skin, took the reins, and continued driving. She was so intent on beating the worst of the storm, which was still mounting, that she didn't think much about herself. But after they were safely at home and dry in a complete change of clothes, Amy began to suffer a pain which persisted throughout the evening. Ada insisted that she call the doctor, who came promptly. He discovered a distension of the stomach muscle that might mean she had an umbilical hernia caused by the heavy lifting. He ordered her to take complete rest for a few days, and the quiet appeared to soothe the strained tissues, so for a time Amy forgot about this latest physical problem. However, the whole experience, which seemed only a trifle at the moment, eventually proved to be fatal. From this point on, the pace of living, which involved writing and producing at least one book a year in the more sanguine stretches between the jagged peaks of pain and suffering, became a kind of frenzied race with Time.

CHAPTER XIII

Success Follows Success

For Amy, the important event of the fall of 1916 was the publication of *Men, Women and Ghosts* on October 18. In the manuscript she had also dedicated this volume to Ada, but Ada persuaded her to remove the dedication. Amy could not comprehend the self-effacing devotion of her companion, who had done much research for this new work, which contained a collection of narrative poems dealing with the Napoleonic Wars ("Four Bronze Tablets") and five contemporary "war pictures." Half of the book was in free verse, a third in rhymed meter, and the rest in Amy's specialty, polyphonic prose. In making up the dummy, she had been shrewd enough to place "Patterns," which had been an instant success when it appeared in the *Little Review,* in front, as an "opener," and she was confident it would mean surefire success for the book as well. It was the perfect lead-off for a volume of poems on themes of love-and-war, and it could be interpreted in any number of ways.

The "stiff, brocaded gown" that the eighteenth-century lady longs to shed could be the moral shackles of the poet herself (as indeed it was to begin with), or it could represent the strictures confining any woman who dreams of freedom. And the last line could be antiwar or anti-middle-class morality, or both; its expletive could be sacred or profane—or both, as it was no doubt meant to be—as a deity-invoking oath: "Christ! What are patterns for?" She was not mistaken; the poem proved to be one of her most popular and is still included, as pointed out earlier, in contemporary anthologies. In this and other personal poems, "love is treated exclusively from the woman's point of view," to quote Foster Damon; and there are indications of the poet herself as lover, emphasized in later volumes (particularly in *Pictures of the Floating World*). The historical poems required close checking of material, especially of dates and names. Ada's assistance had been of prime importance, and, aside from a feeling of love, Amy thought her friend should get the credit for making such poems possible; but Ada remained adamant in her refusal. "You're hopeless, Peter," Amy told her fondly.

As usual, the pressures of launching a book, Lowell fashion, took a heavy toll. The strain of waiting for reviews, refuting attacks, and accepting praise was hard—too hard to bear, in fact. She much preferred the activity of promoting a book to the agony of waiting to see what its fate would be. She once wrote: "The life of a poet is by no means the dreamy aesthetic one most people imagine it to be. A mixture of a day-laborer, a traveling salesman, and an itinerant actress is about what it amounts to." (For many writers her description is equally, if not more, true in 1974, with TV talk shows, radio interviews, and "benefit" appearances.) At any rate, she had a compulsion to push her work in every way she could, which invariably brought on an acute attack of gastritis, followed by jaundice and a general neurasthenia. Now, however, her health was also threatened by the imminent umbilical hernia. She had to postpone a lecture at Washington University and collapsed in bed immediately after the new book appeared.

Men, Women and Ghosts received wide acclaim; eight days after publication a second edition was ordered, but Amy was so ill she could hardly enjoy its success. On November 1, she and Ada drove to Boston to see a window display of her books at the Old Corner Bookshop, but it was a mistake. She could not get out of the car; her chauffeur parked for a few minutes in front of the shop while Ada went in and talked to the proprietor. Amy had to be content to "drink in the display" through the window. She went to bed on their return and had to stay there throughout November and most of December; the doctor forbade her to do any work for five weeks. During the second week in November the internal pain became so severe that she was kept under morphine, at times double doses of it. In the midst of her suffering, the tragic news came that Percy had died suddenly of a cerebral hemorrhage on November 12. He had been forced to take long periods of rest since 1897, just after his discovery of Planet X, when he experienced the same sort of extreme exhaustion from overwork that Amy and at least half of the Lowell family seem to have inherited from their great-grandfather, "John the Rebel."

Amy was too ill to be told of the death for several days. When she was finally informed, the shock of losing her brilliant, adored brother * was mitigated somewhat by Ada Russell's calm, rocklike presence and tender sympathy. Amy must have been more than thankful that "Peter" was with her, that the curse—"along the parching high road of the world no other soul should bear her company," as she had written in *Dome*—had been lifted, and that she had been sent a soul mate of such great understanding. Without her friend to buoy her spirits, it is doubtful that Amy could have recovered and continued at her breakneck, unrelenting pace as she did time after time.

The knowledge that her books were going well made her eager to get back into harness as she began to feel better. *Six French Poets* was selling more copies than anyone had expected, and when she heard that the publisher promised a third printing of *Men, Women and Ghosts* soon, Amy was enraptured. With her keen sense of rivalry, her first reaction was: "I do wish I could beat Frost on a book!" (She was no doubt referring to Robert Frost's latest volume, *Mountain Interval,* which had received such acclaim.) Before long, she was once more in the vortex of the swirling renaissance in the poetry world, which was still on the upswing. Her friendly enemy, Josephine Peabody, became a full-fledged enemy in a turbulent election of the New England Poetry Club, when she lost the race for the presidency to Amy, whose reelection she had challenged. The contest took place while Amy was in the midst of preparing her lecture-study of Frost, and she had sent him

* Before he lost consciousness, Percy said, "I have always known it would come like this, but not so soon." For an excellent account of his career and magnetic personality, see Ferris Greenslet, *The Lowells and Their Seven Worlds* (Boston: Houghton Mifflin Company, 1946).

a telegram asking for some patriotic poems, followed by a letter describing the fracas in the Poetry Club. In an unpublished letter, dated March 1916, the quixotic Frost wrote her: "You are too sudden for me. I can't tell patriotism from decadence. But here are these to choose from." He had enclosed a few poems. On Josephine Peabody he commented: "I am sorry Mrs. Marks has gone to war with you. What is the matter with her? She ought not to let herself be made unhappy by another person's success." To receive such a remark from a poet she admired gave Amy singular satisfaction.

At about the same time she heard from D. H. Lawrence, who complimented her on the new volume at the end of a long letter. "These things are your best, by far," he said. Among his special choices were the "Spring Day" series; a related one, "Towns in Colour"; "The Hammers"; and some of the Stravinsky-inspired lyrics. "The shock and clipping of the physico-mechanical world is your finest expression," he told her. He did not care for the ghost stories, but he liked the tales of "human beings" with living emotions.

She needed all the praise and encouragement she could get from her Imagist colleagues and friends like the Frosts and the Untermeyers, for the second offensive in the poetic war continued to be waged all through 1916–17, whether Amy was feeling well or ill, whether she was tired or rested, whether she was forewarned of opposition or not. Her travel arrangements became more elaborate than ever. In addition to rooms for herself and Ada and a sitting room, she would also rent those on either side, so they would not be disturbed by noise from other hotel guests. Telephone messages were sent to Ada, who also entertained friends, saw reporters, ordered meals at odd hours, while Amy prepared for the lectures. As soon as they were over, Amy would relax for a day or two, and, in New York or Chicago, give dinner parties in her suite as she had done at the Berkeley in London.

One evening late in her career when the guests were all assembled—besides the Untermeyers, Sara Teasdale, and Ernest Filsinger (the man Sara eventually married instead of Vachel Lindsay), and perhaps Elsie Sergeant and Bobby (Robert Edmond)

Jones, or Jessie Rittenhouse and one or two other members of the Poetry Society among Amy's supporters—room service seemed especially long in coming. (The waiters usually appeared promptly in order to make sure of a sizable tip.) Finally, after the literary gossip had been exhausted, Amy said to her friend: "Peter, dear, do telephone room service again. I can't imagine why they are so late." Ada went into her room but came back in a few minutes to announce in a mock-tragic voice: "I'm afraid we aren't going to get any dinner—the waiters are on strike!"

Such news was all Amy needed to go on the offensive. She stood up and marshaled her company with a sweeping gesture. "Come along, everybody; I'm sorry we have to go downstairs, but we'll get dinner all right!" According to Jean Starr Untermeyer, who used to tell the story with great relish,* they arrived in the main dining room en masse, and, since no captain was on duty, Amy marched them to a corner table and motioned them all to take places. They did, and they sat there, along with a sprinkling of would-be diners at other tables, but no waiters came. After a good deal of cussing and stewing, Amy's mouth closed tightly with determination; she rose with a wrathful gleam in her eye and strode toward the kitchen. None of her guests dared to laugh until she emerged from the kitchen moments later. Beaming triumphantly and resplendent in a dark green satin suit gleaming with sequins and the jeweled chains she always wore around her neck, she carried a steaming bowl of soup in each bejeweled hand and set down her cargo without spilling a drop. Then they all roared and burst into applause. It was a great act, and Amy joined in the laughter with the same gusto she showed in her clowning days at school. Like a victorious general, she seated herself at the head and claimed her spoils, and dinner was "grudgingly served by the glum staff."

It was because of episodes like these that Amy Lowell acquired the reputation of having robust health and of being a powerhouse in action. The latter was certainly true, but she threw

* As included in *Private Collection* (New York: Alfred A. Knopf, 1965), her book of memoirs, the anecdote does not have the flavor she gave it in the telling, with different embellishments each time.

herself into every endeavor with such ardor that she burned up her energy and collapsed in exhaustion when the "campaign" or press of work was over, as she had at the time of Percy's death. And from then on, she had to contend with the hernia, for which she was, within a year, to have the first of four operations. Early in 1917, she had recovered her strength sufficiently to embark on the new lecture series, settling into her New York hotel for a stay similar to the one just described. (Whenever she had engagements in the New York metropolitan area with a brief space of time between them, she remained in New York during the interval.) Edwin Arlington Robinson was the subject of the first lecture given at the Brooklyn Institute of Arts and Sciences. It was received well enough and without explosive aftermath, as there was hardly anything controversial in it, but Robinson would not attend: He wasn't taking any chances. However, afterward he did meet with Amy over a glass of bitters to discuss possible changes in the material before publication. The following Thursday she spoke on Robert Frost; next came Masters and Sandburg, and finally "The Imagists," which of course produced the controversy she expected. At Princeton, Amy was attacked, not by the students, but by the faculty, who denounced the principles and practices of Imagism. Following the lecture, they tried without success to convince the aspiring undergraduate poets of the demerits and dangers of Imagism. "They fought hard, but were silenced and demolished to a man," wrote John Peale Bishop, president of the senior class, soon to make his own name known in modern poetry circles.

College students of both sexes enjoyed Amy Lowell's forthright and even rowdy approach. With her special reading lamp, her books, notes, pairs of glasses of different strength, she put on a whole show by way of prologue—she knew it and assumed that the audience knew it. Quite by accident at Wellesley she had hit upon a trick that never failed to win her listeners. After hearing the first poem, the students couldn't seem to make up their minds whether to applaud then or wait till the end—or perhaps they were puzzled by the poetry itself—Amy couldn't tell. At last she demanded impatiently: "Well?—Clap or hiss, I don't care which, but for Christ's sake, do something!" The result of course was a burst of laughter and applause; from then on, she had the listeners in the palm of her hand. (In relating the original incident, Foster Damon did not include Amy's profanity, but it occurs in Winfield Scott's version; and it is likely that if Amy did indeed give vent to her feelings in this way—profanity was not uncommon in her daily speech—she herself probably deleted it in appearances before groups like the Omaha Women's Club.) As time went on, however, she did not need to prod her audiences into applause. Her resonant voice and the compelling storytelling quality of her delivery brought forth enthusiastic and instant hand-clapping.

In the meantime, the plot loosely hatched by Witter Bynner and Arthur Davison Ficke the year before had thickened considerably. When, after Amy's appearance in Chicago, Ficke had sent her the beautiful Japanese print, he had inscribed it, "With the admiration of the enemy," which Amy thought rather odd at the time. She knew that neither Bynner nor Ficke had endorsed the Imagist movement, but she did not consider them enemies. (Most people were under the impression that, as Virgil Thomson remarked, "Amy had the whole Poetry Society in her lap for about ten years"; but the truth was that she never at any time had more than half its members in her more-than-ample lap.) Along with the print, Ficke had sent a copy of his article, "Modern Tendencies in Poetry" (published later in the September issue of the *North American Review*), and had disarmingly asked her if she would criticize the piece before he sent it in. She obliged and read it with an open mind. In the conclusion, he casually mentioned the "Spectrists" among the newest of contemporary schools. Amy told him in her generally favorable critique that she had never heard of them.

She could not know that the "Spectric school" consisted of Bynner and Ficke, or that it had been invented by Bynner on the spur of the moment one night during the intermission of *Spectre de la Rose*. With the friend who had accompanied him to the ballet, he was discussing the epidemic of new schools that had broken out since the onset of the Imagists, and his eye fell on the title of the ballet program. Hence the name of Spectrists, born on the spot! Taking the pseudonyms of Emanuel Morgan (Bynner) and Anne Knish (Ficke), the two poets proceeded—half in fun, half out of malice born of their "genuine indignation at the charlatanism of some of the new schools of poetry"—to write a spate of poems parodying free verse. These they managed without much trouble to publish in various literary magazines, including *Poetry*. And in June 1916, *The Forum* carried an article on "The Spectric School of Poetry," by Mr. Morgan and Miss Knish. They outlined their credo as Amy had done in the preface of the first Imagist anthology.

The Spectrists claimed the entire span of light rays—the entire spectrum—for their verse; they went so far as to discard "the chains of free verse," which should have given away the hoax, and almost did, as far as Amy was concerned. She was still skeptical when a little volume called *Spectra,* published by Kennerly, appeared around the same time as *Men, Women and Ghosts.* In a crowning spoof of the spoof, Witter Bynner himself had reviewed *Spectra* in the pages of the *New Republic.* The new group, he said, rooted out all the rest: The Vorticists, the Imagists, the Futurists, the Chorists (a group who wrote dance poems)—all were now passé. What made the whole thing credible was that both Bynner and Ficke were too talented to write poor poetry, and some of their wildest concoctions were gems of humor and brilliant wit. ("Hope/ Is the Antelope/ Over the hills;/ Fear/ Is the wounded deer/ Bleeding in rills; Care/ Is the heavy bear/ Tearing at meat; Fun/ Is the mastodon/ Vanished complete . . ." is a sample of Bynner's creation; and "If bathing were a virtue, not a lust,/ I would be dirtiest," the opening of Ficke's "Opus 118," is a direct hit at Amy Lowell's "Bath.")

While many were fooled—and *Spectra* and its authors enjoyed far greater notoriety than they ever expected—Amy was not swayed in her feeling that the authors were insincere. She did not acknowledge the presentation copy of *Spectra* sent to her. In January 1917, then, when she sat next to Witter Bynner at a party Jessie Rittenhouse of the Poetry Society gave for her at the completion of her lectures, and he asked her point-blank what she thought of the Spectrists, she looked him straight in the eye and said, "Bynner, I think they are charlatans." At that moment she had no idea that he and Ficke were the real authors, but she had read his praise of *Spectra* and had caught his slur at her and the Imagists. He had taken the occasion to "quote Mr. Morgan" as saying that "while he found the Imagist insistence on natural cadence and clear-driven expression salutary, they would not count so much themselves as in their jacking up of the technique of the poets through whom vibrate richer matters than the tickling of a leaf on a window-pane or the flickering of water in a bathtub." Now (at the party) she noticed that Witter Bynner stared at her rather strangely for a long moment, and offered no retort to her branding *Spectra* the work of charlatans. It was almost as if he suddenly felt a true respect for her, but he said nothing and quickly changed the subject.

Toward the end of the year, she received a note from Robert Frost asking her to "have Lesley over from Wellesley some day to see you where you sit enthroned." Frost could never resist teasing Amy, but he did want his oldest child, who had just begun college, to see Sevenels and meet the leader of the Imagist movement who had given him his first important review in a general literary magazine (not to mention her lecture on Frost, which would soon be published). Amy lost no time in sending Lesley an invitation for tea; and her father's letter briefing her for the visit is both typical and perceptive: "Read Amy's *Men, Women and Ghosts* if you can possibly find time right away," he bade his daughter, "so that if Amy invites you over to see her you'll be ready for her. You won't perhaps care for the longer poems & of course you won't go far in any poem that doesn't get hold of you. Find something to like though. I think you can. Be fairer to her than some people have been to you. She's not going to examine you & see how well you like her. You simply won't want to feel lost in the dark should she happen to illustrate what she means by cadence, rhythm, and such things from her own work. She won't talk about *metre*. She scorns the word. Prosody too she hates the name of. She may try to tell you what determines the ending place of a line in free verse. She'll be interesting. You'll find that there'll be a lot in what she says." Then he seems to have had sudden doubts about Lesley's ability to cope with Amy, for he ended: "But perhaps if she writes to you and invites you just now, you can say you will feel safer to wait till I can come in and show you the way across the city. Tell her I shall be in town toward the end of the week. I mean to get to Wellesley on the coming Thursday or Friday. Love, Papa."

His letter came at about the same time as Amy's invitation, but Lesley had no intention of waiting for her father to take her to Sevenels; she preferred the adventure of going alone. The prospective visit had caused much excitement among her classmates, especially after Amy's successful reading at Wellesley. She had no trouble finding a copy of *Men, Women and Ghosts;* virtually all the girls knew "Patterns" by heart within a few months after the book came out. "I think the whole freshman class went with me to buy a dress for the occasion," Lesley recalled. Such was Amy Lowell's fame and popularity at the time.

The visit was entirely different from her expectations. Unfortunately, Amy was suffering from a serious flareup of the hernia condition, which threatened to require surgery before long. Lesley, who had been looking forward to seeing the library her parents had described in glowing detail, was, to her disappointment, shown directly up to Amy's third-floor bedroom as soon as she arrived. When she entered, three or four other guests—women friends of Amy's—were seated in a semicircle having tea; three or four of the sheep dogs were stretched on the floor around the foot of the bed, where Amy was half-lying, half-sitting, enthroned on her pillows. Her pain had been temporarily diminished by pills, and she hailed Lesley with a hearty welcome. Then, after introducing "Robert Frost's daughter" all around, she reached under a pillow and pulled out a box of her Manilas. "Will you have a cigar?" she asked.

Lesley, though she later smoked cigarettes, had not yet so much as taken a puff of any tobacco; and although she knew very well that Amy smoked cigars, she had not expected to be offered one almost before she had a chance to catch her breath. She was by no means a shy or retiring girl, but the sight of Amy Lowell—bulking large under the covers, with books, papers, and notebooks all over the wide bed, holding out the box of cigars—was enough to make the eighteen-year-old hesitate. So she murmured politely,

"No, thank you, I don't smoke." But she has often said since that she regretted "ever afterward" that she did not just reach out calmly and accept a cigar with a brief thank you and light up like "an old pro." As it was, she accepted a cup of tea from Ada Russell, who was presiding at a small tea table near the bed, and took a small sandwich from the silver tray offered by Elizabeth Henry (Amy's private maid), while Amy herself lit a fresh cigar from the one she had been smoking. Between puffs she paused long enough to ask, like an inquisitor: "What do you think of Keats?"

Lesley realized then, as she sat down on the only empty chair (completing the semicircle of guests), that the books, papers, pamphlets, filing cards, and other paraphernalia that spilled over the bed, littering the floor, and those piled on chests and tables, were all about Keats. Amy's main topic of conversation was "Keats, Keats, Keats," from beginning to end. Lesley did not get a chance to inform her that she was so well versed in *Men, Women and Ghosts* at the moment she could think of nothing else. All the comments about the book she had carefully stored up were left unsaid or went unheeded. Surely the Mad Hatter's Tea Party was not as mad as this one in Amy Lowell's bedroom at Sevenels! If any proof were needed in regard to Amy Lowell's research for her biography of Keats, Lesley Frost could prove it was thorough and long.

She could not know that Amy had just completed the manuscript and makeup of her forthcoming book, *Tendencies in Modern American Poetry*. Based, like *Six French Poets,* on her recent lectures, it would be published the following month. Lesley's already famous father and Edwin Arlington Robinson were first among the three pairs of poets under discussion. As usual, Amy was exhausted, the hernia was aggravated, and she had had to go to bed. She made use of her time to continue the labor of love she had begun as early as 1912, her projected biography of John Keats, and Ada had just brought this load of material from the library. Amy's enthusiasm of the moment always dominated her conversation, and just now she was championing Fanny Brawne, sole beloved of Keats, and accused of causing his terrible frustration and consequent early death by her refusal of his love. Amy's purpose was to exonerate Fanny, while at the same time sympathizing with Keats—which she did almost to the point of assuming his identity. She also aimed to unmask Severn, the poet's pretentious friend (in Amy's eyes), who had placed the guilt on Fanny's head in his famous memoir of Keats's last days.

Amy's preoccupation with Keats took on the intensity of fanaticism at times, and this was one of them. She could not help holding forth on the subject any more than she could on Imagism and the new poetry at other times. But Lesley found that she *was* interesting, and there was "a lot in what she had to say." If only she hadn't used such a lot of words to say it! But that was Amy.

Tendencies in Modern American Poetry appeared on schedule, at about the same time as the third volume of *Some Imagist Poets,* which continued to do unexpectedly well. As with the other two volumes, Amy, who was beginning to recover, took pleasure in dividing the royalties into six equal parts and sending checks to her five Imagist colleagues, who hailed her with delight. For Lawrence and Frieda, as well as H.D. and Aldington (who had not yet separated), those checks proved a lifesaver more than once. Lawrence wrote in one of his rare bursts of optimism that the Imagist anthology seemed to be a "real gold mine, no end to its yield."

Tendencies was widely accepted as an important critical work and did much to improve Amy Lowell's position as an authority in the world of modern poetry, particularly *American* poetry. In her preface she made it clear that "We are no longer of this or that other land, but ourselves, different from all other peoples whatever." Her division of the book into three sections, dealing with three pairs of poets, key figures in the development of the new poetry, was in itself a sign of her gifts for organization and promotion. Conversational in tone, the book appealed to the average reader with its clear-cut portraits of Robinson and Frost, representing "Evolution"; Masters and Sandburg, "Revolution"; and H. D. and Fletcher, the full-fledged modern point of view as outlined by the Imagist creed.

She treated each poet as both person and artist, with a running appreciation of the works as related to their authors' lives.

(Elinor Frost later, in an unpublished letter,* wished to have a "paragraph or two of the most personal part" deleted. The portion dealing with Frost's early life, she wrote, "seems to attribute to me a grim determination to be educated at all costs, whereas the fact was I said again and again I was willing to leave college and be married as soon as he was earning enough money to rent *one room* somewhere, but that I couldn't consent to be a burden to our parents. Some humorous, extravagant remarks of Robert's when they first met apparently made a great impression on Miss Lowell's mind.)

Foster Damon, after giving some background literary data, calls *Tendencies* "the most important critical work produced in America for many years." ** At the time the book appeared, he himself had recently become part of the circle at Sevenels, by a route indicating Amy's indomitable, tireless persistence in seeking out recruits. Not long after Carl Engel's marriage, Amy had heard from John Fletcher that a Harvard graduate student, as a candidate for the Bowdoin Prize, had written a paper on "Free Verse and Imagism," which Fletcher thought was quite remarkable and certainly "worth looking into," and he enclosed a copy. Amy was so impressed with the insight the young writer showed that she immediately started tracking him down. (The thesis had to be submitted anonymously.) She first asked her brother Lawrence to try to find out who had written it, but his staff was unsuccessful. Next she contacted the Harvard *Crimson,* the *Lampoon,* and the Hasty Pudding Club, but as he was not connected with any Harvard publications or clubs, she gave up the search for a time, while letting it be known that she was eager to talk to him.

He finally heard that he was being sought after by the famous "Miss Lowell of Brookline" (now no longer known as "the president's sister" but as "the leader of the Imagists"). Astonished that she would go to such lengths to find him, he summoned his cour-

* To Dorothy Dunbar (later) Bromley, then secretary to Stanley Bromley, one of Frost's editors at Holt. Dated December 27, 1923, the passage concerns a quotation from *Tendencies* to be used in the introduction to a new volume of Frost. On second thought, they decided not to delete it.

** S. Foster Damon, *Amy Lowell, A Chronicle* (Boston: Houghton Mifflin Company, 1935).

age and called her on the phone. He was working on another project—a book that "would open up the language of Blake," as Virgil Thomson put it—but had heard she was interested in discussing his views on Imagism.

Her answer was: "How soon can you come for dinner?" They set a date within a day or two; and when the neat blond young man with a neat blond mustache, a friendly smile, and a gleam of high intelligence in his eyes stood up as she came into the library (early, for her), she knew she had found another ally. He was pale and slender, but his ideas were not. That same night after dinner they had a literary argument which continued until he had to leave to catch the last trolley car. His ideas showed that he had studied not only Imagism but the whole subject of free verse and that he had given considerable thought to its origins. As impressed as Amy had been with his thesis, she disagreed with him on the point that the stanza was the basis of free verse, and it was this that brought on their diverting argument. The young man stuck to his guns firmly but pleasantly. (Later he inserted a paragraph on her views in his essay before it was published.)

There was a lively feeling of intellectual give-and-take to the discussion that made her think of former evenings spent with Carl Engel. Like Carl, Damon also had an interest in modern French music, particularly in the piano works of Eric Satie. In a couple of years, as a Harvard English instructor, he was to bring these works to the attention of Virgil Thomson, along with the volume of Gertrude Stein's *Tender Buttons* (both of which changed Virgil Thomson's life, according to his own testimony). In return, Virgil, after the two became friends, introduced Foster Damon to the charms of peyote, the drug drawn from a Mexican cactus that sent young men on "trips" in the late teens of this century. The two would take this potion together, enjoying its euphoric, hallucinatory effect, sometimes with another poet and English A instructor, Robert Hillyer. If Amy knew of these excursions on Foster's part, she probably saw nothing wrong with them—any more than she did her own smoking of cigars—as long as they did no harm to his brains. No one could actually take Bibi's place. He had been Amy's mentor in many ways, whereas Foster Damon became her disciple. Like any disciple, he was more inclined to show his ardor, sometimes in ways which amused and touched Amy and Ada.

In the Lowell files are such items as a valentine to Amy; a tiny note in free verse, "To the American Sappho," written in gold ink, and sent to Amy as late as 1920, when Damon was on his way to Europe for a lecture tour on Blake, and, in Denmark of all places, on Amy Lowell. In another note, he exclaims: "I wish I could tell you how much you mean to me—O, splendid woman, miraculous woman!" And he always sent his affectionate regards to "Mrs. Russell," who remained his close friend and adviser when he was writing his 700-page *Chronicle* of Amy's life. There can be no doubt that he was a welcome addition to the Sevenels salon from late 1916 to the end. When *Tendencies in Modern American Poetry* was published in late 1917, he was already one of the inner circle.

CHAPTER XIV

Wartime Poet: Personal Catastrophes

THE ACTIVE ENTRY of the United States into the war in Europe in 1917 with the deployment of the American Expeditionary Force in France had brought certain changes to the life at Sevenels as to all American households. The rationing of meat, butter, sugar, and tobacco demanded sacrifices even in an establishment as well provisioned as Sevenels. Strange as it seems now, "cigarettes for the dough-boys" was a patriotic call, and all tobacco was at a premium. It was then that Amy ordered 10,000 of her imported cigars from the Philippines, stacking the boxes in a closet after a chest was filled. She also managed to obtain an enormous supply of sugar, which was stored in a huge barrel, hidden in a long, low closet under the eaves in her third-floor bedroom. If anyone had accused her of hoarding, she would have denied the charge vigorously; *she* was doing the rationing herself: Every Monday morning, like a supply sergeant, she doled out to the cook enough sugar to last the week, and she was strict in keeping her regulation.

One day during lunch the secretaries mentioned to Ada that they were both so fond of a certain apricot dessert they wondered if they could have it again soon; it had not been served for some time. "I think that can be arranged," Ada told them with an amused smile. "I'll ask the cook if we can have it tomorrow." But the next day when they came into the small dining room for lunch, she had disappointing news. "Cook says the apricots take too much sugar. You know Miss Lowell only gives her so much and no more to go on for the whole week," she reminded them.

Mary Sands was ready to accept the decision, but the other secretary, a vivacious Irish-American girl, flashed, "Oh, I'll furnish the sugar! I'll bring a little sack from home." And in a day or two she handed the cook a little brown paper bag half-filled with sugar; the following day the girls and Ada were served the promised dessert, which they all enjoyed. But after Ada left to rush off to the library for Amy, the other girl whispered to Mary, "Do you know where the sugar came from?"

Surprised, Mary said, "I thought you said you brought it from home."

Her coworker giggled. "I said I'd bring a sack, and I did. But I got the sugar—*out* of the barrel *upstairs!*"

Mary's jaw dropped open. Shocked, she exclaimed, "How could you! How did you manage it?"

"Easy," was the answer. "While Miss Lowell was in the bathtub, I snuck into the closet and swiped a shovelful." (Amy had a silver sugar shovel that she used for "rationing.")

Mary was still shocked. "She'd kill you if she knew." But she was giggling, too.

"I know it." The other's eyes were dancing. "That's what made the dessert extra delicious!"

Stifling their laughter, they went upstairs to take the daily dictation. If Amy noticed any conspiratorial looks or suppressed smiles, she did not give evidence of it. She was completely occupied with the business of compiling lists of books for the poetry libraries she had proposed for training camps. Poetry in wartime, she felt, was more necessary than ever, and she offered to make it available to servicemen. To her surprise, the idea was taken up immediately, and the initial trial library that had been set up had been so successful that she had received requests for thirty-four additional ones at as many training camps. (This was one of the reasons Ada had rushed to the library in Boston.) It is not likely that Amy noticed that the sugar level had gone down slightly the next time she doled out the week's ration, but if she did, or if for any other reason she suspected her secretary of pilfering some, she probably felt the girls deserved it. They were working on alternate Saturday afternoons now—at no extra pay—because there was such a press of work, not only for the libraries, but for Amy's new volume of her own poems, which involved correspondence and extra typing.

As a rule, Amy had a sharp eye and ear for every detail of life at Sevenels. She would make a fuss if she noticed gray streaks on the floor; and once, as she was dictating to Mary, she stopped in the middle of a sentence and listened intently. Her ear had detected an alien sound in the lawn mower down in the meadow! From the noise coming in the window on the warm Indian summer air she could tell something was wrong. "Go down and see about it," she said to Mary. "Tell them to fix it before they go any farther. Sounds like a nutmeg grater!"

When Mary went down to the grounds, one of the gardeners was pruning the roses. Long-stemmed blooms were scattered around on the beds as they fell from the clippers. Many were still in good shape, and she asked if she could have one. "Sure. Take a couple," the man said. She selected a single yellow rose, still almost perfect, but as she came into the library, the other secretary warned her, "Don't let her see you with that rose—she'll kill you! We're never supposed to pick the flowers."

Mary explained how she had acquired the rose. "And anyway, look at the flowers in here!" she said, indicating the bouquets that were always on the polished tables. The rejoinder was: "Miss Lowell picks those herself, and you know it. And she hardly ever touches the roses. It's got something to do with her father. Anyway, don't let her see it!" So Mary gave the rose to the cook to keep in a glass of water until she left for the day. From the back kitchen, she could hear the dogs barking in the kennels. The girls often heard the dogs, but they rarely saw them nowadays.

Amy had not been able to lay in a supply of top-round beef for her beloved sheep dogs—the advent of the freezer was far in the future—and there was no way to get around meat rationing. She had had to substitute horse meat for their daily fare, and they could not stand the change. They developed a ptomaine poisoning which eventually took the life of two. (Three were ill the day Lesley Frost was there for tea.) By February 1918, they were all so emaciated that there was little chance they could survive. Heartsick, Amy told Ada to arrange to have them chloroformed—all but Prue, the oldest, who was going to be cared for by Carl Engel's sister at her request. ("If I could take care of them myself, I might be able to cure them," Amy said. "But I can't do it anymore and they need my love and attention, I know," she told the Frosts one evening. She was both too ill and too often away from Sevenels to look after them personally, as she had in the past.) She could hardly bear to think of having them chloroformed, but it seemed to be the best thing to do. "Don't tell me until after it's over," she said to Ada, who, as always, promised to take care of everything, and told her not to fret. It was at the end of February, and Amy's sense of loss was so great she could not work for a solid week.

She realized it would be folly to get any more dogs, yet she and Ada both wanted a pet, and after a time, they acquired Winky, a handsome black cat, who was made famous in several of Amy's poems. (Needless to say, many of her guests felt relieved by the replacement.)

It was a trying, troubled winter, difficult for everyone. Amy caught a cold early in the winter, the ultimate result of which was the loss of her younger secretary, who had caught one before her. When the secretaries came up to take dictation on a mean, chilly day, they found Amy sneezing and coughing into a handkerchief. She apologized for interrupting herself so often, then turned an accusing eye on Mary and said balefully: "It's *your* fault that I have a cold!" Before Mary could ask why or how, she shook a forefinger in the astonished girl's face. "You're the one who gave it to me—coughing right at me all the time I was dictating yesterday! What's the matter—didn't your mother teach you any manners?" And she scolded the girl unmercifully for about ten minutes.

Mary finally managed to put in, apologetically, "I'm sorry, Miss Lowell, I didn't realize I was that close—I didn't mean to give you my cold." At that Amy cut off her tirade abruptly and said, "All right, let's get back to business. Where was I?" Mary could not collect herself, but the other girl read back a few words from her shorthand, and Amy took up where she had left off. She coughed intermittently but did not refer to her cold again.

An hour or so after they had gone downstairs, Mary appeared

in the doorway again. She knocked but did not cross the threshold. Amy, still in bed because of the cold, looked up from the book she was reading, pencil in hand, a notebook beside her. "Oh, Mary," she said and smiled absently.

"Is it all right if I talk to you from here?"

Amy's smile grew broader. "You don't have to stay that far away! Come in, child. What's the trouble?"

"I'm giving my notice," Mary said simply.

"Your notice? But why? I don't understand." Amy seemed genuinely puzzled. She had either forgotten all about the flareup or pretended that she had. "You can't leave now; I need you! Aren't you happy here?" she asked. She could not imagine that the people in her employ led lives of their own, had their own ambitions, their own friends, their own doctors. She once admitted to Elsie Sergeant, half-frankly, half-jokingly, that she would like to enslave all who came within her orbit. And it is likely that at Sevenels she thought of herself as a benevolent ruler, in spite of all her demands, temper tantrums, and eccentricities. And in a sense, she *was* benevolent; she was a masculine matriarch who won the loyalty of most of her staff. The other secretary, in fact, who had been there before Mary came, stayed on long afterward. But Mary could not be dissuaded from leaving. She did not tell Amy she had already lined up another job, tentatively, but the crux of the matter was that Amy Lowell was too erratic, difficult, and exacting as an employer, and the day's scene had made up her mind. She admired Amy in some ways, but she was not willing to be a slave to genius, and she knew she could not go far in a job of this sort. "I won't leave until you've found somebody else," she promised, however. It is interesting to note that the position Mary had applied for was at the Fogg Museum, where she became secretary to Alfred Barr, then a young curator, who also had ideas of his own. In a few years, with his assistant and one other staff member, she came to New York, and the little staff of four people set up the Museum of Modern Art, as much a rebel and pioneer in its field as Amy Lowell was in modern poetry. During an interview in April 1973, Mary (now Mrs. Thompson) said of Amy Lowell: "She was a terrific worker for the ideas and people in the arts that she wanted to have around her; she would do anything to get her own way, and she could be an awful snob. But sometimes she surprised you by her humility in regard to her poetry. She was terribly masculine, of course, but feminine, too; more like a woman when she had those tantrums. Working for her was a real experience, but I couldn't have stayed."

The winter of 1917–18 wore on. More and more American doughboys marched to their death in the war that was to "make the world safe for democracy," but they could not seem to stem the tidal wave of the "advancing Hun." Amy had written poems dealing with the war as early as the month following Britain's declaration of war, in one of which, "August 14, 1914," she produced one of her most striking images, depicting "the long, snail-slow serpent of marching men," and asking, "This is the war of wars?/ And the cause? Has this writhing worm of men a cause?" Remarking, "A dust speck in the worm's belly is a poet," she was perhaps referring to Rupert Brooke, one of the first to enlist. And she ended: "This is the war of wars,/ From eye to tail the serpent has one cause: PEACE!" She now began to examine earlier wars, historic battles, and "causes and effects" in preparation for a volume of historical poems. When she felt up to it, and her rations permitted, she continued to give dinners at Sevenels. Guests were literary people, for the most part, or those involved in the arts—the John Livingston Loweses, whom she had met in St. Louis at one of her lectures (after Lowes joined the Harvard faculty they became close friends); the Untermeyers, with whom she conceived the idea for a new anthology, *An American Miscellany,* which she and Louis were compiling; Robert Frost, occasionally with Elinor; Padraic and Mary Colum; the Marshes (of Macmillan); the Ferris Greenslets; Foster Damon; the Carl Engels; the E. B. Hills. Yet the talk was most often about the war. In one way or another, the war affected everything.

Even the Spectric school of poetry, the hoax perpetrated by Witter Bynner and Arthur Ficke, which had built up to amazing proportions, was wearing thin. The affair that started when the two poets retreated to a second-class hotel in Moline, Illinois, across from Ficke's home in Davenport, and, "from ten quarts of excellent Scotch in ten days extracted the whole of the Spectric philosophy," in Ficke's words, had continued to gather momentum after Amy denounced the movement to Bynner. The two pranksters had tried to enlist Edna St. Vincent Millay, who was close to both of them (first as a sort of disciple, then as the avowed lover of Arthur Ficke); but she was too much of an artist to become a "disciple" of a school whose purpose was to parody another school, and she flatly refused. She had nothing against the Imagists or Amy Lowell; their form of poetic expression simply was not for her. (Amy in turn admired Edna Millay's early work, particularly *Aria da Capo,* Millay's antiwar verse-drama written at this time, but not published till 1920; though she later became critical of the younger poet, probably out of jealousy when the latter won the Pulitzer Prize in 1923, becoming the first woman to receive it. Amy, who considered herself more deserving of the award, was piqued and angry. She also felt threatened by "Vincent's" sylphlike beauty and popularity, but her sense of fairness forced her to give credit where credit was due. There never was much rapport between these two: Each was too individualistic and too dominant a personality.)

Ficke and Bynner did find another recruit for the masquerade, however, Marjorie Allen Seiffert, a fairly well-known poet of the Chicago chapter of the Poetry Society and dinner-party friend of the conspirators. She chose the name of Elijah Hay, and published, under the banner of the Spectric school, poems that brought her literary correspondence with Dr. William Carlos Williams, Alfred Kreymborg, and other recognized poets. The movement went merrily on its way, with far more success than either Ficke or Bynner had foreseen. Amy, after one brief mention of the Spectric school when she spoke at a Harvard "smoker" (where she was "smuggled in and kept quiet with cigars while the undergrads heckled her, but she managed between puffs to hold her own"), did her best to ignore or discount the Spectrists. She could not dismiss her intuition that the whole Spectric concept was a fake. There were too many false notes in the preface that made her suspicious of its intent, which she was quite sure had been meant as a takeoff on her own prefaces; and the dedication of the volume *Spectra* to

Remy de Gourmont was most suspicious of all. Still, the credibility of the public and the popularity of the movement continued to mount. As William Jay Smith points out in his diverting account, *The Spectra Hoax,* "Indeed the hoax might well have continued months longer had it not been for America's entry into World War I; but it soon became impossible to joke about anything, even the state of American letters." *

Arthur Ficke had gone to France as a judge advocate wearing a U.S. Army captain's uniform in late February or early March (and even there the "specter" of the hoax haunted him in an eerie and hilarious episode). But before he left, he, Bynner, and Mrs. Seiffert had purposely let the nose of the cat out of the bag. Little by little, more was allowed to be seen, and on April 26 Witter Bynner was challenged as he was delivering a lecture at the Twentieth Century Club in Detroit, just after he had quoted his (Emanuel Morgan's) "Opus 62," hinting that those lines contained a ray of hope for the future of American literature, whereas most "schismatic poetry" was nothing but rot. At that point a young man raised his hand and asked him outright: "Is it not true, Mr. Bynner, that you are Emanuel Morgan and that Arthur Davison Ficke is Anne Knish?" Confronted head-on, Bynner found himself unable to tell "a direct and large lie," so he simply answered, "Yes." And he proceeded, to the general amusement of his audience, to trace the history of the hoax from its extemporaneous origin to that moment.

Spectra became a legend in that hour; but the repercussions from it, especially for Amy Lowell and her two antagonists, lasted a long time.

It seems unbelievable today that the exposé of *Spectra* should have caused a literary upheaval, but it did, beginning with an item in the *Detroit News,* which commented a few days after the revelation: "Brush off the dusty form of Mr. Barnum's Cardiff giant, and put it away forever; there is now revealed a greater hoax than this." And *Spectra* was credited by some with being the most dastardly as well as "one of the greatest literary hoaxes ever perpetrated in America." Editors who had been taken in by it were

* William Jay Smith, *The Spectra Hoax* (Middletown: Wesleyan University Press, 1961).

naturally miffed (notably Harriet Monroe, who had accepted five recent poems by Emanuel Morgan and two by Elijah Hay and now refused to print them); and those who had been skeptical were quick to crow. But newspaper columns across the country gave full accounts of the story and their reactions one way or another. Arthur Ficke wrote to Bynner from France: "I see by the papers that you have removed the last lingering bit of the cat's tail from the leaky bag, and that it has made a first-class Roman holiday." The two read all the editorial and journalistic opinion with great interest, and Bynner took Harriet Monroe to task for refusing to print "Morgan's" poetry. But the reaction they were waiting for was that of the person who had "inspired" the hoax in the first place—Amy Lowell.

At Sevenels, meanwhile, Amy had been too involved with writing poems for her newest volume, compiling lists for training-camp libraries, and other activities when she was not suffering from her physical problems to keep track of *Spectra*'s progress except for an occasional checkup. When, therefore, she opened the *New York Times Magazine* of June 2, 1918, and saw a long article by Thomas Ybarra, with photographs of Ficke and Bynner, who would, it said, in effect, "take their places beside the great literary hoaxers of all time," she called out in astonished delight, not unmixed with indignation, "Peter, take a look at this!" It was her turn to crow. "What did I tell you, right in the beginning!" she exclaimed triumphantly, while Ada Russell shook her head, laughing at the incorrigibility of creative artists. Amy remembered with glee having told Bynner at the Rittenhouse dinner party that she thought the Spectrists were "charlatans," and she recalled the peculiar look he had given her. But as she remembered other things she grew angry, and she grabbed paper and pencil to jot down notes for a letter not perfected till three days later. (It was one of those her secretary had to type several times.) When Amy was satisfied, the letter, dated June 5, 1918, was a masterpiece of sarcastic wit and feline, polite recrimination:

Dear Emanuel,

You certainly did well with "Spectra." And how glad I am that I always said it was charlatanism! I verily believe that you began to respect me from the very moment that you asked me what I thought of it, and I told you that I thought the authors were insincere. Of course, I had no idea it was a genial hoax. I simply thought that Miss Knish and Mr. Morgan were trying to gain notoriety out of a singularity in which they themselves did not in the least believe, and perhaps you will remember that I never acknowledged the presentation copy which you so kindly sent me.

But I must say I think you sailed a bit close to the wind in your review in "The New Republic," where you said, . . . "If I have overestimated the importance of *Spectra,* it is because of my constant hope, that out of these succeeding schools something better may develop than an aesthetic dalliance of eyeglass and blue stocking." *

Was this quite cricket?

Perhaps you thought you had a right to treat us in that way, believing us to be insincere also. But, dear me, that is all past, isn't it! And now I understand the reason for Mr. Ficke's sending me one of his beautiful Japanese prints after my first lecture in Chicago, inscribed, "With the admiration of the enemy." This was his *amende honorable,* and yours, I take it, was your defence of "Guns as Keys" ** at the Poetry Society last year, for which I am most grateful. In what terms should a lady acknowledge a gentleman's admission that perhaps he made a mistake in trying to cut her throat?

Still, your stiletto has not quite lost its keenness, since in this interview in "The Times" I notice that you again refer to us as a part of the dubious company of "Gists" and "Cists." ("Ah, Saul, Saul, it is hard for thee to kick against thy pricks!")

It is very "sporting" of you to attempt the dual personality plea; but how will it affect the dear public, so ignorant, so fearful of being made a fool of? And how will it affect your serious lectures? But that is for you to decide, and please believe that although the specific instance of your early hostility is news to me, the general attitude certainly is not; and that, barring this return on your track which your present remarks seem to indicate, I freely forgive you, even to the extent of sending you my new book as soon as it comes out, and I trust you will like it.

The hoax was a bit of fun, but the way you pushed the hoax—ah, well, permit me to quote from the immortal Emanuel:

"Asparagus is feathery and tall

* Amy was sure that "eyeglass and blue stocking" was a reference to her and her pince-nez.

** One of the poems for her new volume.

And the hose lies rotting by the garden wall."
The only question is whose hose.

Sincerely yours,
AMY

If revenge is sweet, this moment was one of the sweetest triumphs in Amy's professional life. She had been vindicated in her beliefs beyond her wildest dreams. She gloated over her victory, and Ada was relieved to see her so elated after the depressing events of the winter, the deaths of the sheep dogs two months before, besides the constant worry of her own condition. However, the sweetness of that hour was soon to sour; she probably would have been wiser not to crow quite so loudly, or show such vindictiveness in her letter, justified as it may have been. While "Hal" Bynner (as he was known to intimates because of his first name, Harold) laughed at Amy's own thinly disguised "stiletto," he also felt its steel jabs. In a flash of retaliatory, razor-edged wit, he referred to Amy as "the Hippopoetess." It was passingly funny, even hilarious to Bynner's friends in the Poetry Society's New York and Chicago chapters; but it was the unkindest cut of all to Amy Lowell. She was deeply wounded by the epithet, and helpless at first to combat the equally damaging and vicious publicity that the tasteless but "unshakable label," as Fanny Butcher recently called it, brought forth from countless columnists.

Miss Butcher herself, in her gossipy book of memoirs,* pins a half-mocking label on Amy Lowell, calling her "the grand panjandrum of free verse," who "was so fat that she literally waddled," a gross exaggeration according to the testimony of those who saw Amy at close range. Not only her intimate friends like Nell Belmont, Jean Starr Untermeyer, Foster Damon, Ferris Greenslet, and John Farrar, who might have been prejudiced in her favor, but people who saw her on the lecture platform and off it, have commented on the grace and ease with which she carried her enormous body. Jean Untermeyer has said that "after one or two meetings, one forgot all about Amy's unusual proportions." That this was true Fanny Butcher's own further brief glimpse

* Fanny Butcher, *Many Lives—One Love* (New York: Harper & Row, 1972).

corroborates, for she mitigates her tone of mockery in describing her sole encounter with the "panjandrum" at the time of Amy's lecture in Maurice Browne's Little Theatre. There Fanny, as secretary and general factotum, was delegated to look after the speaker. Amy, true to form, settled herself in a big chair, lit a cigar, and proceeded to explain to the pretty young girl what the "whole new movement in poetry was about." The part that the future literary editor of the *Chicago Tribune* most vividly recalled was Amy's informing her that she, herself, had not created free verse or Imagism, as many readers believed, but that she had been "converted" to broad experimental writing by reading the French free versifiers. Fanny found this "very sporting" of her, since few people had even heard of the French post-Symbolists then, and "she could have taken credit for her own original thinking." Miss Butcher's summary of Amy—"A real eccentric, she was fascinating"—seems to point to Amy's ability to win people over so completely as to make them forget her size.

Foster Damon has recorded that Bynner replied "without rancour on July 11" to Amy's letter of June 5, that she wrote him again on July 22, and that "a friendly correspondence ensued" thereafter. The columnists, however, seized upon the epithet as a choice and juicy morsel to be mouthed over whenever a little spice was needed to perk up their daily stint. They did not actually name Bynner as the originator of "Hippopoetess." (Incidentally, what made the term so odious not only to Amy but to the feminists of the time was the designation of gender—a fight still going on in the arts; women sculpture-artists today are insisting that they be called *sculptors.* Then, the term "poetess" especially carried an implication of the precious or amateurish; in one of her earliest statements, Amy declared she was a *"poet."*) Some journalists attributed the Bynner quip to Ezra Pound, but he was too far removed from the scene, though an interesting sidelight is that he thought the *Spectra* preface was directed at *him,* judging from a letter he wrote to Margaret Anderson of the *Little Review* (he was now its overseas editor, and Amy had withdrawn her financial support). Other columnists thought it might be Ogden Nash, since Christopher Morley carried it among his items one day, and he and Nash were close friends and collaborators in a theatrical venture producing old-time melodramas. But almost everyone knew that it was one of "Witty" Bynner's inspirations, and Amy must have had an inkling of the source. Smith has said in *The Spectra Hoax* that although she continued a friendly correspondence with Bynner for some time, she never completely forgave him. He became her "official enemy"; and apparently he did not realize how bitter she felt toward him till the (Florence Wheelock) Ayscough–Amy Lowell letters were published in 1946. But he should have known.

Amy was inclined to be overly aggressive in always wanting to "run the whole show," but she was extremely touchy about her weight. Too, she often quivered with emotion—whether in anger, zeal, love, or hearty laughter. There were times when she looked as if she might burst into tears, though, contrary to reports, she never did. Bynner was not an insensitive person, and he himself was open to jibes. Wags called him "Twitter," and for obvious reasons. His adobe home in Santa Fe, New Mexico, was, like Auden's summer home in Kirchstatten, Austria, a haven for handsome homosexual young men, mostly poets of varying degrees of talent. He was never known to have a serious relationship with a woman; he proposed marriage once, but he did this out of gallantry—to save Edna Millay from embarrassment—he knew, as she did not, that Arthur Ficke (ever her beloved) was about to elope with the woman who became his second wife. But when Edna, confused and emotionally upset, half-accepted his proposal, Bynner retreated like a scared rabbit.* Basically kind, and not without his own sexual and emotional problems, one would have expected him to show more understanding of Amy's.

In Fanny Butcher's version of the *Spectra* hoax, though she had no part in the unveiling, she recalled Bynner, Ficke, and herself "laughing outrageously" over the whole business at lunch one day in New York. But what was just a lark, especially to Bynner, was a continuing, if intermittent, obstacle in Amy Lowell's other-

* For a full account of this strange triangular relationship and tragicomedy of errors, see Jean Gould, *The Poet and Her Book, A Biography of Edna St. Vincent Millay* (New York: Dodd, Mead & Company, 1969).

wise increasingly smoother professional path. Finally, after another year and a half of journalistic ribbing, she took several firm, contemptuous swipes at the columnists in an interview, published on December 27, 1919, in the *New York Evening Post*. Realizing that she was well on the way to becoming a national joke as well as a national force in favor of the new poetry if she allowed the wisecracks at her expense to continue, she said in part: "One of the hardest battles that the new poetry has waged has been against the pettiness, the stupidity and the ignorance of the so-called 'free press.' There is an incurable desire prevalent in all American newspapers to make fun of everything, in season and out. . . . Look at the 'colyums' in the daily papers. These are not funny, and yet they pass as being so. . . . They are ghastly and pitiful. . . ."

For once, the writers of well-known, "bright" columns found themselves on the defensive. Franklin P. Adams, "F. P. A.," whose "Conning Tower" was supposed to be a literary beacon for aspiring authors with a bent for witty prose and verse, disagreed vehemently in the *Tribune* of December 30, claiming that newspapers gave the poets publicity and that "Miss Lowell, in her attack, was merely seeking publicity in her own way." Others, too, protested that she was not only seeking notoriety but was unfair in her assault on their worth. On February 20, all of them—Don Marquis, Christopher Morley, and Baird Leonard, besides F. P. A.—felt compelled to combat her accusations again; but, from then on, they kept a strict silence concerning all of her activities and turned a deaf ear to anecdotes about her that might make the rounds of literary circles. This had been her purpose, of course, as she was to assert later: "There was a method in my madness; I realized that after a little adverse screaming, the columnists would leave me alone, for I personally was more willing to do without the notoriety they conferred for the sake of the dignity their silence would bring. . . . Not one of them seems to have been bright enough to understand that that was exactly my object."

The *Spectra* affair was never finally closed until long after the exposé of the hoax. It lingered hauntingly during the lifetimes of two of the principals and extended far into the future; in fact, an epilogue of sorts has recently come to light. While it deals only indirectly with *Spectra,* it reveals the extent of Amy Lowell's impact on American poets and poetry. In the summer of 1943, nearly twenty years after Amy's death (according to a letter received by the author in September 1973), Arthur Ficke's daughter-in-law, Jane, the wife of his only child, Stanhope, was visiting Arthur and his second wife, Gladys, at their home, Hardhack (close to Edna Millay's home, Steepletop). Jane Ficke was a young actress who had been a member of Elmer Rice's brilliant but short-lived Living Theatre Company. Stanhope was overseas in the service, and Jane, "suffocating with love and loneliness," often spent the weekend at Hardhack. During lunch there one day, probably because of the war, which then seemed endless, Jane mentioned Amy Lowell's "Patterns," declaring at some length how much she liked the poem. Arthur's reaction was "lightning fast and explosive." He stared at her incredulously and replied: "You don't! You can't!"

Jane has given a graphic picture of Arthur Ficke in action: "I had learned to be chary of Artie and his verbal tricks," she wrote. "He would . . . try to get an argument going and lead the unwary into an intellectual maze far too complex for them and when they were well off balance, pop dazzling bits of more or less logical fireworks at them. (He wasn't a smart lawyer for nothing.) This was great fun but I wasn't up to it at the moment. He went on to pronounce that the poem was contrived and artificial and technically not very something-or-other. . . . Then he went on to say with great distaste how outrageously fat she [Amy] was and what awful cigars she smoked and how Hal Bynner had cruelly but truly dubbed her the Hippopoetess. Arthur gave quite a nice performance, I enjoyed it. . . . When he wound down, I said, 'That may all be true, but I still like *Patterns.*' '*Why??*' he cross-examined."

Jane's answer was germane: "Because it ACTS well!" she blared. Without knowing it, she may have hit on the key to the success of "Patterns"—and to much of Amy's poetry. It is good theater; since Amy's second love was the stage and she read dramatically, it was only natural that her narrative poems should "act" well. But to Arthur, his daughter-in-law's reply must have seemed irrelevant and illogical. He stared at her again for a moment and muttered,

"For God's sake!" The amazing thing is that Arthur Ficke should have felt such acrid bitterness toward Amy Lowell after so many years. Obviously he, like most people, never knew how much she suffered. He himself was very ill by this time, and he died within a year or so (1945).

The only explanation for his acrimony—aside from his own innate flair for giving a performance—is that Amy Lowell's campaign for the new poetry must have been eminently successful. Arthur Ficke's forte had been the sonnet. Perhaps his finest volume was his *Sonnets of a Portrait Painter,* the fountainhead of Edna St. Vincent Millay's superb love sonnets and sonnet series, *Fatal Interview,* and *Epitaph for the Race of Man.* By the late 1930s, both of them were writing free verse in large measure. As early as 1935, Ficke's *The Secret and Other Poems* included a long free-verse poem, "Hospital." It describes his ordeal in undergoing an operation for cancer and contains passages of philosophic thought written while he was still in a half-conscious state from an anesthetic. They are fascinating and represent the rambling, conversational style he had accepted more and more, in spite of his vaunted satire of the free-verse cultists in his *Spectra* poems. This may have been due to the fact that the critics and editors who had accepted the Spectric poems in good faith, Alfred Kreymborg for one, contended that the work of Emanuel Morgan and Anne Knish was superior to anything that Bynner and Ficke had published under their own names. Bynner reported that when Arthur left for France he said, with a distinct note of grief in his voice, "Do you know, some of my best work is in *Spectra.*" (Some time afterward, when Bynner was relating the whole episode to mutual friends at dinner, he remarked that many people thought they wrote better as Knish and Morgan, and he added: "Once in a while we think so ourselves." Arthur's "lightning" retort was: "Inaccurate, Hal. We never think that, as applied to *our own poetry,*" he explained; "but we thoroughly think it about *each other's.*") In spite of this horseplay, he became more experimental than Amy herself was after his return from France; and his last two volumes, *The Secret* and *The Tumult,* were closer to actual prose than Amy's polyphonic prose ever was. But both of these were dismissed by the few critics who reviewed them as being too philosophic and analytic to merit much attention as poetry, and his failure may have been one cause of his antipathy toward Amy.

Following his lead and her own feminist, liberal leanings, Edna Millay produced a mélange of poetry in a verse-drama, *Conversation at Midnight,* published in 1937, which, while it contained some good moments, was too diffuse in its different styles. The late Edmund Wilson, in reviewing it, lamented the fact that, in her verse-play, "you see metrics in full dissolution." But, with his astute judgment, he stated that he did not "complain of this state of affairs; it was all on the cards." And he added, "Miss Millay at her most relaxed is livelier than most of our poets at their brightest." It is significant that, barring his and everyone's bad opinion of her propaganda poetry, Edmund Wilson never wavered in his estimate of Edna Millay's position as "one of the few poets in a predominantly prose age who had attained to anything like the stature of great literary figures." * The year before he died, in a letter to this writer early in 1970, he wrote: "I agree with you that Edna Millay is scandalously underrated today.**

Yet, true artist, lyrist, and superb sonneteer that she was, in *Conversation at Midnight,* which marked the beginning of the decrease in her immense popularity, Edna Millay was not able to blend the various forms as Amy Lowell did in *Can Grande's Castle,* the historical pieces she was completing in 1918 when the exposé of the *Spectra* hoax occurred. The poem she referred to in her letter to Witter Bynner, "Guns as Keys," was based on the stories that August Belmont had told about his grandfather, Comdr. Joseph Matthew Perry,*** the naval officer who had played a key role in the flash war that swung wide the trade gate to the Orient. Amy and Ada usually saw Nell, very often with her husband, when they were in New York. They frequently met for dinner at the Belmonts' or in Amy's eighth-floor suite at the Belmont Hotel. August Belmont always had a fund of anecdotes and episodes from

* From Wilson's tribute to Millay in 1952, published in *The Shores of Light* (New York: Farrar, Straus & Cudahy, 1952).

** Part of her correspondence with Wilson following publication of the present author's *The Poet and Her Book.*

*** Oliver Hazard Perry, hero of the battle of Lake Erie, was his great-uncle.

his colorful family history to recount, and Amy was a good listener; if a tale was absorbing, she would ask detailed questions, tucking the answers away in her mind for further reference. In this case, she had brought up the subject of his grandfather's exploits in the Far East to gather material for a poem she had already conceived as the second in her new volume.

However, when Eleanor Belmont (whose role in the formation and early history of the Red Cross is a fascinating story in itself) returned from a five-month mission in Europe in the first half of 1918, Amy unexpectedly picked up poetry material. On a visit to Sevenels, Mrs. Belmont described an air raid she had watched (against instructions) from the balcony of her Paris hotel room, and Amy seized upon it on the spur of the moment. She had found the finale to bring her four-part historical volume up to date!

In a letter to Nell, she included a scene of current "family" visitors that represented a domestic victory on her part, for Lorna and her first child (she was pregnant) were at Sevenels. The letter inadvertently gives a clear picture of Amy's modus operandi. After commenting on Nell's "priceless" honesty in returning some stamps she had borrowed while there, Amy protested: "You might have at least have accepted the paper pad in return for your description of the air raid. . . ."

The letter continues, "And, by the way, the poem is done, and Ada thinks the air raid is good. It will amuse you to know that I read aeroplane books for a week, but in none of them did I find anything like the vividness of description or the poetical perception which characterized your account. You ought to write a book, or better still, from my point of view, you ought to talk, and talk, and talk to me, and then let me write books. I shall not send it to you, however, but let you come upon it in my new book, which of course I shall send you as soon as it is out. . . .

"We have Lorna and the baby here now for some weeks, and they are coming back again later to pass the Summer with us. *You see how foxy I am. By this process I keep Ada instead of losing her to Salt Lake City.** We have a sand pile in front of the house, and

* Italics mine.

Mr. Man, with his hair cropped short like a real boy, disports himself in it from morning till night; but it is a sad comment on the inferiority of woman that he prefers the men in the garage to any of us.

"I wish you would come here, and inhabit my other barn-like spare room while they are here, and join the group. Then, indeed, Ada's family would be all together. Do think it over, and in the meanwhile, with many thanks for the stamps, and a great many more thanks for the air raid, Affectionately, Amy."

So it was that, little by little, Amy managed to keep Ada by her side for most of the year. Since Lorna now lived in Washington, it was not hard to persuade her to come up to Sevenels with the children—she had three sons in quick succession and a fourth somewhat later—to spend the whole summer. It was like Amy to admit openly how foxy she was, making light of her possessiveness and her very great need. Here was an example of the "half-frankness," as Elsie Sergeant called it, that disarmed people before they had a chance to accuse her of having any ulterior motive. There is no doubt that she was genuinely fond of Nell Belmont, who was charming and bright and good company, but having her at Sevenels would also add another binding tie to Ada and her "family," as she said.

There was another reason why Ada may not have pressed the issue of going to Salt Lake City this particular summer. On one of the trips to New York to deliver another lecture at the Brooklyn Institute, Amy could not sleep, and, hoping to get more air near the window, perhaps to lie and look at the moon, pale though it was by city lights, she got up and thoughtlessly moved the bed herself instead of calling a porter. As she lifted one of the big brass posts, she felt something give way inside, almost a tearing of flesh: The stomach muscles had separated. Now she had an unmistakable hernia. This time there was no chance of avoiding surgery. The doctor said she must have an operation. She tried to get Grace Parker, a nurse who had seen her through other illnesses, whom she regarded as a good friend, to come; but "Porky," as she was known, was nursing the wounded in France and could hardly return, although she was ready to try. Then the doctor told Amy that the operation could wait until September; in the meantime, she was to rest often, and try to build up her strength for the ordeal. Luckily, her book was in press, and neither she nor Ada cared about going to Dublin this year. In fact, the house there would not be large or convenient enough to accommodate everybody for a whole summer; Amy had just about decided to sell Broomley Lacey.

As if to compensate for the unpleasantness connected with the exposé of the *Spectra* hoax, several communications from kinder, more "kindred" spirits buoyed up her own. A long, appreciative letter came from Donald Evans, the young poet who had published Gertrude Stein's *Tender Buttons,* and whose own *Sonnets from the Patagonian* had won him a favorable reputation. A year earlier he had requested an autographed poem from Amy to be sold for charity. Now he was writing from a training camp where he was serving as an enlisted man, though he could have been an officer. Someone had sent him four of Amy Lowell's books —his sole reading material in camp—and she had inspired him to write again after a long arid period of depressing, unproductive endeavor. As a token of his gratitude he was sending her a new edition of his *Sonnets,* with a new preface on poetry and war. She was touched and pleased, despite the fact that she did not care for either Stein's work or his. Her answer was both compassionate and outspoken; it contains as revealing a picture of Amy's mental and emotional approach to her profession—her professional creed—as the letter to Mrs. Belmont reflected her personal life.

After thanking Evans for the "sumptuous" edition of *Sonnets,* she said in part, "I must admit that I am not particularly in sympathy with the key in which this earlier volume of yours is written. . . . I am such an elderly person that I lived during the 1890's. My twenty years saw the annual reappearance of the 'Yellow Book,' and those 'mauve joys' and 'purple sins' were the 'very latest thing' during my adolescent period so that I must be pardoned for finding their manner somewhat dusty and, indeed, a good deal like a cotillion favor resurrected from a bureau drawer. I understand how that sort of thing intrigued you. I agree that it was part of the search for beauty, but . . . personally I find so much beauty in the world, so much lurking in my imagination (getting it out is another matter) that I do not seem to have to hunt for it down back alleys.

"Sometimes I wonder why you like my work. You glory in your pose, as you say yourself; *I detest pose, and have never found the need of being other than straightforwardly what I am.*" Then she buoys him up and upbraids him at the same time: "I think you are better than your pose. Do not tell me that anybody ever enlisted as a private soldier for the sake of a pose." Like Gertrude Stein, Amy Lowell often took a maternal attitude toward young writers. "Courage, mon enfant! En avant! Of course we need more beauty in the world; of course that is what we are all fighting for; and of course, that is what we must make the world safe for. But do not let us lisp this creed in a kind of dying languor; *let us shout it lustily—and dare be happy—and dare be robust—and dare be a thousand things which mean poetry just the same.**

". . . I think you are a plucky fellow. I am sorry you feel obliged to deny it in pursuit of a pose, and I think if I were you, I should believe enough in beauty and brains to become an officer if I had the chance. I have a curious feeling that if a poet is any sort of a poet, he ought to be able to do the other things of the world better than the people who can do nothing else. *Therefore, being a soldier, I should wish to be a general; being a cook, nothing but the chefdome would satisfy me.*** I am afraid I put the poet on a higher level than you do. I think he should be an inclusive kind of creature, not side-tracked, but universal. . . ."

The letter is probably one of the most significant that Amy Lowell ever wrote to a younger colleague; and although she may have revised it three or four times with an eye on posterity, as she always did, even with personal mail, according to her secretary, it still is an important clue to the phenomenon of her life-style,

* Such a statement can be interpreted as relating to many areas of Amy's (or anyone's) life; and when one considers that it was written in a state of apprehension about the upcoming hernia operation, it is even more remarkable; perhaps it was an effort to buoy *herself* up.

** This was written fifty years before Robert Frost's discursive poem, "It's Hard to Keep from Being King When It's in You and in the Situation" (1968), which employs the analogy of the cook. (Italics all through are mine.)

her career, and her undeniable influence on the generation of poets that followed.

Her letter brought an immediate reply, full of gratitude. Evans also gave a candid self-analysis of the reasons for his enlistment, his reactions toward the war, and repeated that "because, my dear lady, I had your four books I am writing, I truly believe, better than I ever have before." In his next book, *Ironica,* a long poem, "Before the Curtain," was dedicated to Amy Lowell.

At about the same time, she received one of Lawrence's inimitable letters, in which he told her that he had dedicated his new volume of poems, *Coming Awake,* very simply, "To Amy Lowell." He added, "You must let me know if you would like this to stand." In an earlier letter, after commenting that "those Imagist books seem to blossom into gold like a monthly rose," he had given *his* views about the war, very different from young Evans's, very definite and defiant views. "Thank God they did not make me a soldier," he wrote. (He had had to join up and spend one night in barracks, after which he was given a total exemption.) "The whole thing is abhorrent to me—even the camaraderie, that is so glamorous . . . the Achilles and Patroclus business. The spirit, the pure spirit of militarism is sheer death to a nature that is at all constructive or social-creative. And it is not that I am afraid or shy: I can get on with the men like a house on fire. It is simply that the spirit of militarism is essentially destructive, destroying the individual and the constructive social being. It is *bad.*" (It might have been better for young Evans, a poet of such promise, if he had taken such an attitude: Disillusioned, he committed suicide after the war, in May 1921.)

In the later letter, Lawrence sent his thanks for the "nice things" Amy had said about him in the lecture she gave at the Brooklyn Institute. "I don't mind what people think of my work," he told her, "so long as their attitude is *passionately* honest—which I believe yours is."

The word "passionately" applied to Amy was appropriate, and Lawrence was one of the few people who realized it. Her insight into his then not yet fully recognized powers is a credit to her literary judgment that either has been forgotten or was never fully granted. The lecture, "Imagism Past and Present," was given in two sessions. In the first, she traced Imagist principles back as far as Theocritus (perhaps stretching things a little), on through Blake, Coleridge, and Emily Dickinson. In the second part, dealing with Flint, Aldington, and Lawrence, she concentrated on Lawrence, since there was much she wanted to make known about Lawrence, especially concerning his erotica, for which he was condemned so widely. "He has no prototype that I can find. He is a poet of sensation, but of sensation as the bodily efflorescence of a spiritual growth. Other poets have given us sensuous images; other poets have spoken of love as chiefly desire; but in no other poet does desire seem so surely 'the outward and visible form of an inward and spiritual grace.' Mr. Lawrence does not do this by obscuring passion in a poetical subterfuge; he gives the naked desire as it is; but so tuned is his mind that it is always the soul made visible in a supreme moment. . . . Mr. Lawrence has been spoken of as an erotic poet, and that is true, but it is only one half of the truth. For his eroticism leans always to the mystic something of which it is an evidence. Not to understand this is to fail to comprehend the whole meaning of his work. . . . I do not hesitate to declare Mr. Lawrence to be a man of genius. He does not quite get his genius into harness; the cart of his work frequently overturns or goes awry; but it is no less Pegasus who draws it. . . . Mr. Lawrence's last volume of poems, *Look! We Have Come Through!* is an amazing book. It is to my mind a greater novel even than *Sons and Lovers. . . .*" For Amy, with her "proper Bostonian" background to praise and promote a novel considered outré, not to say obscene, in 1918 is proof of her literary judgment as well as of her "passionate honesty." The book was not actually banned in Boston, as obscenity legislation was still in the future, but it was suppressed by libraries. Some months later, when Amy accidentally discovered, to her horror, that "*Sons and Lovers* was 'locked up' in the Scruple Room of the Boston Athenaeum," she was enraged. What was a "superb novel" like that doing there, branded with the apothecary's symbol as unfit for public consumption? She raised one of her well-known rumpuses, demanding, as a member of the board, that it be brought out onto the open shelves, along with Compton

Mackenzie's *Sylvia Scarlett,* which she also admired. (A pioneer against literary censorship, she had earlier signed a petition, at H. L. Mencken's request, against the activity of the Comstock Society's campaign to suppress Theodore Dreiser's novel, *The Genius.* In returning the petition with her signature, she wrote to Mencken: "Nothing could be more pernicious to the future of literature in America than to have it in the hands of bigoted and fanatical people, who judge it for reasons quite other than its artistic merit. No country can hope to develop itself, unless its authors are permitted to educate it. I wish every success to the cause.")

Lawrence's offer to dedicate *Coming Awake* to her, asking her twice if the inscription was agreeable to her—at the end he said, "Just let me know about the inscription"—arrived at a time when she very much needed such a mark of affectionate esteem, and she accepted his offer gratefully. Other items from England brought additional comfort. An issue of the London *Sphere* arrived, with a full-page illustrated article by Clement K. Shorter, entitled, "A Literary Letter: The Art of Amy Lowell," in which he proclaimed that "he had no hesitation in proclaiming [her] one of the most remarkable figures in the history of English-speaking countries." And Winifred Bryher, whom Amy had not yet met, but whom she knew about through H. D. and a few Imagist poems Bryher had written, had "discovered" Amy's books, particularly *Six French Poets,* and had been inspired to write a pamphlet on the works of Amy Lowell. It is almost embarrassingly full of adulation, but after the drubbing Amy had received from Lytton Strachey in derision of her work on the French writers, Bryher's words were salve to Amy's wounded soul, all the more because they had come unsolicited and unexpected. She felt that she might at last be gaining a foothold on recognition in England. She hoped Pound would see these two pieces in London and that Witter Bynner had taken note of a long article about her by William Lyon Phelps which had appeared in the *Bookman* around the same time on the American side of the Atlantic. This was the sort of publicity she wanted and needed to combat the literary conservatives and the columnists who poked fun at her.

The summer of 1918 was a relatively quiet one. Because of her impending operation Amy did not go anywhere, but a number of guests (besides "their" family, for Amy considered Ada's family hers as well) came to Sevenels. First among them was Amy's old friend, Florence (Wheelock) Ayscough, who was back in the United States to deliver a series of lectures and to exhibit her collection of Chinese paintings. She and Amy had already talked about translating some Chinese poetry, and she brought her scrolls of Chinese poetry in ancient calligraphy to Sevenels. The two spent several days going through the collection; and Amy made the discovery that the ancient characters were actually pictograms. In classical script the word "mo" (sunset), for example, outlined the sun "disappearing in the long grass at the edge of the horizon." Amy, excited when Florence pointed this out, said they must do a whole volume of the translations, using the pictorial characters; they would give so much more meaning to the lines! She would have started right away if she had been able to. Mrs. Ayscough had not thought of using the characters in translation and felt that Amy had made an important discovery; four years later the idea was to come to fruition.

In July, Malcolm Cowley, one of the young Harvard poets introduced into Amy Lowell's circle through Foster Damon, returned to the United States from overseas, where he had been on ambulance duty. He brought some poems to show Amy, and she liked them so much that she promised to sell them for him. She often spent as much time on placing the work of an aspiring young poet, if she thought it worthwhile, as she did on her own. In August one of her poems appeared in *Poetry;* entitled, "Appuldurcombe Park," it was a lurid tale of adultery during the Revolutionary War. The opening line—"I am a woman, sick for passion"—repeated several times through the poem, was an interest-grabber, and Amy knew it. As she expected, the usual ripples of varying reaction swirled through the mails, some slapping her in the face, others touching her more gently. One that brought a good deal of satisfaction was a dispatch from William Carlos Williams. He commented that no one had ever before dealt so skillfully with the difficult Revolutionary period, but in the next sentence he had a few constructive suggestions to offer. Delighted and amused, she answered him the same day. "I am very glad indeed that you liked 'Appuldurcombe Park,' " she told him. "Your criticism is an excellent one; I wish one could get more of such sensible criticisms." Then she played his own game by telling him how much she liked his "Orchid thing" in the last *Egoist* (a London review now edited by Pound) but adding that she "regretted the repetition of the word 'spray.' . . . It is so fine each time that it is a pity to spoil the shock of it by having it repeated."

So she passed the days. The doctor had forbidden her to do any real work, mental or physical. She dared not garden for fear of straining the abdominal muscles still further; at night there was no sitting at her desk, writing. She went to bed when "Peter" did, or even earlier. She was uncomfortable much of the time, and she read detective stories by the dozen to take her mind off of her condition. Or she sat out on the front lawn with "Peter" and Lorna beside the large sandbox she had the carpenter build for Ada's grandson. It was six feet long and four and a half feet wide, and she was part of the "admiring audience," with his mother and grandmother watching him make sand pies and "having a beautiful time." She was glad Lorna and "Sonny" were there; it was a diversion and a solace to feel that she had a "family."

The operation finally took place on September 12 in a Brookline hospital. It was the first of four such operations Amy was to undergo within two years, though she had no idea then that there would be more. The surgery was pronounced successful, and, typically, Amy felt ravenous: She insisted, against the doctor's and her own better judgment, on eating two large beef sandwiches as soon as she came out of the ether! She was a difficult patient, she admitted. Quite naturally, she was in pain, and when she was suffering, everyone near her knew about it: She was "just an animal raging for comfort not to be had." Her one great comfort was Ada. She probably could not have survived these crises without her. "Peter's" ever serene presence at her hospital bedside, her infinite patience with Amy's foibles, her understanding of the poet's psychological as well as physical trials and tribulations, were extraordinary. Amy herself marveled at her, and had recorded her devotion in many poems she had been writing more or less on the side. She would be firm about publishing them in the next volume. One of these, the quiet, beautiful "Madonna of the Evening Flowers," picturing her friend in the garden at twilight, as Amy had come upon her once when she had been looking all over for her, had been published already. It appeared early in the year, in the February issue of the *North American Review.* Within a few days a note had come from Professor Lowes, telling her how much he liked the poem, and asking if the "Madonna" was not Mrs. Russell —he thought it must be. Amy answered his question with another, as positive as a statement: "How could so exact a portrait remain unrecognized?" And with these few words she left little doubt that she worshiped the "Madonna."

CHAPTER XV

"Amy Lowell, Leader of New Poetry": The Show Must Go On

"PETER" WAS BY HER SIDE throughout the first day in the hospital, but she could not stay all night, nor did either of them think it was necessary. Early the next morning, however, after Amy awoke, still feeling drugged and no doubt uncomfortable, she rang for the nurse again and again, but no one came: The current had been accidentally cut off for four hours. She had to get out of bed to summon a nurse, though the doctor had given her strict orders to lie flat for two days. The bellow of her call could be heard the length of the corridor; she got results, but at some risk, as she made a point of informing the selectmen of Brookline as soon as she could dictate letters again. (That was on the eighteenth of September; the operation had been performed on the twelfth.)

She came home, but she had to stay in bed until the end of the month. On the thirtieth, she tried going downstairs for the first time, but felt so exhausted after an hour that she had to return to her bed. Amy Lowell was a restless soul, to say the least, and it annoyed her to be forced to cancel lecture dates, delay plans for new books, and submit to the healing process. Applying the bandages, which had to be wound around her waist in a certain way to support the inner muscles, seemed to take forever; sometimes they had to be rewound. Then Amy's irritation would change to angry frustration, and Ada would have to calm her, usually by reminding her that the wound would take longer to heal if she allowed herself to become aggravated, and adding that she might as well enjoy being lazy while she could. Then Amy would laugh and try to take her friend's advice. Moreover, she was not completely idle, and the thing that kept her busy was also a source of pleasure: Her new volume, *Can Grande's Castle,* came off the press as scheduled on September 24; the sight of it, and the duty of sending out advance copies to reviewers, was partial compensation for the pain.

She had been eagerly awaiting publication of the book, which she hoped would convince adverse critics and gossip columnists that she could write poetry of epic proportions, dealing with events in history which she could not possibly have experienced, so they would have no grounds to make personal quips and jokes about her. "Can Grande," Dante's stone tower of refuge, was *her* refuge, and she made a point of choosing a title that would eliminate the "ivory tower" charge. Here was no escape from the war they were all suffering through now. Rather, she offered a comparison of the present war with those of the past, bringing to the fore the strange phenomenon of man's self-destructive instincts—and the indestructibility of art. She emphasized the art every civilization was capable of creating before decay and destruction overtook it. The theme was of course inspired by World War I, and it was Amy's purpose to show how life and love went on in the face of holocaust and destruction, as well as to stress the never-ending struggle between commercialism (a basic cause of war) and art. In four crucial episodes depicting the terrifying but inevitable eras of war and its consequences on civilizations, she sought to show that art survived, no matter how self-destructive man becomes.

This was a considerable task, and to accomplish it, she employed the whole repertoire of her poetic styles. Using principally polyphonic prose, she varied it with rhymed and unrhymed vers libre, traditional lyrics, and dramatic dialogues, according to the mood and scene of the segment of history she was relating. And into the historical panorama she threw love and lust, greed and nobility, the colors of a carnival and the headiness of a bacchanal. She began with a famous love affair—the oft-repeated story of Admiral Nelson and his fateful love for Lady Hamilton (not by accident did Amy Lowell choose her heroine from among leading figures in the theater)—but she gave it a dramatic presentation and used techniques no one else had. The very title, "Sea-Blue and Blood-Red," suggests the series of flashing, flaming, color-filled scenes thrown helter-skelter on the screen of time, juxtaposing battle and boudoir scenes as in D. W. Griffith's film spectacle, *Intolerance* (released in 1916)—the episodic technique by which Amy gave her own original version of history. She had a reputation for being eclectic, and she was; but she made no bones about it: She was the unabashed borrower of her time. She borrowed openly, grandly, acting on the theory of music composers, whose "variations" on the themes of other composers are not considered less original because they originated in others' works. Amy considered Carlyle's *French Revolution* a great epic poem, and it probably had an influence on her method.

She was a *poetry* composer, and the things she did with her borrowed material were certainly original, whether one considers the results poetry or not. "She was a story-teller if not a poet, who had studied her art in Chaucer, in Keats, and in Browning," Van Wyck Brooks wrote in 1941.* And, *"Can Grande's Castle,* cinematic in style, remained perhaps her most characteristic. The excess of vivacity wore one out. It was charged with enough electricity to burn one's hand off. But . . . Amy Lowell exulted in her strength, her feeling for ships and battles, barbarism and heroism, pageantry and pomp, dash and fanfarole. . . . She was Lady Hamilton; she was Nelson; and Commodore Perry in Japan. No New England historian since the days of Prescott and Motley had given the world such brilliant historical scenes." Damon says: "Amy Lowell's attitude towards 'quivering, bloodswept, vivid Lady Hamilton' is best summed up in 'The woman is undoubtedly mad, but it is a madness which kindles.' The whole poem is kindled by her; yet Miss Lowell also felt her to be somewhat of a fool." **

She was most successful as Commodore Perry in "Guns as Keys: and the Great Gate Swings," the section of the book dealing

* Van Wyck Brooks, *New England: Indian Summer* (New York: E. P. Dutton, 1940).

** S. Foster Damon, *Amy Lowell, A Chronicle* (Boston: Houghton Mifflin Company, 1935).

with the theme of commercialism versus art. (Whether because of the firsthand descriptions she had heard from the Belmonts, or because they were closer to her own history, the two most valid segments of the book are this, the second, and the last part of the fourth section with the closing episode of the air raid in 1915.) "Guns as Keys" has much that is both cogent and prophetic.

> . . . Let the key-guns be mounted, make a brave show of waging war, and pry off the lid of Pandora's box once more. Get in at any cost, and let out at little, so it seems, but wait—wait—there is much to follow through the Great Gate!
>
> They do not see things in quite that way, on this bright November day, with sun flashing, and waves splashing, up and down Chesapeake Bay. On shore, all the papers are running to press with huge headlines: 'Commodore Perry Sails.' Dining-tables buzz with travellers' tales of old Japan culled from Dutch writers. But we are not like the Dutch. No shutting the stars and stripes up on an island. Pooh! We must trade wherever we have a mind. Naturally!

Other passages are as powerful, and, coming from a descendant of the Lowell and Lawrence economic royalists, all the more interesting:

> . . . Commerce-raiding a nation; pulling apart the curtains of a temple and calling it trade. Magnificent mission! . . .
>
> Romance and heroism; and all to make one dollar two. . . . For centuries men have pursued the will-o'-the-wisp—trade. And what have they got? . . .
>
> A locomotive in pay for a Whistler; telegraph wires buying a revolution; weights and measures and Audubon's birds in exchange for fear. Yellow monkey-men leaping out of Pandora's box, shaking the rocks of the Western coastline. Golden California bartering panic for prints. The dressing-gowns of a continent won at the cost of security. Artists and philosophers lost in the hour-glass sand pouring through an open Gate.

(The above could have been written by Auden forty years later.) Another eerily prophetic line is: "You have blown off the locks of the East, and what is coming will come."

In the air-raid scenes, Amy shifted from Mrs. Belmont's Paris to Venice at the time of Italy's entrance into World War I. This section, called "The Bronze Horses," embraces four Italian civilizations, beginning with the fall of Rome. In coming to the present, she describes the bombs streaking across the sky and, in separate scenes, the effect of the explosions. There is a feeling of reality here and in the first poem of the section that one does not feel elsewhere. Incidentally, the first poem, which describes a languid patrician lady of A.D. 71 lolling in her bath, is far more sensuous than the famous "Bath" of "Spring Day." A few lines seem to be thrown in the faces of those who had been shocked by and critical or derisive of her earlier "Bath":

> Her breasts round hollows for themselves in the sky-green water, her fingers sift the pale water and drop it from her as a lark drops notes backwards into the sky. The lady lies against the lipping water, supine and indolent, a pomegranate, a passion-flower, a silver-flamed lily, lapped, slapped, lulled, by the ripples which stir under her faintly moving hands.

Much of *Can Grande's Castle* seems wordy and overwritten today, too heavily weighted with philosophic and historical content. In her desire to prove that she could deal with other than surface subjects, that with her polyphonic prose she was more inclusive than the exquisite but limited concept of the Imagists, she tried to include too much. In summarizing, it should be mentioned that the third and shortest section of the book dealt with England, the tight little island-empire, with its coaches and hedges, just before the age of industrialism caused the handsome coaches to "vanish in a puff of steam." Her enormous conception encompassed too great an area in space and time. The last section alone, with its four civilizations, through which the bronze horses always survive, is monumental. Here, too, she infused in the poem the basic elements of fire, earth, water, and air, though she claimed when Foster Damon pointed it out to her that she had not done so. Such fare is too heavy for the poetry lover to digest at one, or even a dozen, sittings.

However, at the time of its publication, Damon records, "the reviewers were all but uniformly dazzled by the brilliance of the coloring, the sonorities of the orchestration, and the scope of the panorama." She and Ada read these notices happily as they appeared, and when she was well enough to have guests for dinner again, the circle of intimates joined them in tallying the scores of favorable comments. Incredible as it seems today, the *New York Sun* called the work "the biggest thing since Whitman." The *Boston Transcript* said that Amy Lowell had replaced Poe. Only three reviews voiced adverse criticism—those by Conrad Aiken, Harriet Monroe, and Ben Hecht—and even among those, Amy found enough praise to extract a few sentences to send to the publisher for possible use on new dust jackets. Within three weeks, the publisher decided to order a second printing before Christmas, but copies sold so fast that the second printing was sold out by mid-October, and a third printing followed for the holiday gift sales.

Damon himself, writing more than ten years later, proclaimed: "*Can Grande's Castle* was Amy Lowell's first completely original book—original in metre, method, structure and meaning. It has a glory and exultation to it that reminds one of Blake's *America:* turning the pages is like an increase of light on the retina." (It must be remembered that Damon was a Blake scholar and interpreter.) "Never did she produce anything more purely splendid, though some of her later work was richer."

Congratulations from friends and colleagues poured in, one of the first from the composer Charles Loeffler, who was effusive in his praise; other composers, including E. B. Hill, seemed to have found a relationship between Amy's "cadenced" lines and musical composition which was to lead her to writing in another field. Sara Teasdale was ill with the flu, a victim of the terrible epidemic that took the lives of half a million people at the close of the war; but when the book arrived, and her husband began reading it to her, they were both so excited that she forgot her illness. Then by the end of the first section she was so exhausted she had to rest a while. Fletcher was stunned by the brilliance of Amy's achievement, which he was sure time would consider her most important; he at first chose "Guns as Keys" as his favorite, but a week later expressed a preference for "Bronze Horses." D. H. Lawrence had sent her a note of abysmal discouragement in September in regard to his own efforts because no publisher would "risk" his last novel, and he was working on another he feared would be similarly received. Yet he kept on, not knowing "how we shall ever find a future. Humanity as it stands, and myself as I stand, we just seem mutually impossible to one another," he wrote. Amy had replied with a long letter of condolence, advised him to "simply use an India rubber in certain places" and telling him she was sending him a copy of her new book. She did not think he would like it because it was "objective" and he preferred "subjective" poetry. But she wanted to know what he thought about it.

He was surprisingly enthusiastic. "You are wrong when you say I only like subjective poetry," he told her. "I love visions, and visionary panorama. I love 'thunderheads marching along the sky-line'—and 'beautiful faded city'—and 'fifty vessels blowing up the Bosphorus'—and English coaches. . . . I love the pomp and richness of the past—the full, resplendent gesture. The sordidness of the present sends me mad—such meagre souls, all excusing themselves." Then he tactfully rebuked her for her advice: "No, Amy, again you are not right when you say the india-rubber eraser would let me through into a paradise of popularity. Without the india-rubber I am damned along with the evil, with the india-rubber I am damned among the disappointing. You see what is is to have a reputation. I give it up, and put my trust in heaven. One needn't trust a great deal in anything, & in humanity not at all."

Of her close literary associates, Thomas Hardy was the only one to appear baffled by the book, mostly because he had not yet "mastered her argument for polyphonic prose. He wondered if it could be the same style that they used to call 'word-painting' forty years earlier." But he appeared to enjoy the stories for their narrative value as his wife read them aloud (his eyesight was fading). "Let's read some more of Cousin Amy!" he would say, a mark of affection and esteem which gave her a real glow. (Louis Untermeyer apparently considered the volume an achievement, for as late as the 1940s, when *The Complete Poetical Works of Amy Lowell* * was published, he wrote in his "Memoir" introduction

* Boston: Houghton Mifflin Company, 1955.

a brief analysis in admiring terms of "the long, flowing cadences of her polyphonic prose . . . to achieve a contrapuntal form with orchestral sonorities.")

Another person might have accepted all this approval and adulation and be content to coast a while, but not Amy. She did take a few days' vacation in New York as soon as she felt strong enough to travel. Her recovery from the operation was delayed by a "family" crisis: Lorna was stricken by the flu in October, when the epidemic was at its height (on the first, two hundred people had died in Boston alone). In Washington, D.C., no nurses were to be had, and it was feared Lorna would also develop pneumonia; if she got any worse, she was certain to lose the baby she was expecting in December even if she survived. Amy helped "Peter" locate a nurse to accompany her to Washington, and for once bade her Godspeed. She herself was so sick with anxiety that her incision refused to heal, and the abdominal muscles failed to go back into place. She called Washington nearly every night; by October 24, the crisis had passed, and Ada told her over the phone that Lorna was out of danger. Amy was able to relax a little then, but the doctor still would not permit her to work. She could, however, catch up on her correspondence, try to sell Bryher's and Malcolm Cowley's poems, and publish a review she had written of Sandburg's *Cornhuskers*. When she learned that Lorna was up and around again, she arranged to meet "Peter" in New York City, and they spent ten days at the St. Regis Hotel, entertaining and visiting with friends. (This was the occasion of the waiters' strike, and of the unforgettable dinner that took place as a result.)

They probably saw the Belmonts and Elsie Sergeant, who was soon to leave for France (directly after the war) to cover the scenes of the deserted battlefields for the *New Republic*. They were in New York from the sixth till the fifteenth of November, and so were able to witness the scene of wild rejoicing when the Armistice was signed on November 11. When they returned to Sevenels, Amy was feeling so much better that she again started working with a will and, on one night, did not stop writing until eight o'clock in the morning. Toward the end of November she received a special invitation to join the MacDowell Club of New York and was appointed to its Judges Committee on Literature. In accepting, she arranged to read "The Bronze Horses" there in January 1919, at which time she was also to lecture and read at Columbia. The satisfaction she felt at receiving such recognition was counteracted by the sad news from Carl Engel's sister that the last of the sheep dogs, Prue, had died in spite of all they tried to do for it. Amy could send only a brief note: "The thing is too close to me to write about," she confided to Carl's sister. "I can only thank you for having been so good to her."

She herself "caught a bug" and was ill again for several weeks over the holidays. While she was ill, she wrote "Der Tag," a poem on the surrender of the German fleet, and sold it to the *New York Tribune*. The editor was so pleased with it that he not only paid her fifty dollars—more than she had asked—but devoted an entire page to the poem, illustrating her lines with comic marginal sketches by the caricaturist, Gropper. It appeared on December 22 before she had any idea of the presentation. She and Ada were both horrified at the feature's lack of taste; and Amy's outburst of indignation when she was well enough to send it is an indication of the distance she had come; perhaps it also crystallized her own views toward publicity now, as well as her goals: "You think a poet wants to touch 'the great mass of the people who never read a poem at all,' but that is not so. A poet—or at least this poet—wants to touch the people with a spark of poetry in them, be they blacksmiths or millionaires, but she has not the slightest interest in the rest of the world nor their opinion. Also, I detest the idea of poems as propaganda. If they are not enjoyed as poetry, I do not care whether they are enjoyed or not.

"I have no desire to live in an ivory tower, but, on the other hand, I must be presented with dignity. I have no objection to boldness; I have objection to vulgarity. I think those pictures were vulgar and utterly out of key with my poem. You say that the *Tribune* has never published a more successful 'stroke.' I am very glad to know that, but that some of the public are of my opinion, not yours, is evident from the following letter from an unknown admirer. . . ." Here she quoted a fan letter which objected to the illustrations.

"As to putting myself in your hands, *that is what I have never been willing to do to any editor or any publisher.** Now look here," she continued with the passage already quoted in an earlier chapter, "I started in the world with one of the greatest handicaps that anyone could possibly have. I belonged to the class which is not supposed to be able to produce good creative work. I was writing in an idiom which was entirely new and to most people extremely disagreeable. I knew not a single editor and had entrance to no magazine nor paper. Will you say that I have engineered myself badly in five short years? . . . I do need you, and you can help me a great deal, but only if you will be somewhat guided by me in the presentation of my work; otherwise," she finished prophetically, "I am as bad as Napoleon, I believe in my star, and I have not a doubt that in following it I shall reach the goal, although I confess I personally may be dead before that happy day arrives. . . ."

Certainly Amy Lowell never wrote a saner, more mature, or more definite letter; and those who accused her of childishness in her dealings, of being always a "spoiled child," have presented only one part of her makeup, granting that she often gave them grounds to prove the charge. It was this highly intelligent side of her, however, that brought her the respect and the friendship of editors like Ferris Greenslet, Frederick Marsh, Herbert Croly, James Oppenheim, and John Farrar,** in spite of her foibles and eccentricities.

As she was about to leave for her January speaking engagements in New York, a second wave of the dread flu epidemic flared up. Amy had a severe relapse, and only by a hairbreadth escaped pneumonia. She had to postpone readings in Richmond, Virginia, and at the centennial celebration of James Russell Lowell's birthday the day after her own forty-fifth, which she had to spend in bed, attended by a trained nurse. To add to her health problems, a new complication set in: high blood pressure, which was to persist stubbornly, in spite of precautions the doctor told her she must

* Italics mine.

** Soon to become editor of the *Bookman,* and to appoint her chairman of the Book Committee for Planned Reading Programs.

take. (She did not always follow them, it is true; if she had not driven herself to produce such enormous output, and had not made such extended lecture tours whenever she was well enough to travel, the pressure might have subsided, and her life might have been prolonged. But she knew, as "Peter" knew, that she might as well try to stop the tides from being drawn by the moon as to try to stop herself from giving in to her surging creative energy.)

The strange part of it was that when she was performing, whether at a poetry reading or on the lecture platform, few people realized that Amy was a sick woman at best. Very often she was dangerously ill, but a kind of exhilaration took hold of her when she began to speak that carried her along and spread contagiously among her audience. On February 27, she read at the Copley Theatre in Boston, as part of a program arranged by Mrs. Jack Gardner. Though she had to sit during the reading and was exhausted afterward, the audience, from the sound of its enthusiastic applause, never knew that she was fighting back weakness. When someone once remarked on this ability of hers, she said, "What you forget is that I come from a family of orators, that public speaking is natural to me, that it is no more effort for me to give a lecture than it is to talk in a drawing-room, that I enjoy reading poetry to an audience as I should enjoy acting a play to an audience, because it is one side of my genius." At such moments Amy Lowell did not suffer from any inferiority complex; in fact, especially since the advent of Ada Russell in her life, she had overcome her feelings of inferiority to a remarkable degree. She was never to be entirely free from inner stress, from the turbulence wrought by her high-powered emotional and mental makeup, but she was no longer overly worried about measuring up to her illustrious family or about marrying and begetting Lowells to continue the line; if she was occasionally troubled about such things, she submerged herself in work—her own kind of creation. She loved, and was loved by, someone who was not only worthy of love but who was also a continuous inspiration and an object of adoration. And the volume she was preparing to publish in 1919, which she began assembling during the hours she had to spend in bed, was to contain a whole section of poems that portrayed her love and her "impassioned heart" for those who had the eyes to see it or the antennae to sense it.

Toward the middle of February she began to entertain again. Vachel Lindsay came to dinner, and they had a good poetry talk for once, though she never had any real affinity for Lindsay's evangelism. And by the end of the month, she was hard at work on a lecture which the music department at Harvard, probably at the instigation of Ned Hill, had asked her to deliver for the benefit of the American Friends of Musicians in France. She decided to call her subject "Some Musical Analogies in Modern Poetry," and on Sunday evening, March 2, she and her dinner guests, the Hills and Heinrich Gebhard, conferred about the compositions she planned to mention in her text. (When Lindsay was at Sevenels, they had discussed his poem, "Congo," with its chant of "Boom-lay, Boom-lay, Boom-lay, Boom-lay, Boom!" which she cited as an example of the use of "rag-time" in poetry.) The lecture, delivered the next day at Paine Hall, was the first by a woman ever presented under the sponsorship of the university. It was a complete success and did much to widen the scope of her literary reputation. Among other things, she discussed the way she had developed polyphonic prose from the experiments of Paul Fort. She wanted an "orchestral effect, in which the delicate flute tones of *vers libre* could be augmented by all the other instruments at the command of the poet. In this way, her subject could be phrased musically, dramatically, lyrically and pictorially at the same time." To illustrate, she ended by reading the colorful Venetian carnival from "The Bronze Horses."

Not long afterward, she received a letter from Paul Fort asking for a contribution to his new magazine, *Le Monde Nouveau.* Another French writer, preparing a series of articles on American poets, sent for information about her technique as well as for biographical material. Her friend Magdeleine Hutchinson (formerly Carret), who had helped with the translations in *Six French Poets,* was doing a French translation of *Tendencies.* Amy felt she was well on the way to being recognized in France; but, ironically, she still had to conquer England's literary bastions. She had not forgotten Strachey's devastating sarcasm, now somewhat mitigated by the request from Paul Fort himself; she hoped Strachey would hear about it. She was shocked to learn that Bryher, in her glowing pamphlet on Amy Lowell, had felt she was presenting practically an "unknown poet" to British readers. Finally, as a result of this lecture, the distinguished *Musical Quarterly* asked her to publish the lecture as an article.

She was almost fully recovered by the middle of March, and on St. Patrick's Day delivered her twice-postponed lecture in Richmond, Virginia. With southern hospitality, the members of the Woman's Club took her sightseeing, and, among other historic sights, showed her the Confederate Museum, which she found frightening and wearing. At the lecture, she was tired and wobbly as she was being introduced, but as soon as she started to read, the fatigue seemed to disappear, and her voice rang out clear and strong. "Peter" said she had never heard Amy read more superbly, and some of the young writers there were "permanently liberated" from the old conventional forms. Afterward there was a dinner given by Ellen Glasgow, who was gaining an enviable reputation for her novels. She and Amy discovered that they had been born in the same year, and both were coming into their own in their separate fields. It was a pleasant occasion, and Amy was at her best.

On the way back, she and Ada stopped in New York with the intention of combining business with pleasure, and they set up headquarters in Amy's eighth-floor suite at the Belmont. She read "The Bronze Horses" at the MacDowell Club on March 20 to start things off, and then, in a round of visits to editors, sold no less than seventeen poems. Next, she arranged the contract for her new book, to which she had given the title *Pictures of the Floating World*. Oriental in flavor (actually, "floating world" is a translation of the Japanese word *ukiyoye*), perhaps she chose it to disguise the intensely personal quality of this collection of lyrics, which she had been writing over a period of at least five years. She had no difficulty in getting the terms she wanted, after which she planned to enjoy herself with a little socializing among the literati. She met Percy MacKaye at a tea, and no doubt discussed verse-drama with him. (MacKaye was almost as prolific a writer as she, and was as well known if not as notorious; yet his name is much less known today than Amy Lowell's.) He and the famous Indian poet, Kahlil Gibran, were also at a dinner party she and Ada were invited to at Mrs. Simeon Ford's; and Sara Teasdale came to the Belmont for dinner in their rooms one night, when they spoke of their mutual adoration of Eleonora Duse "and her great art, which had served as their Muse."

Amy was looking forward to other engagements, but, more than anything else, to the arrival of her nephew, Maj. James A. Roosevelt, who had distinguished himself in the battle of the Argonne, and who was at last returning from the war. His mother (Amy's sister Katie), his wife and children, were, like Amy, all planning to meet the transport ship to welcome him. Then terrible news came: Major Roosevelt had caught spinal meningitis aboard ship and had died suddenly the night before the transport was to dock. The tragedy was a paralyzing shock to everyone. Amy, who was just beginning to experience relatively good health after her operation and the flu, was again overcome by weakness, and she canceled their further dates. She and Ada remained in New York for the funeral on March 29 and went back to Brookline directly afterward.

The tragedy affected her for some time. Amy had followed her favorite nephew's moves throughout the war, and her letters had been full of reference to his achievements in the two years he had been "over there." The fact that he had survived the war, was on his way home, and then was cruelly snatched away by a fatal illness the night before being reunited with his family seemed to make the blow almost too difficult to bear. "I practically brought him up," she wrote Winifred Bryher in relating the sad event two months later, "as my sister was [then] an invalid, and he was almost like my son. The result of this, coming immediately after the influenza, was to diminish my vitality and nervous force again." And to Jean Untermeyer in April, she confided, "I feel only an immense languor—partly the remains of the 'flu,' I think, and partly the results of fatigue and emotion. . . ."

She did manage to work a little, and the first of many reviews she was to write for the *New York Times* appeared in the *Book Review.* Although it dealt with Edward Waldo Emerson's mild

Early Years of the Saturday Club, which brought to Amy a recollection of the time Longfellow had carried her around the table in a wastebasket at one of those meetings, her remarks somehow aroused controversy and resulted in a flood of replies to the paper. These required firm rebuttal on her part, which served to divert her from her stress and grief. She also found solace in her garden, except that the spring bulbs were late in coming along; she concentrated on her indoor gardening in the greenhouse. She wrote no poems at this time, but took great care in preparing the format for her new book. She wanted these personal poems to be printed in a certain order—almost, but not quite, chronological—to indicate a progression of feeling. Ada said absolutely *no* to the matter of the dedication, and for once Amy did not press her.

A long, commiserating letter from D. H. Lawrence, in which he mentioned the definite desire and intention he and Frieda had of coming to America, both fascinated and disturbed Amy. Everyone in England had been bitten by the flu, too, he told her. H. D. had had pneumonia, and had almost lost her baby, but it had been born safely—it was a girl—the previous week. (Apparently she and Richard Aldington were already separated by then; and not long afterward, H. D. went to live with Bryher, giving the upbringing of her child over to the latter, who dubbed the baby "the lump," and was spoiling and dominating her unmercifully, though there was no hint of this in Lawrence's letter.) He continued in terms that might have applied to the present: "the world is all at cross purposes, and gets worse: everything seems tangled in everything by a million bits of string. I want awfully to come to America—first to the north, then later to go south, perhaps to Central America. It is what I intend to do when the world becomes sane again, and oneself free.

"Here in England nobody cares about anything, literature least of all: all bent on scrambling uneasily from day to day, as if we were all perched on a landslide, and the days were stones that might start sliding under one's feet. I don't know why it all seems so uncertain, so irritable, such a sequence of pinpricking moments, with no past to stay one, and no future to wonder over. But it is so. And it is hateful to have life chopped up into disagreeable moments, all gritty.

"I agree with you, the poetry of the future, and the poetry that *now* has futurity in it, is rhymeless, naked, spontaneous rhythm. But one has an old self as well as a new. . . .

"I do hope you are well and happy. I would love to see your garden, particularly to get the scents at evening. . . ."

As if responding to his wish, the hyacinth and narcissus beds bloomed, sending up a rich, musklike fragrance. And in the greenhouse, one of the orchids which she had been tending with special care—a *Cattleya thayeriana,* a species probably named for her friend, Mrs. Bayard Thayer, a well-known horticulturist—produced eighteen blooms on a single stalk and won a prize at the spring exhibit of the Boston Gardeners' and Florists' Association on April 17. For all her relatively quiet life, her blood pressure stayed at the dangerously high level of 240, and her eyes bothered her increasingly. The doctor forbade her to work, but she was determined to send her manuscript off in time for fall publication, and she put it in the mail on May 3. Then on May 5 she and Ada took the train to Cincinnati, where Amy was to give a reading before the Ohio Valley Poetry Society. Several members of the society insisted on showing them the sights on the day they arrived, which was too strenuous for Amy. By the next day when she was to speak, she had a fierce headache and had to take "thirty-six grains of phenastine" even to get herself to the hall; but her appearance was deceptively healthy, not to say formidable. Usually when she started to read, her listeners forgot her looks, but today they seemed unmoved by her introduction, and uncongenial to the idea of the new poetry. Her first poem was met with dead silence. Those before her did not give her puzzled looks, as audiences frequently did; nor did they seem uncertain whether or not to applaud. Somehow her stock line did not seem appropriate, so "with dangerous sweetness," she merely said, "I will read it to you again." Still there was no response. Ada, sitting in the front row, could see the signs of a coming tempest and tried to get Amy's attention by shaking her head no, but Amy, her head aching, her blood pressure mounting, gave the ladies a good, round scolding for not listening with open minds as well as ears, and she tried again to explain what the new movement in poetry was attempting to do. By the time she finished reading, the atmosphere was less stiff. The applause was adequate, but hardly enthusiastic, and only a few were interested enough to ask questions.

When later, in the hotel room, Ada scolded her for "losing her temper in public," Amy was surprised and defensive—she had merely given them a good piece of her mind; and anyway, those women needed a little education in modern poetry. Afterward in a letter to the poet Grace Conkling, she confessed, "Ada said I lost my temper and gave them a scolding, which I am afraid is true," and she mentioned her headache as an excuse. Although she may have been at fault, such outbursts as this often roused her provincial audiences into seeking new approaches to reading and writing poetry. It was so in other middle- and southwestern cities as well—in Omaha, Dallas, Fort Worth, Austin, in St. Louis and Des Moines, Grand Rapids and Milwaukee—she awakened the sleeping impulses of poets too long comfortably lulled by late-nineteenth-century verse. (Chicago, of course, was an exception, since *Poetry* magazine had been the mouthpiece of modern poetry two years before Amy discovered her own Imagist and modern poetic tendencies in its pages. Even in Chicago, however, her visits sparked up the movement.) As Van Wyck Brooks was to say, "Wherever she went, she touched off a fuse."

This time she went right back to Brookline, while Ada went on to Salt Lake City, promising faithfully to be back by the middle of July. Amy hated to see her go, for, besides her eye trouble and high blood pressure, the umbilical hernia had still not healed completely; every so often she felt a twinge of pain from the stitches. And she was prey to a nagging, nameless anxiety—one that she refused to confront—that her days were numbered and that she was not going to get everything done before the end. Finally, she had a growing fear that her citadel—the family fortress of Sevenels and the whole structure of the Lowell manufacturing empire—was going to be attacked. This fear was fed by the postwar hysteria as well as by the Russian Revolution and the fall of the Kerensky government (bringing back the letters she had received at the time the stables burned and occasionally since then). The waves of strikes, particularly in the textile industry, had not escaped her, though she had no time to dwell on them or on the conditions that caused them. She had feared the military autocracy of Germany during the war, and she still feared it.* But she gave very few outward signs of all this. She told "Peter" she would count the days till her return, and urged her to come back before the middle of July if possible.

At Sevenels, she learned that her headaches had been caused by weakness in the retina muscles of her eyes, a side effect of the high blood pressure, which, though it had subsided temporarily, rose and fell according to the strenuousness of her activity or the degree of her emotional excitement. Naturally, her long hours of night work strained her eyes and brought on the headaches. The doctor forbade her to work for two weeks. Amy could not be idle that long, so she devised a means of avoiding eyestrain: She had a set of glasses made, "in a scale of increasing strength," identifying each with a different-colored string. She started with the weakest, and as the night wore on, she changed glasses according to the hour, going through the entire spectrum by the time dawn came. Although the scheme was not perfect and was hardly scientific, it did help. On tours, she carried the set of glasses in a basket, like a stage prop, and made capital of their entertainment value as she changed from one to another.

She made some effort not to overstrain her eyes, but it irritated her to have to give in to physical weaknesses. She wrote the Engels that she was an "enraged gardener" by day and that she entertained literary friends at dinner or had overnight guests who kept conversation going till all hours, so she did not have too much chance to work anyway. The Untermeyers stopped at Sevenels on their way up to a boys' camp in New England, where they were taking their son, Richard, for the summer; it was an overnight visit that became an annual event for several years. Foster Damon frequently came for dinner, along with the Ned Hills, and

* She had read John Reed's article against the war in the *Seven Arts* and wrote Oppenheim that, while she found it "interesting and very well written," she did not agree with it. Amy deplored war as such, but she felt the United States would have to fight alone later on if Germany became any more powerful. She felt, as most people did in World War II, that we were fighting for our very existence. "I myself am a complete individualist," she said, "more of an individualist than any of the men who call themselves socialists, . . . but there must be a certain amount of banding together to make life possible."

they talked of setting to music, perhaps for a ballet, a long poem Amy was writing, based on an Inca legend; she knew Carl would be interested. She was not going to open the house in Dublin this summer, especially since Ada was away; in any case, by the time Ada got back the summer would be half over. Amy was thinking of selling Broomley Lacey, as Brookline was becoming "more and more the mart of fashion," she wrote to a friend; and before the season was over she did sell the country place, on her own, and within two weeks of her decision to put it on the market.* The Engels took a place near Marblehead, and when Ada returned, the two drove down and spent the day with them, going out in a launch all around the islands, an excursion Amy found so delightful that she decided to hire a launch in Boston to cruise among the islands in the harbor. (It was also much more effective in helping her sleep than pills, which she frequently had to take.)

Elizabeth Sergeant came back from France, having narrowly escaped death at the start of her assignment for the *New Republic.* On the first battlefield that she and other journalists were inspecting—Elsie was the only woman among them—one of the men picked up a supposedly dead grenade; it exploded, killing him instantly, blowing the arm off another, and splintering the bones in both of her ankles. She was in the hospital there for weeks, and during the long, painful convalescence, she wrote her first book, *Shadow-Shapes.* Now that she was back, Amy invited her to come right out to Sevenels to read her manuscript. This required several visits, and on one evening, Elsie brought with her a young lieutenant she had met in France, whose volume of poetry, *Blindman,* had just been completed. He also read his manuscript to Amy, who was much impressed with his ability, but had a few improvements to suggest, and, as he was studying at Harvard's summer school, she asked him to come again. The poet was Hervey Allen, who became one of the circle of young men Amy took under her literary wing. She considered him among the most talented of the new poets; and if he had not written his enormously successful novel, *Anthony Adverse,* he might have fulfilled his promise. At

* She sold Broomley Lacey for $15,000, and removed only the Dutch tiles from three fireplaces and some furniture.

any rate, he and Amy remained friends as long as she lived. (One might note, in passing, that, in spite of her "enemies," real or imagined, Amy Lowell's friendships, usually instantaneous, were also enduring.)

One matter that troubled her was that D. H. Lawrence had written that he was coming to America at last. He hoped to earn his way at first by giving a few lectures; he wondered if she could arrange some dates for him in Boston. She was forced to tell him that she had found his book in the Boston Athenaeum's "Scruple Room," and that raising a ruckus had done no good. She and Ada would welcome him and Frieda with "the greatest of pleasure," but New England would not. "There is a mistaken and ridiculous prejudice against your books, and that is the long and short of it; because it is undeserved it makes me want to weep. . . . If I cared less for you, I should put you off with some platitude . . . but it is almost impossible to make the general public understand, particularly when your books are prejudicial to their preconceived notions. . . ." She also warned him that he must not look for El Dorado in America, "because it is anything but that."

He answered immediately that he understood, especially about lecturing. "As for an El Dorado," he said, "when I set out to look for one, I shall find one: for nothing is easier to find than money, if a man sets out straight for it. I don't want El Dorado: only life and freedom, a feeling of bigness, and a radical, if preconscious sympathy. I don't want to lecture—never did. I only want to be able to live. And I believe that, once in America, I could soon do that by writing." He hoped that he could come to Sevenels, to stay a week or two, but he was afraid of putting a burden on her friendship. For some reason, Amy was afraid his plans would never work; she also feared there would be prejudice against Frieda because of the continuing American bitterness against Germans. She wrote to each of them separately, advising them earnestly not to come. Then she agonized to Ada over the effect her advice might have on the Lawrences.

The country continued its restless postwar readjustment during the hot weeks of July and August. The final galley proof of *Pictures* was corrected by August 21. With "Peter" to help her, the task was not so hard on Amy's eyes, but when that was done, she began work on pages and pages of notes for the Chinese translations she and Florence Ayscough were doing, and the eyestrain became so intense that the headaches returned. The doctor forbade her to use her eyes at all, and Amy fretted over the delay in her professional enterprises, as well as over the dire implications of the rising tide of social-industrial revolution that was visible all around them. On September 11, the Boston Police Force itself went on strike. For three days, bedlam reigned: Before the National Guard could be called out by Governor Coolidge, bands of hoodlums broke shop windows, stole clothes and sporting goods, and—most flagrant of all to proper Bostonians—shot craps on the Boston Common. Amy was alarmed: Would Sevenels be safe without the fierce barking of sheep dogs to ward off intruders? Now one of the main reasons she had had for choosing such large, noisy dogs became apparent. She acquired a revolver, which she kept loaded and handy in the library table drawer when she worked at night. (She continued her nocturnal hours of hard labor at the least let-up of eyestrain.)

The police strike was not too serious in itself, but to Amy it was symptomatic of a general state of affairs that affected everything and everyone, including her, both as poet and as property owner. The scheduled publication date for *Pictures of the Floating World* was September 24 (a year to the day after *Can Grande's Castle* came out), and the first edition was completely sold out before then; but the second, which was supposed to appear immediately, was delayed by a printers' strike. Amy, frustrated and impatient, decided to go to New York for a consultation with her publisher, and she also made appointments with a number of editors in connection with reviews of the book. As usual, she and Ada got in touch with their friends, among them the Untermeyers, who planned to give a small dinner party to celebrate the new book. Besides Amy and Ada, they had invited a few close friends—Ben Huebsch, the publisher, and George Plank (with whom Amy had come close to launching a new magazine of verse), Sara Teasdale and her husband, Ernest Filsinger, perhaps one or two more. Jean had urged Amy to be on time if possible, since she had only one maid (whereas Amy had twelve "domestics"), a general housekeeper who went home at night, and it was difficult to keep the meal waiting. But as usual, Amy and Ada showed up an hour late, Amy full of apologies. Everything was ready—the pitchers of ice water, the saltcellar flanking Amy's plate—and they sat down immediately. In spite of the delay, the dinner went smoothly, Louis and Amy exchanging quips, entering into brilliant paths of discussion only to veer off on another track a moment later. Ben Huebsch, "genial and skeptical," put in a word or two of "sanative deflation" occasionally, while the rest of them exchanged winks and amused glances as the sallies sailed across the table.

About halfway through dessert, Sara Teasdale brought up the battle going on in the Poetry Society over the activity of George Sylvester Viereck. In various writings during the war he had voiced opinions that were strangely pro-German. Literary gossip had it that his ancestry was somehow connected with the Kaiser, and there was a movement on foot to oust him from the Poetry Society on the suspicion that he might have been a spy. The Untermeyers and Ben Huebsch formed a firm trio against such action, since the suspicion had not been verified and it was probably just another sign of the hysteria they were determined to quash. One instance of that hysteria was the suppression of German music and musicians during the war; and Amy herself, just a few weeks earlier, had run into it when she cabled a bid for the famous letter from Shelley inviting Keats to stay with him in Italy, which was being sold at auction: The censor stopped the message because she also included a bid for some letters by "Huns"—Schumann and Brahms. Frantic, she repeated the bid, and then appealed to the State Department. Her cable was delivered in time, and she acquired the letters (the Shelley-to-Keats at fabulous cost). Now, however, she upheld the case for Viereck's expulsion. The opposition at the dinner table contended that if the Poetry Society was to uphold its own tenets, it should drop Viereck as poetically ineligible for membership, but on no other grounds. And they twitted Amy for her melodramatic poem, "The Cornucopia of Red and Green Comfits," published in the *Independent* of November 1917, based on a story that German aviators were dropping poisoned candy for the starving children at Bar-le-Duc. It was one of the most effective at readings given just after the United States entered the war. Jean remarked in her memoirs that what they thought was gross exaggeration of heinous German behavior in World War I became "a frightfully staggering reality in 1942," and Amy's sense of drama may have given her a prophetic if accidental insight into the future Nazi capacity for brutality. While refilling the coffee cups, Jean said, to emphasize their point, "You and the magazine weren't exactly upholding the Court of Reason, Amy."

At her accusation, Amy's voice suddenly took on an edge of the hysteria they had all been decrying, an unusual tone for her in these discussions. "You don't know what you're talking about," she shot back at Jean. "Times are changing—we're all of us in danger." Now all the fears she had been hiding came out in a rush: "A lawless element may take over at any moment. It's people like myself that they'll go for. I tell you, I feel it. How many nights when I sit writing in my library, nobody awake in the whole house but me and my Winky [her black cat], I think I hear intruders—blackguards—and I grasp my revolver, ready to shoot. I feel these things, and I will *fight!* I am the last of the barons—the last of the barons!" she shouted, pounding her small fists on the table. Her blows set the silver clinking on the glass-topped table; the plates rattled; and the maid "came running in from the kitchen with round, scared eyes to find out what the commotion was about." Ada looked alarmed, but uncertain what to do. The others stared at Amy in astonished silence. But Jean had noticed the dangerous red spots that flared in "Amy's usually controlled and alert face"; and she had heard, as they all had, the strange, hysterical tone of her voice. She was afraid Amy would have apoplexy in another minute. She rose, took hold of the poet's hand, and led her into the bedroom. Amy made no protest, but went with her, "docile as a child." Continuing to hold her hand, Jean sat her down in a boudoir chair, where, "after a few incoherent sputterings," Amy grew calm.

When they rejoined the others in the living room, where talk had resumed, no one mentioned the outburst or reverted to the subject that caused it. Amy talked and laughed as though nothing had upset her. Ada, placing the footstool under her feet when she first sat down, gave her a quick glance of concern and affection; realizing that a crisis had been averted, she cast Jean a look of gratitude. Amy made an effort to be charming, and talk was buzzing along at a great rate when the bell rang to announce the cab that Amy had ordered. After she and Ada had gone, the party delved into speculation and excited comment on Amy's latest scene, "a really disturbing exhibition." Hardly more than ten minutes had passed and they were still in a huddle, and Sara Teasdale, whose delicate nature could not stand controversy, was berating herself for bringing up the subject of Viereck, when the doorbell rang. It was Amy, who stood in the doorway looking rather sheepish. She had come back for her footstool, she said, which they had forgotten. (This in itself was odd, because ordinarily Ada would have come back for it.) Louis quickly found it and handed it to her, but still she stood there, looking from him to Jean, "brightly but uncertainly." At last she said, "Louis, I'm sure, will forgive me, but I'm afraid Jean is angry with me. Will you forgive me, Jean?" The answer she received was typical: "It's not a question of forgiving," Jean said. She held that ignorant people might give way to their prejudices and that the times were bad, it was true; but it was up to people like themselves to keep things in balance. When someone like Amy went off the deep end, it *was* disturbing. At that Amy became doubly remorseful, and she made Jean promise to visit her the next day at the hotel as soon as she got up, about one o'clock. Then, perhaps hoping to throw them off the track of her terrifying premonitions as she had revealed them in her blowup, she turned just as she was ready to go and said: "You'd feel the way I do if a German officer had pushed you right off the pavement. That's what happened to me," she said, recalling the panicky day in London in 1914 when she had been caught up in the mobs of people trying to get out of the country. With this Parthian shot, she went down to meet Ada, who was waiting in the cab.

Jean and Louis carried her final jab back to the company, where they all grinned at the idea of the "unequal contest." "I can't imagine anyone pushing Amy around," George Plank said, laughing. (He had written Jean, in recalling the incident for her in 1961: "Dear Amy Lowell, I hope she is smoking celestial cigars and resting plump jeweled fingers on the shelf of her bosom!—that was an enchanting party.") * But Ben Huebsch observed, "I don't know, it just may be that Amy is right about the future. . . ."

And shortly afterward, possibly on this same trip to New York, she and Ada attended a performance of Gerhart Hauptmann's *The Weavers* with the Untermeyers. The play dealt with mill workers in the early days of the industrial revolution. And Amy, who was sitting next to Louis, again went through a violent, involuntary experience: Her reaction to the plot was similar to her reaction to Jean Untermeyer's remark at the dinner party. She naturally felt the implications of the drama with strong impact, relating them to the source of her own wealth. As she watched "the scene of the pillage in which the starving Silesian workers destroy the machines which have deprived them of work and then proceed to smash the home of the manufacturer," she could not control her guilt and fear. She was mortally afraid that the deplorable conditions in the mill towns founded by, and named for, her great-grandfather would in some way destroy her—"the last of the barons," as she had called herself at the Untermeyers' dinner party. She was visibly trembling, and almost by way of explanation, she whispered to Louis, as the curtain fell: "This is the future. That is what is going to happen to me!" **

It was a fear that continued to haunt her from time to time. Apparently it never occurred to her that she could have done something to benefit the workers, such as altering conditions in the factories. Poetry—the new poetry—was her cause, and she worked as hard as any millhand, and from a health standpoint, under conditions just as severe, and often more painful than poverty.

* In his letter to Jean, George was not sure whether the year was 1916 or 1919, the two he had spent in New York. He thought it might have been 1916, because the war was over by 1919, and "there would have been no point in Viereck being a spy." But he was wrong: The spy-hunt scare was worse after the war; and Amy did not get Winky till after the dogs were gone. She had just bought the revolver in September 1919. Jean placed the incident incorrectly in 1916.

** The incident at the performance of *The Weavers* was recalled by Louis Untermeyer in his "Memoir" introduction to *The Complete Poetical Works of Amy Lowell* (Boston: Houghton Mifflin Company, 1955).

CHAPTER XVI

"Two Speak Together"

As IF TO VERIFY her instinctive warnings about the future, in *Pictures of the Floating World,* Amy found herself with a best seller in nonfiction, but without books to sell because of the printers' strikes. (In a way, the difficulty of obtaining a copy added to the success of the volume.) *Pictures* contained her most personal and deeply felt poems, some of the finest free-verse lyrics she was ever to write. If she had not been so apprehensive about the changing times, or so impatient over the delay in publication of the second edition (which was not issued until late November), she might have savored the satisfying flavor of her success a little more. Though the poems have been passed over lightly by nearly every critic of, and commentator on, Amy Lowell, the section entitled "Two Speak Together" (the second in a six-part division called "Planes of Personality") contains the heart of her psyche. More important, perhaps, it disproves the almost universal judgment that hers was a "surface" art.

The title "Two Speak Together" itself might well be said to epitomize the relationship between Amy Lowell and Ada Russell. Certainly they did speak the same language from the beginning, and in these poems Amy revealed that much of it was the language of love—on her side, love that sometimes seemed to amount to adoration.

"It is almost impossible to tell the degree of intimacy between intimate friends," she wrote in the preface to her last and longest book. She was referring to the relationship of the painter Joseph Severn and John Keats, and the book of course was her biography of the poet. However, the statement could easily be applied to her relationship with Ada, as she perhaps (consciously or unconsciously) meant it to be a warning to speculators about them not to jump to conclusions. The poems were written over a period of at least four years. Most of them were first published singly in magazines, but Amy wanted to assemble them in one place as a lasting public testament of the love that had brought meaning to her life. Two years before, in 1917, she had written to Professor Phelps: "I have a volume of lyrics which I have been wanting to bring out for two years . . . but the publishers have insisted on these more timely poems of mine coming first. . . ." And to Aldington she described the volume as "a collection of short lyrics which I have been writing at odd moments for the last four years"; but some were five years old, and a few were fairly recent. Foster Damon brushes hastily over the section "Two Speak Together," merely citing them as "chiefly love poems, including the popular 'Vernal Equinox,' and the famous 'Madonna of the Evening Flowers.' " At the same time, and in the circumstances, he could hardly say more; but these are not so much "love poems"—in which desire and sexuality predominate—as poems of love, that is, of love in its combined physical and spiritual totality.

These poems deal with devotion, admiration, tenderness, and gratitude, as well as with passion and desire for the beloved. The word *ukiyoye* ("floating world") was "applied by the Japanese to their 18th century art, which delighted in the passing frivolities of life," according to Damon; but the poems in "Two Speak Together" are anything but frivolous. Those in this section, simple, reflective, unpretentious, free of bombast, are among Amy Lowell's most moving—and most modern—poems. She may have chosen the title as a veil to hide her "impassioned heart," as she wrote of herself in *A Critical Fable*. Yet it is thinly veiled indeed, and it may be that she was of two minds about it: She wanted to proclaim and disguise her emotions at the same time. For all her exhibitionism, she exercised extreme discretion in expressing her romantic feelings. This had been the core of her conflict as an awkward adolescent, and the conflict was still part of her, although her companionship with Ada had eased it to a great extent.

"I remember my brother's telling me what an awful time he had to free himself from his inhibitions. Possibly his freedom helped mine, as he was nineteen years older than I, and a constant influence on my childhood . . . ," she wrote, on October 23, 1917, to Helen Bullis Kizer, who had written a long article on Amy Lowell for the *North American Review* about the time *Tendencies* was published. (Mrs. Kizer, who became Amy's devoted admirer and reviewer, was killed instantly by a fall from her horse four days before *Pictures* was published, and now, almost two years to the day from this letter, on October 19, 1919, Amy's piece, "In Memoriam: A Tribute to H. B. K.," appeared in the *New York Times*.) In this 1917 letter, Amy refuted charges that her style was "careless" and that she had been "startled" by some of the pieces in *Spoon River*. "I would be willing to bet a good deal that nothing can 'startle' me," she asserted. Then, in a few sentences, she vigorously voiced views about Freud—or more accurately—about the frenzy with which his theories were being accepted at the time.

"There have been few things which have done so much harm to the world as the promiscuous publication of Freud's theories," she maintained; and she made the valid point that it takes a "trained psychologist" to put them in the light in which they belong. "If you will read his book on 'Dreams' you will see how dangerous a theory can be when ridden too hard. To suppose that all life under the surface consists of violent sexual desires crushed out or sublimated, that all personal relation is a war of sexual antagonisms is to see life through a perfectly distorted medium. We have run mad on the subject in this country, as a few years ago we ran mad over Christian Science. That the Victorians refused to give sex its proper weight is of course true, but that we are over-emphasizing it, and particularly its perversions, is equally true." Her statement could be made today, considering the present rage for sex-permeated books and pornographic films. Time and again she emphasized that the quality which made D. H. Lawrence an artist of such stature in her eyes was that he envisaged life whole and complete, including the spiritual as well as the physical. (She considered *Women in Love,* which he was soon to write, one of his "very finest books," and its suppression "made her sick," she wrote him.)

In "Two Speak Together," three short lyrics alone hold a world of eloquence: "A Sprig of Rosemary," highlighting Ada's hands—

I cannot see your face,
When I think of you,
It is your hands which I see.
Your hands
Sewing,
Holding a book,
Resting for a moment on the sill of a window.
My eyes keep always the sight of your hands,
But my heart holds the sound of your voice,
And the soft brightness which is your soul.

"A Decade," drawing an unmistakable image of both passion and contentment—

When you came, you were like red wine and honey,
And the taste of you burnt my mouth with its sweetness.
Now you are like morning bread,
Smooth and pleasant.
I hardly taste you at all for I know your savour,
But I am completely nourished.

And "Opal," depicting the conflict of the "impassioned heart"—

You are ice and fire,
The touch of you burns my hands like snow. . . .

When I am with you,
My heart is a frozen pond
Gleaming with agitated torches.

So striking was the effect of these three little poems that Carl Engel seized upon them for setting right away. Amy was both proud and pleased; when G. Schirmer's prepared to publish them in 1922, she suggested that they be combined in a printed song pamphlet. "The Letter," like "The Taxi," must have been composed during one of the times Ada went to visit her family. The last stanza reads:

> I am tired, Beloved, of chafing my heart against
> The want of you;
> Of squeezing it into little inkdrops,
> And posting it.
> And I scald alone, here, under the fire
> Of the great moon.

The meditative, nostalgic, but slightly apprehensive "Penumbra" is surely autobiographical. The poem opens with a description of a quiet summer night, with the flower scents coming in from the garden, the silence broken only by the lonely wail of a train whistle. The poet recalls the garden in her childhood, rolling her hoop along the paths, playing Indian with bow and arrow; as if speaking to someone beloved, she senses her own early death, and she asks, "What will it be like for you then?" She describes the room they are in, easily recognizable as the library, especially in the lines:

> You will see my narrow table
> At which I have written so many hours.
> My dogs will push their noses into your hand,
> And ask—ask—
> Clinging to you with puzzled eyes. . . .
>
> You will sit here, some quiet Summer night . . .
>
> But you will not be lonely,
> For these things are a part of me.
> And my love will go on speaking to you
> Through the chairs, and the tables, and the pictures,
> As it does now through my voice,
> And the quick, necessary touch of my hand.

The beautiful restraint of such lines only enriches their meaning. And in "The Garden by Moonlight," which gives a clear, accurate picture of flowers and flower perfume coming out at night, are these poignant last lines:

Ah, Beloved, do you see those orange lilies?
They knew my mother,
But who belonging to me will they know
When I am gone.

The fact that it is a statement, not a question, gives the thought a sad, almost tragic touch. Some of the poems present pure passion; others, admiration of physical perfection as in "The Wheel of the Sun":

For I am blinded by your beauty,
And my heart is strained,
And aches,
Before you.

In the street,
You spread a brightness where you walk,
And I see your lifting silks
And rejoice; . . .

Another describes the gorgeous colors of the crystal boughs of the trees after an ice storm, but finds that the beloved, walking under them at ten o'clock in the morning, is more brilliant than the ice trees; and though the dogs are barking "like sharp hammer-strokes on metal" all around her, their barking does not speak as loudly as her quietness. And then, of course, there is the acknowledged portrait of Ada in the lovely "Madonna of the Evening Flowers":

All day long I have been working,
Now I am tired.
I call: "Where are you?"
But there is only the oak-tree rustling in the wind.
The house is very quiet,
The sun shines in on your books,
On your scissors and thimble just put down,
But you are not there.
Suddenly I am lonely:
Where are you?
I go about searching.

Then I see you,
Standing under a spire of pale blue larkspur,
With a basket of roses on your arm.
You are cool, like silver,
And you smile.
I think the Canterbury bells are playing little tunes.

You tell me that the peonies need spraying,
That the columbines have overrun all bounds,
That the pyrus japonica should be cut back and rounded.
You tell me these things.
But I look at you, heart of silver,
White heart-flame of polished silver,
Burning beneath the blue steeples of the larkspur,
And I long to kneel instantly at your feet,
While all about us peal the loud, sweet *Te Deums* of the
Canterbury bells.

There are several poems suggesting the early death of the poet. One, "Frimaire," which closes the section, pictures both Ada and herself as autumn flowers, a crimson and a purple aster, and wonders which one will die first:

You or I—and I am a coward.
Surely frost should take the crimson.
Purple is a finer colour,
Very splendid in isolation.

So we nod above the broken
Stems of flowers almost rotted.
Many mornings there cannot be now
For us both. Ah, Dear, I love you!

It was not until 1957 that these and later poems of love by Amy Lowell were properly recognized as an expression of deep emotion and poetic beauty, worthy of reassessment and evaluation. They are now considered to rank with such enduring poems as "Patterns," "Lilacs," "Meeting House Hill," "The Boston Athenaeum," "Congressional Library," "Nuit Blanche," "The Basket," "In the Stadium," and the six sonnets to Eleonora Duse, the selections most often appearing in anthologies today. In a small volume, entitled *A Shard of Silence* (1957),* a collection of sixty poems, edited and selected by G. R. Ruihley with the assistance of John Ciardi, the essence of Amy Lowell's exceptional love in its many facets as expressed in her poetry is offered as proof of her unique talent. The excellent introduction written by Ruihley, perceptive of her emotional struggle, refutes the charge that Amy Lowell was a poet of "surface" forms and feelings. "Both the forms of Amy Lowell's life and the record of her poetry suggest a nature shaken by inner stress"; and it was this inner torment, caused by her physical deformity and deep disappointment of her youth—"the promise given and withheld"—that heightened her emotions so that "common experience took on a new meaning." The editor points to "the sight of withering leaves along a path," a spray of mignonette, a garden fountain splashing over a stone figure, the orange flash of a darting fish in the aquarium, the shiny white of "Thompson's Lunch Room" ("Towns in Colour"). All these things touched her far below the surface of objects held up naked to the eye of the reader. "That it was a tortured life, and that in consequence her ultimate development was remarkable, gives the poetry of Amy Lowell its peculiar meaning and expressiveness," the author of the introduction in *A Shard of Silence* indicates. He goes on: "To a degree remarkable in the history of poetry, Amy Lowell was conscious of the emotional impact of material forms . . . and she succeeds in defining their relationship to our life." (He admits that "much of her printed verse is unworthy of her talent" and, as indicated in the present study, that the narratives, while they may express color and movement, are often labored. They probably did "spring from the will," as so many critics perceived and condemned her for; unfortunately, she believed she had to produce a massive volume of work if it was to endure; but "a fair appraisal does not stress failings.")

Fortunately for her, she "found her innate mode of expression" in the principles of Imagism, which started her on a true literary career and brought relief from the sterile life at Sevenels. A personal solution to her emotional life came through her meeting

* G. R. Ruihley, Ed., *A Shard of Silence,* Selected Poems of Amy Lowell (New York: Twayne Publishers, Inc., 1957).

with Ada. "The pronounced affinity between them ripened into an extraordinary love. . . . Safe in this warm garment, Amy could face the pain and disillusionments of her daily life. It was the sight of Mrs. Russell, seated in the garden or reading in a corner of a room, that touched Amy's life with joy." (Here Ruihley refers to "A Sprig of Rosemary": "The rich chambers of feeling newly opened to her softened and deepened her poetry. From the whispered contentment * of 'Penumbra' to the rapture of 'In Excelsis,' her poems sang of her love.")

The 1957 collection, divided into sections, has only one poem in the first: "Patterns." The second is headed "Ada Russell" and contains nine or ten titles, starting with a later poem, "Song for a Viola d'Amore," but most of them are from "Two Speak Together," published in *Pictures of the Floating World.* In the latter volume were recently published poems like the melodramatic "Appuldurcombe Park," which brought the immediate letter from William Carlos Williams, and, with its opening line, "I am a woman, sick for passion," repeated several times in the poem, was usually successful at readings. It was often coupled with "Patterns," but it was not nearly as finely wrought; nor was the opening line and refrain autobiographical, except possibly as a recollection of Amy's early days of loneliness. The poem "A Bather (After a Picture by Andreas Zorn)" is another glorification of a woman's naked body—"Triumphant in smooth, supple roudness, . . ./ Cool, perfect, with rose rarely tinting your lips and your breasts,/ Swelling out from the green in the opulent curves of ripe fruit . . ."—and offers this provocative stanza:

Oread, Dryad, or Naiad, or just
Woman, clad only in youth and in gallant perfection,
Standing up in a great burst of sunshine, you dazzle my eyes
Like a snow-star, a moon, your effulgence burns up in a halo,
For you are the chalice which holds all the races of men.

Amy's fierce admiration for the female body was well known. John Farrar has recalled one occasion of her frequent fury that

* "Penumbra" hardly expresses contentment, but rather a calm, contemplative view of love's triumph over death.

was connected with female nudity. She met him around this time (1919 or 1920),* and though he was editor of the *Bookman,* he soon became one of the circle of young men toward whom Amy adopted a matriarchal air. ("Tell Mama your troubles, Johnny," she would say to him if he seemed downcast about anything.) He met her and Ada first at a performance of the Dorothy Stockbridge group, Stocks, which produced original plays by group members, including a few of Farrar's. Amy's interest in the enterprise had been aroused by two of its patronesses, Mrs. Enrico Caruso and Mrs. H. Noble McCracken, and it so happened that John was playing one of the roles that night in Dorothy's *Jezebel.* Amy had her little footstool, placed under her feet by Ada before the performance began; and, as she settled her great bulk on the rickety bench, she caused quite a stir in the little Village shop that served as the theater. She was pleased with his performance, and when she learned he wrote poetry, she wanted to see some of it. She was equally pleased with his poems and considered him one of the "promising youngsters" in the movement. They often argued about the relative merits of the "cadenced" and the "metred" line. But, according to John, the "sorest" Amy ever got at him, and there were many times when she flared up at him, occurred on the night he invited her to a meeting of another Village group. These young artists choreographed poetry (perhaps a leftover of the Chorists), and several of John's poems were performed. One in particular, "The Slave Girl," was interpreted dramatically by Margaret Severn, a dancer friend of John's. As he read the poem aloud, she danced to the rhythm of it, wearing next to nothing. Afterward, as he approached Amy to ask how she liked it, he could see at a glance that she was furious, and before he could say anything, she demanded: "How *can* you compete with naked women?" Hers was such a startling reaction that mild-mannered John Farrar, with his humorous eyes, could do nothing but laugh, which only made her angrier. Amy flailed the air with her small fists and said, "Don't you realize that no verses can equal the poetry of a young girl's naked body?" That was the same Amy Lowell who

* He was not sure which year it was. These anecdotes are from an interview with Mr. Farrar in April 1973.

wrote so sensitively of the female body, so tenderly of her personal love.

Pictures included a graphic self-portrait of Amy at Sevenels in "Dog-Days," one of the best poems employing the Imagist technique, the first three lines of which have often been quoted:

A ladder sticking up at the open window,
The top of an old ladder;
And all of Summer is there.

Great waves and tufts of wistaria surge across the window,
And a thin, belated blossom
Jerks up and down in the sunlight;
Purple translucence against the blue sky.
"Tie back this branch," I say,
But my hands are sticky with leaves,
And my nostrils widen to the smell of crushed green.
The ladder moves uneasily at the open window,
And I call to the man beneath,
"Tie back that branch."

There is a ladder leaning against the window-sill,
And a mutter of thunder in the air.

This is Amy at home, tending her property, relaxed, giving orders to the gardener on a hot August afternoon. But there were not many such moments in Amy's life from 1919 on. There was always "a mutter of thunder in the air." She packed her hours so full that it was no wonder she had a heart attack in late fall. Her schedule would have been enough to fell a well person—and she was ill. She knew it, but she would not yield to the fact. *Pictures* went into the second printing in mid-November as had been promised (a third would be out before Christmas). In connection with that event and her lecture engagements, she and Ada went to New York and nearby points a number of times. On one occasion she met and entertained John Drinkwater and his wife, who had come to New York for the opening of his play, *Lincoln*. Amy was not able to attend the opening performance, but she and the Drinkwaters formed another of her instant, lasting friendships, and she promised to see the play as soon as possible.

In her writing, she was rapidly becoming a "woman of letters" as well as a poet: In addition to composing two long "legends" for a new volume devoted solely to old tales, she wrote three introductions for other people's books. One of these was for a volume of poems by eight-year-old Hilda Conkling, daughter of her friend, Grace Conkling, whose poems, in the tradition of Adelaide Crapsey, an earlier child wonder, Amy thought were remarkable for their intuitional insights. Another introduction was written for translations of three diaries of Japanese court ladies, made by Elsie Sergeant's aunt, Annie Shepley Omori, who had married a Japanese and lived in Japan many years.* Some engagements had to be canceled because of Amy's high blood pressure, but she had been invited by the Contemporary Club of Philadelphia some time before to give the featured lecture at its celebration of Walt Whitman's centenary, on November 12, and she considered it important to keep that date. She felt well enough to keep another for a reading in Montclair, New Jersey, and two in New York (one at St. Mark's Church-in-the-Bouwerie, a reading before 921 people, more than capacity; and the other before 720 students at Columbia University). Ada had advised her in vain to save her strength for the lecture. Amy enjoyed readings, and she had expressly stipulated that there was to be no debate, discussion, or question period after the lecture, so she thought she could manage to get through everything all right.

They arrived in Philadelphia on November 11, when A. Edward Newton, of the museum staff, was to give a dinner party for her. But she was suddenly seized with shortness of breath and pains in her chest and left side. Ada called the nearest doctor, who pronounced it a heart attack. The dinner had to be canceled, but Amy insisted on staying for the lecture the next evening. She promised she would rest in bed all day. Ada knew it was useless to try to dissuade her. As it turned out, Amy wished she had listened to her friend, for that lecture produced the biggest—and last—public row over the new poetry she was ever to experience.

* As a point of current interest, a recent study has been made of these diaries in connection with "Women's Lib" (1972) which shows that women were the real intellectuals of eighteenth-century Japan.

The Contemporary Club was playing up the centenary, as it was the only club Whitman had ever joined. Amy's speech, "Walt Whitman and the New Poetry," took his greatness for granted, assuming that her listeners would realize that his genius was a point of departure for the creative works of "contemporary" poets. If the club members lived up to the name of their club, she felt, they would certainly acknowledge that the time of "the good gray poet" was past. To show the changes sixty years had brought, she read several of Sandburg's *Chicago* poems; and, in conclusion, she specified Whitman's faults as well as his virtues. He was "a great voice, and a silly, flattered old man," she said (if the other speakers on the platform gasped, she didn't hear them—or she went right on anyway), ". . . a powerful original poet, with a somewhat disconcerting dash of the poseur. . . . Singer, prophet, orator, lover of beauty, sentimentalist, and often slovenly workman, his poems are that splendid paradox—himself. . . . Let us be thankful for him as we are thankful for Theocritus, and Dante, and Chaucer, and Browning. But our skies are not his, and he would be the first to wish us 'God speed' under them."

Certainly there was nothing in her remarks to warrant more than a possible protest against characterizing Whitman as a "slovenly workman," but the subsequent outburst amounted to "the most stupid and virulent attack" to which she had ever been subjected. The third speaker denounced the whole new poetry movement. Amy, at first astonished, quickly grew angry, and when the man began to defend Whitman, recalling his lack of recognition and the sufferings he had had to go through, she broke in: "What do you think I am going through now?"

Laughter swept through the hall, but he replied haughtily over the noise, "Madam, I hope you are going through a reformation." And he continued his abuse. The chairman made no effort to stop him until Amy, reminding him of the stipulation that there would be no discussion, threatened to leave the platform. The next speaker, however, took up the tirade with even greater force. Pointing a finger at her, he called her "a literary hand-grenade thrower." If Amy had not been so angry she would have laughed, and indeed hisses now began hurtling in his direction from her supporters. At the condemnation of the modern poets she had mentioned, especially Sandburg, whom nobody took seriously, she "slammed back good and plenty," she wrote the Chicago poet afterward. But when her adversary finally finished, and she rose, she was so angry that she choked and was unable to speak for a moment. A dangerous redness rose in her cheeks, and Ada was afraid from her agitated expression that she might have another heart attack—no one else knew about it. After a moment, however, she seemed to calm down. There was no point in name-calling, so she merely stated again that she had made the stipulation that there would be no discussion, which had been agreed to by the club secretary, and she said she felt they had broken faith with her. She had nothing more to say. Proud of her, and vastly relieved, Ada watched her leave the platform in dignified silence.

That should have been the end of it, but the next morning the *Public Ledger,* in a story headlined "Tears Punctuate Stormy Spots in Vers Libre Debate," alleged that Amy Lowell had burst into tears and had choked out protestingly between sobs. Reporters, who called the Bellevue-Stratford Hotel throughout the morning to verify the tale, were told repeatedly she was not up yet. Consequently, a story in the next edition stated that Amy Lowell was suffering from a nervous breakdown as a result of her treatment at the Contemporary Club. When she rose at her usual hour, she was astounded and outraged in equal proportions. She said to Ada, "Call the papers, Peter, and tell the reporters to get over here fast." She had Elizabeth Henry take special care with her hair and her grooming. When she chose, there was no one who could be more imposing or poised. She could treat men in a manner "both regal and fraternal," as her friend Elsie Sergeant said.

"Well, boys," she said in her man-to-man tone of voice, "do I look like a person suffering from a nervous breakdown?" They had to admit she definitely did not. "As for those 'tears,' I was just *plumb mad,* and I don't weep when I'm mad," she went on. "Do I look as if I were a weeping woman?" Hardly, they agreed. She let out a hearty laugh, and then set them straight, telling them of the no-discussion stipulation and referring them to the club secretary. Later, in a gesture of public apology, the secretary showed reporters the advance correspondence regarding the lecture, and he assured Amy he had no idea the other speakers would abandon their subjects to attack her. One happy result of the whole thing was that every copy of her books then in Philadelphia bookstores was sold, and New York bookshops "were being drained of their quota to meet the Philadelphia demand." But Amy wanted no more of such publicity, and she knew that the time for discussion and defense of the new poetry was past: It had already won acceptance in contemporary literature. (It was shortly after this that she silenced the columnists.)

She should have gone right home from Philadelphia, but instead she returned to New York to give two more readings. She saw the Drinkwaters again, and, unfortunately, caught the flu bug from which John was just recovering. Amy's illness took the form of a severe cold, and the constant coughing irritated the wound of her first hernia operation, from which the nagging pain had been increasing before she caught cold. Now there was a swelling near the wound. A stitch had broken, the doctor said. The operation would have to be repeated; and, from the looks of things, this time it would be more difficult. But when he said it didn't have to be done immediately, Amy, typically, postponed surgery till after her January lecture tour.

Then, knowing that she had at least a month of grace, she enjoyed the Christmas festivities to the full. Amy had great capacity for the enjoyment of life as well as for work; she possessed enormous lust for life (unlike Sara Teasdale, a semi-invalid, whose frail health made her languid much of the time). It was one of the tragic instances of "the trial by existence," as Frost called it, that Amy had to spend so much time recovering from one health crisis or another. Her glandular and general health problems combined to produce a vicious circle: She often threw herself into activity to surmount pain and suffering, but her nature was such that she overdid almost everything, which then aggravated her situation. At the Lowell family dinner on Christmas Day, she and Ada acted like a pair of mischievous youngsters in their efforts to grab the party favors for Lorna's children. These came from "crackers," most of which contained paper caps with little toys. Amy wanted to snatch all she could for Sonny and the baby, Allen, now about a year old. Her niece, Katherine Putnam (now married with a family of her own), who sat across from her, looked over and saw her "hugging a little figure of Pickwick." She begged: "Do give me that, Aunt Amy. You haven't any children."

At that, Amy "secreted it jealously" in the folds of her napkin. "Certainly I have," she said indignantly. "And I'm not going to let anybody have any more!" (She had given a couple to her nephew, who also had a family now.) Katherine of course had touched a sore spot, and although Amy made a game of it and later felt that she had "really behaved abominably," she also really didn't care: Ada's family was *her* family, Ada's children (or grandchildren) were hers also, and she wanted everybody to realize that they came first with her. Between the two of them, she reported in a letter to Lorna, she and Ada managed to grab five figures, a ten-pin set, and a gridiron. (The little figures she decided were absolutely necessary to be customers in the toy grocery shop she had sent Sonny for Christmas, recalling her own childhood shop, around which she had written her first stories.) She tactfully warned Lorna that the paint might come off the little figures, which was "too bad, as Allen would probably enjoy sucking them."

The holidays brought a cold snap and heavy snow, keeping Amy indoors for a week; but the doctor had told her to stay off her feet, anyway, and not to overexert herself by writing late into the night. She fretted some about Winky (who had figured in three poems in *Pictures*) because he fell in love with the snow, insisted on staying out in it for four hours, and had to be sent to a veterinary hospital. But he was apparently none the worse for his misadventure when he came home, and Amy might well have wished that she had nine lives, so she would be sure of surviving the coming operation. She tried not to think about it and spent most of January 1920 in "desperate lecturing, made miserable by her dropped stitch." She had to move very slowly to avoid pain and jarring. One of the important lectures, which had been long deferred, was a repeat of "Some Musical Analogies in Modern Poetry," originally given at Paine Hall at Harvard. Now, at Columbia University, in spite of the way she was feeling, the lecture created such a strong impression that she was invited to publish it as an article in the *Musical Quarterly*. Amy was like the girl who couldn't say no to any proposal where her writing was concerned, and she agreed. In connection with the project, she made an appointment to consult with the editor of the magazine; but when she got there, at some inconvenience to herself, the secretary informed her that "Mr. Sonneck is out of town." When she had made the appointment with Miss Lowell she had forgotten that he had made a lecture engagement elsewhere on that date.

Whether because she was feeling especially miserable, or simply because she had no patience with inefficiency, Amy exploded. The secretary apologized and said she would make another appointment, but Amy barely heard her and stomped out of the office. "I don't know what I said to her," she reported to Ada. "But I certainly gave her a piece of my mind! I would have rested today if it hadn't been for that appointment!" "Peter" sympathized with her, but she remarked, "I hope you didn't insult the secretary too much; everybody gets dates mixed sometimes." When they returned to Brookline, they found out what Amy had said, among other things. A letter from Mr. Sonneck apologized for the mixup in dates and expressed the hope they could fix another one. Then he wrote, "Madam, I do not know if it is customary in Brookline, whatever the provocation, to call a secretary a 'goose'; in New York, it is not."

"Now I remember, I called that girl a silly goose," Amy admitted. Ada shook her head. "Oh, Amy, Amy!" "Well, she was," Amy said. The article did eventually appear in the June 1920 issue of *The Musical Quarterly*. (Recently, it figured in an article on Amy Lowell as musical apprentice to Carl Engel in the October 1972 issue of the *Quarterly*. A copy of Sonneck's letter, preserved in the magazine's files, came to light in 1973.)

After a number of delays, the operation to "pick up the dropped stitch" was finally performed. As the doctor had predicted, it was a much more difficult and serious operation than the first one, and it cost Amy a number of restless, semi-sleepless nights; pain killers were never very effective for her. The doctor said the surgery was successful, however, so she bore the discomfort as well as she could. But of course she was unable to do anything. Then, just as she was emerging from the worst of it, word of tragedy came from Washington: Little Allen, the baby Lorna had been expecting at the time of Amy's first operation, had died suddenly of the croup; Lorna was prostrated. Ada, who, as before, had been Amy's mainstay, and, with the secretaries, had taken over her correspondence, had to rush to Washington, leaving Amy almost as shocked and shaken as she. And again her recovery from a difficult operation was seriously delayed.

The mail brought news of the outside world and comforted her in various ways. Among the correspondence was a letter from Lawrence in Capri, where he and Frieda had finally found refuge: "My dear Amy, Today I have your letter, and cheque for thirteen hundred Lire. How very nice of you to think of us this New Year. But I wish I needn't take the money: it irks me a bit. Why can't I earn enough, I've done the work. After all, you know, it makes one angry to have to accept a sort of charity. Not from you, really, because you are an artist, and that is always a sort of partnership. But when Cannan writes and tells me he has collected a few dollars—which, of course, I have not received—he wrote to tell me he was collecting a few, but never wrote again. Cannan annoys me with his sort of penny-a-time attempt at benevolence, and the ridiculous things he says about me—and everybody else—in the American press. I am a sort of charity-boy of literature, apparently. One is denied one's just rights, and then insulted with charity. Pfui! to them all. — But I feel you and I have a sort of odd congenital understanding, so that it hardly irks me to take these liras from you, only a little it ties me up. However, you must keep one's trust in a few people, and rest in the Lord.

"I am extremely sorry you are not well, and must have an operation. Such a thought is most shattering. Hope to Heaven it won't hurt much and will make you right. — Blackwell is a good publisher for getting at the young life in England. He's much more in touch with the future than old Macmillan.

"Secker has done another edition of my *New Poems,* properly bound now. I shall have him send you a copy. I asked Beaumont to send you a copy of a tiny book of mine, 'Bay,' which he has hand-printed. He is not very responsible. Tell me if you have received it.

"No, don't go to England now, it is so depressing and uneasy and unpleasant in its temper. Even Italy isn't what it was, a cheerful, insouciant land. The insouciance has gone. But still, I like the Italians deeply; and the sun shines, the rocks glimmer, the sea is unfolded like fresh petals. I am better here than in England. — Things are expensive, and not too abundant. But one lives for the same amount, about, as in England: and freer to move in the air and over the water one is, all the while. Southwards the old coast glimmers its rocks, far beyond the Siren Isles. It is very Greek—Ulysses' ship left the last track in the waves. Impossible for Dreadnoughts to tread this unchangeable morning-delicate sea.

"Frieda came down to Florence from Germany: a bit thinner and wiser for her visit. Things are wretchedly bad there. I must have food sent all the time to F.'s mother from England, and for the children—there absolutely isn't enough to eat.

"We have got two beautiful rooms here on the top of this old palace, in the very centre of Capri, with the sea on both hands. Compton Mackenzie is here—a man one can trust and like, which, as far as the first goes—is more than one can say of Cannan. — But Capri is a bit small, to live on. Perhaps I shall go to the mainland—perhaps not. Anyway this address will always find me. I have just begun a new novel.

"I feel we shall see you in Italy. I do hope you will be better. Is Mrs. Russell with you always? A thousand greetings from both."

A few days later, a short note came from Lawrence, this time from Taormina; Mussolini was on the march with his Fascist forces; there had been some trouble about the check, so Lawrence asked her to stop it and send another in dollars. "Italy feels shaky—Europe altogether feels most insecure. There'll be another collapse soon. . . ." Still, he hoped she and Ada would come to Italy if she was well enough. "I do wish you felt well and strong. . . . Send me a line to say how you are."

Lawrence's letters always provided a diversion and stimulant, but this one, with his felicitous phrase about the "congenital understanding" between them, as well as the "partnership" they had in being artists, brought her a feeling of warmth and pride, the kind of comfort she needed at the moment. Lawrence was not an idle flatterer; he had no hesitation in telling her when he felt her work was inferior to her ability as an artist. And because she realized that he was a great artist (recognized or not), she appreciated his comments all the more.

The announcement in the mail that the famous library of H. Buxton Forman contained a rare first edition of Keats's *Lamia* proved to be a diversion—but, indirectly—a disastrous setback to her health. Amy's collection of rare books and manuscripts was considerable and was growing all the time. Just before her operation Mr. Newton had sent her the proof sheets of Whitman's *Passage to India* as a recompense for her unhappy experience at the Contemporary Club. She was delighted, since she already owned the original manuscript of *Passage*. The day after that unfortunate lecture, she was also given a dinner by Dr. A. S. Rosenbach, the distinguished curator of books at the Philadelphia Museum. (It was one of the most "exotic affairs" she ever attended; after dinner, they wandered through the galleries; and as they went over the treasures in the book division, Amy gave a running commentary the curator found fascinating.) He was a rare-book collector himself, and now Amy, reading that the copy of Keats's *Lamia* to be sold at auction on March 15, was not only a first edition, but was Keats's presentation copy to his beloved Fanny Brawne, inscribed "F. B. from J. K.," felt that she must have it for her collection. She decided to engage Dr. Rosenbach to bid for her. (That way she would prevent *him* from acquiring it.) After an exchange of several letters, she sent him a telegram on March 15: "Get it and good luck!" That evening, he telephoned from New York; the coveted copy was hers—for $4,050, the highest price paid for any single book on the opening day. Amy was so elated she forgot about her misery from the hernia.

But it was still another week after the operation before she was able to go downstairs for dinner. Ada arrived home the same day, and Foster Damon, who had been in the habit of coming for dinner each time he finished a chapter of the book on Blake, reading the manuscript aloud afterward, was there also. (He had paid

Amy a visit and had sent her flowers, but had not been at Sevenels for dinner in two months or more.) Amy was still excited over the acquisition of the Keats book, and as soon as the meal was over, she opened the safe behind the sliding panel in her library to make sure her collection was intact. As the door swung back, the three saw a "ghastly sight": The whole inside was "leprous" with mildew; every item was soaking wet! Amy gasped, "O my God!" and, without thinking, lifted a heavy pail of water someone had left inside. Only half-aware of the strain on her stomach muscles, she set it down immediately and began removing the manuscripts; the pail of lime that was always put beside them to absorb any moisture in the airtight safe had been useless in preventing the evaporating water from being absorbed by every scrap of paper.

Her mouth in a grim line, Amy ordered the furnace drafts opened wide, and all the fires in the fireplace lit. Then the three of them—Ada and young Damon following her instructions—went to work drying things out. Over the registers and in front of the fireplaces all the "great dead"—in Damon's words—were spread out: Blake and Mme Pompadour and Jane Austen and Ben Johnson and Charlotte Brontë and Voltaire and Beethoven and all the rest. Amy herself took charge of her prized *Eve of St. Agnes* manuscript, of such thin tissue that every time she passed it, it fluttered off the back of a chair and sailed toward the searing fire.

They worked like Trojans, but Foster had to leave just after midnight to catch the last car to Boston. Ada pleaded with Amy to go to bed then, but she would not. "You go, Peter dear," she said. "I know you're worn out from your trip and all that happened; but I can't leave until these things are all dried. They're my greatest treasures!" And she worked on till dawn. When Ada rose in the morning and went to Amy's room, she found her not only pale and haggard but alarmed about her wound: A muscle had slipped; when it returned to place, a strange lump persisted in protruding. "I guess we'd better call Dr. Eastman," she said. He told her not to lift anything and to await developments.

She had to go back to bed. And before long, she was facing another operation—the outcome of which would be extremely doubtful, the doctors warned her. She had saved her collection, but at what cost! A consolation arrived: Mr. Newton sent her a lock of Fanny Brawne's hair which he had bought at the Forman sale. Amy was so ardent a collector that she was utterly delighted, especially since her study of Keats was to be devoted in large measure to exonerating Fanny Brawne of guilt for Keats's early death. She did not seem to give a thought to the probability that, because of this traumatic experience, she never again was to be wholly free of hernia complications.

Moreover, she was generally run down from the recent operation. She promised to stay quiet and not to make any more engagements until June 1, when she was to deliver the Phi Beta Kappa poem at Columbia. She planned to recite one of the "Legends"—this one about Indians in North America—on which she had been working. She wrote to Elsie Sergeant, who was in Santa Fe on a government mission connected with Indian reservations in New Mexico. Amy was extremely interested in the Pueblos, and she said she "would give anything" to see a Hopi snake dance or a corn dance. She asked Elsie to send her local-color notes, capturing the atmosphere as Elsie had managed to do in her description of France after the war. But mostly Amy had to rely on books: She read sixty-three volumes—all that could be found on Indian poetry and ceremonials. And for these it was Ada again upon whom she relied. Ada haunted the libraries, hunting up reference books and other material on Indian lore. The friends who figured in "Two Speak Together" drew closer and "spoke together" more than ever from this point on, working as a unit, one complementing the other.

CHAPTER XVII

Active Invalid

AMY WAS NOW A VICTIM of obesity, high blood pressure, hernia, retina deterioration, sporadic gastritis, and heart trouble. But, as she liked to boast when she was ambulatory, nothing affected her "brains," her tremendous energy, her vitality, or her lung power. And even while in bed during her convalescences, she read, took notes, wrote when possible, dictated letters, and got her friends out of their own beds in the middle of the night for lengthy telephone calls.

During this waiting period—no one knew what the lump was going to do—she not only prepared her Phi Beta Kappa poem but took on the job of organizing the American branch of the committee to raise funds for buying (and restoring) Wentworth Place, the house in Hampstead where Keats wrote the "Ode to a Nightingale." She had never done any fund-raising, but she could not resist an appeal from the mayor of Hampstead for a purpose that was so closely allied to her own lifetime project. She initiated the Boston branch (no doubt in another bedroom conference) and invited prominent people to establish branches in New York, Philadelphia, Providence, and Chicago.

She also sponsored a reading of Siegfried Sassoon's poetry—since he was, in her words, "the first important voice to protest against the sentimental glorification of war." (As patriotic as she had been, she was fully aware of the horrors of war and of the falseness of glorifying it, as her poem, "In the Stadium," one of those in the last section of *Pictures,* clearly shows. She portrayed Marshal Joffre reviewing the Harvard regiment as "a little old man/ Huddled up in a corner of a carriage,/ Rapidly driven in front of throngs of people . . ."; and she gave a terse summation: "This is war:/ Boys flung into a breach/ Like shovelled earth;/ And old men,/ Broken,/ Driving rapidly before crowds of people/ In a glitter of silly decorations.") Amy paid a third of Sassoon's fee herself and gave a dinner for him at Sevenels before the reading on April 29; and the whole party drove to the Harvard Union, arriving in good time. That was her first outing after the operation, and it was successful and exhilarating.

Her correspondence included a letter of advice and terms to George Antheil, the young, far-out composer of his time. Her advice was valid: "Do not think that to be different and queer is necessarily to show originality. Do not be afraid of the old any more than you are of the new. Be yourself." (Lawrence's advice to her!) "The bizarre may be enormously original, or it may be simply the weakness of a personality not strong enough to find its own idiom. . . ." Then she got down to business: She usually charged ten dollars apiece for settings of her poems, but as she thought fifty dollars might be a "staggerer" for him, she suggested they wait until she had heard the settings. "I shall not hold you up on money if I like your songs. It is no use setting these things of mine in old-fashioned modes, and I shall be glad to see somebody with your point of view and energy have a try at them."

In May, after a thorough medical examination, the verdict was that the mysterious swelling, which had not disappeared, was caused by a stretched fascia, the band of tissue holding the muscles together. It was inoperable; there was no cure for it, but she must always be very careful to avoid any strain that might increase the sagging of the tissue. For the time being, Amy accepted the findings and the fact that this was just another thing she would have to live with, so she resumed her schedule of public appearances.

She and Ada left for New York on May 31, and on June 1, Phi Beta Kappa gave a dinner for Amy, after which she read her newly completed "Many Swans" as the poem of the occasion. She was elected a member of the fraternity's Delta chapter and was thereby entitled to wear the key, an honor which both tickled her sense of irony and pleased her: For Amy Lowell, who never could sit still long enough to learn her lessons and had not completed even a formal high school education, to become an honorary member of an honor society because of her poetry was both a joke and an accomplishment. She felt the same way about the next event: From New York they went on to Waco, Texas, where Amy was to receive a doctor of letters degree from Baylor University at a Jubilee commencement celebrating its diamond anniversary. Fifty-six honorary doctorates were to be conferred, five of them on poets—besides Amy, Edwin Markham, Vachel Lindsay, Judd Mortimer Lewis, and Harriet Monroe.

There were two days of various programs and events, including a luncheon for the poets, at which the other honored guests read, but Amy was asked to give a special lecture at three o'clock on "Vers Libre and Imagism," illustrated with selections from her poems. When she received the degree (shining in silk gown and velvet hood and beads of perspiration, since it was 106 degrees in the shade!), the president's citation read in part: "By virtue of your versatility as a poet evidenced on our platform here, evidenced and reechoed by your fellow scholars, we have pleasure in conferring upon you, the honorary degree of Doctor of Literature, and admitting you to all the rights and privileges. . . ." She was on her feet much too long, marching in the procession on campus at 9:00 A.M.—the middle of the night for Amy—and kept up all day long, "movie-pictured and kodaked," as she said, and generally feted. One interesting note is that, in the official record of the occasion, published in 1921, Amy's official photo was on page 47, an outline of her lecture on page 48, while page 49 "was filled with 'Madonna of the Evening Flowers.' " Amy had purposely included the poem in her selections, no doubt thinking that it would probably be selected for quotation. She was always looking for some way to have Ada share in her achievements, though Ada always said the pleasure of seeing Amy recognized, and happy over it, was recognition enough for her.

When they got home, Amy was inspired with a "poetry-burst" and began writing poems and answering letters at a lightning-fast rate. Full of his old spirit, Lawrence had sent a long letter from Taormina containing fine descriptions of the surrounding landscape. He was writing again, too. He closed by saying, "Well, I hope your health is good, that's the chief thing. Your garden will be gorgeous now. . . ."

But her health was not good. She was busy with a dozen things, and various guests came and went. But she could feel the fascia was stretching more and more. Though the garden was tempting, she did not care to be active physically. She could walk along the paths on Ada's arm for only a few minutes. The Carl Engels were taking a house in Peterborough, New Hampshire for a month and invited her and Ada to visit them, but she could not even think of it. She wrote to "Dearest Bibi," giving him the names of some friends there, but she knew she dared not take any more trips for a time. At last she consulted another doctor, and his report was "anything but reassuring." "Apparently the whole thing is to happen over again," Amy wrote to another friend, "and it looks as if another operation would be imperative. I myself feel that no operation will be successful, but I am to see a specialist in New York shortly and get his pronouncement on it." She wrote much the same thing to her brother Lawrence, who had gone to England to receive degrees from Oxford and Cambridge. After explaining the seriousness of the coming operation, she said, "I do think I have had enough illness in my life, and it is hard to keep up a career and do all you want to do under these difficulties. Of course we manage somehow; meanwhile I try not to think about it any more than I can help." She also told him of difficulties she was having with her publisher and added, "I hope you get home early enough to advise me what to do. You know I have always owned my own books, and now I am selling so many that Mr. Brett [of Macmillan] has decided he wants to own them in the future." Amy had a fairly good idea of what she would do, but she wanted her brother's opinion. This letter also contains one of her few references to politics, and shows her individual assessment of issues in the upcoming presidential election, her solid Republican background notwithstanding: "The nomination of Roosevelt for Vice-President has greatly helped the Democratic Party, helped it over the edge, I am afraid. People seem to consider Cox and Harding, and stand off in horror; but there is no doubt that Roosevelt is more universally popular than Coolidge. The mere nomination of Harding, a machine politician, has discouraged a good many people with the Republican Party, and *the fact that Harding is against the League is doing a great deal of harm.** Bessie has thrown herself heart and soul into Harding's election, and has even gone so far as to say she thinks him not a bad choice. I do not think that so; in fact, I am very blue as to the result. . . ." (Since Harding's dark record has been revived in connection with Watergate, this is doubly interesting, except that the latter makes the Teapot Dome scandal of the Harding administration look like a relatively mild political brew.)

Operation or no, Amy was determined to keep two speaking engagements at the Summer School of the University of Chicago. Both were given at Leon Mandel Hall, which had a capacity of 1,200, but were so well attended that people were standing in the aisles on each occasion. The first was a reading; one of the poems presented to this audience was the newly completed "Lilacs," and it was an instant success in this debut. She was to read "Lilacs" many times in the next few years, until it became almost a trademark of an Amy Lowell reading. In fact, if she didn't include that poem on the program, someone in the audience would ask for it as an encore, and after a while she said she was tired of always getting requests for it. However, if it *wasn't* requested, she was equally irked and disappointed. She once said to Nell Belmont (who was at Sevenels for the weekend) and "Peter," as they were all driving home after a highly successful reading at Harvard, "But nobody asked for '*Lilacs*'!"

Though it was not published in a volume until after her death in the Pulitzer Prize-winning *What's O'Clock* (1925), the poem first appeared in the September 1919 issue of the *New York Post* "Literary Review," and it is still included in anthologies. It is by no means a sentimental poem (as one might expect from the title and the first six or eight lines). It is a solid yet heartwarming poem, containing a philosophical truth in the relation between people

* Italics mine.

and their native lands, succinctly tracing the history of Eastern and Western civilizations while apparently epitomizing New England. In other words, it is universal, and one of Amy Lowell's happiest creations.

You are the great flood of our souls
Bursting above the leaf-shapes of our hearts,
You are the smell of all Summers,
The love of wives and children,
The recollection of the gardens of little children,
You are State Houses and Charters
And the familiar treading of the foot to and fro on a road it knows.

They stayed over a day or two after the lecture and, on one evening, had dinner with the Sandburgs at Elmhurst, a Chicago suburb. The visit was so enjoyable that after she and Ada returned home, Amy wrote a poem, "To Carl Sandburg," and sent it right off to him. Crossing it in the mail, on the way to her, was a poem Sandburg had written about the evening, with a typical Sandburgian title: "Three Notations on the Visit of a Massachusetts Woman to the House of Neighbors in Illinois (For Amy Lowell)."

About the middle of September her appointment with the New York specialist came due, so the second week saw Amy and Ada in their suite at the Belmont with plans for accomplishing several things before the examination. Most important was the confrontation with George Brett of Macmillan. He was even more obstinate and unbending about the new contract terms than Amy had implied in her letter to Lawrence. To her the situation was intolerable, and she canceled all her contracts with the firm then and there. She telephoned Ferris Greenslet at once and informed him she was returning to Houghton Mifflin. He was delighted. The next day she and Ada were at the New York docks to meet H. D. and Winifred Bryher, who were now living together. They were stopping briefly in New York on their way to California to visit H. D.'s parents. Amy gave a small dinner party for them in her rooms, offered them advice on travel in America, and read some of her poems. Bryher, who was short and slight, with dark hair in a dutch cut in bangs across her forehead and keen blue eyes that took in everything, was anything but shy. In fact, she was a tyrant in her own way, as H. D. was to discover; but that night, her first meeting with Amy, she sat and watched her perform in amazed silence. When the waiter began serving the vegetables in small, individual sauce bowls, Amy fixed him with a baleful eye and demanded: "Haven't I told you never to serve me with those little bird baths?"

He did seem awkward and nervous, and, in apology afterward, explained that he was preoccupied with worry over his wife, who had suddenly been taken to the hospital. Amy, trying to submerge her own anxiety about another hospital bout, was filled with remorse, and, Ada told Jean Untermeyer later, tipped the waiter so generously he was "overwhelmed." (The Untermeyers were the only other guests.) After they saw their friends off at the train, Amy and Ada went to the specialist's office. As she feared, he prescribed a third operation as soon as possible. He could not guarantee complete success, but he assured her that nine cases out of ten had been arrested if not cured, so she agreed to undergo surgery again, at the end of October.

Back in Brookline, she wrote to Bryher on September 23: "I do not fear the operation at all, but I do terribly fear and dread the long weeks flat on my back, when I am not myself, but a hysterical maniac, feeling that the ceiling is pressing itself down on my throat and I cannot breathe, and all the real world and its interests seem dissolved in a nightmare of pain and discomfort. . . . There is a certain awful breathlessness about these weeks preceding an operation which makes it difficult to settle down comfortably and work."

Being Amy, she did some work, of course, laboring mostly over the Chinese translations. One of the visitors earlier in the summer had been Florence Ayscough, who spent three days at Sevenels, and during her visit they translated eighteen poems. Florence, now in her forties, was herself an imposing woman by this time, and was as exhausted as Amy, if not more so. In addition, Amy wrote an article on Louis Untermeyer entitled "Critic, Parodist, and Poet," in which she reviewed *The New Adam,* published in the *New York Times* of October 10. On October 19, she gave a reading at Harvard to a "cram-jam" audience, a "delightful experience," as she never expected to be so honored in her own community; it was an experience enhanced by the fact that Cox had chosen that night to speak at the Harvard Union, so the boys in the Poetry Club had expected only a scattering of people.

It buoyed her up for the operation, which took place on October 29. Five doctors and three nurses took part. The incision was enormous; layers of excess fat had to be lifted before the surgeon could get at the muscles. And the operation was a long one. The following three weeks were sheer hell—"the most dubious three weeks she ever passed." One unexpected complication in her care was that large amounts of alcohol were needed to bathe the wound. Prohibition had been in effect nearly a year, and the legal substitutes irritated Amy's skin, so she, who never drank hard liquor, had to employ a bootlegger. (Amy had no use for Prohibition, anyway. She felt that congressmen had let themselves be talked into a foolish law by a lot of fanatics. She gasped in astonishment at the orders of Secretary of the Navy Daniels, dubbed "Grapejuice Josephus," that the U.S. fleets be sent out without the proper stimulants.) For a while her condition was touch-and-go, but by the end of November she was able to go down one flight of stairs to Ada's room, and by the middle of December she could get downstairs for dinner. But the hour kept getting later and later: The elaborate bandages she had to wear * now took three-quarters of an hour to be wound around her "middles," and, if they didn't seem to fit just right, the whole thing had to be done again. And then the wound began to develop abscesses which had to be lanced; it was enough to try the patience of Job, and Amy could not have borne it without Ada's constant support and companionship. As before, she took over the correspondence, read to Amy, and sometimes simply held her hand.

On December 22, after the doctor had said the operation was a success in spite of the side effects, Amy felt strong enough to go into Boston to the Houghton Mifflin office to see about her new

* In this connection, four letters at the Houghton Library from Theodore Amussen, Lorna's husband, deal with the question of some special bandages Amy wanted to order from Germany. He informed her that the "Elastiche Idealsbinden" were unavailable, but he would get others.

book, *Legends,* for which she had signed a contract just before the operation. She had been working on the format as well as on the manuscript. But the excursion left her spent, and she could not go to her sister Katherine's for the annual Lowell family gathering. Nor was she able to hold the concert she had planned: Eva Gauthier, a Canadian soprano noted for her authentic interpretations of contemporary composers—Schönberg, Ravel, Poulenc, Satie, Honegger—had been engaged to give a song recital at Sevenels, including the three poems to Ada that Carl Engel had set to music. Amy had to let "Bibi" know that, as much as she had been looking forward to hearing "their" songs, she simply was not up to holding a big affair. She and Ada spent the holiday quietly, entertaining only the Loweses for Christmas dinner.

As she began to improve by the end of January, Amy began to accept invitations at intervals. One which she could not resist was an immensely rewarding request to deliver the Keats Centenary Address at Yale on February 23, and she began work on it at once, even though she was suffering from her customary postoperative cold. Ten days before the Yale engagement they went to New York so she could study the Keats material in the Morgan Library, and, incidentally, give her Whitman lecture at the Brooklyn Institute.* Bryher was also in New York, married on Saint Valentine's Day to Robert Menzies McAlmon, whose poems she had read in *Poetry,* and whom she had just met at a party in Greenwich Village, given by some friends of H. D. Amy had "the blushing pair" up to the Belmont suite for dinner, and, "with a quaking heart," she gave them her blessing. Later the news was featured as an international romance between a millionaire's daughter and a penniless poet, but one cannot help wondering if Amy realized it was anything but a romance—rather, a marriage of convenience, on Bryher's part at least, so McAlmon could serve as a father figure for H. D.'s child. (According to McAlmon's diary, even he was not aware of the true situation until after they had been married some months. He stood her tyranny as long as he could and finally sued for divorce; with the settlement he received, he began the small

* Subsequent to the harrowing experience of the first time, Amy had no more hecklers on the Whitman lecture.

publishing firm which led to his bringing out Gertrude Stein's *The Making of Americans.* In the Lowell correspondence at Harvard are seventy-five letters from Bryher, and while there are hints of discord, most of them deal with professional matters. If Amy did know something, it was the result of her intuition. H. D. and Bryher stayed together for years, H. D. evidently putting up with her domineering ways because of the child.) *

The Yale lecture on Keats, for which Amy drew on her own collection of unpublished Keats material, was an enormous success. She wrote to Foster Damon: "I had something very closely approaching an ovation . . . they had to put a sign on the door announcing that no more could be allowed in. Mrs. Russell says the applause afterwards was very long and enthusiastic. . . ." And to Ferris Greenslet she wrote: "It would have amused you if you could have seen the boys at Yale running up to the platform with books for me to sign." She lost count somewhere between thirty and fifty. She was surprised at how many copies of *Dome,* her first book, were brought up, until she remembered that "it sells for 25 cents less than the others" and wondered if they hadn't set the price too high at two dollars. She finished: "However, that shows you what stimulation of interest my going to a place will do." (No wonder T. S. Eliot called her a "demon saleswoman.")

Ada insisted that she go right home and rest in bed until the next engagement or she wouldn't be able to make any more appearances. The hernia wound was bothering her, so that she went to bed as soon as they got home. While resting she kept busy: The manuscript of *Legends* was ready for the press, and since she could not go to the Riverside Press of Houghton Mifflin, she "summoned the Press to her bedside," and still another conference took place in her third-floor haven, which in these years was becoming less of a retreat than a reception room. Ada, who, more than anyone, knew what she was going through, and how important these professional matters were to Amy's need for fulfillment, served both as her guardian angel and as her emissary. When Harvard

* The only person who seems to have realized that Bryher was no shy violet was Thornton Wilder, who said, after one meeting with her, "Bryher is Napoleonic; she walks like him, she talks like him, she probably feels like him."

asked for permission to exhibit her Keats collection, Amy sent Ada to Cambridge with it, to make sure the items were properly displayed. They read the proofs of *Legends* together, Ada doing a double check to make sure all corrections had been noted. Yale wanted to publish the Keats lecture, which made Amy all the more determined to write the full-length biography of the poet she had always idolized, and it would be Ada who did at least half of the research, checking the data when she finally began it. They went to New York again in April, Amy to give a couple of readings, consult the Keats material in the Morgan Library, and, much as she hated to, see the hernia specialist. He confirmed her fear that a stitch was sagging, but he told her that all would be secure if the condition was corrected at once. Since there was no rational alternative, she agreed to have her fourth operation in two years.

The publication of *Legends* had been delayed by another strike, and the Keats biography would also be delayed to some extent owing to the latest operation, so Houghton Mifflin decided to bring out the translations of Chinese poems late in the fall. Luckily, Florence Ayscough arrived about the first of May with the last sixty-seven poems to be translated, and they both worked with a kind of frenzy to finish them before the operation—and finish they did, just twenty-four hours before it took place. Amy was very tired and nervous—but the thing was done! She and Ada had been invited to her brother's for dinner the night before the operation; and, perhaps to divert her, he got out a family volume of *A Fable for Critics* by their great-cousin, James Russell Lowell, and began to read aloud the clever rhymes and puns James had used to characterize the prominent writers of his day. She and Ada discussed it when they got home, and, since Amy could not sleep much, she kept her mind off the coming operation by trying to portray Frost and Robinson in the same way.

The operation proved to require only the sealing of a small hole. The rest of the incision was holding; if she would only be careful, the doctor said, she would be well. But that was a big if. For *Legends* was published three days after the operation, and as soon as Amy was allowed to sit up, nearly three weeks later, she began thinking about the production of *Fir-Flower Tablets,* the title she and Florence Ayscough had chosen for the Chinese poems. June brought a heat wave, causing her more discomfort, and Amy, who usually enjoyed hot weather, now suffered from it. Abscesses "caused by non-absorption of the kangaroo sinews used in the stitches" began to appear, and they became unbearably painful before they were lanced. Yet, in spite of this, she arranged the "dummy" for the new book and dictated letters trying to sell the poems yet unprinted to various magazines. Toward the end of June, the garden was so beguiling that, with the help of Ada and Elizabeth Henry, she went out twice and afterward felt so revived that—as often as she had repeated them when she was a child—the lines "What is so rare as a day in June?/ Then if ever come perfect days . . ." from her cousin's poem, *The Vision of Sir Launfal,* must have taken on new meaning for her.

She kept thinking about his *Fable for Critics,* and of her own effort to satirize Frost and Robinson in the style of James Russell Lowell. It would be fun to try it with the others she had included in *Tendencies,* and all the other leading poets of the day, including herself; the project would help to pass the painful, tedious hours of convalescence, without the strain of research. Furthermore, if it was good enough, she might publish it anonymously—it would be a hoax of her own to rival *Spectra!* The mere idea of it amused her no end. The only person whom she told about her scheme besides "Peter" was Ferris Greenslet: "Not a word about my modern fable to *anybody,*" she warned him. "It may never be good enough to see the light of day, and if it is, the whole fun will be springing it on the unsuspecting public, so don't you dare whisper it. It amuses me, anyway." (This was Amy Lowell's occupational therapy—an intellectual exercise that was both entertaining and relaxing, and one that furthered her career at the same time!)

Comfort came from many friends, but the gesture that touched her heart most came from D. H. Lawrence. When he heard about her latest operation, he wrote to Ada Russell, suggesting that his next share of the Imagist royalties, now dwindling rapidly, be spent on a "fuchsia tree" for Amy. She dictated a reply to his letter herself when she "at last got far enough to answer him with her own voice if not her own hand." As touched as she was at his "sweetness in wanting to buy her a pot of fuchsias" with the pittance of royalties now coming from the anthologies, she wouldn't feel justified in not sending the check. But, she said, "The bond between us is intensified by your picking fuchsias, as they are one of my favorite flowers." And she recalled those that hung over the door in Devonshire when she was there with Miss Dabney, recovering from her nervous breakdown many years before. It was a long letter, commenting on his novel *Women in Love* at greater length than before; reporting the progress she had made in placing some of his poems; and, in a postscript, telling him she was sending him a copy of her new volume, *Legends*. "I hardly know whether you will like it or not," she added.

His answer gave her one of the great satisfactions of her literary life. First he told her, "I had your letter and the eight dollars yesterday. I had much rather you had had the fuchsia tree. There are lovely ones here." (He and Frieda were then in Austria.) After thanking her for looking after his poems, and saying that he hoped the operation was successful and *final*, "& that you can live your own life freely," he wrote: "I read *Legends* last night—and again this morning. I like them the best of all your poems. You have always written of the existence & magic of *things*—porcelain and rain: and of *things* you catch an essence: even cannon and ships. But in this book it is life and death superseding things. So I like this book the best.

"I like best *Many Swans* which I have read twice and which I feel really speaks inside my unexplained soul. I should not like to try to explain it, because of the deep fear and danger that is in it. But it isn't a myth of the sun. It is something else. All the better that we can't say offhand what. That means it is true. It rings a note in my soul. Then I like Blackbird, & Witch Woman. But I doubt if you quite get her—the Witch Woman. . . . I must read Yucca and Passion Vine again. I don't quite get it. But it is the most *interesting*, after Swans. . . . I hope you'll have as much pleasure as you wish out of the public reception of this book. . . ."

The last-mentioned reference was to the Inca legend of the rape of the moon by a fox—or the attempted rape, for the love-starved fox is hurled to his death, the only trace of her "defilement beneath the passion vine" being his paw marks—as the explanation of the spots on the moon. (It is strange that Amy, whose adored brother was an astronomer, should have been so preoccupied with moon worship, the moon as a love object, all her life. Was it the lure of the unattainable that appealed to her? On the psychological level the poem is fraught with Freudian symbolism. In planning the ballet that was to be made from the poem, she wrote to the dancer she had in mind that the fox was to be part animal, part human, as the faun in Debussy's *L'Après-midi d'un faune.* (One is also reminded of Gauguin's painting, *The Fox,* with a paw resting possessively on a woman's breast.) She wrote the dancer that the fox should be "unctuous, lascivious, cunning, and exceedingly wheedling and attractive. . . . There seems to me to be the scope here for your remarkable, imaginative symbolism." The weighty title, *Memorandum Confided by a Yucca to a Passion Vine,* was symbolic in itself, and Amy made good use of the golden temple of the sun as well as of the silver temple of the moon.

The legend of "Many Swans," which spoke so deeply to Lawrence, concerned the Indians of North America, including the Alaskan, the Plains, and the Pueblo tribes, and was a "double allegory," as he had divined. It dealt with the destruction of the Indian races by "the all-imposing power of the white man," as Amy explained. She was criticized for one line, "And a poison leaf from Gethsemane," but she introduced it "with malice aforethought," as she said, to symbolize both "the extinction of the Indian before the march of the white man, and the crowding out of the Indian religions through the unwise and non-understanding attitude of some of the Christian missionaries . . . to show that all religion was the same in essence, and that in suppressing the natural expression peculiar to the Indians, the white man has reduced the Indian nation mentally to ashes. . . ." In the light of recent rebellion at Wounded Knee, South Dakota, her thesis makes "Many Swans" the most timely of the *Legends.*

It is also highly possible that this poem, and "The Witch Woman," an old tale of the Yucatán, served as the genesis (in his "unexplained soul") of Lawrence's novel, *The Plumed Serpent,* the chief product of his sojourn in America. The story deals with the aborted revolution of Mexican Indians who wished to follow the religion of Quetzalcoatl, the ancient Aztec god, combining elements of Christian, Aztec-Indian, and Freudian philosophy. In fact, the sections of Lawrence's novel, *Written Hymns of Quetzalcoatl,* and other verse stanzas of the book show the immediate influence of "Many Swans" and some of the Indian songs in Amy's later, posthumously published, *Ballads for Sale.* Rereading Lawrence's *The Plumed Serpent* after reading Lowell's "Many Swans" leaves one with little doubt that her work spoke as deeply to him as his letter indicates.

Now, in her reply to his extraordinary reaction to *Legends,* she wrote: "I wonder if you have the slightest idea how much pleasure your letter about 'Legends' has given me. I know what you mean by my insistence on *things.* My things are always, to my mind, more than themselves,* but I do believe I have laid too much insistence upon them, and obscured the more important issues beneath them for my readers. I am trying not to do this now except in poems that are apparently only things, and that you see what you do in 'Many Swans' makes me very happy, because it was exactly what I tried to put into that poem. Sometimes I wonder whether I shall live long enough, and grow enough, to be able to put into my poetry what I want to have there. I don't know, one can only live and try to go on growing. The technique of poetry is easy, very easy to anyone born that way; life is not easy, and it is still less simple to express in words the real throb, and misery, and gusto which it has. That is what you do, and that is what I wish I could learn of you."

A more self-revelatory analysis or one with more humility toward her work could scarcely be expressed. It was this side of her volatile employer that Mary Sands Thompson discovered when she was one of Amy's secretaries, and a memorable instance occurred in connection with this book. The girls had typed a poem about the hanging of a poor boy whose only crime had been to

* This was the facet of Amy Lowell's work that nobody seemed to grasp until 1957, in the aforementioned book, *A Shard of Silence,* G. R. Ruihey, Ed. (New York: Twayne Publishers, Inc., 1957).

steal a sheep for his starving mother. After they had typed the final copy, Mary was sure she had once read the poem among Tennyson's works. The other girl said she must be mistaken—"You know Miss Lowell can't stand Tennyson!"—but Mary looked it up and found the poem, "word for word." With some trepidation she carried the complete Tennyson volume up to the third-floor bedroom and brought the duplication to Amy's attention. To her surprise, "Miss Lowell" did not take offense at the implication that she might have copied Tennyson, the anathema of the modernists. She merely read the poem intently and then thanked Mary, almost gratefully, for pointing it out to her. She had probably set the manuscript aside for several years, and had taken it out again when she needed more material to flesh out the volume of *Legends.* Her version of the incident was that she had found the kernel for the story of "Dried Marjoram" in an old book about Hampshire, as a recorded fact. "Somebody told me it was the same subject as Tennyson's 'Rizpah,' which I had never read. It was very funny to read it afterwards and see how two generations treat the same idea."

It is possible that Amy was telling the truth as far as the fact-finding was concerned, but that when she began to write the tale the first time, the Tennyson poem came back to her subconsciously from the days when the pupils in Miss Cabott's school had to learn Tennyson's poetry by rote, and, working in the middle of the night, she simply set down the lines as they came to her. When Mary pointed out the similarity, she changed the treatment but not the style: This was one of the few poems in metered rhyme in the book. And she herself put the incident in writing before anyone could accuse her of copying Tennyson's idea, especially since she had decried the fact that his influence was a major cause of static poetry in the last decades of the nineteenth century.

She was still mortally afraid of her "enemies," almost to the point of paranoia, which seems not without some justification from the attacks she had suffered. They had subsided to a great extent, but nothing Ada said could convince her that "they" were not waiting to pounce on her at the slightest provocation. Two thousand copies of *Legends* sold within three weeks, and she was able to report to Lawrence that reviews had been universally favorable, although she didn't think anyone understood the book as well as he.

If only she had been willing to let her reputation rest there a while, and had perhaps worked quietly on her biography of Keats and on occasional poems that forever kept forming in her mind, she might have saved herself much mental and physical grief. But she could not rest; she had to best her "enemies." While she was recovering from her fourth operation, she had written *A Critical Fable* in a month's time for "relaxation," which it proved to be. But when she heard that Witter Bynner was working on a book of translations from the Chinese, she insisted on completing the book she and Florence Ayscough had been compiling. The poems were all but done, but the preface and introduction, and an elaborate appendix of notes and cross-references of words had to be constructed. Florence came to Sevenels again later in the summer of 1921, and they worked assiduously. Jessie Rittenhouse, secretary of the Poetry Society, was in Boston for a few days, and called Amy, who told her to "come right out." When she reached Sevenels, she was shown up to the third-floor bedroom. Amy, wearing a "voluminous white robe," half-reclining on her wide bed, looked like a presiding swami. "Sit down," she said, waving Jessie to a chair with a regal air. "We're finishing up *Fir-Flower Tablets.* The doctor says I'm supposed to lie flat for another three weeks, but I've given enough time to this damned hernia. . . ." And she launched into an outline of the aims and method of the book. Florence put in a word now and then, but had no chance to say more. From Jessie, Amy verified the news that Witter Bynner was working on some translations of Chinese poetry, but would not listen when Jessie said he was not nearly as far along as Amy.

"Well, I heard his book was about ready," Amy told her. "And if we don't get ours out ahead of his, I know people will say I imitated him! That's the reason I'm not obeying doctor's orders. We've got to beat Bynner, or our book will fall flat, and the poetry is too fine. . . . Listen to this." And forthwith she began to read some of the poems. She insisted on standing up although

Ada cautioned her not to, and she read majestically, standing there in her long white robe, giving the lines "much gusto and fine effect."

The book was published in December, too late for the Christmas sales, but in time for a few reviews, which, unfortunately, lessened its chances for financial success after the first of the year. Arthur Waley, the authority on Oriental literature, realized at once that neither Amy Lowell nor Florence Ayscough were true scholars of Chinese. Florence, although she had been born in Shanghai and had lived many years in China (and whose own books in prose were very successful), knew little of the language, and had had to enlist the help of a Chinese professor in her literal translations for Amy. Waley found errors to point out in his piece in the "Literary Review" of the *New York Evening Post,* but Amy optimistically said they were not as damaging as might be expected from him. *The Chinese Students' Monthly* was far more severe and gave her "a wild headache and a sleepless night." The worst thing, however, was that the poems *themselves* fell flat. In spite of the fact that she had "beaten Bynner" and despite the many laborious hours she and Florence had spent writing the explanatory remarks —or perhaps *because* of them—the poems themselves lacked the customary color and luster Amy Lowell's poems had if nothing else. There was too much exposition, and there were too many long-winded titles, although Mrs. Ayscough's introduction was interesting as her own work, and Amy's notes were informative. But *Fir-Flower Tablets,* although it represented a personal achievement for her, was a mistake professionally, and she knew it.

Even before the book had a chance to prove her hunch correct, she was on the defensive. Early in January, at the Poetry Society's annual meeting, Witter Bynner, the newly elected president, programmed an "all-American" night, with poets from forty states present, and, oddly enough, with a Chinese professor, Dr. Chan Peng-chun, a scholar of Chinese literature, as the principal speaker. When Amy and Ada arrived, late as usual, the entire assembly arose in a gesture of honor to Amy Lowell for her "service to poetry," which was gratifying; and she found the main speaker, who contrasted Chinese and American attitudes, very interesting. But the rest of the program was long and tedious (with the exception of Carl Sandburg, whose Windy City poems woke everybody up). Amy's hernia began to give her pain; the effect of the pills she always carried with her was wearing thin, and so was her patience. She wished Bynner would call on her so she could go back to the hotel and rest. But he waited till the tail end; she was the last speaker—at 1:00 A.M.—and Bynner made what she considered a malicious reference to *Fir-Flower Tablets* in his introduction. So she "slammed back" at him and the society, she wrote Florence, inveighing against the trend the organization was taking toward conservatism. Now, with Bynner as president,* she would probably lose some of her influence, although since the end of the war she had stopped hammering on Imagism, vers libre, or even the new poetry, and had dwelt more on freedom of the individual poet to express a thought or mood in the manner or mode best suited to it.** (Later on in her career she finally received the top award from *Poetry,* the Helen Haire Levinson Prize, for "prominence"; but some of the honor was diminished by Harriet Monroe's article on Amy Lowell which appeared in the magazine a month before the award was made. It opened: "Let us begin by granting Amy Lowell everything but genius." The poetry world seemed to salaam her with one hand and slam her with the other.)

Still, she kept plugging her own work and that of people whose style she admired. The day after that tiresome meeting, she read "Many Swans," with two intermissions of Indian music, before an audience of 950 people at St. Mark's Church-in-the-Bouwerie. The performance was so successful that she repeated it at a MacDowell Club benefit to raise funds for construction of the Colonists' Building, then one of Mrs. Edward MacDowell's principal projects. The only recompense Amy requested was a residence period for Hervey Allen, which was granted. She sent the

* Bynner was president of the Poetry Society from 1922 to 1924.

** She wrote as much to Elinor Wylie, whose volume, *Nets to Catch the Wind,* had just been published. After Amy had read her poems, she expressed to Elinor Wylie her admiration of them, saying that she understood perfectly why they had to be written in rhymed, metered verse. It marked the beginning of another literary friendship. She wrote, in part, "Were you to put any of these poems into cadenced verse they would lose at least half their value." Elinor answered, "I must thank you with all my heart for your letter."

following note in reply: "My dear Mrs. MacDowell: Thank you very much for your kind letter of May 6th. I am delighted that you will make room for Hervey Allen. You will not regret it, I am sure.

"You must be fearfully tired after your fifty recitals, but you must console yourself with thinking what an excellent work you are doing in Peterborough. Really I do not know anything which seems to me so valuable."

Amy once called on Marian MacDowell, and was full of admiration for the slip of a woman, a concert artist, who gave as much energy, vigorous organizing power, and devotion to her cause in promoting the arts as Amy did. She looked as if a sudden gust of wind might blow her away, but she had a good deal more stamina than Amy, whose life from this time on was like a mounting crescendo in some weird orchestral work, composed of lecturing, giving readings, creating, loving, and hating—all permeated by the ever present physical pain—a life that was bound to end in a sudden collapse.

CHAPTER XVIII

Act IV, Scene ii

"A bard of Ireland told me once,/ I should not live long . . . / . . . / Ay, what's o'clock?" *

IN SPITE OF DOCTOR'S ORDERS, Amy kept up with her still breakneck if slightly moderated schedule of public appearances, working at night, entertaining at Sevenels, even gardening occasionally, although she was not supposed to be on her feet or do anything that would put a strain on the already stretched muscles. She must have known she was risking a relapse, yet she kept on in a kind of compulsion. Inevitably, the hernia broke through again, but the doctor said it would not require surgery immediately, and Amy once again promised to try to relax—her blood pressure, constantly high, sometimes reached the staggering figure of 240—because, as she said privately, she resolved never to have another operation. She told Ada she did not think they did "a damn bit of good."

She was determined to begin the actual writing of her full-length biography of Keats this year (1922), but somehow the project kept growing larger and longer. As she became more involved in discovering the sources of Keats's poetry and the motivations of his short life, her beloved friend continued to be indispensable. Without "Peter" to discover the books she needed—and she would not have known many of them even existed if Ada had not ferreted them out—Amy could not have written about Keats

* Shakespeare, *King Richard III*. The lines indude the one Amy chose, significantly, for the last volume compiled during her lifetime, *What's O'Clock* (published posthumously).

with such voluminous detail. (It was during this period that Nell Belmont saw her old friend Ada come home staggering under a load of books, followed by Yates, the chauffeur, with a second load.) Amy and Ada worked together more closely on this book than on any of the previous ones.

During the first half of the year, however, there were previously made lecture and reading commitments to be fulfilled, and they traveled a good deal, laden with Amy's powerful reading lamp (it had blown a fuse at Brown University the winter before, but she continued to tote it around wherever she went, as she could not get through a reading without it), her basket of glasses, her books, her footstool, her "retinue." Since her blood pressure remained high, she suffered from the heat, and on overnight train trips she had difficulty breathing. Once when her compartment was especially stuffy, she called the porter to bring the ladder, and, before his astonished eyes, she climbed up and knocked out the little pane of colored glass at the top so that she would be able to get a whiff of air at least. She handed him her card and told him the company should send her a bill (she never received one). She raised a ruckus in Rochester because the hotel she stayed in there gave her a room with twin beds instead of one with the outsized double bed she had requested. (Through the papers, the story was all over the city the next day, but her reading at the University of Rochester was a big success.)

Toward the end of May, Robert Frost, who, with his family, was staying in Ann Arbor as the University of Michigan's first poet-in-residence, wrote to Amy asking her to come and read there in June. The students had raised money themselves for a "Spring festival of poetry," and Frost was rounding up his friends. They wanted Amy to open the series; he had also enlisted Carl Sandburg (with guitar), Vachel Lindsay, Louis Untermeyer, and Padraic Colum, who would follow her in turn in the four succeeding weeks. When she and Ada arrived with the lighting equipment, Frost informed her at once that it was against the janitor's rules to use any outside lamps; but Amy informed him crisply that no lamp meant no reading. They had arrived late, and the audience was waiting. "Plug it in for me, Robert—there's a good boy," she said.

She tugged the twisted cord one way and he tugged the other while the students giggled. Lesley Frost, sitting next to her mother in the front row, saw her grow first pale, then red with angry embarrassment. When Frost finally plugged in the fixture, there was a slight explosion—the fuse had blown! In the blackout that followed, 2,500 people sat enjoying the ad lib exchange between the two poets till the fuse was replaced.

From the darkness of the hall, a voice suddenly pleaded, "Please smoke your cigar, Miss Lowell!"

"Why don't you smoke?" Frost urged her in a stage whisper. "They'd like to see you do it."

"Don't I know it? Come on out behind the barn," she whispered back.*

After this horseplay, when the lights finally came on and Amy stood to read (as she always did when she felt strong enough) —a huge, imposing figure, and began in dramatic tones, "I am a woman, sick for passion"—an audible titter rippled through the audience. But she paid no attention and went right on, presenting the story of "Appuldurcombe Park," with her usual flair for the histrionic potential of the plot dealing with adultery. Under the spell of her commanding voice, her listeners settled down within a few seconds. She had them with her, and she knew it. The reading turned out to be one of her most successful. In the evening, she and Ada and the Frosts were invited to Dean (of the literature school) and Mrs. Bursley's home. It was a warm June night, and a full moon flooded the Bursleys' garden, which Amy viewed in pure delight. (She had written "The Garden by Moonlight," included in *Pictures,* which, as those who have watched a garden by moonlight know, gives an accurate picture. Her perception of it was enhanced by the quiet presence of Ada, "white like the alyssum flowers,/ And beautiful as the silent sparks of the fireflies." ** Then there was the charming "Planning the Garden"

* Dialogue from Jean Gould, *Robert Frost: The Aim Was Song* (New York: Dodd, Mead & Company, 1964).

** One of the pleasures of reading Amy Lowell's work is found in the wide-ranging, knowledgeable inclusion of flowers and her use of them both as color and as symbols. Throughout her poetry, she expresses varying degrees of emotional impulses, including sexual ones, by means of sensuous flower imagery.

and "Impressionist Picture of a Garden"; and later this summer she would "spin a poem" around a "perfectly beautiful 3½-inch white clematis, white as a moon at night": the sensuous, "Song for a Viola d'Amore," beginning, "The lady of my choice is bright/ As a clematis at the touch of night,/ As a white clematis with a purple heart/ When twilight cuts the earth and sun apart."

Elinor Frost would remind her of this moonlight night at the Bursleys' when she wrote to Amy in December, thanking her for her hospitality when she and Robert had visited at Sevenels during the fall, and expressing the wish that Amy and Ada would visit them at their "little farmhouse" sometime. "I mean I wish there was any hope of you *thinking* we could," Elinor wrote revealingly of their limited ability to make Amy comfortable. "I believe we could really." The letter was signed, "With our best love to you and Ada."

From Ann Arbor, in June 1922, Amy and Ada went to Chicago, where Amy lectured on Chinese poetry for the Moody Foundation at Mandel Hall on the University of Chicago campus. It was jammed to capacity, with 1,100 people; others were "turned away by the hundreds." Then, reluctantly, Amy saw Ada off on the train to Salt Lake City, consoling herself with her friend's promise to be back before Lorna and the children came (after little Allen's death, Lorna became pregnant almost immediately, and the baby was another boy). Ada also promised not to make any more trips to Salt Lake City until the Keats biography was finished. She knew how much the completion of that work meant to Amy, and she was quite concerned about the precarious state of the poet's health at this point. Amy was already feeling the effects of the trip—her digestion as well as the hernia were affected—and instead of going to Hanover, where she was slated to give a lecture at Dartmouth College, she went home immediately, postponing the lecture. She wrote an account of her travels to Elsie Sergeant, mentioning a critical attack on her poetry that had followed her Chicago lecture. "The more successful I am, the more I am hated," she said. "I meet with no jealousy from men who have arrived, like Frost, Lindsay and Sandburg, but I meet with nothing else from those of lower rank. Meanwhile, my books increase their sales. . . ."

Her poem, "The Sisters," opening with a meditation on the "family" of women poets, was published in the *North American Review*. This was the poem in which she stated her views on the "queer lot" they were: ". . . Why are we/ Already mother-creatures, double-bearing,/ With matrices in body and in brain?" These lines were written one night when she had been in labor over another poem, and the creative process to her was truly being "in labor." Her description in the Keats biography of the creation of a poem closely resembles childbirth: "Every nerve, even every muscle seems strained to the breaking point. The poem will not be denied; to refuse to write it would be a greater torture. It tears its way out of the brain, splintering and breaking its passage, and leaves that organ in the state of a jelly-fish when the task is done." In "The Sisters" she paid tribute to three poets she much admired. Of "Sapho" she said: "And she is Sapho—Sapho—not Miss or Mrs." But the next poet, "Mrs. Browning," of whom she is very fond, she would never dream of calling "Ba," and says bitterly, ". . . as if I didn't know/ What those years felt like tied down to the sofa./ Confounded Victoria, and the slimy inhibitions she loosed on all us Anglo-Saxon creatures!" The third "sister," Emily Dickinson, she could not bring herself to address as "Miss Dickinson," or send in a formal visiting card; in her fantasy meeting with Emily, she "climbed over the fence, and found her deep/ Engrossed in the doing of a humming-bird/ Among nasturtiums." She called Emily a "Frail little elf,/ The lonely brain-child of a gaunt maturity," who "hung her womanhood upon a bough/ And played ball with the stars—too long—too long— . . ./ Until at last she lost even the desire/ To take it down." Amy blamed not only Queen Victoria again but also Martin Luther, "And behind him the long line of Church Fathers/ Who draped their prurience like a dirty cloth/ About the naked majesty of God."

She wondered how many people would "jump on her" for blasphemy, and how many Emily Dickinson lovers would denounce her. But to her surprise, she received an enthusiastic letter from Millicent Todd Bingham, whose mother, Mabel Loomis

Todd, was both the editor of, and the person really responsible for the publication of, Emily's hidden "letter to the world." The mass of poems had been known only to a few, among them Thomas Wentworth Higginson, editor of the *Atlantic Monthly,* who gave her advice on her poetry-writing. In reply, Amy said, after expressing her pleasure at Mrs. Bingham's letter, "To my mind, Emily Dickinson is one of the greatest women poets who ever lived. I wish I could claim to be a pioneer in this, but really everybody agrees as to her merit today. She wrote half a century ahead of her time, that was all. There is not, to my mind, a sadder page in history than the picture of good, well-meaning Mr. Higginson trying to guide Emily's marvelous genius." And with her usual hospitality, she invited the Binghams to come to Sevenels.

Mrs. Bingham's husband, Walter, a professor at the Carnegie Institute of Psychology, had been wanting to analyze the creative process of a poet, and he tried to persuade Amy to be his subject; but she could not bring herself to undergo such vivisection. She had done some experiments with a Professor Patterson in connection with rhythm timing of cadences in free verse, but that had entailed a mechanical breakdown of the cadenced line and she was interested in the findings. Bingham's request would involve her own emotional conflicts and the real struggle it cost her to bring forth a phrase or a line, let alone an entire poem. And she no doubt feared that more than her professional secrets would be revealed in such an analysis. Her friend John Lowes was already hard at work on *The Road to Xanadu,* his monumental analysis of Coleridge's sources, and she admired his scholarly research, his insight into the materials of Coleridge's inspiration (which they often discussed when the Loweses came for dinner). But Coleridge and his circle of intimates had been long dead, and Amy Lowell, ill as she was, considered herself very much alive. And, although she was forthright and open about her life-style, she would not allow the invasion of her deepest privacy. She did let Bingham give her a free-association word test one evening after dinner, but of course it was a farce, and she was well aware that her zany answers would make him give up. But she wrote a ballad, "To a Gentleman Who Wanted to See the First Drafts of My Poems in the Interests of Psychological Research into the Workings of the Creative Mind," which states her feeling, her categorical "No," very clearly and cleverly:

So you want to see my papers, look what I have written down
'Twixt an ecstasy and heartbreak, con them over with a frown.
You would watch my thought's green sprouting ere a single
blossom's blown. . . .

Don't assure me that your interest does not lie with me at all.
I'm a poet to be dissected for the good of science. Call
It by any name, I feel like some old root where fungi sprawl. . . .

. . . By no means do I find your prying hands
Pleasure bearing and delightful straying round my lotus lands.

Not a word but joins itself with some adventure I alone
Could attach consideration to. . . .

Seize the butterfly and wing it, thus you learn of butterflies.
But you do not ask permission of the creature, which is wise.
If I did consent, to please you, I should tell you packs of lies.

Surely she was thinking of Ada in the next lines:

To one only will I tell it, do I tell it all day long.
Only one can see the patches I work into quilts of song.
Crazy quilts, I'm sure you'd deem them, quite unworthy of your
prong.

You mean well, I do not doubt it, but you're blind as any mule.
Would you question a mad lover, set his love-making to rule? . . .

Take my answer then, for, flatly, I will not be vivisected.
Life to me is more than learning. . . .

Therefore unequivocally, brazenly, I tell you "No!" . . .

But she had one thought to add, which might well have served as her epitaph:

Though I shudder thinking of you wandering through my beds
of bloom,
You may come with spade and shovel when I'm safely in the tomb.

The big event of the year was the anonymous publication of *A Critical Fable,* her own hoax, which, if she could succeed in concealing her authorship, she hoped would "beat Bynner's" in *Spectra*. She had evened the score in one way to begin with, by omission: Bynner and Ficke were conspicuous by their absence in her roster of poets worthy of appraisal. Her list included all those she had discussed in *Tendencies,* with the addition of herself, Conrad Aiken, Sara Teasdale, Hilda Conkling (the "child-wonder" poet), Alfred Kreymborg, Louis and Jean Starr Untermeyer, T. S. Eliot, Ezra Pound, William Rose Benét, Wallace Stevens, Edna Millay, and Maxwell Bodenheim. The book was hardly off the press before she noised about the rumor that Leonard Bacon, whose piece of light verse, "Banquet of the Poets," she had enjoyed, was the "brilliant" author of the *Fable*. He felt flattered but denied it indignantly. She wrote a long letter to John Farrar, speculating on who it could be, implying that she had not the faintest idea. When she herself was accused by Louis Untermeyer, she pointed the finger at him. It became a sort of literary game to guess the author of *A Critical Fable* for quite some time, and, as an indulgence to lighthearted mischief, it served as a diversion from the arduous task of the Keats biography.

Undoubtedly the two best portraits were those of Robert Frost and herself:

> There's Frost with his blueberry pastures and hills
> All peopled by folk who have so many ills
> 'Tis a business to count 'em, their subtle insanities.
> One half are sheer mad, and the others inanities.
> He'll paint you a phobia quick as a wink
> Stuffed into a hay-mow or tied to a sink.
> And then he'll deny, with a certain rich rapture,
> The very perversion he's set out to capture.
> Were it not for his flowers, and orchards, and skies,
> One would think the poor fellow was blind of both eyes
> Or had never read Freud, but it's only his joke. . . .
>
> He's a foggy benignity wandering in space
> With a stray wisp of moonlight just touching his face,
> Descending to earth when a certain condition
> Reminds him that even a poet needs nutrition. . . .

He's an unexplored mine you know contains ore;
Or rather, he acts as a landscape may do
Which says one thing to me and another to you,
But which all agree is a very fine view.

Frost came first, followed by Robinson in the *Fable,* the reverse of their position in *Tendencies,* which may have been due to her closer relationship to the Frosts in the years in between.

In the presentation of her own characteristics, Amy used an amusing device: She had set the whole piece in a framework of a conversation with an old man, or perhaps a ghost, for whom the past holds beautiful traditions, and when he asks about women, and she names Emily Dickinson, he refutes her, so she mentions " 'Amy Lowell, for instance,' I spoke a bit clammily./ 'Good Heavens!' he shouted, 'not one of the family!' " But she goes on to describe herself with candor, insight, and humor:

Conceive, if you can, an electrical storm
Of a swiftness and fury surpassing the norm;
Conceive that this cyclone has caught up the rainbow
And dashed dizzily on with it streaming in tow.
Imagine a sky all split open and scissored
By lightnings, and then you can picture this blizzard.
That is, if you'll also imagine the clashes
Of tropical thunder, the incessant crashes
Which shiver the hearing and leave it in ashes.
Remember, meanwhile, that the sky is prismatic
And outrageous with colour. The effect is erratic
And jarring to some, but to others ecstatic,
Depending, of course, on the idiosyncratic
Response of beholders. When you come to think of it,
A good deal is demanded by those on the brink of it.

Here she coined a phrase which followed her around:

Broncho-busting with rainbows * is scarcely a game
For middle-aged persons inclined to the tame.

Then come the telling lines:

Despite her traducers, there's always a heart
Hid away in her poems for the seeking; impassioned,

* Italics mine.

Beneath silver surfaces cunningly fashioned
To baffle coarse pryings, it waits for the touch
Of a man who takes surfaces only as such.

This was her answer to those who claimed she was a poet of things and superficialities, without emotion or heart. Nor did she spare herself:

Every book that she writes has a preface to guard it
Which spits fire and cannon-balls, making each hard hit
Tell, and mow down its swathe of objectors.
But critics have ever been good resurrectors.
Since she keeps the fight going, they rise to do battle,
When the whole mess is only so much tittle-tattle.

The game lasted about a year and a half. Once, at a literary party, when she accused Conrad Aiken of being the author, while he said he was positive she was and she kept denying it, he finally flung at her: "All right, if you're not, I'll say what I really think of it: I say it's damn rotten!" Amy winced, but would not concede. Like Bynner a few years before, she changed the subject; but in this case, Aiken was being acid and meaner than he needed to be; for, despite his constant attacks on her, she had written him a letter of hearty congratulation on his *Punch, the Immortal Liar,* written in 1921, and had reviewed the book glowingly in the *New Republic.* She had not been as generous to him in the *Fable,* however, and he was probably smarting from the jabs of her pen. Others who featured in the guessing game were Don Marquis, Christopher Morley, and, "to his mingled consternation and delight, Ferris Greenslet." Finally, fearing that she was becoming an inveterate liar, Amy wrote the exposé of herself as the author of *Fable* to John Farrar, after she tried, as chairman of the *Bookman*'s poetry committee, to have the work put on the recommended list for women's clubs. The English *Who's Who* of 1923 revealed the authorship publicly.

Greenslet summed up the *Fable* accurately: "When we consider the low physical state in which it was composed and compare the facility, force, and justice of her appraisal of her contemporaries and herself, with the same qualities of Cousin James'

Fable for Critics written by its author at a period of 'whoreson health,' it is evident that Amy and not James was the supreme literary exponent of Lowell animal spirits."

The two-volume biography of Keats was of course still the principal project at Sevenels, with Ada (and the secretaries) almost as involved in the work as Amy; but she kept up her book reviewing—one title was V. Sackville-West's novel, *The Dragon in the Shallow Waters,* which came about as the result of an unexpected, interesting letter from the English author: "Dear Miss Lowell, Two years ago I had a book published,—"Heritage"—and in the Richmond (Va.) *Times* of my American press was a quote of a favorable opinion you had expressed of the book, so I am venturing to send you a new one which has just been published, & which I hope you will accept with my grateful thanks for your appreciation of Heritage. This present one is shortly to be published in America by Putnam.

"Of course I am familiar with your work and may I say how *much* I admire it? its originality, its vitality, and its courage? I hope you will not mind my writing to you and sending you my book, but as a matter of fact a friend of mine—George Plank—has just been staying with me and suggested I should do so; he tells me he knows you.

"I have often wondered what the *Richmond Times* was quoting? Was it from a review by you? Yours sincerely, V. Sackville-West."

This hitherto unpublished letter provides a link between the Bloomsbury circle and Amy's Imagist movement, and proves that she was respected by the English group in spite of Lytton Strachey's withering attitude toward her. It is also a measure of Amy Lowell's literary position at the time. *Dragon* was a weird tale of two demonic brothers, one of whom was blind and the other deaf and dumb; yet by sheer force of body and character they have established a dominance over their fellow villagers. Amy could not help being fascinated by the story told in V. Sackville-West's forceful style, and decided to review it some months after receiving the copy. Her review, "A Breaker of Moulds," appeared in the *New York Times,* March 26, 1922.

Her entertaining continued to be lavish. She invited Elinor Wylie to stop at Sevenels for dinner on the way to the MacDowell Colony; she enjoyed the beautiful, meticulously styled, and sharp-witted poet as much as her unique, penetrating poems. As always, Amy maintained her voluminous correspondence. D. H. Lawrence wrote to her from San Francisco. He was in America at last, on his way to Santa Fe and Taos, New Mexico. She could reach him in Taos in care of Mabel Sterne—formerly Mabel Dodge, famous or infamous for her salons in New York and Europe, for her affair with John Reed and sundry others, and for her marriage to Sterne, whom she divorced to marry Tony Luhan, a Taos Indian. Amy's quick and hearty "welcome to America" went out to Lawrence at once. She hoped he and Frieda would come to Sevenels soon, but she warned him that in Santa Fe he would run into a nest of her "enemies"—Witter Bynner and Alice Corbin (Henderson), associate editor of *Poetry*. However, Elsie Sergeant was living near Santa Fe, Amy said, and "she will make you happy if you tell her you are a friend of mine."

Lawrence's next letter was from Taos, where he and Frieda were settled in "a gay little adobe house on the edge of the desert, with the mountains sitting round under the sun, the Indian reservation about two miles off, and the Taos pueblo only one mile. We don't see much of the world save Mabel Sterne and her visitors. The land I like exceedingly. You should see Frieda and me trotting on these Indian ponies across the desert and scrambling wildly up the slopes among piñon bushes. We go to the hot springs and sit up to our necks in clear, jumping water. America does what I thought it would—just *bumps* me." Then he told her that they "slept the first night at Witter Bynner's in Santa Fé and Alice Corbin was there." Both spoke of Amy, but not like "an enemy." He went on to observe that he always expected literary enemies, if that was what she meant: They could tear him to shreds. Later Lawrence did meet and become friends with Elsie Sergeant, who probably told him of Bynner's mocking epithet for Amy, which may explain the satiric portrait of Witter Bynner in the first part of Lawrence's *The Plumed Serpent*. Bynner, angry, shocked, and bewildered by the character—obviously modeled on himself, emphasizing the "twitter" side, and unnecessarily dragged in, since he has nothing to do with the story and leaves the scene early in the book—could not understand why Lawrence had attacked him.* The mystery is explained if one realizes the loyalty and sympathetic understanding Lawrence felt for Amy Lowell. Because of her illnesses, he never did get to Sevenels, though a visit was planned, and was almost realized when he was in New Jersey on a brief trip.

Meanwhile, the constant carousel of work, work, work, and play whirled around at Sevenels, with Amy only the occasional barker now. Given the opportunity, she would shout and "blow the trumpet," as she said, for related fields. In the fall of 1922, she wrote "Bibi" (now in Washington at the Library of Congress) that she was to go to New York to speak at the League of American Composers on jazz. The other two speakers were to be Ned Hill and Gilbert Seldes, the latter then editor of *Dial* magazine. In November, the magazine printed T. S. Eliot's *The Waste Land,* which prompted Amy to write Seldes that, though she found "interesting passages" in it, the work as a whole left her cool, "cooler even than Ezra's *Cantos.*" It was here that she said it was as if Eliot "had laid a fire with infinite care but omitted to apply a match to it." Almost apologetically, she concluded, "Forgive me if you can, for I know that I shall require forgiveness in your eyes. I think you were quite right to print the poem, and time will prove which of us is right." In her attitude she showed more diplomacy and generosity than some of her critics had given her credit for.

She was not as generous toward women poets who showed signs of becoming a threat to her. She was nettled more than anything else when Edna Millay was awarded a Pulitzer Prize in 1922, the first woman ever to win the award for poetry. Amy undoubtedly felt that her output, being far greater, was more deserving, not to mention her position as elder stateswoman of the renaissance of American poetry; but there was little she could say in protest since the award was given in large measure for eight

* Bynner took his revenge nearly twenty years later, when, in 1951, he wrote *Journey with Genius,* an invidious account of his trip to Mexico with Lawrence, one of the last unfriendly books about the controversial British novelist.

love sonnets by Millay published in *A Miscellany of American Poetry,* the anthology that Amy and Louis Untermeyer had compiled. Amy herself was well represented, as were both Untermeyers, and the original new poets. The *Miscellany* was a steady seller for several years.

At the end of January 1923, Amy and Ada set out on their final lecture tour, which lasted till March 10. There were times when Amy thought she would have to cancel a date, but somehow she always rallied, "like a real trouper," Ada said. But when it was over, Amy (richer by $1,825) declared she was through with tours until the biography of Keats was in press. And work they did, Amy sometimes straight through the night. Spring weather was late in coming that year, so she was not tempted to do any gardening, and rested when she was not writing. The season was lovelier than ever when the weather finally changed, and Amy sent a long description of the garden to a former nurse, commenting at the end, "I do not think the place has gone down at all since Papa's time, *except that I do not grow so many roses.*"* She may have been the child who sprang late from her father's loins, and she was proud of being a Lowell, but she was *Amy,* not Augustus, and Sevenels was hers, by right of purchase, and she felt no constraint to preserve his preferences.

Nell Belmont came for an overnight visit, and her two friends accompanied her to her room for a second good-night, Amy asking what she would like to read. Her answer—"A detective story"—revealed the fact that Amy, whose relaxation books (as is often the case with poets, including Edna Millay) were detective stories, had the guest room well stocked with them, and had "put three or four good ones" on Nell's night table. The one she chose, *The Mystery of the Boule Cabinet,* had been written by Burton Stevenson, compiler of the great standard anthology, *Home Book of Verse,* which no doubt attracted Amy's attention to it. This may have been one of the times Amy stopped by her room at eight o'clock in the morning, on her way to the third floor, to greet her and have a sip of coffee from her breakfast tray. Amy looked tired, but not as tired as she might have at such moments, for she recently had be-

* Italics mine.

gun to sleep a couple of hours on the sofa in the library before attempting to climb the two flights of stairs. She did not want to move to a lower floor, or have a small elevator installed, as people in her circumstances often did. She may have considered it a kind of self-discipline to climb, laboriously, to her own quarters. At any rate, Eleanor Robson Belmont, with her theater background, told Amy that Stevenson's detective story was not only "good," but "held a play" in its plot, and the book went home with her. Being a woman of action herself, and one who got things done, she contacted Harriet Ford, who had adapted *Audrey,* one of Eleanor Robson's hit roles, for the stage, and the two became partners in a playwriting venture.

It was a busy, full summer. Lorna and the children came from Washington for several weeks, and Ada saw to it that the little boys did not disturb Aunt Amy unless she wanted to be. Ada, indeed, became a regular watchdog during these months of intense work. One of the painters-in-residence at the MacDowell Colony in the summer of 1923 was Theodore Spicer-Simson, noted for his portraits of well-known people. He had completed a portrait of Thomas Watson, the inventor and partner of Alexander Graham Bell, on July 2. He was, in his words, "keen to have the celebrated poet Amy Lowell" sit for him while he was in the Boston area, and phoned her one evening. At first Amy seemed indifferent, but she always paid attention to people from the MacDowell Colony, and as they talked, she grew interested in the idea of sitting for a portrait, though she had sworn she never would. She went so far as to ask him to call on her at Sevenels. Unfortunately, he didn't know that she was a night worker (like Graham Bell), and showed up while she was still asleep. One would hardly recognize Ada from his description, "who was as rude as she could be without actually saying much." Quiet Ada was firm, but she did give him the chance to leave his card and some photographs of portraits he had done, promising to give them to Miss Lowell for inspection. Amy was sufficiently impressed with the reproductions to ask Spicer-Simson to come for dinner a few times, and she and Ada discussed the question of whether or not she should sit. She finally decided she would; but she did not want to do it during the summer while

Lorna and the children were there, and she made arrangements to have the portrait painter "run up from New York" in the fall. They set a date in October.

In August, a huge box of Sherry's chocolates arrived from Nell, who was already well into the project of dramatizing the detective story, having the usual struggle with dialogue. Amy's delighted (and deliciously frank) letter of thanks to "Dear Nell" needs no comment, but speaks worlds:

"Your bounty is beyond words, and the worst of it is that I have, with the most meagre assistance, eaten it all up. I have been afraid to weigh myself since the deed was — Ah, but I do like Sherry's chocolates! . . . The joy is only so much enhanced because it partakes of the nature of forbidden fruit. With every delectable drop, I feel a pound going on, and only when I recollect how short is life, how fleeting, do I reflect that it makes very little difference whether a skeleton was once fat or thin. This consoles me greatly, and I eat on, unmoved and unmoving. . . .

"Both Ada and I feel a distinct desire for recreation, so I think we may drop into your town somewhat sooner than we expected—October, perhaps, or early November. There are such things as P.E.N. dinners. You have heard of that literary dining club got up last winter? I think they have monthly dinners, and I think we shall time our trip to coincide with one of them. I ought not to break away even for a day, but I have been attending to Keats for so long that I do crave a brief vacation.

"Ada read me your mournful letter. Poor Nell, you have had a time! I am sorry the play is sticking. But don't get discouraged, things often do that. I do think you will have to write the dialogue yourself if you want it to snap. . . . You will get confidence as you go along. . . .

"I do hope you will become so exhausted with the labour of authorship that you will have to take a rest, and that you will take it chez nous. I do so like to have you here, and of course Ada remains on the grill from the moment you come till the moment you go. Your coming here would be the best kind of vacation for us. Now I must go and eat my supper, being 4 A.M. The others would send messages, but they are fast asleep." She had just signed herself "affectionaly," when she was interrupted, and added a postscript: "Ada has appeared on the scene, and says this is spelt wrong from beginning to end. She is so savage at dawn, and she has no business to be awake anyhow. It is the bad habit the children have taught her."

Lorna and the children left in September, and Amy doubled her efforts, with the assistance of Ada and the secretaries, to get on with the manuscript, which was now piling up. Elinor Frost wrote early in October to ask: "Would you like to have Robert and me spend a day or two with you, coming to you either the 24th or the 25th of October? We are to be at Wellesley two or three days, and I am not quite sure when we are expected to leave. . . . Please be quite frank if you are not feeling well, or if, for any reason it is not perfectly convenient for you. . . ." With her usual hospitality, Amy told them they would be welcome at Sevenels, and then she received momentous news that made her cancel or change all her appointments: Eleonora Duse was returning to the United States for a tour in the 1923–24 season, after twenty-one years, and had expressed a desire to see Miss Lowell! Amy shifted her whole schedule. The sittings with the painter were indefinitely postponed; the first date with him was broken at once, much to his disappointment. She did arrange another, but it was indefinite, and the portrait was never painted.* The Frosts came to spend a Sunday, and said they would spend a weekend later on. Right now everything was of secondary importance, even the biography of Keats. Duse was touring in *Lady from the Sea,* which evidently opened in Boston, since she came out to Sevenels after a performance. She "fell in love with the place" and said she would like to come back to visit when the tour was over. She was very frail, but still possessed an eloquent and breathtaking beauty. Little was said, however, as Amy and Ada spoke very little Italian, Duse no English, and her companion was a poor interpreter. The only sentence that came out clearly was: "The past is dead; the future alone has life." But Amy was ecstatic, and she wrote a poem, "To Eleonora Duse, 1923," containing lines considered too intimate

* From the autobiography, *A Collector of Characters: Reminiscences of Theodore Spicer-Simson.* Coral Gables, Florida: University of Miami Press, 1962.

to publish at the time: "The sight of you is piercing as a cry,/ Your loveliness betrays my eyes to tears,/ . . . I am no hero-worshipper,/ Yet for your sake I long to babble prayers/ And overdo myself in services./ Is this not love, then?" The great actress was pitifully thin and could eat virtually nothing; the only thing that seemed to sustain her was champagne. Amy furnished her with all that was left in her cobwebby cellar from pre-Prohibition days and, when that was gone, found ways to get more.

Of course Amy and Ada went to New York where, Eleanor Belmont wrote in her autobiography, Duse's "final performance in *Lady from the Sea,* at the Metropolitan Opera House, was one of the great moments in the American Theatre, an imperishable memory." While Amy was in New York, she arranged with the headwaiter at the Belmont to procure champagne (undoubtedly at an enormous price) for her idol; and after the New York run was over, she made special trips from Brookline to the hotel, to be sure that the headwaiter was still providing the great actress with champagne. The bottles were carefully wrapped against breakage, packed in a suitcase, consigned to a traveling friend, and carried by hand to Duse wherever she happened to be playing. The idea of Amy Lowell of Sevenels, Brookline, Massachusetts, descendant of the lordly Lowells, serving as "bootlegger for Duse" appealed to Nell Belmont's fancy and touched her heart, as it did that of others who knew about it, and who knew that Amy also smoothed the way for the actress by arranging with friends in different cities to put her up and take good care of her so that she would not have to stay in hotels. She wrote six sonnets to Duse during this time.

It was an exciting, emotional period for all. Nell Belmont's play (which she and Harriet Ford finally called *In the Next Room*) opened at the Vanderbilt Theatre on November 27, 1923; it was produced by her friend Winthrop Ames and coproduced by Guthrie McClintic, a first venture in that capacity for him. Opening night was a huge success, and when the enthusiastic audience called "Speech, speech—author, author!" Eleanor Robson Belmont told the audience, "I had no idea that my reentrance into the theatre would be made on a crime wave," though she could not remember saying it. The play looked as though it would run for several years (which it did), and the godmothers to her brain-child, Amy and Ada, rejoiced with her. Whether it was because of the general excitement, the long hours of writing when at home, or a combination of the two, Amy suffered retinal hemorrhages in both eyes and lapsed into a state of exhaustion that kept her in bed again for several weeks. While recovering, she received a letter from Duse which had to be read aloud to her after a hasty translation by someone who knew Italian. The tour had ended in Baltimore, and Duse was resting there. She had received an offer to make a second, shorter tour and had accepted it because she did not know when, if ever, she would return to America. She would be glad to come to Sevenels for an extended visit. Luckily, Amy's eyes began to clear; while she was still recovering, she got an Italian dictionary and translated Duse's letter, which was written in purple ink in a hand so fluid one could hardly make out the words. But Amy discovered that the translation which had been read to her contained nothing of the compassion and tenderness she discovered in the letter. She immediately wrote another poem, "To Eleanora Duse, In Answer to a Letter," addressing the actress as "Dear lady of the great compassion,/ All tenderness enmeshed in withes of truth. . . ." She sent copies of both long poems and the six sonnets to Sara Teasdale, who had also found her first inspiration in Duse. Sara was moved, and wrote, " 'Eleanora Duse, 1923' is the finest of the poems, I believe, and next, 'In Answer to a Letter.' I don't know that I have ever read finer praise from one woman to another. Sappho's praise of Anactoria being out of the running as representing a wholly different sort of thing."

Amy sent telegrams to friends in the cities that Duse's second tour included; and when she recovered, she saw to it that champagne followed the actress again. She also prepared to modernize the main guest room by installing a tile bath, everything included, to make things more convenient for the ailing actress when she arrived. (The old copper tub, always highly polished, had been there all the years, and the commode was down the hall, out of earshot.) These things attended to, she settled down again to work on the biography of Keats. February 9 was her fiftieth birthday, but she did not want any formal celebration as her friends and colleagues suggested, because she was too deeply immersed in completing the manuscript.

Two months later, suddenly, word came that Duse, now at the end of her tour, was desperately ill with pneumonia, stricken while playing in Pittsburgh, where she was staying with Amy's friends, Professor and Mrs. Bingham (the Professor Bingham who had wanted to analyze Amy). Nightly telephone calls revealed that the doctor had prescribed injections which at first seemed to help, but after a brief rally, the actress faded rapidly and died before dawn on Easter Monday, April 21. She was brought to New York for the funeral. The casket was surrounded and banked with flowers from dignitaries and celebrities around the world, lying in a small chapel of St. Vincent Ferrer Church. The numbers interested in expressing their sympathies and devotion to the actress, whose greatness was legendary, led to the necessity of issuing tickets for the services. They were in demand, but Nell Belmont was able to secure three tickets through the Italian consul, and she took Amy and Ada. They were seated in the fourth row among the chief mourners, as indeed the three felt themselves to be, Amy in particular. She sent a long account of the funeral to Millicent Bingham, describing the flowers and the tearful crowds. It had been a chill, gray day, but suddenly the sun shone through the stained-glass windows of the church and sent prismatic light playing over the flower-laden casket. Amy, a far from religious person, felt it was a sign of spiritual peace that had come at last to the tragic artist. After the service, the three devoted admirers followed the cortege down to the docks, but the crowds were so tremendous that they could not see the casket being placed on the ship that carried Duse back to Italy for burial.

Back in Brookline, Amy and Ada concentrated on the Keats manuscript once more, Ada taking particular care to see that day-to-day life was made smooth for Amy. Toward the end of May a letter written by Elinor Frost in Amherst gives an interesting picture of the Frost family, their friendship with Amy and Ada, and Ada's role in Amy's life and career. The letter speaks of the

Frosts' leaving the next day for Pittsfield, Massachusetts, where Lesley and Marjorie were going to open their bookshop. "We are all very much excited over it. They are going to pay postage to any part of New England and Lesley would be grateful for an order from you sometime. We have to be at Breadloaf the first week in July, though Robert wishes there were some way of getting out of it. We want you to come here for a lecture or a reading some time in November. Do you think you can? If you do, I wish Ada could come here for a night beforehand, to see if she doesn't think you could be made comfortable in our house instead of going to a hotel in Holyoke. We have a large house, six bedrooms and three bathrooms, and I could get in a good cook for a few days. *Ada could assume charge of the house and give her own orders for your comfort.** I think it would be easier for you, and we should enjoy it. There is, you see, plenty of room for you and your maid. Love to Ada and yourself. Affectionately. . . ."

How could Amy resist such a cordial, concerned, not to say urgent invitation? Obviously she could not, and she did not, for by the middle of November, Yates, her chauffeur, delivered her 1,160-page manuscript of *John Keats* to Ferris Greenslet, who was to have exactly ten days to read it and give the doughty author his considered opinion. An appointment was made for five o'clock at the Houghton Mifflin office at 2 Park Street. Though he could not know it, Amy fretted and stewed during those ten days, fearing the book would not be understood, or that she had left something out, though Ada assured her she couldn't have squeezed in one more intimate detail of Keats's short life. Amy knew "Peter" was worried about her. The day of her appointment with Greenslet the bandages seemed to take forever to be properly adjusted. She was late by an hour and a half, arriving at 6:30 for a 5:00 P.M. consultation. Yet there was no sign of her inner agitation when she walked into the editor's office, "apologetic and as always completely disarming," according to Greenslet.

"Well, Ferris, what about it?" she demanded, taking her capacious cigar case out of her equally capacious handbag, lighting up, and offering him one at the same time.

* Italics mine.

"Amy, it's a great book," he began, "but you have given the reader the whole process of your research and your thought, not just the results, which are what he wants. I have put faint pencilled brackets about some sentences and paragraphs which would be better out. The more the marble wastes, the more the statue grows." If he thought this reference to art would help him, he was mistaken.

"Ferris, you are a dear good boy, but you don't know a thing about biography, not a damned Thing!" Amy told him flatly. They took off from there, but got nowhere, though the interview was prolonged and the offices deserted by the time Amy rose to leave. In the end, the biographer embraced her editor-publisher, patted him on the shoulder, and reassured him that he was "a good boy," but not one word of the 1,160-page manuscript was deleted. (Much later Greenslet recalled Carl Sandburg's remark to Florence Ayscough: "Arguing with Amy is like arguing with a big blue wave.")

Amy felt triumphant but tired as Yates drove her back to Sevenels in the "mulberry motor," as Ferris called her car. She had written to Louis Untermeyer (and other friends) that *Keats* was "nearly killing her" when she was in the midst of it, and now that the manuscript was on its way to press, she felt stone-dead tired; yet she could not rest for long. She began to prepare another book of lyrics and short pieces; she wanted to bring together all her poems of a personal nature without delay. She felt more and more that there were not too many hours left in store for her. Like Richard III, she kept asking herself, "What's o'clock?"—words she had already chosen as a title for the book.

It was an upsetting autumn. Amy was either ill or working and did not go out often. Her sister Bessie's husband, William Lowell Putnam, died, and Amy, accompanied by Ada, attended the funeral. On December 10, tragic word came from New York: August Belmont had died suddenly and unexpectedly. A violent infection had invaded his blood cells, evidently caused by a hypodermic injection of a simple drug used frequently to increase red corpuscles in cases of anemia. Ada got ready at once to rush to her friend's side, while Amy penned a heartfelt note: "Dearest Nell," she wrote quickly, "I cannot let Ada go on to you without sending you my love and very deep sympathy. You know how I wish there were anything I could do, and you know also that our house is always a welcome resting-place for you whenever you will come to it and for as long as you will stay. I know that to be with Ada will be the greatest comfort you can have, and I want you to feel that it is not only Ada who longs to take care of you and comfort you, but I also, as far as it is in my power. Come to us then, Dear, as soon as you can, and always consider this as another home. Lovingly always, Amy." Only Ada and Nell could know fully how generous and warmhearted this note was on Amy's part.

The publication date for *John Keats* was set for February 10, 1925. As soon as Ada returned from New York, she and Amy got busy on the galleys, checking and rechecking them to be sure they missed no typos. It was to be a two-volume work, and everyone in the family was interested in the biography that had occupied half of Amy's time for years, and, during the last four, almost all of it. Her sister Katie could hardly wait till the book came out, and even Lawrence said he wanted to read it. But, on February 4, tragedy struck again, unexpectedly, as before. Katie, who was president of the Women's Municipal League in Brookline, had gone to New York for a conference of some kind. No one knew quite how it happened—Katie had been subject to dizzy spells for years—but a terse telegram announced that she had been killed instantly by a fall from the window of her room in the Hotel Vendome. It was almost too much to bear. If Ada had not been with her, Amy was sure she could not have stood the shock and confusion—the whole family rushed to Sevenels, where the funeral was held. On February 11, Amy wrote the last (extant) letter to "Dearest Bibi," who had called from Washington as soon as he heard the news: "You never fail me, and I count on you always, and love you dearly. Katie died like a captain on his quarterdeck, serving her beloved Municipal League. It was almost horrible to receive advance copies of my book the morning after her death.* She was waiting for it so eagerly.

* Damon states the arrival of the advance copies on the same day as the news, but this letter indicates that he was mistaken (*Amy Lowell, A Chronicle* [Boston: Houghton Mifflin Company, 1935]).

"I can't write, Dear. I am so tired. They brought Katie here, to her old home, and there was much to do for Katherine Reeve [Katie's married daughter]. I wish I could see you. Please give our love to Helen. Always your affectionate Amy."

The two "stout red volumes" of *John Keats* were released on schedule, February 10. On the same date, a second printing, not yet available, had already sold out; and three more printings were ordered within five days. This work at last was dedicated to Ada, with her consent; but Amy took advantage of the opportunity to do what she had wanted to do for years: She added a phrase to the initials, so there would be no doubt in anyone's mind about the extent of her friend's share in her life and creativity. The dedication reads: "To A. D. R., This, and all my books. A. L." Ada was more pleased and touched than vexed, and, as the work seemed to be the most successful of all Amy's books, she must have felt more than a little proud of her share in it, which was considerable. The secretaries, too, received a paragraph of appreciation in the Acknowledgments. They had "worked their hands to the bone," Amy admitted privately, especially toward the end, when Amy's eyes were so weak that she had to dictate each page, which the girls took down in shorthand before typing, often working late.

Reviews in America were uniformly good. The critics could all agree on this book by Amy Lowell at one level at least: The biography of Keats was a "monumental" work, a scholarly contribution as a reliable source book. And many went so far as to commend her interpretation of Keats, her self-identification with his "cult of the moon"; her clarification of Fanny Brawne's behavior; her treatment of Keats's relationship with the men that formed his circle, particularly Joseph Severn. And American readers loved the book. At first Amy and Ada thought this was one book that would be free of controversy. But when the reviews began to arrive from England, they were shocked: Almost without exception, the critics were hostile. They seemed to feel that Amy Lowell had invaded English literary territory. She had had the effrontery to negate Sidney Colvin's long-accepted theory of Keats's life. How did she know so much? (They may not have realized that there was more Keats material in America than in England. The poet's brother had emigrated to Virginia, and the close correspondence between the brothers was located in the United States. Amy herself had one of the best collections.)

Amy was angry and heartbroken. She did receive a good review from "A. E." (George Russell, the Irish poet) in the *Irish Statesman,* and Thomas Hardy sent a comforting letter to "Cousin Amy," telling her not to pay attention to the critics. She also received invitations to speak at Oxford and Cambridge, and at Keats's residence, Wentworth House (which, as already related, had been bought and restored largely through her efforts), so she planned a trip to England to speak on Keats's and her own behalf. The doctor had told her a sea voyage might be dangerous because of the risk of strangulation of the hernia, but she was willing to take the chance. She and Ada made plans to sail on the *Berengaria,* due at Southampton on April 21. In the meantime, she wrote tributes to celebrate the fiftieth birthdays of Robert Frost and Percy MacKaye. (Actually, Frost was going to be fifty-one, the same as she, but he didn't bother to correct the error in his birth record; if people wanted to make him a year younger than he was, it was all right with him.) Though Amy's fiftieth birthday had been more or less ignored (except in the press) because of her work on Keats the year before, this year, because of Katie's death, there was no thought of a birthday celebration. However, her many friends and associates decided that a "Complimentary Dinner" should be given early in April as a belated fiftieth birthday celebration and as a mark of recognition for her contribution to modern American literature. Naturally, she and Frost received invitations to each other's parties (his was on March 26 at the Brevoort in New York, but Amy was not sure her health would permit even a short trip to New York if she wanted to sail).

On February 27, Elinor wrote her a friendly letter, enclosing a writeup in the Amherst student paper about Amy's reading there, and saying how much they had enjoyed the visit with her and Ada. Then, referring to the "Complimentary Dinner," she wrote, "Robert says to tell you that he'll be on hand for your party if there is anything left of him by that time—he has 12 or 13 reading engagements, lots of travel, besides his college work, and doesn't know how he'll manage. Then there is his own party on the 26th, which will of course be a nervous strain, though a pleasure. I wonder if anyone will come to his party. *Please change your mind and come yourself.* I hope you reached home none the worse for your little trip to Amherst." She sent her love to both Ada and Amy and closed, "We'll look forward to a jolly time with both of you and Louis and Jean."

However, Amy did not feel well enough to attend Frost's party, but she did send along the fine tribute she had prepared for delivery in person, which was read by one of their colleagues at the Brevoort. As the date for her own celebration drew near, however, she grew nervous; she was full of anxiety about what Louis and Robert might say. Perhaps they would be critical of her for not showing up at Frost's party. Though everyone knew she was ill, no one knew how serious her condition was. (Several years earlier she had writen Louis, "Do try and get here as early as possible before they have quite minced me to pieces and swept me up in the dustpan," but she didn't mention the double hernia as the cause.) On a sudden impulse she called the Untermeyers the night after Robert's party; she knew the Frosts were spending the weekend with them. (As usual, it was around 1:00 A.M., but luckily Robert and Louis were still up, talking.) Amy began by saying how sorry she was she couldn't make the celebration at the Brevoort, wanted to hear all about it, and then said she was looking forward to seeing them at her dinner, adding, according to an account by her friend Elsie Sergeant (in the latter's biography of Frost): "You and Louis come here first, and *I'll tell you what you will each say at my dinner.*" She probably didn't realize how imperious she sounded, and since neither of her colleagues knew the state she was in, her words were enough to make both of them decide to bow out.

On March 29, Elinor Frost sent Amy a tactful but firm note: "My dear Amy—I am writing to say what we ought to have said decidedly in the first place—that it's simply out of the question for Robert to speak at your dinner. He just isn't able to. He is tired now, and has three lectures ahead of him this week, with much traveling. He is sorry, and we hope very much that it won't greatly disarrange your plans. And we hope very much, too, that the occasion will be a happy and satisfactory one for you. I am sure it will be. With love to you and Ada—Faithfully yours, Elinor Frost." It was a distinctly cool note compared with the others from her in the Frost file at the Houghton Library.

In spite of these personal complications, the "Complimentary Dinner in Honour of Miss Amy Lowell" in the ballroom of the Hotel Somerset in Boston was a beautiful event, according to all accounts, including Elsie Sergeant's, for she was there along with most of Amy's friends in the Poetry Society. Nell Belmont, who at first hesitated to accept, being in deep mourning, was assured by both Amy and Ada that it would not be a social gathering "in the usual sense of the word," and they insisted that she come. Afterward, she was always grateful that she had attended. Not long before, Ada had confided to her that she was extremely anxious about Amy's health, but Nell was not prepared for the ominous change in the poet within the two months since she had seen her. Amy was pale and her eyes were darkly circled. She was near the point of collapse with fatigue, and she was, for her, thin, down to 159 pounds. Dressing for the event was a terrible strain, even with all the help she had. The bandages took longer than ever; but at last she was ready, and somehow she managed to look regal, almost like her usual self by the time they reached the ballroom, then already filled with more than four hundred guests. Her old friends, Mrs. Bayard Thayer and Mrs. Montgomery Sears, had gathered flowers from their own greenhouses. Her place at the main table was marked by a silver bowl of exceptionally beautiful orchids * to be carried home with her as a gift. The total effect of the flower arrangements was breathtaking, a garden in itself.

The hundreds of distinguished persons present were decidedly gratified when, with the coffee, the guest of honor pulled out her "capacious cigar-case." And the speeches began. The supply of praise for every phase of Amy Lowell's work seemed inexhaustible. Glenn Frank, editor of the *Century,* speaking early

* Orchids were Amy's favorite plants in her own greenhouse gardening.

to catch the train back to New York, nominated her for President of the United States. Some of the other speakers were John Livingston Lowes, E. B. Hill, Elinor Wylie, Foster Damon, Hervey Allen, and Archibald MacLeish. It was past midnight when John Farrar's turn came. He knew Amy was not well and was exhausted by this time, so he discarded his prepared remarks and said, with true fondness, "I wish Miss Amy Lowell long life and happiness, but the best wish I have for her is that one day a biographer would write of her with as much love and understanding as she has written of John Keats." At 1:00 A.M. Amy stood up (with some difficulty, though no one noticed) and made the observation that she hadn't recognized herself in the evening's speeches but hoped her cat Winky would when she got home. Then, appropriately, she read "Lilacs" and "A Tulip Garden" (the latter inspired by Mrs. Thayer's famous tulip beds). Tired as she was, she read in her best style.

After receiving myriad congratulations and the silver bowl of orchids, exhausted but thoroughly happy, she left with Ada and Nell for Sevenels, where the three talked over the glowing occasion to the last detail for more than an hour. That night Amy did not sit up writing. She went to bed when the others did, she and Ada accompanying Nell to the guest room she had remodeled for Eleonora Duse. She rested most of the next day, but soon began to make more precise plans for her upcoming tour in England. She lined up a total of sixteen lecture dates. Ada was worried about the venture; Amy kept losing weight, involuntarily. It was puzzling, frightening. And on April 10, the hernia flared up again. This time the muscles became widely separated, and, though surgery was indicated, it had to be deferred—her continuing loss of weight made an immediate operation too risky. Absolute quiet was ordered; the sailing had to be canceled. In terrible pain, she wrote her last letter to Ferris Greenslet on May 2, enclosing a list of corrections for *Keats*. "I have two nurses now, and I am no good at all for anything," she wrote. "The sooner we get through these corrections the better."

On the same day she received an engaging letter from Lesley Frost, written on stationery from The Open Book, telling her how sorry she was that she was ill and had to postpone the trip to England. She hoped it would not be for long and that Amy would be there "to see an English spring come in," and added, "That's something I'm always homesick for—their spring." She thanked Amy for autographing copies of *Keats* for the bookshop and told her they had just won a battle to have a "showcase" within a couple of feet of the pavement instead of the twelve-foot frontage demanded by the city. "We are making your books the first 'show' to celebrate!" she finished. Ada read the letter to her, and Amy must have felt pleased, not only to hear about the display of *Keats,* but because it told her that she must not have offended Robert Frost irrevocably. She had the note put in her files till she could answer it. A couple of days later in talking on the phone to Mrs. E. B. Hill, who hardly recognized Amy's voice in the hoarse whisper that came over the wire, she said, "Alison, I feel like hell!" She did not know when she could even get back to her correspondence.

It was finally decided that an operation was necessary, risky or not. The date was set for May 13. On the twelfth, she woke up in despair. "Peter, I'm done," she said wearily. "Why can't they leave me alone!" Her friend said she might feel differently when she got up, for, miserable as she was, and steadily growing weaker, Amy had insisted on being up part of each day. As she was sitting in front of her dressing table, letting her maid and the nurse wind the bandages around her, she started to pin the left side herself, but suddenly stopped, as if puzzled. "My hand hurts," she said. Ada, standing behind her, holding the braided crown to place on her head as always, gave a little laugh, trying to make light of it. "Mine often hurts," she said. Amy tried again, and faltered. "But it's numb; I can't use it," she said. Suddenly, catching sight of herself in the dressing-table mirror, she saw the right side of her face drop and recognized her tragic fate. "Pete," she gasped in a low voice, "a stroke."

As she sank in a half-conscious state, the nurse and her maid moved her in her chair to a sofa and were able to get her onto it while Ada hurried to phone the doctor. When she came back, she bent over Amy and took her hand. "Get Eastman," murmured

Amy, issuing orders with her last breath, which brought a tender smile to her friend's face. "I have, dear," she said. She could not be sure, but she thought she saw the ghost of an answering smile flicker across Amy's face as she sank into unconsciousness.

An hour and a half later, at 5:30 P.M., May 12, 1925, Amy Lowell died, at the climax of her career, before the usual running time of life's drama is over.

Ada called Nell Belmont, who came up to Sevenels at once. It seemed symbolic that Amy should die in lilactime, and the bloom was especially bountiful that spring. They gathered armfuls of them on May 15, the day she was cremated—at her own behest—for she who had trumpeted so loudly during her lifetime had stipulated that there be no formal funeral or gathering, and no religious service. So, as a fitting memorial, they filled the house with "Lilacs,/ False blue,/ White,/ Purple,/ Colour of lilac,/ . . . great puffs of flowers," gathered from the garden to which she gave so much of her cherished time. Only the Lowell family, Ada, Mrs. Belmont, and Elizabeth Henry were present to accompany her ashes to the family plot at Mount Auburn Cemetery. Her will was filed on the same day. Her magnificent collection of books and manuscripts was left to Harvard, along with the furnishings from her library if the university wanted them. The portrait of Amy as a debutante was presented to Lowell House. Sevenels was to be Ada Russell's home for as long as she wanted to live there, and there was a trust fund for Ada set up to last the rest of her life. It had been agreed that she be appointed Amy's literary executor—no small mission and a demanding one, which required both the skill and the understanding only she could give it.

CHAPTER XIX

"In Excelsis"

THE NEWS OF Amy Lowell's sudden death shocked the world, especially the literary world. Telegrams and notes flowed in upon Ada, inundating her with emotional expressions of condolence. As might be expected, the Frosts and the Untermeyers were filled with remorse at their hasty retreat from Amy's commanding presence in refusing to attend the last great occasion of her life. If only they had known—but nobody except Ada and those who lived at Sevenels knew how ill she had been for years. Robert Frost wired Ada: "All Elinor and I can think of at the moment is our personal loss and yours. We can hardly accept it." (As he thought about Amy, and the Imagist leader she had been in the first years of her decade, the cogent image of "the immortal wound"—a Frostian phrase soon to become well known, one he had been mulling over for some time—crystallized in his mind. When he spoke to his students on "The Poetry of Amy Lowell," he found himself bringing forth the fruit of this concept that had been germinating, and he realized that Amy had planted the seed.)

The Engels were of course concerned. "Bibi" wanted to know what he could do, and whether Ada wanted to come to Washington to stay with them for a while. But there was too much to be done at Sevenels. Lorna came up with the boys for a visit, and the oldest, Theodore, spent the summer with his grandmother. After the letters of condolence were answered, the first job was to go through Amy's papers and burn the ones Amy expressly wished to have her destroy: Her letters from both Ada and Carl Engel—Amy had kept the letters "Peter" sent her from Salt Lake City locked in her desk drawer along with those from "Bibi"—she wanted them all to go up in smoke. Summer came in early on a heat wave, and on a hot Sunday morning in the back garden, Ada, following Amy's wishes, made a bonfire of boxes full of letters. She wrote to "Bibi," describing the task before her: "She kept everything—a note or telegram of no interest or value to anyone. . . . I wish to tell you also, Bibi, that all your letters to her were burned, *unread. She wanted me to do that*—clear out the drawers of her desk in her own room. Also I burnt all mine and that was easy in one way, only it was hot, and I watched it all. . . ."

Watching it with her was her grandson, Theodore Amussen, then only ten years old, but as he saw the boxes of letters and other papers in flames he felt, for some reason, that it was not right. Years later, when he was executive officer and editor in chief of two New York publishing houses, he realized what a terrible "archival disservice" had been done.* But Ada felt that "the hard thing will be to go through all the papers and all the files and decide what is worth keeping for posterity and the biographer—for the files mean a perfect history of the whole poetry movement. . . ."

Then she had to see *What's O'Clock,* the last volume Amy had prepared, through the press. It had already gone to the printers and appeared in October, only a few months after the poet's death. This volume contained (with the exception of the sequence, "Two Speak Together") some of her most personal, and moving, poems of love. Here was a whole sheaf of poems obviously written with Ada in mind: "The Anniversary," marking ten years of a shared life, with a hint of her oncoming fate—"Blowing asunder,/ Yet we shall be as the air/ Still undivided." Then comes the "Song for a Viola d'Amore"; a seven-line lyric, "Prime"; and the extraordinary "In Excelsis," with the lines, already quoted, immortalizing the beloved's hands. And, though she spelled it differently, Amy was writing the seventeen-syllable, three-line poems (haiku) so

* From a letter by Theodore Amussen to William C. Bedford, in "A Musical Apprentice: Amy Lowell to Carl Engel," *The Musical Quarterly* (October 1972).

popular today: "Twenty-Four Hokku on a Modern Theme," carefully structured, anticipates "The Anniversary," also in seventeen-syllable, three-line stanzas. The theme is the brevity of life: "When the flower falls/ The leaf is no more cherished./ Every day I fear."

These, along with such poems as "Lilacs," "Purple Grackles," and the lately anthologized, symbolic poem, with the provocative title, "Which, Being Interpreted, Is As May Be, or Otherwise," suggests a fantasy or deviate love (a frequent theme in Amy Lowell's work), represent her personal feelings. They precede "The Sisters" (the "queer lot" of women poets) and "Fool o' the Moon," a moon-cult poem, and one of the numerous lyrics glorifying the naked body of a woman. "The Green Parrakeet" is still another of these, a fascinating, perplexing poem. The volume closes with the six sonnets to Eleonora Duse. Certainly one of the most consistently valid of all of Amy Lowell's volumes, *What's O'Clock* was awarded the Pulitzer Prize on May 3, 1926, nearly a year after her death. It was not, as her detractors like to imply, merely a gesture of posthumous honor to her position as an important figure in the poetry movement. *What's O'Clock* itself included enough good poetry to warrant the award. It is a sad fact that Amy did not live to receive it in person.

At about this time, Sevenels had to be closed in preparation for its sale. Ada had just finished preparing *Ballads for Sale,* along with *East Wind,* a volume of dialect folk tales Amy had collected; and the files of papers had all been culled and organized. Harvard, at first accepting the furnishings of the library, had understandably reversed the decision after much discussion; the fire hazard was too great. Amy had deeply hoped that the library, her pride and joy, would be preserved to house her book collection just as it was at Sevenels, and Ada and those close to her were disappointed by the decision. The mansion itself was too large for Ada Russell to live in alone. She did not do much entertaining on the scale that Amy had maintained, and so she moved to a charming, smaller, more practical home on Chestnut Hill Avenue, not far from Sevenels. She often had Foster Damon and his roommate, John Marshall, over for dinner, and here she carried on the tradition of Sevenels, as Amy would have wished her to do. "For example," Mr. Marshall wrote to the present biographer in 1973, "she had in the library where we sat before and after dinner a large table covered with recent books. They were sent to her, as they always had been to Miss Lowell, by the Old Corner Bookstore, on approval. Miss Lowell looked at the books that came for a certain time, then sent back those she did not want, as did Mrs. Russell." (As Amy had written it would in "Penumbra," her love "went on speaking to Ada through the chairs, and the tables, and the pictures"; Ada could use only a few pieces of the furniture at Sevenels, but she did keep the library table.) Speaking of the dinner, Mr. Marshall continued: "The tradition of the table was the same. Sherry was served with the soup, in good Boston fashion. In the mid 1920's, the wine was usually Chateau Ponte-Canet, Miss Lowell's favorite wine, of which she laid in a large stock before prohibition. Her cigars were still offered. In fact, after her death Mrs. Russell gave both Damon and me a box of them, because again Miss Lowell during World War One had bought an enormous supply....

"Mrs. Russell was of course herself a great lady. . . . She was charming, thoughtful and cultivated, a true companion for Miss Lowell." *

East Wind and *Ballads for Sale* appeared in successive years right after *What's O'Clock*. The former consisted of thirteen stories and legends in New England dialect; one of them, "The Gravestone," presents an actual incident told to Amy by Robert Frost. In this connection, she and Frost enjoyed endless arguments about New England speech patterns, no matter whether it was "north of Boston" or down East, each poet contending that the other did not know true New England speech. Amy finally confessed in a letter to Albert Feuilleret and to Helen Kizer that her knowledge of New England and New Englanders and her use of dialect was "atavistic," rather than based on personal experience. And for those who have claimed that she was pure New England—a "New England vestal" (probably because of the last lines of "Lilacs," beginning: "Lilac in me because I am New England,/

* Letter from John Marshall to the author, May 16, 1973.

Because my roots are in it, . . .")—she stated that her background was "cosmopolitan." She admitted that she had little firsthand knowledge of rural New England and that Frost was more "sympathetic" than she toward New England farmfolk. The stories in *East Wind* are almost all neurotic and even—in the case of the old man "cossetin' the apples"—psychotic. Amy referred to it as "Freudian." If one had to categorize her, Amy was urban New England, the *im*proper Bostonian, although she spoke of herself always as "Amy Lowell of Brookline."

Ballads for Sale, with its subtitle, *Fresh, New Ballads, with the Ink Scarce Dried upon Them,* shows Amy as "barker" beginning her spiel preceding the poems: "Have a ballad, good people/ A sheet of song-words just pulled from the press," and, after describing them, ending: "Step up, good people,/ And buy a fine ballad crisp from the press,/ with the ink scarce dried upon it." To use her own term referring to the "Songs of the Pueblo Indians" in this book as "Side-shows" produced while she was working on "Many Swans," the volume was a series of sideshows of various vintages, moods, and methods, an experimenter's carnival or songfest of all sorts of poems. For example, the two long poems to Eleonora Duse, which were considered "too intimate" for *What's O'Clock,* were included here, as were the Indian songs and a series of "dance" poems, including "Jazz Dance." Here, too, was the "Portrait" containing the initials "E. R. B." in parentheses, which Ada sent to Nell Belmont after Amy's death with the following note: "Dearest — Inside is the poem—It is lovely, I think—if not an exact portrait. How sweet you are—how good you have been and how I love you. Your Dada [an old pet name for Ada]." The poem describes a certain mood of both the painter and the subject of this portrait (as mentioned earlier). It was published without the initials in the *Selected Poems* of 1928, but included with them when it was published again in *The Complete Poetical Works.* It was undoubtedly written before Amy knew Ada's friend very well and may have represented an initial impression of Amy's awed admiration of Nell's beauty and innate culture, combined with a sturdy, grass-roots hold on life that would not bow to every passing wind. Or, as earlier suggested, it may have been evoked by E. R. B.'s reaction during one of the times Amy created a scene over Ada's visits to Salt Lake City. Mrs. Belmont herself has written: "This application [to herself] was just a mood of the artist and did not indicate her real feeling, as you can judge by the fact that when my husband died she wrote me a letter inviting me to come and live with them." * In any case, Ada was correct in judging the "Portrait (E. R. B.)" a "lovely" poem, unusual in its images.

The question of a suitable biographer for Amy Lowell came up about this time. Her friend Elsie Sergeant, in a book composed of a series of "portraits," which first appeared separately in the *New Republic, Harper's, Century Magazine,* and the *Nation,* entitled *Fire Under the Andes,* published in 1926, had led off with an almost surrealist picture of "Amy Lowell," subtitled, "Memory Sketch for a Biographer." The introductory chapter notes that Amy died after the book was begun, "just before her own chapter was to be written and who still lives for me." While it caught the quintessential qualities in Amy Lowell's life and the excitement she engendered, the picture of the conflict between her masculine and feminine impulses was perhaps too accurate to suit the family. Lawrence, as president of Harvard, felt that a Harvard professor should be his sister's biographer and that John Livingston Lowes was suitably eminent. But Lowes was editing her *Selected Poems* and making corrections on his own *Road to Xanadu,* just published in 1927, so the family turned to Foster Damon, now on the faculty at Harvard, as their second choice. He was, after all, closer to Amy and Ada than John and Mary Lowes were, and, although young, he was an ardent scholar as well as an admirer of modern poetry. Too, in a sense he was a protégé of Amy's since that first paper he had written on Imagism; and he had lectured on Amy Lowell and William Blake in Denmark. In addition to all this, he knew her household life well, and was certain to do a thorough job. (His *Chronicle* of her life, published in 1935, is evidence that he did just that.**)

* Letter from Mrs. August Belmont to the author, May 24, 1973.

** S. Foster Damon, *Amy Lowell, A Chronicle* (Boston: Houghton Mifflin Company, 1935).

Ferris Greenslet edited a book of her essays (entitled *Poetry and Poets*), studies in modern literature, which championed D. H. Lawrence among others, and was published just two months after his death on March 2, 1930. Damon observed in his 750-page biography: "Again a publication of Amy Lowell's proved timely: this posthumous acclaim of her dead friend was so opportune as to be the first important voice in the establishment of his fame." There is something fascinating, not to say eerie, that she, who was among the first to promote D. H. Lawrence while they were both alive, should be the first to hail his work when they were both so recently dead—it was almost as if they had met in the Beyond and Amy somehow arranged to blow the trumpet for him. Lawrence's recently revived plays (1974) were a part of his creativity which she alone encouraged. He sent her the manuscript of several of his dramas.

Naturally, Amy's presence was felt for a long time by those near to her, particularly by Ada, who was working with her papers. In March 1927, Jean Untermeyer—whose world had collapsed in the two years since Amy's death—paid a visit to Ada. Jean had just lost her son and only child, Richard, who had committed suicide, and her marriage had broken up. Warmhearted Ada had invited her to visit so that she could offer her some comfort, and it was a comfort to both of them to be able to talk freely about "the two loved ones they had lost" (as Jean said), including, inevitably, the relationship each had had with the one who was gone. In her memoirs, Jean stated that on that visit she learned, at close range, why Ada had taken such a part in Amy Lowell's life. She did not elaborate except to say that she found so much of it so interesting that she begged Ada to write the story of her own life, both in the theater and at Sevenels.

Self-effacing Ada said she had no talent for writing, though she showed great ability in handling and editing Amy's posthumous work. Her life with Amy (again in Jean's words) "had enriched her without taking from her any of her own quiet strength." But she confided that she had recently been troubled because Amy had appeared in her dreams several times, "shaking her head and moaning, 'You were right, Peter, it was a mistake;

the cremation was a mistake.' " The dreams worried her, not from a religious standpoint, for she had long ago rejected all religious creeds, living a personal religion that meant giving her love and understanding to others. Since she was still working with Amy's papers at the time, it is likely that the cremation of her dreams subconsciously represented the burning of the letters that undoubtedly held the key to Amy's emotional life.

It is indeed an unfortunate fact that she wrote no biography of her own, not only because of what she could have provided for other biographers of Amy Lowell but also because of what she herself could have contributed to the understanding of human behavior—especially to those troubled with a psychosexual conflict such as Amy Lowell's. Right after her death, many statements were made about her achievements and her personality. Robert Frost in his remarks to his Amherst students, printed on May 16 in the *Christian Science Monitor,* spoke of "the immortal wound" taken by the reader of a good poem, and went on: "How often have I heard it in the voice and seen it in the eyes of this generation that Amy Lowell had lodged poetry with them to stay. . . . The breathless swing is between subject matter and form. Amy Lowell was distinguished in a period of dilation when poetry, in the effort to include a larger material, stretched itself almost to the breaking of the verse. Little ones with no more apparatus than a teacup looked on with alarm. She helped to make it stirring times for a decade to those immediately concerned with art and to many not so immediately. The water in our eyes from her poetry is not warm with any suspicion of tears; it is water flung cold, bright and many-colored from flowers gathered in her formal garden in the morning. Her Imagism lay chiefly in images to the eye. She flung flowers and everything else there. Her poetry was forever a clear resonant calling off of things seen." His observations, unsentimental but deeply poetic, showed clearly that Robert Frost did not realize the emotional value that flowers and all those "things seen" had for Amy; nor, for all his insight, did he grasp her psyche.

Louis Untermeyer, in the "Memoir" he wrote as introduction to *The Complete Poetical Works,* cites an early letter Amy wrote him regarding his piece on Imagism, Pound, and Lowell: "The only thing I object to in your article is your saying that it was under his leadership that 'the Imagists became not only a group but a fighting protest.' It was nothing of the sort. The Imagists, during the year and a half in which he headed the movement were unknown and jeered at, when they were not absolutely ignored. It was not until I entered the arena and Ezra dropped out that Imagism had to be considered seriously. . . . The name is his; the idea was widespread. But changing the whole public attitude from derision to consideration came from my work." And he goes on to relate that "She began waging a battle on two fronts. She fought with equal ardor as propagandist and poet; she stalked the ramparts of her own beleaguered citadel, went forth to shout down her critics and stormed enemy battlements clear across the country."

Amy's friend Elsie Sergeant began the final strokes of her "Sketch" in which she had shown both "the buccaneering maleness" and the feminine sides of Amy's makeup by observing, "Her death is like the fall of a dynasty," a variant of which was quoted by Damon and other biographers. It is true that Amy had had a regality about her and had been a militant leader for Imagism and free verse, but she had been not so much a ruler as a slave to her muse in the realm of poetry, which she never wholly conquered. If she had not tried to encompass so much she might have produced more lasting art in the area in which she excelled—personal poetry, not merely the "calling off of things seen," but the impression the images of the eye made upon her inner being, like her fine apostrophe to lilacs—but most of all in the poems of a deep and tender love, expressed in fresh, free terms.

One of the most colorful tributes paid her was written by the illustrious journalist Heywood Broun; his comments on Amy Lowell appeared in his "It Seems to Me" column in the *World* on the same day as Frost's (May 16, 1925) and show a good deal more insight: "Since Dr. Johnson there have been few so much addicted to conversation and so able in the art. . . . I have always hoped for a Heaven. Mostly I want it for myself, but I also like to think of it in relation to Amy Lowell. I like to think of her arrival. St. Peter and others of importance would be brushed aside, I believe, when she came to the great gate. Nor would she, in those first moments, ask, like the others, for the King of the celestial city. Rather I see her striding by the saints and crying out: 'Where is John Keats?' " And, to the critics who claimed that Amy had all the qualities a poet needed but passion, that she had perception but lacked feeling, Broun flaunted his disagreement in a figure as flamboyant as any of Amy's: "She was upon the surface of things a Lowell, a New Englander and a spinster. But inside everything was molten like the core of the earth . . . given one more gram of emotion, Amy Lowell would have burst into flame and been consumed to cinders."

Unquestionably she was an outstanding influence "in the American art of her time," as Elizabeth Sergeant said. She cleared the path for her younger contemporaries like Marianne Moore (who was just beginning her career when Amy died); Wallace Stevens (whose poetry she was among the first to recognize); e. e. cummings (whose lower-case and other typographical tricks she criticized as affectations, but who was the first to point out that in content he was an Elizabethan lyrist); Archibald MacLeish; William Carlos Williams, with whom she disagreed but whom she admired; and Babette Deutsch and Louise Bogan, also just beginning. Moreover, her pioneering groundwork paved the way for a later generation of poets. Among the women Muriel Rukeyser, Denise Levertov, Elizabeth Bishop, the late Anne Sexton, May Swenson, and that tragic genius Sylvia Plath come to mind; among the men, Williams' disciple, Allen Ginsberg (though Amy would have decried his "obscenities" as she did Joyce's, she nevertheless led the way for the experimenters); James Dickey; Howard Moss; L. E. Sissman (whose "Mt. Auburn: 1945" narrative might have come from her storytelling poetry); and even, though he disclaims any but a distant relationship, the present-day poet of her family, Robert Lowell, with his powerful, raw realism. Of course, there were other significant influences: Eliot's *The Waste Land,* whether it moved Amy Lowell or not, changed the course of modern poetry. But if it had not been for Amy's initial campaign, modern freedom of expression in poetry, whatever its form or lack of it, might have taken much longer to evolve and may have, one might guess, evolved differently. Contemporary poetry, like contemporary music and painting, can take any turn its creator pleases—though one may reject this as a thing totally good in itself—and although no one writes Amy's polyphonic prose today, it was an important milestone along the road. (At the MacDowell Colony in 1973, one contemporary poet expressed astonishment at "The Basket" in a recent anthology, and at Amy Lowell's use of "the image in the eye." She exclaimed: "That's the same concept as mine!")

The amazing thing about the odd scheme of Amy's life-style, her whirlwind existence, is that *it worked,* as her friend Elsie Sergeant said. "Amy Lowell accomplished ten times as much in the last fifteen years of her life as the rest of us in half a century, and there was no conflict, I believe, between her aims and pursuits. This was due in great measure to the unselfish seconding and the stimulus which Mrs. Russell brought."

Ada lived till about 1952. One of the last letters to Eleanor Robson Belmont,* a cherished note to her "Dearest Child," full of the love she gave freely to those close to her, was dated August 9, 1938, from the Chestnut Hill Avenue house. No one knew better than Ada the trials that Amy had had to overcome, and the tremendous courage of the "stout-hearted fellow" in her, even stronger than the one which beat in the breast of her grandfather, John Amory Lowell, whom she admired, or that of her twice great-grandfather, the "Old Judge," whom she remarkably resembled. To Amy herself, her triumph in the world of literature, as represented by the elite among editors and poets at her testimonial dinner, meant also the undeniable victory of her poetic revolution—the ascendancy of the arena she had chosen to enter over the aristocracy of her birthright, the conventional world of high society. If her impetus toward heterosexual love had not been checked—to her a tragic disappointment at the time—she might never have been more than a Boston clubwoman and society matron running a semiliterary salon.

* Published in Eleanor R. Belmont's autobiography, *The Fabric of Memory* (New York: Farrar, Straus & Cudahy, 1957).

In his remarks preceding his evaluation of Amy's contribution to poetry, Robert Frost, who liked to equate art with love, said: "Permanence in poetry as in love is perceived instantly. . . . We throw our arms wide with a gesture of religion to the universe; we close them around a person." Amy Lowell closed hers around Ada Russell. And nowhere did she do so with more finality, more complete adoration than in her poem of love, "In Excelsis":

You—you—
Your shadow is sunlight on a plate of silver;
Your footsteps, the seeding-place of lilies;
Your hands moving, a chime of bells across a windless air.

The movement of your hands is the long, golden running of light
    from a rising sun;
It is the hopping of birds upon a garden-path.

As the perfume of jonquils, you come forth in the morning.
Young horses are not more sudden than your thoughts,
Your words are bees about a pear-tree,
Your fancies are the gold-and-black striped wasps buzzing among
    red apples.
I drink your lips,
I eat the whiteness of your hands and feet.
My mouth is open,
As a new jar I am empty and open.
Like white water are you who fill the cup of my mouth,
Like a brook of water thronged with lilies.

You are frozen as the clouds,
You are far and sweet as the high clouds.
I dare reach to you,
I dare touch the rim of your brightness.
I leap beyond the winds,
I cry and shout,
For my throat is keen as a sword
Sharpened on a hone of ivory.
My throat sings the joy of my eyes,
The rushing gladness of my love.

How has the rainbow fallen upon my heart?
How have I snared the seas to lie in my fingers

And caught the sky to be a cover for my head?
How have you come to dwell with me,
Compassing me with the four circles of your mystic lightness,
So that I say "Glory! Glory!" and bow before you
As to a shrine?

Do I tease myself that morning is morning and a day after?
Do I think the air a condescension,
The earth a politeness,
Heaven a boon deserving thanks?
So you—air—earth—heaven—
I do not thank you,
I take you,
and live.
And those things which I say in consequence
Are rubies mortised in a gate of stone.

A Selected Bibliography
Including Sources of Background Material

Works by Amy Lowell (listed chronologically)

1. Volumes of Poetry:

A Dome of Many-Coloured Glass. Boston: Houghton Mifflin Company, 1912.
Sword Blades and Poppy Seed. New York and London: The Macmillan Company, 1914.
Men, Women and Ghosts. New York and London: The Macmillan Company, 1916.
Can Grande's Castle. New York and London: The Macmillan Company, 1918.
Pictures of the Floating World. Boston: Houghton Mifflin Company, 1919.
Legends. Boston: Houghton Mifflin Company, 1921.
A Critical Fable. Boston: Houghton Mifflin Company, 1922.
(Posthumous): *What's O'Clock.* Boston: Houghton Mifflin Company, 1925.
East Wind. Boston: Houghton Mifflin Company, 1926.
Ballads for Sale. Boston: Houghton Mifflin Company, 1927.
Selected Poems (Ed., John Livingston Lowes). Boston: Houghton Mifflin Company, 1928.
Complete Poetical Works. Boston: Houghton Mifflin Company, 1955.
A Shard of Silence, Selected Poems of Amy Lowell (Ed., G. R. Ruihley). New York: Twayne Publishers, Inc., 1957.

2. Anthologies:

Some Imagist Poets (with a Preface on Imagism). Boston: Houghton Mifflin Company, 1915.
Some Imagist Poets, Vol. II. Boston: Houghton Mifflin Company, 1916.
Some Imagist Poets, Vol. III. Boston: Houghton Mifflin Company, 1917.
A Miscellany of American Poetry (compiled with Louis Untermeyer). New York: Alfred Harcourt, 1917.
A Miscellany of American Poetry, Vol. II. New York: Alfred Harcourt, 1918.

3. Prose Works:

Six French Poets (essays drawn from lectures). New York and London: The Macmillan Company, 1915.
Tendencies in Modern American Poetry. New York: The Macmillan Company, 1917.
John Keats (biography, 2 Vols.). Boston: Houghton Mifflin Company, 1925.
Poets and Poetry (essays published posthumously). Boston: Houghton Mifflin Company, 1930.

4. Translations:

Fir-Flower Tablets (with Florence Ayscough, translations of ancient Chinese poetry). Boston: Houghton Mifflin Company, 1921.
Works of modern French poets discussed in *Six French Poets, Appendix.*
Verse plays by Edmond Rostand and Alfred de Musset (unpublished but produced).

5. Uncollected Poems:

"The Cornucopia of Red and Green Comfits" (1915?).
"Der Tag" (Sunday *Herald-Tribune,* December 22, 1918).

6. Letters. (Published and unpublished, in various library collections.)

McNair, Harley F., Ed. *Florence Ayscough and Amy Lowell:* Correspondence of a Friendship. Chicago: University of Chicago Press, 1946.

Biographical and Critical, also Peripheral Material

Aiken, Conrad. *Skepticisms: Notes on Contemporary Poetry.* New York: Alfred A. Knopf, 1919.
Anderson, Margaret. *My Thirty Years' War.* New York: Horizon Press, 1969. Reprint of 1930 edition.
Belmont, Eleanor Robson. *The Fabric of Memory.* New York: Farrar, Straus & Cudahy, 1957.
Bogan, Louise. *What the Woman Lived: Selected Letters.* New York: Harper & Row, 1974.
Brinnin, John Malcolm. *The Third Rose.* New York: Grove Press, 1961.
Brooks, Van Wyck. *New England: Indian Summer.* New York: E. P. Dutton, 1940.
Butcher, Fanny. *Many Lives, One Love.* New York: Harper & Row, 1972.
Bynner, Witter. *Journey with Genius: Recollections and Reflections Concerning the D. H. Lawrences.* New York: John Day, 1951.
Carpenter, Margaret H. *Sara Teasdale.* New York: Schulte Publishing Company, 1960.
Damon, S. Foster. *Amy Lowell, A Chronicle.* Boston: Houghton Mifflin Company, 1935.
Fletcher, John Gould. *Life Is My Song.* New York and Toronto: Farrar & Rinehart, 1937.

Gould, Jean. *Robert Frost: The Aim Was Song.* New York: Dodd, Mead & Company, 1964.
——. *The Poet and Her Book, A Biography of Edna St. Vincent Millay.* New York: Dodd, Mead & Company, 1969.
Greenslet, Ferris. *The Lowells and Their Seven Worlds.* Boston: Houghton Mifflin Company, 1946.
——. *Under the Bridge.* Boston: Houghton Mifflin Company, 1952.
Gregory, Horace. *Amy Lowell: A Portrait of the Poet in Her Time.* New York: Thomas Nelson & Sons, 1958.
—— and Zaturenska, Maria. *History of American Poetry from 1900 to 1940.* New York: Harcourt, Brace & Company, 1947.
H. D. (pseud., Hilda Doolittle). *Tribute to Freud,* 1936.
Hughes, Glenn. *Imagism and the Imagists: A Study in Modern Poetry.* Stanford: Stanford University Press, 1931.
Kreymborg, Alfred. *Our Singing Strength.* New York: Coward-McCann, 1925.
Lawrence, D. H. *Selected Letters* (with An Introduction by Diana Trilling). New York: Farrar, Straus & Cudahy, 1958.
——. *The Plumed Serpent.* New York: Viking Press, 1965.
——. Unpublished letters to Amy Lowell, c. 1914–1924. Cambridge: Houghton Library, Harvard University.
Loggins, Vernon. *I Hear America.* New York: Thomas Y. Crowell Company, 1937.
Lowell, Robert. *Life Studies* (Autobiographical Fragment). New York: Vantage Books, 1959.
Lowes, John Livingston. *Convention and Revolt in Poetry.* Boston: Houghton Mifflin Company, 1930.
McAlmon, Robert, Diary of. Edited by Kay Boyle. New York: Harper & Row, 1968.
Monroe, Harriet. *A Poet's Life: Seventy Years in a Changing World.* New York: The Macmillan Company, 1930.
Moore, Harry T. and Roberts, Warren. *D. H. Lawrence and His World.* New York: Viking Press, 1966.
Morison, Samuel Eliot. *One Boy's Boston: (1887–1901.)* Boston: Houghton Mifflin Company, 1962.
Putnam, Mrs. William Lowell. "A Glimpse of Amy Lowell's Childhood by Her Sister" (unpublished manuscript).
Rittenhouse, Jesse B. *My House of Life.* Boston: Houghton Mifflin Company, 1934.
Ruihley, G. R., Ed. *A Shard of Silence,* Selected Poems of Amy Lowell. New York: Twayne Publishers, Inc., 1957.
Scott, Winfield Townley. *Exiles and Fabrications.* New York: Doubleday & Company, Inc., 1961.
Sergeant, Elizabeth. *Fire Under the Andes.* Boston: 1927; reprint, Kennikat Press, 1966.
Simon, Charlie May. (Mrs. John Gould Fletcher). *Johnswood.* New York: E. P. Dutton, 1953.
Smith, William Jay. *The Spectra Hoax.* Middletown: Wesleyan University Press, 1961.

Spicer-Simson, Theodore. *A Collector of Characters: Reminiscences of Theodore Spicer-Simson.* Coral Gables, Florida: University of Miami Press, 1962.

Stafford, Joan. *Great Women Poets in English* (section on Amy Lowell). New York and London: The Macmillan Company, 1972.

Stein, Gertrude. *The Autobiography of Alice B. Toklas.* New York: Harcourt Brace & Company, Inc., 1933.

Stephens, Edna B. *John Gould Fletcher.* New York: Twayne Publishers, Inc., 1967.

Thomson, Virgil. *Virgil Thomson.* New York and London: Weidenfeld & Nicholson, 1967.

Toklas, Alice B. *What is Remembered.* New York: Holt, Rinehart & Winston, 1963.

Untermeyer, Jean Starr. *Private Collection.* New York: Alfred A. Knopf, 1965.

Untermeyer, Louis. "A Memoir," Introduction to *The Complete Poetical Works of Amy Lowell.* Boston: Houghton Mifflin Company, 1955.

———. "Storm Center in Brookline" in *From Another World.* New York: Harcourt Brace & Company, 1939.

———. *American Poetry Since 1900,* Revised Edition. New York: Harcourt Brace & Company, 1953.

Warren, Robert Penn, Brooks, Cleanth, and Lewis, W. R. B. *American Literature Makers.* New York: Appleton-Century-Crofts, 1972.

White, Katherine Dana. "Recollections of Amy Lowell in Childhood" (unpublished manuscript).

Wilkinson, Marguerite. *New Voices.* New York: The Macmillan Company, 1927.

Wilson, Edmund. *The Shores of Light* (section, "All Star Literary Vaudeville"). New York: Farrar, Straus & Cudahy, 1952.

Wood, Clement. *Amy Lowell.* New York: Harold Vinal, 1926.

Numerous reviews and articles, the most valuable among recent studies, "A Musical Apprentice," by William C. Bedford ("Amy Lowell to Carl Engel,") in *The Musical Quarterly,* October 1972.

"Life On a Cloud," Profile of Margaret Anderson, by Janet Flanner, in *The New Yorker,* October 3, 1974.

Index